ORIGEN

and the History of Justification

ORIGEN
and the History
of Justification

The Legacy of Origen's
Commentary on Romans

THOMAS P. SCHECK

Foreword by Joseph T. Lienhard, S.J.

University of Notre Dame Press
Notre Dame, Indiana

Library of Congress Cataloging-in-Publication Data

Scheck, Thomas P., 1964 –
Origen and the history of justification : the legacy of Origen's commentary on
Romans / Thomas P. Scheck.
p.   cm.
Includes bibliographical references and index.
ISBN-13: 978-0-268-04128-1 (cloth : alk. paper)
ISBN-10: 0-268-04128-8 (cloth : alk. paper)
1. Origen. Commentary on the Epistle to the Romans.
2. Bible. N.T. Romans—Commentaries.   I. Title.
BS2665.53S34   2008
227'.106092—dc22

2008000407

 This book is printed on recycled paper.

Contents

Foreword

In the opening two or three pages of the introduction to his anthology of Origen's writings, Hans Urs von Balthasar sketched, brilliantly and with compact elegance, the history of Origen's thought up to his condemnation at the Fifth Ecumenical Council in 553, and beyond the council to the Middle Ages. Von Balthasar invoked two striking images to make his point.

Balthasar's first image is a sad one: what we have of Origen's writings is like the wreckage of an aircraft after a crash, twisted pieces of metal strewn randomly about a forest or a field. To reassemble the aircraft is difficult, if not impossible, and we can only guess at its original form and even beauty. Because of the ecumenical council's rejection of Origen, most of his writings, in their original Greek, were lost or destroyed. More of his work survived in Latin translation, on the supposition that the saintly translators had removed the poison from these writings and made them safe and wholesome. But still, we piece the picture together only with difficulty and seldom with certainty.

The second image that von Balthasar proposes is more hopeful, and even intriguing: Origen was a vessel filled with precious perfume that was shattered into a thousand pieces, and the perfume has filled the whole house.

The latter image is the one that Thomas Scheck chose to follow. Students of Origen are familiar with the general outlines of the influence he exerted. Negatively, his thought was reduced to a system, and a somewhat heretical system at that, concerned mostly with the beginning and the end of things. It was this system, utterly unfaithful to Origen's inquiring and restless mind, that was condemned in the middle of the sixth century. Positively, Origen's writings, especially his writings on the Bible, were eagerly plundered—sometimes by those who acknowledged their source, and sometimes by those who did not. As a result, the exegetical tradition of the Church, in the West as in the East, owes far more to Origen than has generally been acknowledged in the past.

The last half-century or so saw a dramatic, and happy, growth of interest in Origen's writings on Holy Scripture. Symbolically, at least, this revival goes back to a famous sentence that Henri de Lubac wrote: "Observe Origen at work." What de Lubac meant to do, it seems, was to draw attention away from Origen's speculative works, especially *On First Principles*, and to focus it on his sermons and scriptural commentaries. The Origen of the homilies and commentaries, especially the later ones, is far more pastoral, and more centrist, than the Origen of the earlier, speculative works. The decades since de Lubac wrote that famous sentence have been fruitful: many good translations of Origen's writings on Scripture have been made, and scholarly study of these works has flourished.

One of Origen's works, however, remained a sort of stepchild, neglected and disregarded—that is, his *Commentary on Romans*. A fresh critical edition of the Latin text became available only in the 1990s. Thomas Scheck has undertaken, almost singlehandedly, to bring about a broader knowledge of Origen's *Commentary on Romans* and a greater appreciation of it. In 2001 and 2002 he published, in two volumes, the first English translation of the commentary, in the series Fathers of the Church. Now, in the book here presented, he follows, in a scholarly fashion, the perfume that spread throughout the house, the Church, from the shattered vessel of Origen's learning.

A key word in most of his chapter titles in this book is "reception." In theological usage, the word was first more common in German, in the form *Rezeption*. In this theological sense, reception differs markedly from acceptance. One accepts a material gift, and the acceptance does not change the gift: one accepts a vase and puts it on a shelf. But the reception of ideas, and of the texts that express them, is different. The receiver may ponder and exploit some passages attentively, and glide over others; he may understand them in a way that the author never intended; and he will fit the author's ideas into his own world of thought. Reception, therefore, is a living, dynamic process. No one can simply take another's idea and put it on an intellectual shelf; each idea is integrated into the receiver's own universe. Thus, the study of the reception of Origen's commentary is a complex and intriguing undertaking.

It is a privilege for me to write some "words beforehand" to Thomas Scheck's impressive book. The book serves two great purposes: it brings into clearer light some of the key theological themes of Origen's understanding of St. Paul, and it guides the reader and the theologian along the winding and sometimes bewildering road leading from the third century to the present, as generations of Christians struggled to understand and appropriate St. Paul's great Epistle to the Romans, with Origen leading the way.

Joseph T. Lienhard, S.J.

Acknowledgments
and Dedication

This book began as a doctoral dissertation at the University of Iowa ("The Reception of Origen's Exegesis of Romans in the Latin West," 2004). I am grateful to the members of my interdisciplinary Ph.D. committee for their guidance and support. Thomas Williams was my thesis supervisor. James McCue and Dwight Bozeman were committee members, as well as John Finamore and Craig Gibson. I also received advice from Ralph Keen. The suggestions of all these scholars led to substantial improvements.

From outside the University of Iowa, I received direct help from Joseph Lienhard, J. Patout Burns, Steven Cartwright, and Mark Reasoner. The criticisms of anonymous readers from Brill Press and from the University of Notre Dame Press greatly improved both the structure and the argument of my manuscript. I am grateful to Ralph McInerny, who awarded me a postdoctoral research fellowship in the University of Notre Dame's Jacques Maritain Center. The revision of the original dissertation took place during my two wonderful years at Notre Dame. The result reminds me of Tertullian's prefatory words concerning his expanded edition of his treatise *Against Marcion:* "This present text, therefore, of my work—which is the third from the second, but henceforward to be considered the first instead of the third—renders a preface necessary to this edition of the work . . ." Finally, I am sincerely grateful to two colleagues, Bret Sunnerville and Jay Martin, who showed a keen interest in this research project and offered much intelligent feedback and encouragement. The work is dedicated to my wife, Susan, who is the mother of our six children.

Introduction

In his magnum opus, *Medieval Exegesis*, Henri de Lubac stated that the full significance of Rufinus of Aquileia's Latin translations of Origen for the development of Christian thought and Western culture has not yet been fully measured.[1] For me Lubac's words constitute a challenge, and I hope that the following investigation will contribute in a small way to measuring the influence of one of Rufinus's most important Latin translations, that of Origen's *Commentary on the Epistle to the Romans* (hereafter *CRm*). The following table shows the approximate length of Origen's major writings.

Table 1. Approximate Length of Origen's Major Extant Works (According to the Latin Text That Appears in Migne)[2]

Title of Work (with ancient Latin translator)	Number of Columns in Migne (PG 11–17)
Against Celsus	493
Commentary on Romans (Rufinus)	455
Commentary on John	405
Commentary on Matthew (on Mt 16.13–22.33)	382
On First Principles I–IV (Rufinus)	296
Homilies on Numbers (Rufinus)	220
Commentary Series on Matthew (on Mt 22.24–27.66) [traditionally called *Homilies*]	199
Homilies on Leviticus (Rufinus)	169

Table 1. Approximate Length of Origen's Major Extant Works (*continued*)

Title of Work *(with ancient Latin translator)*	*Number of Columns in Migne* *(PG 11–17)*
Commentary on the Song of Songs (Rufinus)	136
Homilies on Joshua (Rufinus)	123
Homilies on Genesis (Rufinus)	117
*Homilies on Jeremiah (Jerome)	107
Homilies on Exodus (Rufinus)	100
Homilies on Luke (Jerome)	99
Homilies on Ezekiel (Jerome)	96
Homilies on Psalms 36–38 (Rufinus)	90
*On Prayer	73
Pamphilus's Apology for Origen (Rufinus)	72
Homilies on Judges (Rufinus)	40
*On Martyrdom	36
Homilies on the Song of Songs (Jerome)	21
Homily on 1 Samuel (Rufinus)	17
Spurious Works Attributed to Origen:	
Anonymous Commentary on Job	149
*Dialogue of Adamantius on the Orthodox Faith (Rufinus)	85

*Indicates that the work survives in its entirety in Greek as well

In spite of its stature as the second-longest extant work of Origen, second only to *Contra Celsum,* and as the longest of Origen's surviving scriptural commentaries, Origen's *CRm* has been seriously neglected as the subject of research. It received some attention in the twentieth century but not a great deal. As late as 1988 Crouzel could still call it the *parent pauvre,* "the poor relation," of Origen's works and the most neglected of his writings.[3] Even more recently Kovacs observed that "today Origen's exegesis of Paul is largely unknown."[4] And if Origen's exegesis of Paul is largely unknown, the legacy, or *Nachleben*, of Origen's exegesis of Romans would seem to be an even riper field of research and one that is long overdue. Wagner had stated in 1945, "The question of the use made of Rufinus' translations during later antiquity and the Middle Ages would bear systematic study. Hints on this point are not difficult to find."[5] This state of affairs justifies an in-depth examination of Origen's exegesis of Romans followed by a study of the reception of Origen's views in select theologians in the Latin West.

The Use of Rufinus's Version

Origen's *CRm* was originally written in Greek between 244 and 246.[6] Origen himself refers to it in his *Commentary on Matthew* 17.32 and *Cels* 5.47 and 8.65. The Greek text was known to St. Jerome (cf. *Eps* 36, 121),[7] St. Basil (*De Spiritu Sancto* 29.73), and the church historian Socrates (*HE* 7.32.17).[8] Fragments of the Greek original are preserved in the *Philocalia*,[9] the *Catena*,[10] and the Tura papyri.[11] Didymus the Blind (313–98) drew on Origen's Greek exegesis of Romans in his work *Contra Manichaeos*.[12] The anonymous commentator on Paul, writing around the year 400, also used the Greek text of Origen,[13] as did Pamphilus of Caesarea in his *Apology for Origen*. Apart from these references, to my knowledge the Greek version of Origen's *CRm* had little direct influence.[14] However, Rufinus's Latin translation of Origen's *CRm* (406) had an extremely significant *Nachleben*,[15] far more significant than has hitherto been imagined. It appears to me that Heither's statement that Origen's interpretation of Paul was without subsequent influence in the Church is seriously mistaken.[16] The context suggests that what she means is that Origen's central interpretation of Paul's message, as she understands it, was lost to later view, but even so the statement cannot stand. This topic will be the subject of the second half of this book (chapters 2–7). For it was the Latin Origen's Pauline exegesis that was transmitted to the West.[17]

My primary focus in this study is on "Rufinus's Origen" and the legacy of Rufinus's Origen. I will not endeavor to determine the original Greek wording of Origen's expressions, or whether a given statement of the Latin Origen may in fact be a gloss of Rufinus. Such a task would require a separate study of the Greek fragments of Origen's commentary, together with an examination of the entire corpus of Origen's writings. In any case, T. Heither has done that task in large measure on texts that are relevant to this study.[18] My aim instead is to move the discussion forward into the Latin theological tradition and to analyze its engagement with the Latin Origen. This is the aspect of Origen scholarship that has been seriously neglected. This will be more an investigation into *Rezeptionsgeschichte* than *Geschichte*. The question of determining the historical authenticity of the views expressed in Rufinus's translation is an important and indeed complex one, but it is not mine.

On the other hand, I would still like to make a few brief remarks concerning the reliability of Rufinus's translation with respect to Origen's discussions of justification. In the past some theologians have entirely denied the authenticity of the discussions of justification in Origen's commentary. In 1930 Völker declared confidently: "Origen never speaks of justification from faith, for the discussions in the CRm are hardly authentic."[19] Even apart from any other evidence, the suggestion that Origen would "never speak" of a biblical theme like justification by faith strikes me as doubtful. Völker's particular assertion has been proved false by the archaeological discovery of the Tura papyri in 1941.[20] These papyri contain long Greek excerpts from the original commentary, including extensive discussions of justification by faith. Even texts where Origen speaks of "justification by faith *alone*" have been preserved.[21]

Prior to Völker, many German scholars were interested solely in recovering the alleged *verba ipsissima* of Origen and were deeply suspicious of Rufinus's translations. Only the Greek fragments, or very little of Rufinus's translations, were used as sources for Origen's thought. It is true that Völker used Rufinus's translations more freely than did his predecessors. He encouraged scholars to study Origen's homilies that have been preserved in Latin translations by Jerome and Rufinus, an exhortation that fell on deaf ears, according to Lubac.[22] But Völker was still quite distrustful of Rufinus, as the above citation proves. In some cases Protestants were hostile to those who mined Rufinus's Latin translations for information about Origen and denounced the efforts of Roman Catholic scholars to form a "dogmatically correct" picture of Origen's doctrine of justification based on Rufinus's version. Völker criticized Wörter on this issue, and Molland reproached Verfaillie for the same reason.[23]

In large measure this minimalist approach to the use of Rufinus's translations as a source of Origen's thought has been challenged and substantially overcome in recent years through the efforts of such scholars as Balthasar, Chadwick, Cocchini, Crouzel, Danièlou, Hammond Bammel, Heither, Lubac, Roukema, and Schelkle. None of these scholars denies that Rufinus's translations contain post-Nicene Rufinian glosses, especially on Christological and Trinitarian passages, nor do I deny this. But they insist that Rufinus should still be extensively used as a source for Origen's thought. In the specific case of Origen's *CRm*, the Tura find was of such decisive significance that Völker's and Molland's dismissive approach to Rufinus's version had to be completely abandoned. Roukema, for example, prefaced his recent study of Origen's *CRm* with the words "The opinions which were held before the publication of the Tura papyrus will be left out of consideration, since this text has thrown a new light on Rufinus' version."[24] It seems probable to me that most of the Origenian explanations that are discussed in this book are traceable to Origen himself, albeit in a new form of language and theological context.[25] Of the theologians who are investigated in chapters 2–7, only Erasmus had hesitations about the reliability of Rufinus's translation of Origen's *CRm*, and his scruples did not touch the majority of passages that are examined here. In any case, since my focus is on the Latin Origen and his legacy, the reader, and in particular the patristic scholar, is welcome to supply "Rufinus's Origen" wherever I speak of "Origen."

Parameters of This Investigation

This book is divided into two parts: a lengthy first chapter, in which Origen's views on justification are analyzed and discussed; and chapters 2–7, in which the legacy of Origen's interpretations is investigated. I have endeavored to make the initial chapter foundational for the remainder of the investigation. However, because each subsequent Latin theologian responds differently to Origen's *CRm* and calls attention to different aspects of Origen's Pauline interpretation, at times I have discussed important texts from Origen's *CRm* in later chapters which are not mentioned in the first chapter. For example, Origen's interpretation of Rom 5.12 (the transmission of original sin) is discussed in chapters 2 (Pelagius),

3 (Augustine) and 4 (William), but not in chapter 1. (I have avoided discussing this topic in chapter 5 on Erasmus, even though there would have been significant material for reflection here, as R. Sider, the translator and editor of Erasmus's *Annotations on Romans* has shown.[26] Likewise, Origen's depiction of Paul as a tour guide of a king's palace whose commission is to reveal partially the divine mysteries and recruit an army for the king is discussed only in chapter 5 on Erasmus, who found this comparison instructive. Moreover, Origen's texts that comment on Romans 1 ("God handed them over") and Romans 9 (predestination, the meaning of the hardening of Pharaoh's heart) are engaged outside of chapter 1. The first chapter focuses primarily on Origen's understanding of justification, faith, and works, with an excursus on Origen's doctrine of grace.

The initial chapter on Origen's doctrine of justification shows that Origen's anti-Gnostic, anti-Marcion polemic is determinative for some of his theological emphases, especially his focus on interpreting Paul as an untiring defender of the free choice of the will. Yet the anti-Gnostic polemic is not the sole grounds for Origen's views. The heart of Origen's interpretation of Romans is direct reflection on Paul's text interpreted canonically and ecclesiastically. The main result of this rather lengthy examination is the confirmation of Rivière's thesis, that Origen stresses the intimate connection of faith and good works as the two complementary conditions of salvation that must not be separated. Marcion was the first "Christian" to assert that God will not weigh the Christian's works in the judgment. In the face of Marcion's denials, Origen contends for the unity of justice, holiness, and mercy in the one God, which implies that the Christian's good and evil works will be recompensed. Yet Origen regards this teaching as a part of the deposit of faith and not merely a reaction against heretics. That is to say, Origen believed that the Rule of Faith, tracing back to the apostles, upheld the doctrine that good works done freely have meritorious value and secure eternal life for the baptized Christian. Conversely, evil works, including those done by believers, will merit punishment. The first chapter concludes with an excursus covering modern assessments of Origen's doctrine of grace and his relation to Augustinian and Pelagian theology.

The rest of the book comprises six chapters that investigate Origen's legacy in the West as an interpreter of Romans. On the matter of justification, I have found that Origen's discussions cleared a path for later theologians who likewise attempted to demonstrate harmony between the ideas of Paul and James. Origen supplied material for exegesis that was extensively exploited by subsequent theologians. I examine in some detail the use of Origen by seven theologians: Pelagius, Augustine, William of St. Thierry, Erasmus, Melanchthon, Richard Montagu, and, to a lesser degree, Cornelius Jansen.

Pelagius was a natural choice, since he was Rufinus's contemporary and the first Latin theologian to engage Origen's interpretations of Paul in their Latin garb. Pelagius's own *Commentary on Romans* itself became a classic work in the West in a revised form (with orthodox interpolations). It was transmitted pseudonymously, and its authorship by Pelagius was unknown until the twentieth century. Apart from a few "Pelagianizing" blemishes that focus on the doctrine of transmission of sin from Adam (Rom 5.12), it was received in the Catholic tradition as a highly instructive and concise interpretation of Romans. Since it is infused with Origen's Pauline interpretations, the exercise of clarifying Pelagius's indebtedness to Origen is worthwhile in its own right.

Chapter 2 will provide a snapshot of Pelagius, focusing on his *Commentary on Romans,* rather than a comprehensive study of all his extant writings; it will show the extent of Pelagius's borrowings from Origen and the themes around which these borrowings center. Also included are significant discussions of texts from Origen's *CRm* not mentioned in the first chapter, especially ones pertaining to the interpretation of Rom 5.12 and the doctrine of original sin. I endeavor to interpret Pelagius fairly and sympathetically, though I still find grounds for agreeing with St. Augustine, who upon reading Pelagius's *CRm* immediately reproached the author for a faulty understanding of the transmission of sin.

The third chapter focuses on Augustine's possible use of Origen's *CRm.* The importance of this Church Father should be obvious. My research follows the path taken by Bammel, who endeavored to show that Augustine did not neglect the Latin Origen's exegesis of Paul. In some respects, the result is surprising: Augustine viewed the Latin Origen as an ally in the war against Pelagius's understanding of the transmission of sin. On the other hand, Augustine's theological framework is independent and decidedly different from Origen's, especially in his later anti-Pelagian period. There are clear tensions in their respective Pauline interpretations. Still, Augustine was ready to learn from Origen as a Pauline exegete, and his dissent does not focus on Origen's explanation of the constitutive role that faith and postbaptismal good works play in justification, or in Origen's conception of justification as a renovation in the virtues.

In his last works, Augustine explicitly defines Origen's departures from orthodoxy, and his exposé focuses on Origen's eschatology, doctrine of creation, and doctrine of souls. I argue that for all his explicit and implicit disagreements with Origen's understanding of Paul, Augustine does not focus his most serious criticisms of Origen's theology on Origen's exegesis of Romans. This is an important result, for it shows a clear distinction between Augustine and the Protestant Reformers, Luther and Melanchthon, who claimed to be loyal Augustinians.

The fourth chapter focuses on William of St. Thierry, an important though somewhat neglected Augustinian theologian of the twelfth century. In this chapter I first show how the ground was prepared for a favorable reception of Origen's exegesis of Romans in the Middle Ages when St. Jerome implicitly endorsed it in his own Pauline commentaries, and Cassiodorus explicitly approved it in his *Institutiones*. As a result many medieval theologians exploited the Latin Origen's exegesis of Paul. This chapter contains the most detailed textual analysis of any chapter in this book, since William's exposition lends itself to this sort of analysis. William's extensive use of the Latin Origen exemplifies the way a deeply committed Augustinian theologian was capable of receiving Origen in a friendly manner as an interpreter of Paul. Indeed, in his preface William associates Origen with Ambrose and Augustine as a doctor of the Church. While borrowing massively from Origen's exegesis in his own, particularly for the explanation of Romans 1–6, William nevertheless keeps his predominantly Augustinian theological framework intact. The way he does this is by glossing his plagiarisms from Origen with Augustine's anti-Pelagian insights. The result is a new and original synthesis that capitalizes on what William regards as Origen's best insights, while preserving the structures of the late Augustine's doctrine of grace. This chapter also contains discussions of important texts from Origen's *CRm* that are not mentioned in the first chapter, especially pertaining to Romans 1 and 9, the themes of divine election and reprobation. William exemplifies the possibility of an "Augustinian" reception of Origen's Pauline exegesis. William's favorable reception of Origen's exegesis stands out in dramatic contrast with the programmatic rejection of Origen that is found in the professedly Augustinian theologians Luther, Melanchthon, and Jansen.

The fifth chapter focuses on the great patrologist Erasmus of Rotterdam. Erasmus admired Origen as one of the greatest of the ancient exegetes of Romans and assimilated a massive amount of Origen's exegesis into his own interpretations of Romans. However, he did not do so in the plagiarizing manner that William had adopted. Erasmus was the master of the Origenian material, whereas William had been more of a servant of Origen's interpretations. Following Godin, I first identify some of the basic principles of Erasmus's reception of Origen's Pauline exegesis. Then I compare his *Paraphrase on Romans* with Origen's *CRm*. My aim is once again to illustrate Origen's substantial legacy in the West as an interpreter of Paul. In contrast with the work of William, whose *Exposition on Romans* had no subsequent legacy, Erasmus's biblical scholarship was itself extremely influential in both Catholic and Protestant circles. Thus through him Origen's voice was heard and it exerted an indirect influence (though this influence is not discussed here).

Chapter 5 also contains a significant excursus covering Origen's legacy among Erasmus's predecessors in the fifteenth century and his contemporaries in the sixteenth century. I have also appended a discussion of the first printed editions of Origen's writings. This excursus demonstrates how access to Origen's writings was obtained during this period. Also, this material shows that Erasmus was the heir of an Origen renaissance and not its principal instigator, an all too common misconception. Moreover, I contend that Erasmus was no "Origenist," as he is often described; rather he endeavored to retrieve the best of the entire Greek and Latin exegetical tradition, and his reception of Origen was largely determined by the principle of patristic consensus.

The sixth chapter attempts to provide an answer to the question that P. Grech posed in what is probably the most important article in English on Origen's doctrine of justification in his *CRm*, namely, "How would the Reformers have accepted Origen's exegesis?"[27] Because Luther and Melanchthon represent a fulcrum moment in the history of interpretation of Romans in the West, namely the Protestant Reformation, I treat the matter in some detail. The answer to Grech's question is basically that they radically and programmatically rejected the basic structures of

Origen's exegesis of Paul and accused it of being "Pelagian," or rather, anti-Christian. But according to Luther's own account of his conversion experience, his discovery of a new and unprecedented understanding of Romans was determinative for his attitude toward the Church Fathers and his assessment of the value of ancient Christian exegesis. Under Luther's decisive influence, Melanchthon crafted a theoretical justification for the Lutheran Reformation in the form of a decadence theory of Church history. This theory was later perpetuated in the Lutheran *Centuries of Magdeburg*. According to Melanchthon, Origen's faulty exegesis of Romans plays a decisive role in the corruption of the Church's understanding of the Pauline "gospel." He argues that the Protestant schism is the only legitimate answer to such corruption.

My analysis of Melanchthon's critique of Origen shows that the essential criticism turns on Origen's doctrine of justification, not his doctrine of grace or his practice of allegorical exegesis. Moreover, Melanchthon's critique of Origen on this doctrine is identical with his critique of his contemporary Catholic opponents, of St. Thomas Aquinas, and St. Augustine himself. The evidence strongly suggests that the Lutheran Reformation was not directed merely against medieval Catholicism. Instead, Luther and Melanchthon viewed the corruption of medieval theology to be of a piece with the corruption of ancient Christian exegesis, as exemplified especially by Origen, and embracing St. Jerome's interpretation of Paul, but by no means excluding Augustine's. In short, the Lutheran Reformation was *Luther's* Reformation, not Augustine's. Though carried out *publicly* in the name of Augustine as a battle against medieval corruptions, it was *privately* acknowledged, by both Luther and Melanchthon, to be directed *against* St. Augustine's own interpretation of Paul.

The final chapter surveys the reception of Origen's Pauline exegesis in post-Reformation controversies. After briefly mentioning the use of Origen's *CRm* by late sixteenth century Protestants, I then treat in more detail an early seventeenth-century polemical exchange between a Jesuit-influenced Catholic lay apologist, John Heigham, and his Anglican opponent, Bishop Richard Montagu. The latter theologian's amiable reception of Origen stands out in stark contrast with Luther and Melanchthon's. This shows, of course, that Protestantism was not univocal in its attitude toward Origen as an exegete of Paul. Indeed, in a surpising text discovered in the course of my research, Montagu declares Origen to be the "perfect Protestant," and he says this precisely of the doctrine that Luther and Melanchthon believed was Origen's gravest error, namely justification by faith. Montagu's importance is in the many ways he represents and anticipates the friendly reception of ancient Christian exegesis found in an important sector of Protestantism which is clearly distinguishable from the Lutheran and Calvinist branches, namely that of anti-Calvinist Anglicanism and Continental Arminianism. In many ways Montagu also anticipates the later Anglo-Catholic movement of the nineteenth century.

This chapter concludes with a look at Cornelius Jansen's *Augustinus,* in which we encounter another decadence theory that is riveted on Origen's *CRm*. Like Melanchthon, Jansen accuses Origen's *CRm* of being a fatal source of "Pelagian" theology. But Jansen's understanding of "Pelagianism" is totally different from Melanchthon's, whose definition in turn differs from Augustine's. Jansen's accusation of Origen turns on Origen's doctrine of grace and his interpretation of Romans 9 (predestination as foreknowledge, the hardening of Pharaoh's heart). At this point in the investigation, I briefly discuss the Molinist doctrine of election *post praevisa merita* in order to show that one of the accusations that Jansen raises against Origen also lands on prominent Jesuit theologians who were Jansen's contemporaries. This indicates that Jansen's understanding of "Pelagian" is broader than that of the Catholic Church for it embraces positions that the Church (at least the Roman Catholic Church) does not condemn as "Pelagian." This is also confirmed by the fact that the Magisterium censured Jansen's book. That Origen was still the focus of much discussion during these intra-Church controversies demonstrates the ongoing legacy of Origen's interpretations.

This book aims to cover the major periods in the history of Christian thought; though this means that many important theologians had to be left out of the discussion.

The Complementarity of Faith and Works

The thesis of chapter 1 is that Origen demonstrates the intimate connection of faith and good works as the two complementary conditions of salvation that must not be separated. I find solid reasons for agreeing with Verfaillie that Origen's doctrine of justification anticipates the principal affirmations of the Council of Trent's decree on justification. For chapters 2–7, I argue that Origen's discussions of justification assisted later Catholic theologians in demonstrating the equal necessity of faith and postbaptismal good works for justification. Furthermore, I demonstrate that Origen's legacy in the West as an interpreter of Paul was very substantial. Catholic theologians generally read and explained Paul's Letter to the Romans under the tutelage of the Latin Origen. Clearly, Origen's Pauline interpretation exerted a massive direct influence on Pelagius, William, and Erasmus. This is not to say that Catholic theologians received Origen as an unassailable and infallible authority on Paul. On the contrary, Origen's interpretations were always susceptible to disagreement, criticism, and even reproach; but Origen's Pauline exegesis was generally received as Catholic exegesis. Although his anti-Pelagian theological system stands in significant tension with some of Origen's Pauline interpretations, even Augustine did not make Origen's *CRm* the principal locus of Origen's errors. Moreover, on the theme of justification, faith, and works, Augustine does not differ substantially from Origen. Furthermore, that a thoroughgoing Augustinian theologian like William of St. Thierry could still adopt so much of Origen's Pauline exegesis throughout his exposition of Romans 1–6 shows that even Augustinians had found a way of substantially receiving Origen as a guide to the interpretation of Romans.

Luther and Melanchthon mark a significant aberration in this pattern in that they were the first to identify Origen's Pauline exegesis as the principal source of Origen's errors, indeed as the source of deformation that justified their reformation. Their radical challenge to Origen's stature as an interpreter of Paul focused on the conviction that Origen had fundamentally misunderstood Paul's doctrine of justification and the law/gospel distinction. In a similar manner, Cornelius Jansen viewed Origen's *CRm* as the fountainhead of Pelagianism, but in Jansen's opinion this was owing to Origen's allegedly faulty understanding of predestination and grace. Yet the mere fact that such sweeping criticisms of Origen's *CRm* arose and that such decadence theories were spawned confirms my thesis concerning the significant legacy of Origen's commentary in the West. For even Origen's enemies were unable to remain neutral about his Pauline exegesis and were forced to engage it.

Chapter 1

Origen's Doctrine
of Justification

Introduction

Since the sixteenth century, and primarily on account of the Protestant
Reformation, the doctrine of justification has been the subject of an enor-
mous body of theological literature. This pattern has continued through
the twentieth century down to the present day and shows no signs of abat-
ing.[1] In the literature of the early ages of the Catholic Church, however,
this doctrine was not made the object of direct study. The thoughts of the
Fathers on this theme are more or less scattered and occasional. However,
one work from Christian antiquity constitutes an exception to this pattern: Origen's *Commentary on the Epistle to the Romans*. In this work, originally written between 244 and 246, the author responds to numerous
statements of the Apostle Paul in Romans with detailed discussions and
explanations of the meaning of justification in Paul and in the rest of
the Bible. This makes Origen's *CRm* a work of unique importance in the
history of theology, and particularly with respect to the doctrine of justification.[2] Its significance in this respect has not been entirely neglected by
modern theologians.[3]

Survey of Modern Scholarship

Rivière and Verfaillie

In his important article "Justification," Rivière remarked that Origen's treatment of this doctrine in his *CRm* is the best and most complete expression of the Catholic teaching in the pre-Augustinian Church Fathers.[4] This prominent Catholic theologian[5] argued that Origen's discussions cleared a path for later theologians who would attempt to demonstrate harmony between the ideas of Paul and James on justification; for Origen had showed the intimate connection of faith and good works as the two complementary conditions of salvation that must not be separated.[6] Rivière also commended Origen for keeping himself from the excess of one of his disciples, Hieracas, who attached so much importance to the necessity of good works for salvation that he excluded from heaven infants who die after baptism because they had been unable to accomplish any works.[7] Epiphanius reports that Hieracas's followers believed "that children who have not reached the age of puberty have no part in the kingdom, since they have not engaged in the struggle."[8] Clear texts in Origen's *CRm* show that while he affirms the necessity both of good works for salvation and of infant baptism for the forgiveness of sins,[9] he does not draw the negative inferences from these affirmations, as Hieracas had apparently done. If Rivière had a text in Origen in mind where Origen shows such restraint, he may be referring to the passage in the *CRm* where Origen seems to mitigate the responsibility of little children and the mentally incompetent by asking whether they are exempt from the precepts of natural law, since the judgment of right and wrong does not yet exist in them.[10] Origen also explains how death in Rom 5.12–14 stands in a variety of relationships to human beings. It affects children under the age of reason in the least degree, in such a way that although spiritual death affects all human beings, it is final only for those who of their own choice persist in transgression.[11]

Inspired by Rivière's commendation of Origen's discussions, Verfaillie devoted a dissertation to fleshing out Origen's doctrine of justification.[12] Verfaillie was partly reacting to what he considered to be the Protestant exploitation of Origen's statements about justification "by faith alone," an apologetical usage he considered to be entirely naive. In response he crafted a dissertation with a somewhat reactionary and apologetic purpose.[13] Verfaillie concluded that, on the contrary, Origen's understanding of justification in fact anticipates the principal affirmations of the Council of Trent's decree on justification. This applies to several points of fundamental importance: an original Fall but not a total corruption of humanity, the necessity and efficaciousness of Christ's redemptive work, the application of Christ's redemption through the indivisible cooperation of God and the human being, the effective sanctification of the soul through grace, and the meritorious value of the soul's actions in view of glory. "Such are the doctrines opposed by the Church to the Reformation. Yet they are all already found clearly in Origen."[14]

Verfaillie's defense of Origen's Catholic orthodoxy on the matter of justification confirmed Rivière's thesis, that Origen's understanding of justification was essentially Catholic in how it treats the relation of faith and works as an organic and inseparable unity. Both Rivière and Verfaillie argued that in spite of the claims of certain Protestant dogmaticians who had naively tried to depict Origen as a proto-Protestant by exploiting certain isolated statements where Origen had used the formulation "justification by faith alone," Origen was not in fact a Protestant on this issue.[15] It is certainly interesting to note that Origen's explanation of the Pauline phrase "justification by faith" in *CRm* 3.9 was read aloud at the Council of Trent, alongside citations from other orthodox Fathers.[16] It is also remarkable that the magisterial Protestants, Luther and Melanchthon, vehemently accused Origen of corruption on this exact point. They even crafted a decadence theory of Church history in which Origen's doctrine of justification plays a decisive role in the ensuing theological darkness and constitutes a compelling justification for the Lutheran revolt.[17] It seems that any attempt completely to dismiss Verfaillie's main thesis will have to give an account for Luther and Melanchthon's intense hostility to Origen's Pauline exegesis.

Molland and Seeberg

As a secondary thesis, Verfaillie argued that justification occupies a central place in Origen's theology. This assertion is provocative. The Lutheran Molland, for example, claims that justification is a peripheral doctrine to Origen and not related to his core understanding of the gospel.[18] On the other hand, Osborn agrees in principle with Verfaillie and argues that justification occupies a central position in Origen's thought.[19] It will not be possible to explore this particular question here. Molland articulates the difference between Origen, on the one hand, and Luther/Marcion on the other, in these terms:

> In all the works of Origen there is hardly a passage where he conceives of the relation of the Law and Gospel in the Pauline terms of νόμος and χάρις, the role of the Law being to convince mankind of sin and bring all men under the judgment of God, whereas redemption comes by Grace through the Gospel. Of this idea, which is so central in theological thinkers like Marcion and Luther and has determined their whole conception of the Gospel, there are but very faint traces in Origen. To him it is of little interest to contrast Law and Grace, because Grace is found in the Law if it is rightly understood.[20]

Molland rightly identifies their law/gospel definitions as fundamental differences between Luther and Origen. He exemplifies the point that law and grace are not contraries in Origen by referring to Origen's interpretation of Paul's words in Rom 6.14, "You are not under law but under grace." Here *law* for Origen must mean the law that is reigning in our members, of which Paul speaks in Rom 7.23. It cannot be the law of God that is put in contrast to grace. Origen continues, "But if anybody will find the law of Moses in Rom 6.14, he must say that the meaning of the phrase is: We are not under the letter of the law that kills, but under the law of the Spirit that makes alive and is called grace."[21] Origen's nuanced understanding of the Pauline term *law* is one of the distinctive features of his *CRm*.

Based on such statements, Molland concludes that Origen conceives of the difference and contrast of the law and the gospel in terms quite other than those of judgment and grace, as is found in the theology of Luther and Marcion. For Origen the difference is defined in terms of imperfect and perfect religion. Here appears an essential element of Origen's understanding of salvation history and the relation between law and gospel, namely that for Origen law and grace are not contraries; and it is the incarnation of God's Son that determines the transition point from shadow to reality, from imperfect to perfect religion.

The assertion that Origen understands the Pauline terms of law, gospel, and justification in a way that conflicts with the standard Protestant perspective on these terms is admitted by most Protestant scholars. Among modern historians of dogma, the Lutheran Seeberg gives what appears to be a fairly balanced Protestant critique of Origen:

> Origen, in his commentary upon Romans, reproduced the Pauline doctrine of justification, but was not able to maintain himself at the altitude of that conception. Faith is sufficient, indeed, for righteousness, but it finds its consummation in works, and suffices only because it has ever works in view. "Righteousness cannot be imputed to an unrighteous man. Christ justifies only those who have received new life from the example of his resurrection."[22]

Seeberg refers to other texts in Origen's writings where similar views are found, namely where the forgiveness of sins and the salvation and eternal happiness of the human being depend not only upon faith but more upon repentance and good works.[23] Seeberg also cites *Commentary on the Song of Songs* 3.12: "The salvation of believers is accomplished in two ways, through the acknowledgment (*agnitionem*) of faith and through the perfection of works." The essential point of Seeberg's criticism of Origen seems to be that Origen viewed faith and postbaptismal good works as complementary causes of justification that, from a salvific point of view, belong inseparably together. In other words, the criticism states that Origen in his deepest teaching did not locate in faith alone the sole and exclusive condition of salvation. Thus he failed "to maintain himself at the altitude" of the "Pauline" (sc. "Lutheran") conception. It is certainly striking that what for Rivière and Verfaillie is the badge of honor for Origen's conception of justification in the *CRm*—namely, the way it views faith and good works as equally constitutive of justification—is for Molland and Seeberg the grounds for reproaching Origen.

Wiles, Heither, and Reasoner

More recent discussions of Origen's doctrine of justification in his *CRm* by Protestants and Catholics have reached conclusions that in some ways reverse the reader's expectations, but in other ways do not.[24] The

Protestant M. Wiles claims that there is a clear and radical difference of spirit between the ways in which Paul and Origen speak about faith.[25] Generally, Wiles thinks that Origen has "tamed" and domesticated Paul. One way he has done this is by mitigating the apparent absoluteness of Paul's "attack" on the law.[26] Wiles repeatedly accuses Origen of incoherence, and, for example, he finds it hard to reconcile Origen's statements on the relation between faith and works in his *CRm*. He is especially puzzled by texts where Origen says, on the one hand, that the judgment on believers' works may amount to assigning him a place with the unbelievers,[27] and yet, on the other hand, that faith alone saves.[28] Wiles assesses this as follows:

> We might say that Origen appears to assert that faith without any ensuing works will save a man, whereas faith followed by evil works will not be reckoned as faith at all. No doubt there is an element of inconsistency in Origen's thought at this point, but the most significant fact is that at his best Origen is not really prepared to accept the problem at all in the precise form in which it is here posed.[29]

Wiles later says that Origen's comments on Rom 10.9 represent his most fundamental resolution of the problem of faith and works. Here Origen states that the one who confesses Jesus with his mouth must similarly confess himself to be subject to the lordship of wisdom, righteousness, truth, and everything else that Christ is. For Origen, Christ did not merely possess the various virtues accidentally or contingently; Christ is his attributes. Origen makes this point clear not only by John but also by Paul, especially in 1 Cor 1.30. What this indicates is that for Origen our relationship to Christ is automatically our relationship to wisdom, righteousness, truth, and all the other virtues. To be "in Christ" is to be "in" all the virtues; to have Christ in us is to have them in us. To be "in Christ" is the same as to serve him, and to be his servant is to be the servant of all the virtues. To put on Christ is to put on all the virtues, and conversely to put on the armor of God is to put on Christ. Wiles's conclusion from this is the following: "Clearly therefore according to this analysis there can be for Origen no faith without works. Faith in Christ does not need to be supplemented by the virtuous life; it *is* the adoption of the virtues. Thus the connection between faith and works is a logically necessary one."[30] I regard Wiles's analysis here as filled with insight and will return to it below. It amounts to saying that Origen interprets the Pauline phrase "justification by faith" as a synecdoche in the sense of part for the whole. We are justified by faith that embraces and is not exclusive of all the other infused theological virtues. On the other hand it seems erroneous to deny, as Wiles does, that Origen can conceive of faith without works. It is rather the case that Origen would acknowledge such faith but not consider it "living."

T. Heither, in an important recent monograph, *Translatio Religionis,* claims that Origen is at his best as an interpreter in his *CRm,* and he even offers valuable insights for modern exegesis, even if, or rather precisely because, Origen's interpretation antedates the Pelagian crisis and is thus foreign to Western discussions that succeeded from Luther. Citing the work of K. Stendahl and the revolution in Pauline interpretation that succeeded from this, Heither claims that the modern perspective on Romans no longer accepts *a priori* that justification by faith alone is the essential and exclusive concern of Paul in Romans.[31] For Heither, this new perspective opens up good possibilities for allowing Origen to make an important contribution to the modern exegetical discussion.[32] Heither claims that Origen does not view faith and works as contraries, but as fundamentally and indeed organically related concepts. On the other hand, she nevertheless makes the seemingly surprising claim (for a Catholic) that Paul himself does speak of justification by faith *alone* in Rom 4.5 (such a qualification is absent from Paul's text). Heither claims that Origen defends Paul's "radical" doctrine with concrete examples.[33] Heither believes that Origen "resolves" the problem of faith and works in his comment at 4.1.18 (965), where he claims that faith obtains the righteousness out of which works emerge, as branches from a root, and that this relation is not reversible. Surprisingly, Heither does not engage Verfaillie's investigation or make any reference to it.

Finally, the recent monograph by the Protestant Mark Reasoner, *Romans in Full Circle,* treats the reader to a deeply sympathetic presentation of Origen's interpretation of Paul's letter. Reasoner confirms Heither's reading, that Origen's interpretation of Romans is remarkably consonant with the direction taken by the "new perspective" in modern Pauline interpretation. I will return to Reasoner's path-breaking work in the conclusion of this book.

If the weakness of Wiles's study is his inability to see consistency in Origen's thought, the weakness with Heither's investigation is her tendency to be reductionistic by neglecting several important texts in Origen where he explicitly rejects the formulation "justification by faith alone" as a genuinely Pauline idea. These texts will not be neglected in my analysis below. This brief survey of some modern assessments of Origen's doctrine will, it is to be hoped, provide a context for investigating his views in greater depth.

Polemic Against Heretics

Valentinus and Basilides

I would like to begin this investigation of Origen's doctrine of justification in his *CRm* by identifying the heretical backdrop of his discussions. Origen combats heretics throughout the *CRm*, especially the trio of Marcion, Valentinus, and Basilides. Indeed, in the preface Origen says that he was prompted to write his *CRm* because the "heretics" had been making use of Paul's Letter to the Romans to advocate their own perverted doctrines. The chief of these is the denial of the free choice of the will and the doctrine of salvation by natures.[34] To be more specific, Origen says that those who proceed from the school of Valentinus and Basilides teach that "there is a nature of souls that would always be saved and never perish, and another that would always perish and never be saved."[35] Origen also attributes this doctrine of natures to Marcion's school.[36]

Valentinus and Basilides were Gnostic heretics of the second century. The former was an Egyptian who taught in Rome from 135 to 160 and was probably the most influential of the Gnostics. Basilides taught in Alexandria. Valentinus taught a sort of natural predestination that divided humanity into three categories. The redeemer, Jesus, saves people from the world by giving them saving knowledge, or *gnosis*. The *gnosis* is available only to the spiritual (*pneumatikoi*). The second kind of nature is the "soulish" (*psychikoi*) and refers to ordinary members of the Catholic Church, who can achieve some kind of salvation by faith and good works. The third group is the rest of humanity, or the "natural" (*hylikoi*), who have no chance at redemption.[37] Clearly, according to such a system, human freedom in salvation is unreal, since redemption is based on the nature one receives at birth, at least for the first and third categories of humanity. Grech summarizes the heretical teaching as follows: "Many gnostics, in fact, affirmed that the hylics and the pneumatics are born so, only the psychics have the freedom to move towards matter or spirit."[38]

Origen, in contrast, believed that the doctrine of freedom was a part of the apostolic deposit of faith. In *Peri Archon* 3.1, he says that the teaching of the Church includes the doctrine of the just judgment of God, a doctrine that summons its hearers to live a good life and by every means avoid sin; for the doctrine assumes that human beings acknowledge that deeds worthy of praise or blame lie within their own power.[39] In short, for Origen the freedom of creatures and the corresponding merit and demerit of works is an inference from the doctrine of judgment.[40] In order for God's judgment to be just, it must be exercised on responsible creatures.[41] In his *CRm*, it is evident that the Valentinians and Basilidians have provoked Origen all the more by denying freedom altogether. Against their claims, he will make the free choice of the will one of his principal theological preoccupations in his *CRm*.[42] Origen believes that the free choice of the will, not one's nature, is the principle that distinguishes good and evil souls. Consequently, every nature is equally suited for salvation or, if it becomes negligent, for perdition, since freedom of will always abides in rational creatures.[43] Origen articulates this view early on in the *CRm*:

> But out of both sides' support, the duty of choice is preserved. For the matter is not done by force nor is the soul moved in either of the two directions by compulsion. Otherwise neither blame nor virtue could be ascribed to it, nor would the choice of the good earn a reward or the turning aside to evil merit punishment. Instead the freedom of choice is preserved in the soul in all things, so that it may turn to what it wants, just as it is written, "See, I have set before you life and death," "fire and water." Life, therefore is Christ, and death refers to the last enemy, the devil. The soul therefore makes its own decision whether it want to choose life, that is Christ, or to turn aside to death, the devil.[44]

Just as in *Peri Archon* 3 and *Cels* 1, freedom and the corresponding reward, or recompense of merit and demerit, is an inference from the doctrine of the coming judgment. In Origen's view, in light of the divine judgment, the soul must have the power to serve whom it wishes, whether Christ or the devil. It must incline to good or evil not by necessity, as the Gnostics claim, but by free choice. If this were not the case, guilt and reward could not be justly assigned, and both virtue and merit would be annihilated.

In a passage related to this theme, Origen challenges Christians to take heed to keep their bodies and hearts undefiled by means of conversion and repentance and to prepare every day cleaner wedding garments: "Wearing them, let us deserve to enter the palace of wisdom and the chambers of the King's Son."[45] The context shows Origen to be explaining Jesus' parable in Mt 22.1–12 about the future judgment awaiting his disciples. Matthew's text in 22.8 explicitly states that those who are excluded are unworthy. Origen takes Jesus' words at face value and concludes that one merits, or becomes worthy of, entering the palace by using one's free will in a good way, by doing good works and by keeping oneself from sin. Once again, merit and demerit are a direct inference from Jesus' teaching about the coming judgment.

Elsewhere Origen stresses that human beings have a definite responsibility in the matter of their salvation and sanctification. The future judgment would have no meaning if they did not. He says, for example, that we will not be reckoned to be in the flesh but in the Spirit, "if only by our deeds and manner of life we are such that we deserve to have the Spirit of God in us."[46] The gift of the Spirit may be sought by merits and preserved by the blamelessness of one's life, and grace may even be increased in each person according to his progress in faith. "And the purer the soul is returned, the more generously the Spirit is poured into it."[47] Nowhere does Origen deny that God's assisting grace is necessary for this achievement of a blameless life, though he certainly does not stress its necessity. Commenting on the latter text (6.13), Grech writes, "Though righteousness is certainly God's gift, it remains unclear whether the Spirit is also its author or merited by it. Perhaps we can find a parallel in the Catholic doctrine of sanctifying grace which grows with merit."[48] This appears to be a proper analogy for receiving Origen's interpretation.

It seems somewhat paradoxical that, on the one hand, Origen affirms freedom and merit/demerit as being entailed in the ecclesiastical doctrine of the future judgment on our works; and yet, on the other hand, Origen completely repudiates any thought of religious boasting in works. Inspired by Gal 6.14, he insists that not only is all Jewish boasting in works of the law excluded, so is the Christian's boasting in his own virtues. In light of texts like Mt 5.28, Prv 20.9, 1 Cor 1.21, and Isa 64.6, Origen concludes that the Christian's virtues of chastity, wisdom, and righteousness cannot provide him valid grounds for boasting. For the only legitimate boasting is based upon faith in the cross of Christ which excludes all boasting that derives from the works of the law.[49] With respect to Isa 64.6, a text much used in later tradition, Origen says, "And who will boast about his own righteousness when he hears God saying through the prophet, 'all your righteousness is like the rag of a menstruous woman'?"[50] The implied answer is: "No one." Thus in Origen's view, in the Christian dispensation, the human being cannot lay claim to works of any kind *as grounds for boasting*. This includes moral and religious works, in light of the cross of Christ.[51] Merit and demerit are entirely affirmed, but religious boasting is entirely excluded.

In summary Origen affirms the recompense of merit and demerit in some very real sense, as the work and duty of God, who promises to repay good and evil human works in the coming judgment. The fact that the Old Testament prophets along with Jesus and Paul repeatedly threaten believers with the possibility of the exclusion of the unworthy from the kingdom implies the existence of freedom. On the other hand, religious boasting on the part of the human being is entirely excluded. It appears that Origen's polemic against Valentinian Gnosticism is an important factor that leads him to affirm strongly the reality of human merit that accrues to free human choices leading to salvation or damnation. And yet, for Origen, God is a rewarder of virtue and a punisher of vice by nature. Origen has found this doctrine embedded in the apostolic deposit of faith. God's judgment is not based on any sort of natural predestination, but rather, the principle that determines good and evil souls is the free choice of the will.

Marcion

Origen also endeavors throughout the commentary to refute Marcion, the heretic from Pontus who came to Rome around 136–40 and was expelled from the Roman Church in 144.[52] Marcion was scandalized by the problem of evil and other philosophical issues, and his response was to reject his former faith.[53] He thought out a doctrinal system based on the irrecon-cilability of justice and grace, law and gospel, Judaism and Christianity, the God of the Old Testament and the Father of Jesus. He admitted two deities, a good, nonjudicial God (the Father of Jesus), who is not to be feared, and a just but inferior god known as the Demiurge (the Creator of the world = the God of the OT and of the Jews), in whom resides the grounds of fear, anger, severity, judgment, vengeance, and condemna-tion.[54] Marcion so emphasized the absolute newness of the dispensation brought by Jesus that he repudiated the OT in its entirety. He denied that it predicted the coming of Jesus or spoke about the good Father pro-claimed by Jesus. Moreover, he taught his followers that the received form of the New Testament had been corrupted by Judaizing Christians, whom he identifies as the Catholics of his day.[55] He "edited" the Gospel of Luke and ten of Paul's letters and made these documents the canon of his church. And by removing texts even from within these writings which he found incompatible with his antecedent theology, he succeeded in his own mind in severing the link between what he regarded as the original core of the Jesus/Paul religion and Old Testament Judaism.[56]

In the *CRm* Origen associates Marcion with the same doctrine of natures that Valentinus and Basilides taught.[57] Whether or not this is a somewhat stereotyped association,[58] it does seem that, from the Catholic perspective, Marcion implicitly denied the freedom of will and the corre-sponding future judgment on the Christian's works. Tertullian discusses Marcion's view of freedom of will in *Against Marcion* 2.5–8 and 4.41. In these texts Tertullian answers Marcion's cavils against the Creator God, which led Marcion to deny human responsibility for the Fall. Instead, Marcion pinned the blame for sin on the Creator who had made creatures whom he then permitted to fall from obedience into death. Such a God, in Marcion's view, could not be good, prescient, and powerful.

In the first passage Tertullian replies to Marcion by saying that these creatures were endowed with freedom of will, which is the very meaning of their being made in the image of God. Thus the blame for the Fall is on God's creatures, who misused their freedom, rather than on God. In 4.41 Tertullian shows that Marcion's cavils, if applied consistently, would nec-essarily also land on Jesus, who permitted his disciples Peter and Judas to fall into sin. This again points to Marcion's implicit denial of human freedom. The consultation of Tertullian shows that Origen does not seem unjustified in associating Marcion with the denial of the free choice of the will in salvation, along with Valentinus and Basilides. For this was a traditional association. The orthodox Fathers received Marcion's accusations against the Creator God, and his blaming the Creator for subsequent sin, as an implicit attack upon human freedom.

In the *CRm* Origen repeatedly attacks Marcion's doctrine that the good God is not a just judge.[59] Marcion evidently taught his followers that since the God of Jesus is good but not just, he will not take into consideration the merit and worth of their works in the judgment. Faith alone will be the sole criterion of salvation for the Marcionites. This is not to say that Marcion was licentious and antinomian. On the contrary, even Tertullian bears decisive testimony to the exceptional purity of his life and his rigorous asceticism.[60] Marcion apparently firmly held that human beings would be rewarded or punished hereafter according to their deeds in this life. He was obligated to recognize a judgment in some form or other. But this judgment—and this is a point of crucial importance—would not be executed by the Supreme God, whom Marcion represented as pure beneficence. Instead, it would be carried out by the Demiurge.[61] Cocchini summarizes Marcion's doctrine as follows: "In the doctrine of Marcion any judgment proceeded from the just God, whereas the good God, precisely because of his goodness, acknowledged mercy alone, which he gave to all, leaving out of consideration more or less meritorious actions."[62] In short, Marcion has introduced duality into the deity. He posits two gods, which means that, from Origen's point of view, Marcion's claim to recognize a future judgment is utterly meaningless, since that judgment proceeds from a different god and not from the Father of Jesus.

Origen attributes such views to Marcion and Marcion's subsequent followers.[63] In opposition to Marcion, Origen stresses the unity and coherence of the Bible and of the God described therein.[64] In a key passage that comments on Rom 1.17, Origen says:

> But notice that he has not recorded the single cause of faith alone for the disclosing of the righteousness of God, but he also associates the law and the prophets. For faith alone, apart from the law and the prophets, does not disclose the righteousness of God, nor on the

other hand do the law and the prophets [disclose it] apart from faith. The one is rooted in [*haeret*] the other so that perfection comes from both. . . . And so, both, by cleaving to one another [*adhaerens*], are consummated, the one from the other.[65]

In this context the term faith seems to refer to the new religion brought by Christ.[66] The idea of faith being "rooted" and "cleaving" to the law and the prophets will be seen elsewhere in contexts stressing the organic connection between faith and works, where the same verbs appear.[67] For Origen faith and works go together like the two testaments. You must have both for perfection. The current passage seems clearly directed at the Marcionites, who separated their severely truncated body of Christian writings from the law and the prophets. They tried to drive a wedge between the faith and religion of the New Covenant and the previous dispensation of the law and the prophets, going so far as to posit two different gods and to deny that the good God of Jesus is also a just judge.[68] Origen's doctrine in contrast stresses the unity of the testaments and of the God of the testaments.

It seems clear that Marcion's denial that the God of Jesus is just led his sect equally to deny the salvific or meritorious value of good works for the Christian. In 8.2 Origen speaks of persons who do not understand the equal necessity of faith and good works in salvation. He refers to them as he expounds Rom 10.9, "that if you confess with your mouth that Jesus is Lord and believe in your heart that God raised him from the dead, you will be saved":

> For it will seem to some through this that even if the advantages of good works are lacking in someone, even if he does not pay heed to the virtues, nevertheless, in this, that he has believed, he would not perish but is saved and possesses salvation, even if he is unable to have the glory of blessedness.[69]

Based upon Rom 10.9–10, Origen's unnamed opponents seem to have imagined degrees of salvation and the possibility of settling for a low one. Though Origen does not explicitly identify these opponents, it is possible that he is speaking of people who have been influenced by Marcion's thinking.[70] For the language is strikingly similar to that used in 2.4[71] where

Origen refutes the "heretics" who claimed that [the] faith alone can suffice for salvation. That is basically what he says here. In the text in 2.4 Origen insists that the *just* God will pay back believers for their works. We know that the denial of God's justice is a principal tenet of Marcion's system. This suggests that Marcionite views are being engaged here in 8.2.

Origen repudiates a view that denies that Christians will be subject to a just judgment according to works. The inextricable connection between faith and good works for Origen becomes clear in the immediate context, where Origen insists that belief in Christ's resurrection and public confession of his lordship does not profit one at all if his resurrection is not realized in the life of the baptized. In fact Christ is still in the tomb for us, if we have not subjected ourselves to his lordship by giving up sin and embracing the virtues.[72] Similarly, in another passage he says that whoever complies with the lusts of the flesh nullifies the cross and undoes the work of reconciliation.[73]

In a comment on Rom 2.6, Origen says that Paul's words about the just judgment of God refute the heretics who claim that the natures of human souls are either good or evil. They need to realize that God pays back to each one not on account of his nature but on account of his works. Origen then addresses the Christians: "Let the faithful be edified lest they think that the fact alone that they believe can suffice for them, but let them know that God's righteous judgment will pay back to each one according to his own works."[74] In this passage Origen repudiates the heretical doctrine of salvation by natures by an appeal to a final decisive judgment based upon works. Origen also rebukes the view apparently held by certain Christians that there will be no just judgment of works in store for them. I have suggested that this latter group may refer to people who have fallen under the influence of Marcion's doctrine, since their error is explicitly said to be a misunderstanding regarding a *just* judgment according to works. They are deceived, Origen says, if they think that on account of their faith alone, they will be exempt from the just retribution that applies both to recompense and to punishment. For Origen the good works of the justified Christian really do have value and secure eternal life for him.[75]

Origen's comments on Rom 8.33–34 confirm that it is Paul's doctrine of the *justice* of the final judgment that governs Origen's insistence on the meritorious necessity of the believer's good works. He writes:

For unless you are chosen, unless you show yourself to be approved by God in all things, you will have an accuser. For if you have a bad case, if your indictment convicts you, what would an advocate help you, even if it be Jesus who intercedes? For Jesus is truth; therefore, the truth cannot testify falsely on your behalf. An advocate will only be of help to you in this, that you will not be overwhelmed by the malicious charges of the accuser, that your past sins, which were wiped out through baptism, should not be imputed to you. But if after these things you should again transgress and do not wash these things away with any tears of repentance, you will be offering material to your accuser to bring an indictment against you.[76]

In Origen's view the justice of the coming judgment precludes the possibility that transgression will not be punished. Baptism removes past sins, but it does not guarantee the nonimputation of the believer's future sins. For Jesus the good and merciful Savior and Advocate cannot be separated from Jesus the just Judge. It is apparently Marcion who first attempted to posit a contradiction between these indissoluble functions. For Origen, in contrast, Paul's words in Rom 8.1, "There is therefore now no condemnation for those who are in Christ Jesus . . ." cannot be severed from Rom 8.4: "who walk not according to the flesh but according to the Spirit." In other words, in order to be free from condemnation, there is to be nothing deserving of condemnation in us. By freely choosing to avoid sin and walk in the Spirit, the believer keeps and fulfills the law of Christ and preserves the innocence that was reputed to him in baptism. If he fails to do this, if he lives according to the flesh, then he will no longer be judged to be free from condemnation and will not attain final justification. To be sure Origen admits that the Christian will not be judged for his failure to keep the law of Moses, that is, circumcision, Sabbath observance, and so forth.[77] But he will undoubtedly be judged by the law of Christ. For Christ is both a redeemer to be trusted and a legislator to be obeyed. Therefore, obedience and disobedience to the law of Christ will be recompensed at the final judgment. And one of the possible outcomes of this judgment for the Christian is the failure to merit redemption.

In another passage Origen says that both our souls and our bodies must deserve to be redeemed when they come before the judgment seat of Christ. The purpose of this judgment is:

"In order that each one might receive his own reward for what he has done in the body" [cf. 2 Cor 5.10]; and according to what was said, "Instead, fear him who can destroy both the body and soul in hell" [Mt 10.28]. And for this reason each person must suffer and groan in this age, lest, on account of wicked deeds and negligence in the present life, he might not merit to attain to the redemption of his own body, but that sentence that condemns body and soul to the fires of hell should overtake him.[78]

Again the inference that flows from the Church's doctrine of final judgment is that the undeserving will disqualify themselves from attaining to final redemption. Origen is obviously not attempting to assert the human being's ability to save himself by his own powers. His theological aims are not Pelagian. Rather his intention is to take seriously Jesus' threats of judgment. McSorley indicates that such an emphasis is also directed against Marcion's theology:

When the (pre-Augustinian) Fathers argued that free will was necessary for merit or demerit, they were not seeking to extol the power of man to merit his salvation. They were simply taking seriously the scriptural teaching that God judges all men according to their works, and from this theological standpoint—from the revealed truth of the coming judgment of God—they insisted against their pagan contemporaries, Marcion above all, that the God who judges is the good God and that man had to have free will if a judgment of God is to be at all meaningful and just.[79]

Thus it is a serious misunderstanding of the patristic teaching on free will to interpret it as mere "moralism," or as an assertion of autonomous humanism. On the contrary, in its original context it was much more an assertion of the justice and the holiness of the one God. To defend human freedom in salvation is to recognize the original goodness of God's creation and to confess the biblical faith in the coming judgment of our works by God. For Origen the affirmation of freedom is at the same time a declaration of the unity of the person of Christ, as Savior, Advocate, and Judge, which implies that a fruitful reception of God's grace will merit and secure our final redemption; an unfruitful reception will earn eternal ruin.[80]

Origen's General Understanding of Romans

The Translation of Religion

Within this ecclesiastical and dogmatic framework of Origen's proclamation and, more specifically, within the context of anti-Gnostic and
anti-Marcion polemic, I would like now to turn to Origen's general understanding of Paul's Letter to the Romans. Origen believes that Paul's epistle
was written to proclaim a soteriological message: the movement of salvation history from promise to fulfillment, from imperfect to perfect religion.[81] Christ Jesus, who was announced as coming in the law and the
prophets, has fulfilled the promises of salvation that were given to Israel.[82]
Christ stands at the midpoint of salvation history, as it were, with the
prophets of Israel having preceded him and the apostles having followed.
At the beginning of his explanation of Rom 12.1ff., Origen summarizes the
ground Paul has covered in chapters 1–11:

> In the entire preceding text of the epistle the Apostle had shown
> how the essence of religion has been transferred from the Jews
> to the Gentiles, from circumcision to faith, from the letter to the
> Spirit, from shadow to truth, from fleshly observance to spiritual
> observance. Moreover, he showed that these future things had been
> depicted in this way by prophetic voices.[83]

For Origen the theme of Romans is to clarify how the essential core of the
one true religion has been transformed.[84] The Jews alone were the original bearers of true religion. But now, after the incarnation of God's Son
and the outpouring of the Holy Spirit upon the Church, the Gentiles
as well are invited to partake of salvation. The transformation of religion
occurs both in terms of salvation history (from the Jews alone to Jews and
Gentiles together in the Church) and in terms of the transformation of
the individual (from fleshly to spiritual observance). The above-cited late
review of the thematic content of the epistle agrees well with an earlier
synopsis Origen made in 3.1:

> For through the entire text of this epistle he wants to show both how
> salvation came to those who lived according to the law before the

coming of Christ and how, on the basis of Israel's unbelief, salvation was bestowed upon the Gentiles through the coming of the Savior. Furthermore he wants to show that not all Gentiles entirely come to salvation but only those who have believed; nor is the entire nation of Israel rejected but a remnant of believers are being saved.[85]

In this passage, which is preserved in Greek in the Tura papyri,[86] Origen describes the concrete process of how the transformation of religion took place, namely within salvation history. For Origen, Paul's essential concern is a soteriological one that applies to humanity's two main divisions, Jews and Gentiles. The turning point came with the "coming of the Savior/Christ." Salvation is not automatic but requires a human response and choice. In the transformation of true religion, only *unbelieving* Jews are excluded from salvation, and only *believing* Gentiles can be saved.

Paul as Arbiter Between Jews and Gentiles

C. Bammel wrote: "If one looks for a central theme in Origen's *Commentary on Romans,* the relationship between Jews and Gentiles in the divine dispensation is perhaps the most prominent of the various recurrent themes."[87] On repeated occasions Origen describes Paul's conduct in the Epistle to the Romans as that of an arbiter sitting between the Jews and the Gentiles. Paul endeavors both to affirm and to hold in check both Jews and Gentiles, by summoning and inviting both groups to faith in Christ.

> In this letter Paul, like an arbiter sitting between the Jews and the Greeks, i.e. believing Gentiles, summons and invites both groups to faith in Christ in such a way as to not offend the Jews completely by destroying the Jewish ceremonies nor to cause despair in the Gentiles by affirming the observance of the law and of the letter. And whether he is recalling the promises or the punishments, he apportions the word to each people.[88]

In Origen's view Paul is careful not to alienate members of either group, whether Jews or Gentiles, and so he tempers and balances his discourse, as a kind of mediator between the two groups who now together compose the Church.[89] Gorday was impressed here by the way Origen accords real

value to Judaism while arguing for the superiority of the Christian revelation.[90] He found a striking contrast between Origen's relatively benign
approach to Judaism and what he regards as a more hostile attitude in
Chrysostom and Augustine.[91]

In a key passage commenting on Rom 3.9–18, Origen sets forth his
understanding of Paul's core proclamation in Romans.

> "For we have charged that all Jews and Greeks are under sin." But if
> all are under sin, consequently there shall be no grounds for the
> self-exaltation of one group against the other since both come to sal-
> vation not on the basis of their own righteousness but on the basis
> of God's mercy.[92]

Grech concludes the following from Origen's statement here: "Our author
cannot insist more persistently on the fact that both Jews and Gentiles
come to salvation not through their own righteousness but through God's
mercy."[93] For Origen, both Jews and Gentiles who do not believe in Christ
are in the same position, namely "under sin," and must transfer from the
group of those who are perishing to the group of those who are being
saved. They must adopt a new shape for their religious lives by becoming
members of Christ's body, the Church, through faith and baptism. For
Origen, then, the stress in Romans is more on the equality of Jews and
Gentiles than on the revelation of the righteousness of God, though both
aspects are proclaimed. Clearly the ground of salvation is not law but faith
in Christ.

Justification in Origen's *Commentary on the Epistle to the Romans*

The Meaning of *Iustitia*

Let us now turn specifically to the theme of justification in Origen's *CRm*.
How does Origen understand Rom 1.17, "For in it [the gospel], God's justice is revealed"? He says, "The justice of God is revealed in the gospel
through the fact that with respect to salvation no one is excluded whether
he comes as a Jew, Greek, or barbarian."[94] Here *iustitia dei* seems to refer
to the revelation that God wants no one excluded from salvation.[95] Imme-

diately citing Mt 11.28, Origen says that in the gospel, God's justice is shown, that is, the Savior's equity or fairness in freely inviting all to come to him to be saved. *Iustitia* is thus viewed as a juridical characteristic of God, but Origen's stress is not on its punitive aspect but on God's distributive justice[96] or fairness in inviting all of humanity. In contrast with the above depiction, Heither rejects the idea that Origen understands the righteousness of God here as a characteristic of God. Rather, she says, it is identical with Christ himself, who calls everyone to himself who is ready to believe.[97] It appears to me that Heither is right in what she affirms (that Origen identifies Christ as God's righteousness) but wrong in what she denies (that God's righteousness is a characteristic of God).

In the second place, for Origen justice is an inherent quality. Verfaillie has rightly noticed that although Origen does not pose the question of knowing whether justice is imputed or inherent, one can see that the spiritual realism of his psychology favors the latter conception.[98] Indeed throughout the commentary Origen understands "the justice of God" to refer to the person and work of Jesus Christ.[99] Paul's identification of Christ as *iustitia* in 1 Cor 1.30, "God has made Christ to be our justice," is determinative for Origen's understanding.[100] The justice of God refers both to the indwelling presence and to the redemptive work of the Savior, as this is imparted to the believer. To illustrate this, Origen uses the similitude of the human soul as a house into which a person can freely choose to invite Christ, the virtues, including justice (*iustitia*), the angels, and the entire Trinity to come dwell; or, spurning these, to allow the devil, his demons, and the vices, including injustice (*iniustitia*), to dwell within. In this picturesque description, justification is viewed as the reception of the whole Trinity, and especially of *iustitia,* that is, Christ himself.[101] Justifying righteousness, then, is conceived as the divine presence within us; Christ, our justice, justifies us by dwelling in us by his Holy Spirit (cf. Jn 14.23). Those who refuse him entrance, or who later spurn him, cannot be justified.

Similarly, based on Rom 5.5, Origen describes justification (cf. Rom 5.1) as an inpouring of love that enables us to love God: "For the love of God which is greater than everything follows faith and hope, and not only fills our mind but also abounds and is shed abroad into our hearts in view of the fact that it is not sought by human skill, but is flooded through the grace of the Holy Spirit."[102] The following text that comments on

Rom 5.3–5 also stresses that justification is an infusion of grace and has a Trinitarian stress. Rufinus's Origen says:

> Both the Son and the Holy Spirit are to be understood as springing from the one fountain of paternal deity. From the fullness of the Spirit, the fullness of love is infused into the hearts of the saints in order to receive participation in the divine nature, as the apostle Peter has taught [cf. 2 Pt 1.4], so that through this gift of the Holy Spirit, the word which the Lord said might be fulfilled, "As you, Father, are in me and I am in you, may they also be one in us" [Jn 17.21].[103]

Origen's correlation of texts from various canonical sources clarifies Paul's words about the inpouring of divine grace. This shows that Origen conceives the reception of the grace of justifying righteousness as a divinization of the human being, which he calls a gift of the Holy Spirit.

In addition to architectural metaphors, Origen also adopts organic imagery quite frequently to clarify how the grace of Christ is applied to our souls. For example, he says that all who are saved are engrafted into the root of the Lord Jesus Christ, who "supplies the fertility of sanctity to the branches that abide in it; for Christ gives life through the Holy Spirit to those who cling to him and cultivates them by the word, enabling them to produce abundant fruit in the fullness of all the virtues."[104] In this passage, as in the one cited immediately above, the operation of the Son and the Holy Spirit are closely correlated. Christ nourishes us by his word and sanctifies us by entering into us by the Holy Spirit as we, for our part, constantly cling to him. Origen concludes from this that we cannot boast in our fruit bearing, because we have nothing that we have not received from Christ; moreover, by sinning we can easily be cut from the vine.[105] Thus for Origen the infused divine grace sanctifies, yet it does not nullify human cooperation or the possibility of resistance and exclusion.

Finally, it is noticeable that in speaking of justification, Origen often simply follows biblical usage in understanding the term to be synonymous with salvation and the opposite of condemnation.[106] In a comment on Rom 3.28 ("A man is justified by faith apart from works of the law"), Origen cites as explanation the example of the woman in Luke 7, one who was *justified* by faith alone apart from works of the law. He explains: "It was on the basis of no work of the law but for the sake of faith alone that he said to her, 'Your sins are forgiven you,' and again, 'Your faith has *saved* you.'"[107] Origen thus interprets Paul's statement that *justification* is by faith as equivalent to Jesus' teaching that *salvation* is by faith.

In summary, at a definitional level, the *iustitia dei* for Origen seems to refer to God's distributive justice, to the infused grace of the indwelling Christ, and more generally to the gift of salvation. But Origen often seems to identify each of these aspects of the term with Jesus Christ.

Effects of the Grace of Justification

Forgiveness of Past Sins

If justification is understood essentially as an inpouring of the divine grace of Christ, or as the presence of the entire Trinity in the hearts of those who are receptive, what effect does the reception of this gift have in believers? Origen says that justification effects several things within the justified: the forgiveness and destruction of past sins, the enabling of the believer to be constituted righteous by loving God and fulfilling the law, and a real sanctification of the soul. His comments on Rom 3.24 show that he understands that the basic message of Rom 1–4 presupposes the equality of Jews and Gentiles before God. Both groups are invited through the gospel to receive the cleansing of sins and justifying righteousness through faith and not on account of their merits.

> Therefore the righteousness of God through faith in Jesus Christ reaches to all who believe, whether they are Jews or Greeks. It justifies those who have been cleansed from their past crimes and makes them capable of [receiving] the glory of God; and it does this not for the sake of their merits nor for the sake of works, but it supplies this glory freely to those who believe.[108]

God's righteousness is a gift to humanity that is given not for the sake of merits and works, but freely to those who believe. When viewed relative to the past, God's righteousness bestows a cleansing from previous sins which results in a state of purity that renders the soul irreproachable. Immediately after this passage, however, Origen stresses a very serious pastoral concern, namely that this pardon is only the beginning. The remission of sins is given for *past* sins and does not cover future ones. If it did the believer would have a license to sin, which is unthinkable.[109] In this negative aspect of justification, sin is not merely covered over but put to flight and exterminated from our flesh. "For when the remission of sins was granted to us, sin took to flight and was destroyed from our flesh, and the justification of the law began to be fulfilled in us."[110]

Fulfillment of the Law

Origen's words "the justification of the law began to be fulfilled in us" are based on Rom 8.4. They indicate that for Origen the gift of justification can also be viewed relative to the present and future, and not solely to the past. It thus embraces the positive reality of the inundation of grace that makes the soul capable of receiving God's glory or presence and of fulfilling the law. Commenting on Rom 2.13, "the doers of the law will be justified," he says that while the law assuredly cannot have doers accord-ing to the letter, "but [it can have doers] according to the Spirit, through which alone it is possible for the law to be fulfilled."[111] To fulfill the law, Origen says, is the same as to perfect the law, and it takes place in Christ, who said, "I have not come to destroy the law but to fulfill it."[112]

For Origen, then, under the conditions of the New Covenant (Jer 31.31; cf. Rom 8.4), the law has now been given internally to believers and is able to be fulfilled by them through the Spirit. The "law of the Spirit of life" (cf. Rom 8.2) liberates and cultivates the faith of the justified. In fact the relation between God's gift and the believer's fulfilling of the law is so close that Origen even identifies the law of God as the life-giving Spirit.[113] Thus the gospel, as the New Law, is not understood in opposi-tion to law.[114] Origen supports this by connecting Rom 8.2 with Rom 6.14, where, he claims, Paul names the law of the Spirit of life "grace."[115] Ori-gen says:

> Everyone who, while believing in Christ, behaves well and keeps himself from every stain of sin confirms the law of God by living uprightly; but the one who plunges headfirst into sinful vices and without any restraining halter of repentance is stained by the con-stant repetition of evil deeds, this man, even if he may seem to believe in Christ, does not establish the law through his faith but instead sets aside the law.[116]

Roukema comments on this text: "To Origen 'upholding the law' applies to everyone who leads a holy life and soundly believes the Mosaic law, especially in its spiritual sense."[117] Conversely, to practice sin and evil deeds is to set aside the law. In short, for Origen the application to Christians of Paul's words "the doers of the law will be justified" (Rom 2.13) is that the divine gift is intended to effect a renovation of our nature. Actions that are intrinsically good and holy constitute the fulfillment of the law of God and will secure our final justification, as fruits of faith. Opposite actions will earn the opposite effect, since God has imparted to us the power of being justified and of pleasing him or of repudiating this gift.

Conferral of Sanctifying Life to the Soul

Origen stresses that God's grace truly effects a deliverance from sin and a real sanctification. In a comment on Rom 5.17 he says:

> But as for "those who receive the abundance of grace and of the gift of righteousness," not only does death no longer reign in them, which would certainly even in itself be no small grace, but also two other goods are conferred on them. First, instead of death, life reigns in them, namely Christ Jesus. Second, they themselves will likewise reign through the one, Jesus Christ.[118]

The grace of justification is essentially the conferral of divine life to the believer which, seen negatively, puts an end to the reign of sin and death in us, and, seen positively, confers life and the reign of Christ to believers' souls. Origen even says that God justifies sinners in such a way that sin no longer reigns in them, so that properly speaking they are no longer impious.[119] As Grech rightly perceived and as will be seen more fully in chapter 6, this is "an assertion to which Luther would certainly have taken exception."[120]

For Origen, then, justification is a bestowal of life, of intrinsic justice (Christ), and of all Christ's virtues. In justification, Origen says, human beings are enlivened, sanctified, and constituted just (*iusti fiunt*); that is, they become beings in whom the justice of God dwells. Origen repeatedly identifies Christ as this *iustitia* through which all become *iusti*.[121] Christ became obedient unto death for this reason: "in order that those who follow the example of his obedience might be made righteous [*iusti constituan-tur*] by righteousness itself, just as those others were made sinners by following the model of [Adam's] disobedience."[122] In other words, just as humanity's corruption in Adam is real, so is its justice in Christ real. To be constituted just thus embraces the progressive process of interior renewal by means of imitation of Christ. We become partakers of Adam's sin when we imitate Adam by sinning; so we are progressively made partakers of Christ's *iustitia* when we follow him in our actions.

The Necessity of Christ's Redemptive Work

We have briefly discussed the nature of justification in Origen's *CRm*. Let us now turn to the question of why this gift was needed. Origen's comments on Rom 3.25–26 strongly assert the necessity of Christ's redemptive work as the foundation for human salvation, in light of humanity's inability to merit salvation by works.

> Through the sacrifice of himself he makes God propitious to men and through this he manifests his own righteousness as he forgives them their past sins, which they had contracted by serving the worst tyrants at the time when God was tolerating and allowing this to be done. God allowed this so that afterwards, i.e., at this time, he would manifest his righteousness. For at the consummation of the age, at the end of time, God disclosed his righteousness and, for the redemption price, gave him whom he made a propitiator. . . . For God is just, and the one who is just could not justify the unjust; for that reason he wanted there to be the mediation of a propitiator so that those who were not able to be justified through their works might be justified through faith in him.[123]

Reconciliation with God is not possible without the shedding of blood. And it was solely the blood of Jesus that could atone for the guilt of the human race. For Origen, then, God accomplished redemption independent of us. Origen frequently describes Christ's death as a penal satisfaction, as he does here.[124]

This sacrificial character of Christ's death is expressed very eloquently in the following passage, which is an explanation of Rom 5.8–9. Origen finds the substitutionary death of heathen heroes—he is probably thinking of heroes like Codrus,[125] Marcus Curtius,[126] Iphigeneia,[127] and Alcestis[128]—as analogous to the sacrificial death of Jesus:

> Now the question of how Christ died for us and in what way he, since he is the lamb of God, takes away the sin of the world and bears our weaknesses and suffers pain on our behalf, has been frequently discussed by us in other passages.[129] There we have cited instances reported in secular histories, that even among the heathen several individuals are regarded to have averted plagues, storms, and similar things by devoting themselves to death, or to have delivered their homeland or nation from the destruction of a threatening scourge. To what extent these recorded events are actually true, or what significance they may have if they are true, God alone knows. However, none of those concerning whom these stories are told, not even in fiction, is presented as having absolved the sins of the whole world—except Jesus alone, who, "though he was in the form of God thought it not robbery to be equal with God, but he emptied himself." And having taken the form of a slave, in accordance with the Father's will, he offered himself as a sacrifice for the whole world by handing over his own blood to the ruler of this world.[130]

It was *for us* that Christ suffered pain and endured the penalty of our sins, and he alone was capable of bearing it. Although it has some curious secular parallels, Christ's substitutionary death is a unique action in human history by the way it absolves the sins of the whole world. This action constitutes the very foundation of salvation. According to Origen, the bloody ransom price of this act of redemption was paid to the devil, the ruler of this world.

But why did God choose this bloody means of the atonement? Origen does not say. Rivière observes:

> We are told that the substitution was necessary, but were we to ask why, we should receive no answer. It never occurred to Origen to advert to the exigencies of Divine Justice. In other words, Origen has not probed the mystery to the bottom, he has not succeeded in getting below the surface, but at any rate what he does he does well.[131]

According to Rivière, Origen's explanation of the substitutionary nature of the atonement is well conceived, even if it is incomplete. Origen clearly asserts the necessity of the redemptive work of Christ and interprets Christ's sacrifice as a substitution for sinners which absolved the sins of the world.

The Role of Faith and Baptism in Justification

Faith and Baptism, Not Works, Receives Righteousness

Origen stresses that the Church's rule of faith lays down that God's gift of righteousness is received by faith and baptism. "Faith is reputed for righteousness in the converted."[132] Consequently, the pagan's lack of faith excludes him from justification. For the Church's rule of faith establishes that unless one is born again of water and the Spirit, he cannot enter the kingdom of heaven.[133] Elsewhere he says that unbelievers are strangers to eternal life.[134] And in another passage he explains:

> A human being is justified through faith; the works of the law contribute nothing to his being justified. But where there is no faith which justifies the believer, even if one possesses works from the law, nevertheless because they have not been built upon the foundation of faith, although they might appear to be good things, nevertheless they are not able to justify the one doing them, because from them faith is absent, which is the sign of those who are justified by God. . . . Therefore all boasting which comes from the works of the law is excluded.[135]

This is the text that was read aloud at the Council of Trent during the discussions about justification.[136] It clarifies that justification is received by faith; it is not a repayment for fulfilling the works of the law. On the contrary, the works of Jews and Gentiles apart from faith cannot justify. Elsewhere Origen affirms that the boasting that arises from Jewish works of the law avails nothing, "because it does not embrace the humility of the cross of Christ."[137] Origen says that faith is the beginning and foundation, and where it is absent there can be no justification. Surely it was in order to make these very points that the Tridentine Fathers cited this text.

Preparation for Justification

The fact that justification is received by faith and baptism does not imply, however, that works of repentance may not function as a necessary preparation for justification. Repeatedly in connection with the subject of preparing for baptism, Origen insists on the necessity of dying to sin. "If you are still living in sin, you cannot be buried with Christ."[138] "Therefore those who are hastening to baptism ought to take care as a matter of first importance that they first die to sin. And in this way they can be buried with Christ through baptism."[139] These texts seem to indicate that for Origen a preparation for justification is possible and consists in abandoning sin.[140]

Loss of Justification Through Sin, Even with Faith Intact

Origen also says that the grace of justification can be lost through sin, even while faith remains intact. "If anyone acts unjustly after justification, it is scarcely to be doubted that he has rejected the grace of justification."[141] In such cases sin will be imputed to the believer. For only those who abide in the vine will be saved. Those who remain in Christ in name but are found unfruitful in works and deeds will be cut off and cast into the fire.[142] While Origen does say that the proof of true faith is that sin is not being committed, and where sin is being committed, there you have proof of infidelity,[143] yet he simultaneously repudiates the claims of rigorists who denied that believers will ever sin.[144] These latter texts show that in Origen's interpretation of Paul, faith can subsist even when sin is committed. Elsewhere he says that believers' sins will inevitably come to judgment even if their faith is kept intact.[145] In short, Origen does not assume that justifying faith is always living faith. Rather, after justification those who act unjustly can by no means rest assured that sin will not be imputed to them, even if they remain believers. This seems similar to what the *Catechism of the Catholic Church* states (1814–15), that the faith that remains in the absence of hope and love does not fully unite the believer to Christ or bestow living membership in Christ's body.

Examples of Justification by Faith Alone

Of the many scenarios of salvation set forth in Scripture, Origen recognizes that *sometimes* Scripture says that human beings are justified by faith *alone*. In 3.9 Origen paraphrases Paul in Rom 3.28 as follows: "He is saying that the justification of faith alone suffices, so that the one who only believes is justified, even if he has not accomplished a single work."[146] Origen then looks for an instance of someone in the Bible who exemplifies Paul's teaching, that is, one who has been justified by faith alone without works of the law. He finds two examples: the sinful woman in Lk 7, and the good thief who called out, "Lord Jesus, remember me when you come into your kingdom!" (Lk 23.42).[147] Of the good thief Origen says:

> In the Gospels nothing else is recorded about his good works, but for the sake of this faith alone Jesus said to him: "Truly I say to you: Today you will be with me in paradise." . . . Through faith this thief was justified without works of the law, since the Lord did not require in addition to this that he should first accomplish works, nor did he wait for him to perform some works when he had believed. By his confession alone Jesus, who was about to begin his journey to paradise, received the thief as a justified traveling companion with himself.[148]

The good thief was justified apart from any antecedent merit or works. His confession of faith in Jesus alone was adequate for him to begin his journey to paradise as a justified traveling companion with Jesus. Origen seems to understand this to be an exceptional scenario, however, in that the man had no opportunity to be justified by his subsequent good works.[149] The focus of Origen's citation of these examples of justification by faith alone is on the exclusion of works antecedent to faith.

The Role of "Works" in Justification

Good Works as the Necessary Fruit of Justification
On the other hand, one of the central themes of Origen's theology is the necessity of human cooperation in salvation, a cooperation that extends to all that pertains to salvation: election, justification, interior transformation, and perseverance.[150] In light of this fundamental stress, while Origen admits that works before faith and justification do not merit entrance into the kingdom, and that Scripture sometimes describes examples of sinners who are justified by faith *alone*, normally he insists that after justification the ensuing works of righteousness of the Christian are a necessary and

meritorious precondition of final salvation. They are necessary, in Origen's view, because the whole of Scripture (Paul, Jesus, Ezekiel, James) has asserted their necessity; and they are meritorious, because the Church's doctrine of a future divine judgment presupposes that merit and demerit will be recompensed. Those who transgress will be excluded from the kingdom.

In his comment on Rom 5.8–9, Origen affirms the incontestable superiority of Christ's redemptive death for justification. Yet he does not view it as exclusive of our being justified by our faith and works of justice.[151]

> By this he is showing that neither does our faith justify us apart from the blood of Christ nor does the blood of Christ justify us apart from our faith. Of the two, however, the blood of Christ justifies us much more than our faith. And for this reason, it seems to me that, although he plainly said above, "having been justified by faith," here he adds, "how much more then, now, having been justified by his blood"; in order to teach that even if our faith saves us from the coming wrath, and even if our works of righteousness [*opera iustitiae*] save us, nevertheless beyond all these things it is much more the blood of Christ that will save us from the coming wrath.[152]

The redemptive work of Christ has its own proper value as the meritorious cause of our salvation, anterior to any cooperation on our part.[153] It is the original source of the acceptability of our good works and remains constantly the ground for human justification and redemption.[154] In addition, however, Origen says that our faith and our works of righteousness "save us." Origen's language is entirely biblical. He is speaking of the fruits of repentance as the objective effect of an entirely gratuitous initiative of the divine goodness. In the immediate context Origen speaks of both John the Baptist and Jesus requiring these works of their followers. The term "coming wrath" is obviously derived from Mt 3.7, Lk 3.7, and 1 Thes 1.10; and the assertion that our works "save us" reflects the thought of Jas 2.14 and 21 where "save" and "justify" are equivalent: "Can such faith *save* us?" "Was not Abraham our father *justified* by works?"

Thus in Origen's view the doctrine that the blood of Christ justifies does not at all preclude the doctrine that our faith and our postbaptismal good works also justify us. The latter works are inspired by faith and subsequent to conversion. They "save us," not in the sense that they are the original cause of our acceptance before God, or that they cause our sins to be washed away. Rather, the gift of the Spirit can be seen working mightily in our works of obedience and love, with the result that we show our divine sonship by our outward deeds. But these works are posterior to the redemptive death of Christ, which weighs infinitely more in value.

In a graphic illustration of his conception that the grace of Christ and also human faith and good works are indispensable for final justification, Origen borrows language from the gospels to help explain Rom 5.18:[155]

> By means of Adam's transgression a certain access, as it were, was given by which sin, or the death of sin, or condemnation, spread to all men. Thus, in contrast Christ opened up an access to justification, through which life enters to men. This is why he said about himself, "I am the door. If anyone enters through me he will be saved."[156]

Christ is the door to justification, the door to life, to a person's being justified and saved. Origen then refers back to his earlier discussion of this theme where he had said the following:

> But let us see what sort of door he is, in order that we might understand what sort of people they ought to be who would enter through it and have access to grace. The door is truth, and through the door of truth liars cannot enter. Again, the door is also righteousness, and through the door of righteousness the unrighteous do not pass. The door says, "Learn from me because I am gentle and humble in heart." Through the door of humility and gentleness, then, neither the wrathful nor the arrogant may enter. Consequently if there is someone who, in accordance with the Apostle's word, wants to have access through our Lord Jesus Christ to the grace of the Lord in which Paul and those who are like him claim to stand, he must be purged from all these things we have recorded above. Otherwise this door will not allow those who are doing things alien to it to enter through it. Instead it closes at once and does not allow those who are dissimilar to it to pass through.[157]

Christ has opened up an access to justification through which human beings can be saved. By faith in his redemptive act, they enter through this door; but at the same time, access to the Lord's grace requires cleansing and holiness. It requires union with Christ in the virtues. Those who are alienated from Christ's likeness are still threatened with the possibility of exclusion. The Church's doctrine of a future judgment according to works is once again the basis of Origen's claim. Origen illustrates the necessity of being purged from sin in order to attain final salvation by citing the parable of the foolish virgins (Mt 25.1–12) who, "since they did not bring the oil of good works in their vessels, found the door closed when they came too late."[158]

A comparison of these parallel passages shows that Origen equates "access to grace" with "access to justification." Access to this single gift is gained by means of both faith and good works. For the same God warns us that we cannot have access to grace if we lack one of these two conditions.[159] Elsewhere, he refers to Ezek 44.9 and says that those who show themselves to be uncircumcised either in faith (by holding base and unworthy opinions concerning the faith) or in works (by committing unclean and defiled actions) will be excluded from entering the sanctuary of God.[160] Origen repeatedly affirms that faith anticipates good works, which are the necessary fruit of justification. One without the other is condemned, "seeing that faith without works is called dead (Jas 2.17, 26); and no one is justified before God by works without faith." Mt 7.24 and Lk 6.46 are evidence for Origen that "everywhere faith is joined with works and works are united with faith."[161] Faith and works cleave (*adhaerens*) to one another and are consummated.[162] As we saw above, this synthesis explains for Origen why Paul insists in Rom 3.31 that Christians do not make void the law but establish it.[163]

Unity and synthesis seems to be an overriding theme in Origen's interpretation, the unity of the OT and the NT, of the law, the prophets, and the apostles, of faith and good works. Origen speaks of two kinds of faith, a human and a divine. The addition of the latter makes perfect justifying faith. The one is of reason, the other of grace, the special gift of God, and both must coexist.[164] There are also two justifications, one by faith, one by works.[165] The former makes one just in the sight of God; it is forgiveness, known to God alone. The latter makes one just also in the sight of saints and angels. The former is strictly only the *"initium iustificari"*; it is imperfect faith. The faith that was imputed to Abraham for righteousness was perfect faith, which had already manifested itself in obedience.[166] This is "justified by God"—the person is made really and truly righteous. Then one's faith is no longer "imputed to him for righteousness," for he is righteous. Heither finds in Origen's words here no contradiction but rather completion. Origen is faithfully expounding Paul's very Jewish view according to which any polarity of faith and works is incomprehensible.[167]

Origen illustrates the three stages toward justification from Ps 32.1–2: "Blessed is he whose transgression is forgiven, whose sin is covered. Blessed is the man unto whom the Lord does not impute iniquity." First, he says, the soul leaves its evil and obtains pardon. Next by good deeds it covers its sins. "But when a soul forthwith reaches perfection, so that every root of evil is completely cut off from it to the point that no trace of evil can be found in it, at that point the summit of blessedness is promised to the one to whom the Lord is able to impute no sin."[168] Verfaillie comments on Origen's text: "Origen speaks as a moralist here, but his psychology leads to a theology."[169] Origen sees Rom 4.7–8 as describing the soul's conversion in a three-stage progression: remission, covering, and nonimputation of sins. The soul first detaches itself from evil; then it puts the good positively into practice; and finally it arrives at the "summit of blessedness." At the first stage the soul receives the remission of sins when one can scarcely imagine that sins continue to subsist. In the second stage, the soul covers them, that is to say, the evils disappear under the abundance of good works. Finally, when no vestige of sin remains, and God finds no ground for reproaching the soul, it has reached perfection. As we shall see below, at 4.6 Origen will apply the terms faith, hope, and love to these three stages of conversion. The overall stress here is on justification as a process, subsequent to the grace of faith, of being progressively transformed into the image of Christ.

While admitting that faith is primary, Origen insists that it must not be separated from works. He sees the same organic link between faith and works as between the root and branches of a tree.

The Apostle is saying that it is only on the basis that one believes in him who justifies the ungodly that righteousness is reckoned to a man, even if he has not yet produced works of righteousness. For faith that believes in the one who justifies is the beginning of being justified by God [*initium iustificari a Deo*]. And this faith, when it has been justified, is embedded in [*haeret*] the soil of the soul like a root that has received rain so that when it begins to be cultivated through God's law, branches arise from it which bring forth the fruit of works. The root of righteousness, therefore, does not grow out of the works, but the fruit of works grows out of the root of righteousness, namely out of the root of righteousness which God accepts even without works.[170]

Heither summarizes Origen's "resolution" of the problem of the relation between faith and works in this passage by claiming that Origen seeks a synthesis between the two: "Faith obtains the righteousness out of which on the other hand works emerge; and this relationship is not reversible. Only upon the way of faith does man obtain forgiveness of sins, reconciliation with God."[171] "Works are thus not the ground for grace, but the outworking of grace, because grace must be effective in man."[172]

Origen illustrates his understanding of salvation when he says that hope and love cleave inseparably (*inseparabiliter coherere*) to faith. God's promise of salvation will be fulfilled only if faith, hope, and love abide in those who believe:

I consider faith to be the first beginnings and the very foundations of salvation [*prima salutis initia et ipsa fundamenta*]; hope is certainly the progress and increase of the building; however, love is the perfection and culmination of the entire work. That is why love is said to be greater than everything else.[173]

This text correlates with 4.1 cited above. Origen states once again that being justified by God (*iustificari a Deo*) is identical with salvation (*salus*). He views faith as the beginning step (*initium*) and foundation (*fundamentum*) of the process that is nourished by hope and culminates in love. In other words we attain to justification by stages and progressively. The gift of divine grace within us can increase, and it can also perish.

It is noteworthy that Origen speaks of reconciliation and adoption in a way similar to the way he treats justification/salvation. These different ways of describing God's gift of salvation are commonly viewed as a process with a beginning, middle, and end; a past, present, and future. For example, with regard to reconciliation Origen says that Christ's death on the cross killed the hostility between God and humanity (past). This was the beginning of reconciliation (*reconciliationis initium*).[174] But only when we actually resist sins to the point of death, in imitation of Christ's example, does he reconcile humanity to God (present), provided that we keep the covenant of reconciliation inviolate (present). For those who abide in the works God hates cannot be reconciled (present and future).[175] Whoever turns back to sin restores the hostility and rebuilds the wall of separation, thus destroying the work of Christ and making void the cross of his suffering.[176] Likewise with adoption: By our faith in Christ and baptism we already possess salvation, and we already have adoption as sons (past).[177] But salvation is still in hope (future); we wait for it still (future), and have it now as in a mirror and in a riddle (present). When the perfect comes we shall have adoption face to face (future).[178]

Exclusion of "Works of the Law" from Justification

Origen distinguishes postbaptismal works of justice, or virtues, from the Pauline term "works of the law." His comments on Rom 11.6 clarify the manner in which Origen repudiates the idea that Paul is a preacher of a *pecca fortiter, crede fortius*[179] doctrine:

> One should know that the works which Paul repudiates and frequently criticizes are not the works of righteousness [*opera iustitiae*] which are commanded in the law, but those in which they boast who keep the law according to the flesh; that is, the circumcision of the flesh, the sacrificial rituals, the observance of Sabbaths and new moon festivals [cf. Col 2.18]. These and works of a similar nature are the works by which he says no one can be saved, and concerning which he says in the present passage, "not on the basis of works; otherwise, grace would no longer be grace." For if anyone is justified through these, he is not justified *gratis*. But these works are by no means sought from the one who is justified through grace; but this one should take care that the grace he has received should not be in him "in vain" [cf. 1 Cor 15.10] . . . So then, one does not make grace become in vain who joins works to it that are worthy and who does not show himself ungrateful for the grace of God. For anyone

who sins after having attained grace becomes ungrateful to him who offered the grace.[180]

This passage does not exhaust Origen's thought on these themes, but it does make an important clarification. Origen so wishes to safeguard the necessity of the Christian's postbaptismal good works that he explicitly states that the "works of the law" that Paul criticizes in his letters do not refer to the Decalogue or to the moral works of righteousness. Rather the term refers to Jewish ceremonial works (such as circumcision, Sabbath keeping, food laws) apart from faith. Thus Origen restricts Paul's οὐκ ἐξ ἔργων, "not from works" (Rom 3.28), to external ritual law.[181] It is not such ritual works that need to be added to faith in order that the grace of God not be received in vain, but the moral works done in obedience to the law of Christ, by which Christians will most certainly be judged.[182] Reasoner correctly notices that Origen's definition here is an early precedent for the "new perspective" in Pauline interpretation, according to which Paul's words "apart from works" normally means "apart from those works of the law that visibly separate the Jewish people from the nations."[183] This observation will be revisited in the conclusion of this book.

Justification Is Not by Faith Alone

The connection between faith and postbaptismal moral transformation is inseparable. For this reason, Origen says explicitly and on repeated occasions that faith alone is not adequate for salvation.[184] For God requires other theological virtues in addition to faith. Mercy, piety, love, and the other virtues can be reckoned as righteousness, just as faith can.[185] If we do not produce these other virtues by laying aside the old man with his unrighteous deeds, faith cannot be reckoned as righteousness.[186] For Christ justifies only those who have received the new life in the pattern of his resurrection and who reject the old garments of unrighteousness and iniquity.[187] Faith is deservedly (*merito*) reckoned as righteousness when this mortification occurs and when we hold fast to perfection not only in faith but in all the virtues.[188]

In Origen's view justification is above all a sharing of life between the resurrected Christ and the justified. Cocchini summarizes this emphasis in Origen as follows:

Origen has already said that the resurrection of Christ constitutes an example for Christians, and such an example is based on the "new life" that really unites the resurrected Christ to as many as believe in him. The difference then between Christ and the Christians consists, according to Origen, in the fact that whereas for Christ one is dealing with a new life in the most complete sense of the term— since it has already been made completely manifest as such—for Christians one is dealing with a life that, as long as they are not resurrected, one can manifest as "new" above all in the moral aspect.[189]

The point is that it is primarily in postbaptismal moral transformation that the "new" in the "new creation" is visible. For Origen, the justified share in the fruit of Christ's redemptive death and his resurrection life. He bases this on the link made by Paul in Rom 4.24–25: "It will be reckoned to us who believe in him that raised from the dead Jesus our Lord, who was put to death for our trespasses and raised for our justification." Elsewhere Origen says that to be alive to God in Christ Jesus (Rom 6.11) means to be alive to God in all the virtues, which are identified with Christ.[190]

Interestingly, Origen exemplifies the necessity of mortification by returning to the example of the thief on the cross, whom he had earlier cited as an example of one justified by faith alone. He again makes use of organic imagery and says that this thief had fulfilled Rom 6.5–6, in that he had been planted together in the likeness of Christ's death and of his resurrection, and for that reason he deserved paradise since he had been joined to the tree of life:

Christ himself then is the tree of life. . . . His death becomes for us a tree of life as a new and a wonderful gift from God . . . Now I think that one could fittingly say this also about that thief who was hanging together with Jesus on the cross and has appeared to be planted together into the likeness of his death by his confession in which he said: "Lord, remember me when you come into your kingdom"; and he rebuked the other thief who was blaspheming. But it has appeared that he was also planted together in his resurrection by what is said to him: "Today you will be with me in paradise." For truly he was a plant worthy of paradise which was joined to the tree of life.[191]

Origen points to the good thief as a living, or rather dying, commentary on Rom 10.9–10. Earlier in his exegesis Origen had used the good thief as an illustration of one justified by faith alone without works.[192] The current passage seems to make clear, however, that in Origen's view this thief is simultaneously an example of how faith and works cooperate in an organic way in contributing to salvation. The good thief exemplifies the Pauline text about the necessity of dying and rising with Christ.

The good thief freely carried out the just works of publicly confessing the lordship of Christ and rebuking the other thief who was blaspheming. The result is that ultimately the good thief was deservedly justified by a synthesis of his faith and his virtues. By God's wonderful gift of life to him the thief had not only been declared just with respect to the past, with no antecedent works; but he had also become inherently just and worthy of paradise through his active adhesion to the living Christ. Verfaillie synthesizes Origen's theology of grace, merit, and works as follows: "This meritorious character of our acts has its source in the grace of justification and completes the conception of it. Liberated from the death of sin, the Christian soul is united to Christ who gives it new life, by means of which he gives the means of bearing fruit that is pleasing to God."[193] This conception seems to be fittingly exemplified by the good thief.

Reasoner noticed that there are three references to the good thief in Origen's commentary, and that the point of the final citation seems to be the following:

> The necessity of works alongside faith becomes clearer in the final reference to this thief. When exegeting what it means to be planted with Christ in his death in order to share in his resurrection (6:5), Origen cites the thief's confession to Jesus and rebuke of the blaspheming thief as evidence that he was planted with Christ in a death to sin.[194]

Concluding Summary: Justification by Faith as Synecdoche

Many texts have been discussed in this examination of Origen's doctrine of justification in his *CRm*. I have tried to stress, in the first place, that Origen begins with the assumption that the ecclesiastical dogma of a future judgment according to works implies that freedom and merit are mean-ingful concepts. In order for God's judgment to be just, it must be exer-cised on responsible creatures who will be recompensed for their merits and demerits. Since Paul himself speaks of a just judgment according to works that is in store for Christians,[195] Origen's interpretation is direct reflection on Scripture.[196] Secondly, Origen's stress on human freedom and merit owes something to the deterministic heresies against which he is fighting. Heretics have fastened on texts in Paul in an effort to deny the reality of human freedom in salvation. In Marcion's case they have reviled the Creator for endowing human beings with free will and have denied that God is a just judge of the Christian's works. In response, Origen bends over backward to defend Paul against such distortions. He stresses that faith receives justification, but faith is not viewed as the sole and exclusive criterion of God's judgment. Origen clearly makes room for a human con-tribution to salvation; he accords real religious value to our postbaptismal works; but he does not countenance religious boasting in good works.

Origen seems to understand the Pauline slogan "justification by faith" as synecdoche (*pars pro toto*). In the Pauline text the part (faith) is put for the whole (postbaptismal renewal). We are saved by faith, to be sure, but by a faith that is not exclusive of other theological virtues such as hope and love, obedience and holiness. God has made Christ to be our justice (cf. 1 Cor 1.30), so that we are saved by Christ's justice, but Scripture iden-tifies Christ with his other virtues and operations, such as sanctification, redemption, wisdom, justice, mercy, and love; therefore we are saved by all these operations of Christ as well.[197] This synecdochical understanding helps to explain why Origen can say that not merely faith but also all the other virtues can be reputed for righteousness.[198] For Origen justification is more than a nonimputation of past sins. It is an effectual and progres-sive sanctification in which sin is expelled and grace (sc. Christ), in all its aspects, is established in the believer's soul. Grech paraphrases Origen's overall position in this way: "Christian righteousness therefore consists in serving Christ in the Holy Spirit. Paul himself, who received the grace of the Spirit served wisdom, justice and all the other virtues which Christ is said to be. Christ certainly does save, but so does the Holy Spirit."[199]

Recently, Bammel has described Origen's understanding of justifica-tion as being in conflict with that of St. Augustine.[200] Bammel claims that whereas Augustine viewed justification as a process of becoming righ-

teous, which begins at baptism or conversion, in the Origen-Rufinus commentary justification appears to be conceived as a momentary event in
which sins are forgiven and the new convert is accounted righteous before
God.[201] I will discuss Bammel's assertion in greater detail in an excursus
appended to the chapter on Augustine. For the present, I would question
whether the passage Bammel cites from Origen can be fairly described
as his "definition" of justification. Moreover, I would contend that Origen's understanding of justification cannot be reduced in such a way. To
be sure in Origen's view, as in Augustine's, *in the beginning* believers are
accounted righteous with respect to the past when their previous sins are
pardoned; for past sins can only be removed by an imputation of righteousness. But this is only one aspect of the gift of divine righteousness
and an initial one at that. For both Origen and Augustine believers are
not only forgiven but also constituted children of God and therefore they
become inherently righteous progressively and by stages. Indeed, in justification we are adopted as God's children and enabled by God's grace to
fulfill the moral law of God and perform it unto justification.

Excursus: Modern Assessments of Origen's Doctrine of Grace

With regard to the Church's understanding of divine grace, scholars generally concede that the teaching of the Fathers before the fifth century,
especially the Greek Fathers, is less precise than that of the Fathers who
lived after the Pelagian and semi-Pelagian controversies. In spite of this,
accusations against Origen's doctrine of grace have repeatedly been made.
Huet devoted a long dissertation to proving Origen's "semi-Pelagianism."[202]
Likewise, Freppel found Origen's doctrine vulnerable on two points: the
absolute gratuity of grace, and the priority of divine action over human
cooperation.[203] Later in this book we will encounter the various accusations of Melanchthon and Jansen. The former accuses Origen of a faulty
understanding of the nature of justification (as an intrinsic renewal in the
virtues), whereas Jansen accuses Origen of being Pelagian in his doctrine
of grace and predestination. Before concluding this chapter, then, I wish to
discuss briefly several important texts in Origen's *CRm* where his views
on the relation between human faith and merit and the initiative of divine
grace are mentioned. These texts are not directly relevant to the thematic

complex of justification, faith, and works in Origen's *CRm*. Yet they are important passages on a topic that will become an enormously important theme in subsequent theology, and they have provoked a variety of reflections from modern scholarship. This excursus is not intended necessarily to resolve these controversies so much as to call attention to them. It is hoped that this discussion will also help prepare the road for the chapters that follow by briefly comparing and contrasting the doctrine of Origen and Augustine.

Definition of Pelagianism and Semi-Pelagianism

In the first place, a historically accurate definition of Pelagianism and semi-Pelagianism should be given. Pelagianism refers to the basic tenets of Pelagius (d. 420) which were condemned by the Church in 417–18.[204] F. Clark has helpfully summarized these under three propositions: (1) Adam's sin injured only himself, so that his posterity were not born in that state of alienation from God called original sin; (2) it was accordingly possible for a person, born as he was without original sin or its innate consequences, to continue to live without sin by the natural goodness and powers of his nature, and therefore justification was not a process that must necessarily take place for one to be saved; (3) eternal life was, consequently, open and due to a person as a result of one's natural good strivings and merits; divine interior grace, though useful, was not necessary for the attainment of salvation.[205] In opposition to Pelagius's teaching, the Church holds that Adam's sin injured all his posterity; that justification is a process that must take place for the human being to be saved; and that divine grace is necessary for human salvation to take place.

Semi-Pelagianism is probably more accurately termed "semi-Augustinianism."[206] Its advocates were not halfway to Pelagius, but supported Augustine's early views about divine predestination, rather than his later anti-Pelagian understanding of this term. The term *semi-Pelagian* was coined at the Lutheran Formula of Concord of 1577. This term of Lutheran origin was adopted in the Catholic camp as well.[207] It refers to tenets rejected by the second provincial council of Orange in 529, whose canons were approved by Pope Boniface II.[208] Its doctrine was represented by monks of southern Gaul in the fifth and sixth centuries who accepted without question the Church's condemnation of Pelagianism, and held the orthodox doctrine that without divine interior grace one could neither reach eternal life nor be justified. Clark describes their doctrine as an incautious reaction against what they regarded as the arbitrariness attributed to God in the Augustinian teaching on predestination. In response they supposed that God looked for some previous stirrings of good on the part of the human being as a necessary condition for granting him the aids of divine grace and faith which would lead him on toward salvation. Clark writes:

> On such a theory, though grace was absolutely necessary for justification and salvation, the preparatory striving for the *initium fidei,* or the beginnings of that process which would culminate eventually in justification, could be initiated by man's unaided free will. Indeed it was supposed that God had to wait for such a previous initiative on man's part before he could grant the first prompting of grace which would lead on to salvation.[209]

Semi-Pelagianism was rejected by the Church, because it made some purely natural good movement of the human being's free will the *necessary* preliminary before God's salutary grace could come to his aid. In this sense it compromised the revealed truth that is attested by St. Paul concerning the complete gratuity and primacy of God's merciful intervention to save sinful humanity. With these definitions of the terms in mind, we proceed to investigate Origen's various statements.

Anticipations of Augustine

As we have discussed above, Origen's *CRm* had the purpose of demonstrating the human being's free will against the Gnostics. Yet it cannot be said that he excludes divine help. It is even evident that in some passages Origen seems to anticipate the theology of the late Augustine by asserting that faith itself is a gift of divine grace.

> For in the passage where he lists the gifts of the Spirit, which he says are given to believers according to the measure of their faith, he asserts that the gift of faith as well is granted along with the other gifts through the Holy Spirit. For after many words he speaks of it in

this way, "To another faith is given by the same Spirit" [1 Cor 12.9], in order to show that even faith is given through grace. Moreover elsewhere the same Apostle teaches this when he says, "Because it has been granted to you from God not only that you believe in Christ but also that you should suffer on his behalf" [Phil 1.29].[210]

At first glance this text seems to represent a stunning anticipation of the Augustinian doctrine of grace.[211] A position that Augustine himself only gradually came to, that is that faith itself is a divine gift to humanity, is affirmed clearly by Origen. However, this text does not exhaust Origen's thought on the subject. The commentary contains many other statements in which Origen seems to make room for the possibility that human merit can procure grace from God. For example in 9.2, while commenting on Rom 12.3–5 and discussing the grounds for receiving offices in the body of Christ, Origen writes:

> I think that it is beyond our comprehension [to ascertain] whether he himself offers some cause, or whether it is by the will of God, without regard to any causes whatsoever, that this one or that one should be constituted this or that member. But lest those who assert that there are different natures of souls and that they have been constituted by different creators seem to find an opportunity for reinforcing their doctrines, let what we have discussed above about the vessels of honor and the vessels of dishonor suffice even for the present passage. For it should never be conceded that either in the present or in the past or even in the future ages divine providence does not direct each one in such a way that each one's merit, which is acquired through the freedom of will, furnishes material to the one who dispenses. For God is just and there is no injustice with him.[212]

The context here is specifically dealing with membership and office in the body of Christ, and not eternal salvation per se. Origen raises the question as to whether there is a cause in us for the reception of the grace of these offices, or whether this bestowal is wholly determined by God's will. Origen affirms that God's justice requires that merits arising from free will supply material to the One who dispenses. Yet shortly after this Origen seems to say that grace must first be received from God for one to become a member of the body of Christ: "So then, he is declaring that the diversities of the graces are given 'according to the measure of faith' of each so that, for example, *when grace has been received* anyone may become this or that member in the body of Christ."[213] But a little later Origen says that "something is done even by us in this, but the greater part is based upon the generosity of God."[214]

Verfaillie made an acute observation with respect to the first passage cited above (9.2), namely that to take Origen's assertion in an absolute sense, that is, that merit acquired through free will is a precondition for receiving divine grace and is so in an exclusive manner, would be to resolve the very question declared by Origen to be beyond human understanding.[215] This carries weight and casts doubt on any identification between Origen's doctrine and "semi-Pelagianism," as defined above. Origen's admission that this subject is a mystery renders such an accusation suspect. Origen has conceded in his prefatory remarks, "I think that it is beyond our comprehension . . ." Origen's chief concern is visible in the wording of the passage itself: to give no room to the heretical denial of free will and the Gnostic doctrine that souls are of different natures and have been constituted by different creators.

Yet in spite of Verfaillie's caveat, Origen does seem to endeavor to resolve the matter to some extent in what follows when he says that something is done by us but the greater part is based on God's generosity. This seems to confirm that in Origen's view there is room for genuine human effort and merit in the procuring of the grace of membership and office in the body of Christ, indeed in procuring God's grace generally. This agrees with Origen's repeated insistence that because of the existence of free will, it lies within the power of the human being to be saved or to perish, a point that Origen's heretical opponents repudiate by their denial of free will and their natural predestinarian interpretations of Paul.[216] Against the claims of the Gnostics, Origen is convinced that the cause of each person's salvation lies not in an arbitrary decision and determination of God, but, at least in part, in one's own purpose and actions. For Origen this explains among other things why Paul, in spite of his election, still feared the possibility of his own damnation,[217] and why Christians must always fear the treachery of the flesh: because the undeserving will be excluded from eternal life.[218]

Tensions with Augustine

A remarkable un-Augustinian corollary of Origen's claim that the merit deriving from free will is surely to be recompensed by the just God is his claim that even the unbeliever's good works will be rewarded by God. Origen is far from saying that all the deeds of unbelievers are sins.[219] On the contrary, even unbelievers can be "justified" in comparison with members of the Church, if their virtues outshine those of believers, just as Ezek 16.51 says that Sodom was justified in comparison with Jerusalem.[220] Origen does not equate this relative form of being justified with eternal salvation. Yet clearly, Origen seems to take a more favorable view than Augustine does of the prospects of Gentiles who obey natural law.

The tensions in Origen's *CRm* are quite dramatic, especially when they are read through the spectacles of the Pelagian crisis. To illustrate them, we note that Origen clearly accepted the rule of the Church that no one can be saved without the grace of Christ received in baptism.[221] Yet he simultaneously asserted that a person *can* do good works prior to receiving grace or baptism, and that some believers begin with good works and perfect them by the addition of faith.[222] Origen refers to Jacob, for example, who earned the divine election by cleansing his heart of sin through good works.[223] As Burns has observed, the tension between these two assertions is clearly focused in the argument that the Gentiles who are excluded from eternal life by their failure to believe must not lose the reward due the good works they have performed.[224] Origen denies that such good works will go unrewarded.

When Origen says that the good works of unbelievers will be recompensed in the next world, evidently he means that they will be given a higher gradation in the afterlife.[225] Schelkle interprets Origen to mean not heavenly and eternal rewards but earthly and temporal blessings.[226] In any case Origen denies both that these works will go unrewarded and that they will earn their doers eternal life. Origen's interpretation is estranged from Augustine's thought. Eno even raises the perceptive question whether Origen's doctrine here is an early version of Occam's scholastic doctrine: "Facienti quod est in se Deus non denegat gratiam," that is, "God does not deny grace to the one who does what is in his own power."[227]

Defenses of Origen

As mentioned above, based on the texts that seem open to the possibility of good works without divine grace, Origen has been accused of attributing to the human being the sole initiative in salvation. Recently Balthasar has mounted a defense of Origen. He claims that while the late Augustine in his battle against the Pelagians embedded human freedom so completely in divine grace that true freedom actually becomes an effect of grace, Origen's battle against Gnosticism led him to emphasize human freedom. Origen's specific solution to the freedom-grace dialectic is as follows:

> On the one hand all natural powers are given and preserved by God, but the human being is free in using them for good or ill; and that on the other hand, in the area of the virtues, there is for each virtue a human, "natural" virtue to be gained by one's own activity, and a corresponding divine, "supernatural" virtue given only as grace. God gives these gifts of grace to whoever works for the natural virtue, but he is in no way obliged to do so.[228]

This means, according to Balthasar, that Origen undoubtedly emphasizes more strongly than Augustine the human being's freedom of choice and his own activity as distinct from grace. But Pelagian tendencies are excluded, because for Origen God's grace and human cooperation interpenetrate in such a way that grace always remains strictly undeserved and free, and no human work can make the slightest claim to it.

A text that seems to support Balthasar's interpretation, which is extant in both Greek[229] and Latin forms, is Origen's comment on Rom 4.4:

> Now when I consider the eminence of his words, that he says that to the one who works it is repaid as something due, I can hardly convince myself that there could be any work which would demand from God repayment as something due. For even the fact that we are able to do anything at all, to think and to speak, we do as a gift from God granted to us by his generosity. What debt will he have to pay back to us, seeing that his capital came first?[230]

Origen seems to make a distinction here between a proper and improper application of the term *merit* to divine-human relations. Verfaillie noticed that this passage implicitly contains a definition of merit as such—that which demands from God repayment as something due (*quod ex debito remunerationem Dei deposcat*)—and remarked that Origen is strongly inclined not to admit merit in this sense.[231] Likewise Balthasar comments that this is a "strongly Augustinian passage" in which "the apologetics of freedom against a naturalistic Gnosticism recedes into the background and gives way to a genuinely Pauline theology of faith."[232]

In a related passage at 4.1, Origen comments on Rom 6.23: "The wages of sin is death." Origen calls attention to the fact that Paul did not go on to say in similar fashion, "but the wages of righteousness is eternal life." Instead he says: "But the gift of God is eternal life." "For he wanted to teach that wages, which are assuredly comparable with a debt and a reward, refer to the repayment of punishment and death; whereas he registers eternal life as a gift of grace alone."[233] In formulating this contrast between gift and wage, grace and debt, Origen seems to imply that the initiative in bestowing salvation ultimately rests with God alone whose capital precedes our efforts. In light of this passage, Verfaillie resolves the tension between this text and Origen's words elsewhere, where he speaks of eternal life being a reward for human effort, by appealing to Augustine's dictum, "Eorum coronando merita coronas dona tua" (By crowning their merits, you crown your own gifts).[234] That is to say, by admitting that eternal life is a gift of grace alone, Origen is implicitly affirming that God, when he awards salvation to us as a reward for our merits, has become our debtor, not as though he has received something from us, but because he has promised what pleased him. It is a different thing when we say to a human being, You are my debtor because I have given you something, and when we say to God, Give us what you have promised, for we have done what you have commanded. What seems certain is that such texts in Origen suggest that merit means something less than justice in the strict sense, as if one were speaking of two equal and independent parties.

Similarly, Origen says elsewhere that even the mortification of the flesh and of vices does not spring from us but is granted us as a gift through the death of Christ, just as when we walk in newness of life, we do so through Christ's resurrection.[235] In his discussion of these texts from Origen's commentary, Grech states: "Origen's doctrine, therefore, is not far removed from Augustine's thought, although he considers God's help as given more through persuasion and love, as Augustine himself also states, than as direct assistance to willpower."[236] Similarly, Balthasar says, "Everything in the type and spirit that Origen is and the whole system of his thought exclude the possibility that the impulse to conversion (*initium fidei*) comes from the human being."[237]

Likewise, Wiles, writing from a perspective significantly different from that of Verfaillie and Balthasar, thinks Origen's doctrine of grace and merit should not be condemned outright. He notes that the Latin *mereri* and *meritum* carry a stronger implication of "merit" than the original Greek words that they represent, which are ἄξιος and καταξιῶμαι. Wiles points to the fact that on at least three occasions in the New Testament itself those words are used of humanity's relations to its final heavenly reward (Rev 3.4, Lk 20.35, 2 Thes 1.5), which suggests that if the concept of growth in grace has any meaning at all, it must mean that the faithful reception of God's gifts makes us able or fit to receive his further gifts.[238] In fact, one could expand Wiles's assertion by noting that there exist far more than three references to merit in the NT, if we add texts such as Mt 22.8, Lk 12.48, Acts 13.46, Rom 1.32, and other passages where the concept is implicit, such as Mt 25.31–46.[239] Moreover, if we supplement these references by the addition of the OT use of these Greek terms, which Wiles altogether omits mentioning, the weight of evidence shifts even more decisively in Origen's favor.[240]

Wiles adds one caveat:

> On the other hand it must be admitted that on occasions Origen certainly does speak of the merit of our own achievements as something apparently wholly distinct from the God-given grace of the Holy Spirit. But, however much we are forced to admit the presence of this idea of merit in the thought of Origen, it was certainly not intended to imply an exact equivalence of desert and reward. The principle that with what measure ye mete it shall be measured to you again applies, he insists, only to our evil deeds; the "reward" of our good deeds always exceeds our deserving.[241]

In summary, while there does seem to be a meritorious human contribution to salvation in Origen's soteriology, it does not seem to be merit in the strict sense of the word. Grech summarizes Origen as follows: "Man must do whatever is in his power while God intervenes to augment and to complete. It is proper to give the human being his full due, but the *major part* [emphasis Grech's] is attributable to God; good works are an outcome of God's gift and benevolence."[242] Grech assesses Origen's place in the Pelagian controversy by saying that he is certainly not Pelagian in his doctrine about Adam's sin and the total gratuity of righteousness, but he comes close to the Pelagians in his anthropological optimism.

> His insistence on the need for grace to perform good works leads him a good way towards Augustine . . . while Luther would have rejected this commentary outright, for obvious reasons, Trent might have had something to add to on Augustinian lines. The post-Tridentine Jesuit school of Suarez, however, would have welcomed the doctrine of election *post praevisa merita.*[243]

Likewise, Wörter thought that a clear difference between Origen and Pelagius could be articulated: "Between the determination of Pelagius and that of Origen exists then the great distinction that the former excludes grace, the latter necessity; for that reason as well [Origen's view] is not Pelagian."[244] Finally, the Protestant B. Drewery said that Origen was saved from moralism, legalism, and Pelagianism by his "overriding doctrine of divine grace."[245]

Chapter 2

Pelagius's Reception of Origen's Exegesis of Romans

Introduction to Pelagius

Rufinus's Latin edition of Origen's *CRm* was published in 406.[1] The first known student of the work was the British monk Pelagius (360?–420) who was sojourning in Rome at the time the translation was being composed. He was able to make a thorough study of it before writing his own *Commentary on Romans,* which was completed in Rome before 410[2] and was cited by Augustine in 412.[3] Although the Pelagian controversy broke out after Rufinus's death in 411, its themes were evidently being discussed in Rome at the time when Rufinus was translating Origen. The doctrines of Pelagius condemned by the Church in 417–18 have been summarized in the excursus at the end of chapter 1.

The consensus of older scholarship (Fremantle, Westcott, Murphy, Kelly) had been that Rufinus's translation of Origen's *CRm* was carried out in Aquileia, not Rome. This would have put Rufinus far from the center of Pelagius's activities. Hammond calls this assumption into question: "Rather than defending Rufinus against the charge that he was associated with the genesis of Pelagianism, we should be ready to acknowledge the stimulation of his influence in person as well as through his translations on the creative thought of his generation."[4] Among other evidence, the new theory is confirmed by the immediate and extensive use of Rufinus's translation made by Pelagius. Moreover, there is evidence to suggest that texts from Origen's *CRm* played an important role in the wider Pelagian controversy.[5] Both sides cited passages from it to support their interpretation of the disputed themes: divine grace and human responsibility, free will, the relationship between predestination and foreknowledge, the possibility of sinlessness, the propagation of Adam's sin. Hammond Bammel suggests that Rufinus was able to translate Origen "without inhibitions" since the Pelagian/anti-Pelagian camps had not yet become entrenched.[6]

Pelagius's *Commentary on Romans*

History, Legacy, and Style

Pelagius's *Commentary on Romans* is his longest extant work.[7] At this early stage of his career, Pelagius was not yet in open conflict with Church authorities. The commentary seems to be written with a humble and churchmanlike spirit. Ostensibly Pelagius's polemic is directed against Manichaean and Arian interpretations of Paul, not Augustinian views, at least not explicitly. One of its most striking features is its concern for orthodoxy.[8] Like Origen, Pelagius does not dogmatize but often offers a range of possible interpretations of the Pauline text, introducing them with the words *sive* or *aliter*.[9]

After Pelagius's condemnation and death, this particular work of his circulated pseudonymously, in particular in the pseudo-Jerome version, made before 432, and the pseudo-Primasius version, which is a revision supervised by Cassiodorus (485?–580), who at first believed it to be the work of Pope Gelasius. Upon closer scrutiny, Cassiodorus observed that the work was marred by Pelagian errors and consequently revised it. In the Middle Ages it passed as a work of St. Jerome. Erasmus of Rotterdam (1466–1536) printed it in his edition of St. Jerome's writings (1516), but he declared that he recognized that Jerome was not the true author. He had no idea that Pelagius was the author.[10] The original form was rediscovered and printed in 1926 by A. Souter.[11]

In form Pelagius's commentary differs markedly from Origen's. Pelagius's work is literal and terse, whereas Origen's is discursive, speculative, allegorical, and lengthy. Pelagius draws on the entire antecedent tradition, and many tributaries feed into his own independent appropriation of that tradition. Among the authors used by Pelagius are the early Augustine, Ambrosiaster, the anonymous commentator on Paul, Jerome, and others.[12] The direct and particularly strong dependence of Pelagius upon Origen's work was first demonstrated in the modern era by Smith (1919) and has been confirmed by Souter, Bohlin, and other modern scholars. Pelagius had read Origen's entire Latin commentary. He inserts material derived from Origen in various locations in his own commentary and not merely in passages under the same lemma of the Epistle to the Romans. Smith has assembled a series of parallel Latin passages between Origen and Pelagius beginning at Rom 1.1 and continuing through Rom 16, showing that Pelagius has taken not merely thoughts from Origen's commentary, but also phrases and expressions. Pelagius evidently shared the attitude toward appropriating Origen of many of his contemporaries, including Epiphanius, Augustine, Jerome, Rufinus, and Ambrose: he was comfortable with denouncing the errors of Origen without proscribing his works altogether.[13]

Pelagius's Anti-Manichaeanism

Pelagius's commentary is noteworthy for its anti-Manichaean emphasis. Bohlin observes, "Pelagius's system appears to stand and fall with the dialectic deriving from his anti-Manichaeism."[14] Manichaeus, or Mani/ Manes (215–276), was the founder of Manichaeanism, a heresy that threatened the Church for many centuries and even claimed the young St. Augustine as one of its adherents. Manichaeus came from Persia and is reported to have died of torture in prison while chained up by the wrists.[15] He desired to blend Christianity, Zoroastrianism, and elements of Buddhism together. Manichaeus preached an extreme dualism of two independent and absolutely opposed eternal principles, those of good and evil. Like Marcion he denied that Jesus was prophesied in the OT. He said that the good God was characterized by light, while the material world was inherently dark and corrupt. Manichaeus believed that Jesus and other teachers came to release souls of light from prison in material bodies.

The Old Testament was the product of the forces of darkness. Manichaeus also denied the free choice of the will in salvation.

Viciano observes that Manichaeanism had an unusual capacity for syncretism with other religions. As it spread throughout the Roman Empire it adapted to certain aspects of Christianity, particularly to the theology of the heretic Marcion, whose cosmology was dualistic, whereas his Christology was permeated by Gnostic elements.

> Such coincidence with Manichaean doctrine, along with the fact that Marcionism, like Manichaeism, was organized as a church, facilitated such syncretism. Moreover, Mani himself admired Marcion in so far as their respective interpretations of the epistles of Paul had many points in common.[16]

The fact that Pelagius is writing against Manichaeanism suggests that his commentary was never intended to sustain the sort of analysis to which it was subjected by Augustine. For example, Pelagius never discussed how faith originates or the relation between God's contribution and the human being's response.[17] Repeatedly Pelagius refutes the Manichaean interpretation of "the flesh" because of the determinism it implies.[18] De Bruyn suggests that Pelagius's theological tenets were developed precisely to counter Manichaean notions of creation, sin, redemption, and beatitude:

> The goodness of creation, the capacity of all human beings to chose between good and evil, the endurance of that capacity despite the accumulation of sinful habits, the accounting for that capacity in God's plan of salvation—these are basic to Pelagius's understanding of human destiny, and in his stark formulation they are rid of any shadows which to his mind blur the contrast between Manichaean determinism and Christian freedom.[19]

An example of this concern is found in Pelagius's comment on Rom 2.9 where Paul speaks of a judgment according to works. Pelagius writes, "The apostle threatens the soul with punishment because of heretics who say that only the flesh does wrong and deny that the soul can sin."[20] This thought is clarified under the lemma to Rom 6.19 where Pelagius rejects the Manichaean view that it is the nature of the body to have sin mixed in.[21] Under the lemma to Rom 8.7 Pelagius confronts the Manichaeans explicitly by saying, "The flesh itself is not hostile to God, as the Manichaeans say, but the carnal mind is."[22]

We recognize in these concerns a close resemblance to the issues that inspired Origen to write his own exposition of Romans. In particular Origen dealt with the Gnostic doctrine of natures, which affirmed that there are natures of souls that are constitutionally hostile to God and cannot be saved, and souls that are good by nature and cannot be lost, no matter what sin they commit. It is noteworthy that Church writers consistently appealed to the Pauline doctrine of a final judgment according to works as a means of refuting this brand of determinism.

Pelagius's Use of Origen's
Commentary on the Epistle to the Romans

This examination of Pelagius will endeavor to determine the general features of Pelagius's reception of Origen's commentary, more particularly, how he receives the themes outlined in chapter 1: freedom, redemption, justification by faith, and works of the law. I will not attempt to draw a complete picture of Pelagius's theology based on all his extant writings, which would be beyond the scope of this investigation.[23] Rather, my aim is to study the way Pelagius receives certain material from Origen's Latin commentary, transmits Origen with approval, passes over other material in silence, and censures or modifies certain of Origen's views. I will delineate some of the principal characteristics of Pelagius's reception of Origen's Pauline exegesis.

The Main Theme of Romans

At a thematic level there seems to be a large measure of agreement between Origen and Pelagius in their depictions of what Paul is trying to do in Romans. In his prologue, Pelagius describes the "arrogant dispute" between Jewish and Gentile Christians in Rome.[24] The Jewish Christians boast of their heritage, the Gentiles remind them of Israel's repeated apostasy. Paul functions as an arbiter between the two groups.

Thrusting himself between [*se medium interponens*] those who were disputing in this way, the apostle interrupts the questions of the two parties so as to establish that neither of them deserved salvation by their own righteousness; rather, both peoples sinned knowingly and gravely, the Jews inasmuch as they dishonored God by transgression of the law, the Gentiles in that, although they ought to have worshiped as God the Creator revealed by the creation, they changed his glory into idols fashioned by hand. With [irrefutable] logic the apostle shows, therefore, that they are equal, both having obtained pardon in like manner, especially when in one and the same law it [was] foretold that both Jews and Gentiles were destined to be called to faith in Christ. Wherefore humbling them in turn, he exhorts them to peace and [to] concord.[25]

This description of Paul's main concern in Romans is noticeably reminiscent of the way in which Origen set out the principal aims of Paul in *CRm* 2.14 and 3.2. It would seem that from an original insight found in Origen, Pelagius has adopted the view that Paul is acting as an arbiter between Jews and Gentiles in this epistle. Like Origen, he sees the main theme of the letter as the fulfillment of the scriptural promises. God is offering free and equal salvation to believing members of both groups through his mercy, and not through human righteousness and human works.

Free Choice of the Will

Doubtless the two theologians, Origen and Pelagius, show a profound affinity on the questions of free will, grace, redemption, and predestination. Free will is a primary datum for both of their theological anthropologies.[26] For Origen and for Pelagius the possession of free will is a hallmark of the rational creature and the principle of good and evil. In a comment on Rom 6.13 Pelagius writes, "At the same time it should be noted that it is through freedom of choice that a person offers his members for whatever side (*parti*) he wishes."[27] Precisely on this verse Origen had explained, "He is showing that the matter lies within our power, that sin should not exercise dominion in our body."[28] A little later Origen explains Rom 6.16 in these words:

Each person has it within his own power and in the efficacy of his choice that he should become either a slave of sin or of righteousness. For to whichever side [*partem*] he renders obedience and to whichever side he wants to submit, that side claims him as its slave. In this, as I have said, he is showing with no hesitation that there is freedom of will in us. For it rests with us to offer our obedience either to righteousness or to sin.[29]

Both theologians understand the faculty of free will to be implied in Paul's issuing of commands. For Origen these commands refute the Gnostics; for Pelagius they refute the Manichaeans. Dempsey claims that Pelagius's clear defense of free will by itself constitutes no prejudice against the admission of actual grace (transient grace given for the performance of salutary acts), for Catholic theologians have always stoutly defended both freedom of will and the need for actual grace. However, the history of the Pelagian controversy shows that the Pelagians considered them incompatible. Of the author of the commentary, Dempsey writes:

He certainly does not deny the doctrine of grace or mention it explicitly in connection with liberty, but when we turn to his explanation of passages the normal exposition of which would demand a reference to the positive help of God given to the human will, we get a sufficiently clear indication of his mind. . . . God's share in our action is reduced to that of a mere spectator, who, like a teacher before an examination, offers his advice and promises a reward but gives no help in the performance of the task.[30]

Dempsey finds Pelagius guilty of omission, that is, of failing to say something that should have been said. He may be right when he says that the history of the Pelagian controversy shows that Pelagians considered free will to be incompatible with actual grace. However, that does not necessarily impugn Pelagius's words here. There is no reason why we should not instead choose to interpret Pelagius more sympathetically and see here a simple affirmation of free will. Even Dempsey, who frequently finds Pelagius guilty of omission and who thinks that the doctrine of actual grace found no place in Pelagius's theology, admits, "That he was aware of its existence and positively refused to admit it is doubtful. That he was in perfect good faith seems certain."[31]

The natural consequence of human beings' possessing free will is that they themselves then become responsible for their sin. Smith observes that although Pelagius's short glosses on Rom 1.24–32 seem to owe little to Origen's exposition of this same passage, there is nevertheless one important point of contact: they both understand the divine "handing over" in the same way.[32] Pelagius explains Paul's words in Rom 1.26, that "God handed them over," with this gloss: "Because of the reasons noted above they were abandoned to their monstrous behavior."[33] And on Rom 1.24 Pelagius stated: "In the Scriptures God is said 'to hand over' when because of freedom of choice he does not restrain transgressors."[34] Notice the following parallel in Origen's commentary on the same text in Romans: "The duty of choice is preserved. For the matter is not done by force, nor is the soul moved in either of the two directions by compulsion . . . Instead the freedom of will is preserved."[35] Slightly later, Origen writes, "God is said 'to hand over' those whose deeds and mind he shrinks back from and deserts because it turns away from him and indulges in the vices."[36] It seems clear in these cases that Pelagius has appropriated and transmitted the Origenian inheritance on the matter of freedom of will and of human sin as the antecedent cause for God's "handing over." Such a stress in Pelagius was probably aimed to silence the Manichaeans, who denied that souls were responsible for sin.

Predestination as Divine Foreknowledge

The decidedly antideterminist reading of Paul is shared by both commentators. That is to say, in a way that is similar to Augustine in his early efforts,[37] both Origen and Pelagius explain predestination and election essentially as foreknowledge of merits.[38] It is undoubtedly from Origen that Pelagius derived his interpretation that Rom 9.14–19 expresses the view of Paul's opponents, not Paul himself.[39] Earlier in his commentary, Origen had described how Paul was "set apart" for the gospel (Rom 1.1), namely by means of divine foreknowledge of his merits: "The reasons for this and the merits which entitled him to be set apart for this purpose were seen by the One from whom one's mind does not escape."[40] Origen goes on to say that God knew how hard Paul was going to labor as an apostle and chose him in accordance with that foreknowledge of his future deserts. Similarly Pelagius writes on Rom 1.1 that Paul was set apart by God because he "merited the office of apostle by faithful and matchless service."[41]

Dempsey interprets Pelagius more severely: "One thing at least is clear: Pelagius succeeded in explaining this chapter of St. Paul to his own satisfaction without the necessity of appealing to that divine help which was later called actual grace."[42] If this judgment is valid, it would also apply to Origen. In any case Origen's view of God's foreknowledge of human merit is repeated with slight modifications by Pelagius. Smith observes that Ambrosiaster shared this view as well, that is, that predestination is equivalent to divine foreknowledge, and so did Augustine at one time.[43] Moreover, Hermas represented this position in *Similitudes* 8.6.1ff. All this suggests that the view under consideration is embedded in the early Catholic tradition.

On Rom 8.29 Pelagius makes explicit that he identifies election with foreknowledge, but here it is noticeable that in Pelagius the object of the divine foreknowledge differs slightly from Origen's understanding. Pelagius states:

The purpose according to which he planned to save by faith alone those whom he had foreknown would believe, and those whom he freely called to salvation he will all the more glorify as they work [towards salvation]. To predestine is the same as to foreknow. Therefore, those he foresaw would be conformed in life he intended to be conformed in glory.[44]

Origen explains the same text in these words: "They are said to be called according to the purpose of God, who knows that a pious mind and the longing for salvation is in them."[45] As Smith notes, for both exegetes "God's purpose is determined by His foreknowledge of the characters and merits of men."[46] There is, however, a slight modification of the Origenian tradition by Pelagius. For Origen, God foreknew that a pious mind and a longing for salvation is in the human being. Pelagius places greater stress on foreseen faith, indeed on faith alone, and says that God foreknew their conformity in life. This view of election *post praevisa merita* also resembles Augustine's earlier explanation of Rom 9.10ff. in *Expositio quarundam quaestionum in epistula ad Romanos* 60, according to which God does not elect foreseen works but foreseen faith.[47] Indeed, Augustine's work is one that Pelagius has followed here.[48] Moreover, the interpretation also anticipates the post-Tridentine Jesuit school of Suarez.[49]

Redemption

The redemption of humanity by the blood of Christ (Rom 3.24) is explained in the same spirit by both commentators.[50] In what De Bruyn calls a "classic statement of Pelagius's view of baptismal justification,"[51] Pelagius glosses this verse, "'Having been freely justified by his grace.' Without the works of the law, through baptism, whereby he has freely forgiven the sins of all, though they are undeserving."[52] According to Rivière this extremely brief gloss well reveals the theological direction of Paul's soteriology. Pelagius's stress on gratuitous justification by means of baptismal grace logically presupposes an anterior and superior cause, which can only be the death of Christ on the cross.[53] Baptism is the application of this objective work of redemption accomplished by the Redeemer to the believer, both ritually and symbolically. Rivière observes that Pelagius's stress on humanity being "undeserving" of this grace shows that for Pelagius the reach of the mystery of the cross far surpasses the purely psychological effect that this act exerts upon our minds.[54] In short, in Rivière's opinion, Pelagius's theology of redemption is unobjectionable here, and the burden of proof must now rest upon the critic who wants to say that Pelagius didn't really mean it. In my judgment, there is no reason to challenge the correctness of Rivière's analysis.[55]

On Rom 3.25 Pelagius writes: "'Whom God has presented.' He has set him in public before the eyes of all, so that whoever wishes to be redeemed may draw near. 'As a propitiator for faith in his blood to manifest his righteousness.' So that he may be propitious towards those who believe that they need to be freed by his blood."[56] In the same spirit, Origen had written on Rom 3.24:

> Therefore the righteousness of God through faith in Jesus Christ reaches to all who believe, whether they are Jews or Greeks. It justifies those who have been cleansed from their past crimes and makes them capable of receiving the glory of God; and it supplies

this glory not for the sake of their merits nor for the sake of works, but freely to those who believe.[57]

And on Rom 3.25, Origen said:

> Through the sacrifice of himself he would make God propitious to men and through this he manifests his own righteousness as he forgives them their past sins, which they had contracted by serving the worst tyrants at the time when God was tolerating and allowing this to be done. God allowed this so that afterwards, i.e., at this time, he would manifest his own righteousness. For at the consummation of the age, at the end of time, God disclosed his own righteousness and, for the redemption price, gave him whom he made a propitiator. . . . For God is just, and the one who is just could not justify the unjust; for that reason he wanted there to be the mediation of a propitiator so that those who were not able to be justified through their own works might be justified through faith in him.[58]

Common to both interpretations are the elements that both Jews and Gentiles are estranged from God because of sins, that they do not deserve to be set free from the bondage of sin, and that their salvation is grounded upon Christ's objective act of redemption on the cross which places them under the obligation to sin no more.[59] This indicates that the theologies of redemption are similar in Origen and Pelagius. It is noteworthy, however, that Pelagius passes over in silence Origen's long allegorical excursus on the term *propitiatory* and its roots in the OT. Also, Pelagius skips over Origen's interpretation of Christ's death as a ransom paid to the devil.[60] Omissions like these point to a less speculative and more practical frame of mind in Pelagius.

Romans 5.12 and the Transmission of Sin

Pelagius's doctrines of free will, grace, predestination as divine foreknowledge of merits, and redemption resemble Origen's and seem to be partly derivative from Origen. Nor does Pelagius's substantial orthodoxy on these themes seem to be in doubt, when his statements are read sympathetically and in their original historical context and with awareness of his reliance upon the antecedent tradition. On the other hand, we shall now observe that Pelagius has a tendency toward an uncomplicated understanding of the transmission of sin, which does not seem sufficiently balanced. This becomes clearer when we compare Pelagius with his principle source, Origen.

All scholars have noted the affinities between Origen and Pelagius in their interpretation of Rom 5.12. Pelagius glosses the words of Paul "But just as through one man sin came into the world . . ." with this terse comment: "by example or by pattern" (*exemplo vel forma*).[61] And under the lemma to Rom 5.19 Pelagius writes, "Just as by the example of Adam's disobedience many sinned, so also many are justified by Christ's obedience."[62] And finally, under the lemma to Rom 5.15 Pelagius reports the views of those who deny the transmission of sin without the slightest indication that these arguments are to be rejected.[63] When his other notes are compared to this one, one can be confident in affirming that for Pelagius Adam's influence on posterity is reduced to a bad example.

Transmission of sin from Adam solely by example or pattern came to be regarded as a "trademark" of Pelagius's thought.[64] Dempsey argues that Pelagius's explanation of Rom 5.12 is "tantamount to a denial" of the Church's doctrine of original sin, since he was aware of Ambrosiaster's exegesis of this passage and ignored it.[65] Pelagius prefers instead to follow the movement of Origen's interpretation of Rom 5.12, where the whole emphasis is on the personal sins of individuals who have followed Adam's example, rather than on solidarity in Adam's guilt.

Origen's position is clarified in his comment on Rom 5.12: "With an absolute pronouncement the Apostle has declared that the death of sin passed through to all men in this, that all sinned."[66] He then cites examples of human beings who committed actual sins, a list that includes Abel, Enosh, Methuselah, Enoch, Noah, and Abraham. It seems that Pelagius and Origen correspond very well with each other in their interpretation of Rom 5.12 as teaching the personal sin of imitation. However, Origen's commentary also contains material that gives an alternate explanation of Rom 5.12 in which the inherited consequences of humanity's physical solidarity with Adam are indicated. Tellingly these other explanations of Origen, which seem to bear a resemblance to the theory of original sin posited much later by Ambrosiaster and Augustine, were bypassed by Pelagius.

In 5.1, for example, Origen raises the question of why sin entered "through one man," when the woman sinned before Adam and the serpent before the woman.[67] As an answer he suggests that the succession of human descent which became subject to the death coming from sin is ascribed not to the woman but to the man. Then he cites Heb 7.9–10 as a means of explaining the phrase "in whom all sinned." As in the case of Levi, all humanity, Origen suggests, may be said to be in Adam's loins and could have been collectively expelled from paradise with Adam.[68] Later in 5.4 Origen suggests that everyone is in this valley of tears and place of humiliation because they were equally expelled from paradise with Adam, being in his loins.[69] Then in 5.9 Origen refers to the Old Testament sin-offering for newly born babies and the Christian practice of infant baptism as proof that all have the pollution of sin at birth and need to be cleansed from it. That succession from Adam plays a role in this defiled condition is suggested in the passage where he says that only after his sin did Adam know his wife and beget Cain and that because of the virgin birth, Christ only had the *likeness* of the flesh of sin and not the flesh of sin itself.[70] It is true that Origen does not say that all human beings "sinned" in Adam, but that they "fell" with or in Adam. One of the hypotheses Origen appears to be offering is that of a prenatal collective fall of the whole race, as contained in Adam, from the heavenly place.[71]

Reasoner finds it "most significant" that Origen reads a "hard fall" into Rom 5.12; that is to say, Origen asserts that all human beings are affected by Adam's sin.[72] Kelly noted that this particular idea of succession of sin handed down from Adam and of a collective fall runs against the grain of Origen's theology and is in fact incompatible with Origen's famous view of the fall as the personal fall of the individual soul before entering the body. Kelly admits that the alternate view that Origen presents in the *CRm* resembles the later orthodox doctrine of original sin (which omitted the idea of the pre-existence of souls). This similarity led Kelly to suspect that Rufinus must have altered the original material in Origen's commentary in the interest of orthodoxy.[73] Kelly assumes that Origen is a "firm exponent" of the former theory set forth in *Peri Archon* of the pre-existence and fall of all individual souls. He, along with many other modern scholars, argues that this theory is an essential aspect of Origen's theology.

Origen's primary theory was originally an attempt to defend divine justice and the principle of liberty against the Gnostics. It states that in the beginning God out of his goodness created a fixed number of rational essences, all of them equal and alike, and endowed them all with free will. Since these souls were free, it rested with their own volition to advance by imitating God, or to fall away by neglecting him. For a soul to depart from good was tantamount to its settling down to evil. As a result of their falling away, God assigned these souls to bodies.

According to Kelly, Origen's theory entails the abandonment of any doctrine of corporate sinfulness, since it suggests that if human beings are sinful from birth, their wickedness is the legacy of their own misguided choices in the transcendental world, and has nothing to do with the disobedience of any one first man. Kelly further notes that interpreters of Origen have sometimes been reluctant to admit that this was his true teaching. Kelly is aware of the passages in Origen's *CRm* where he appears to accept the doctrine that the whole race was present in Adam's loins and "fell in him," but he does not accept these statements at their face value, since they have only been preserved in the translation of Rufinus, who is known to have adjusted Origen's teaching in the interest of orthodoxy. Kelly writes:

> For example, he [Rufinus] represented Origen as taking ἐφ᾿ ᾧ in Rom 5.12 as meaning "in whom," whereas he [Origen] really understood it as meaning "since" [Kelly bases this on Origen's comments in the *CJn*]. Even in that commentary [*CRm*], however, in expounding Rom 5.12–19, his whole emphasis is on the personal sins of individuals who have followed Adam's example, rather than on their solidarity with his guilt; and, while admitting the possibility that we may be in this vale of fears [*sic*] because we were in Adam's loins, he does not conceal his belief that each one of us was banished from Paradise for his personal transgressions.[74]

Roukema has made a very similar observation without advocating Kelly's view that Rufinus has doctored Origen's text.[75]

Kelly and Roukema seem correct when they say that Origen's whole emphasis in his explanation of Rom 5.12 in the *CRm* is on personal sins. But Kelly, at least, makes two questionable assumptions: first, that Origen dogmatically held a monolithic and uncomplex view of the cause of the fallen human condition, which was announced in his earlier writings (*On*

First Principles, CJn);[76] second, that Rufinus therefore must have altered Origen's original text in his translation of Origen's *CRm* in light of orthodoxy, since he represents Origen as presenting alternate views. To my knowledge Kelly is the only modern scholar who has suspected Rufinus's reliability on this point. Both suppositions are dubious, in my opinion, when we consider the following: (a) that Origen frequently presents alternate views of interpretative problems; and (b) that the timing of Rufinus's translation (406), which antedates the Pelagian controversy and the debate over the transmission of sin, makes it improbable that Rufinus would have doctored Origen's text in this way.

Bammel has addressed the question of the alleged incompatibility of Origen's statements in the *CRm* with his statements elsewhere. She denies the necessity of supposing that Origen's theory of a succession of sin handed down from Adam to his descendants is incompatible with that of the fall of the individual soul before entering the body. She also challenges the necessity of positing that Origen "changed his mind" on this subject. She writes:

> A particular situation (in this case the human condition) can have more than one cause. The individual soul may enter human life as the result of its own previous fall and here be subjected to conditions which are the result of Adam's condemnation. . . . His aim was not to dogmatize or to force his biblical material into a straitjacket, but rather to do justice to the multiplicity, complexity and variety of the biblical pronouncements concerning Adam, human nature and the fall.[77]

Bammel's approach seems sensitive to Origen's general approach to disputed theological questions. It allows for the possibility that Origen made various tentative suggestions about the causes for the fallen condition of humankind without attempting to reconcile them. It is not that Origen's views are "ambiguous,"[78] but that they are diverse and complex. Certainly, for Origen the rule of faith at the time in which he flourished left room for various theories on the causes of the fallen condition of human beings. If the material in the *CRm* is authentic, its presence surely shows the range of Origen's views and the exploratory nature of this theological enterprise.

The relevant point for our current study is that Pelagius is completely silent with regard to other explanations of Rom 5.12, which are found in both Ambrosiaster and Origen. This suggests that Pelagius's appropriation of the antecedent tradition was seriously one sided. As De Bruyn has observed, Pelagius "tended toward an uncomplicated presentation of the issue."[79] To be sure Origen had clearly stressed that all human beings sinned by imitating Adam, and Pelagius adopts such statements in his own commentary. But Origen had also spoken of the physical succession of sin from Adam and of a collective fall of the race in Adam. These suggestions imply that the consequences of Adam's sin can be transmitted by propagation and not merely by imitation. Moreover, Origen had also spoken of infants being already unclean at birth and in need of the regeneration of baptism. Yet Pelagius completely bypasses such material in Origen. De Bruyn summarizes the distinction between Origen and Pelagius by noticing that while Pelagius does concern himself with deliberate sin and spiritual death, he is silent on physical death, ignorance, and concupiscence, all of which figure in Origen's comments on these verses. It is possible, but scarcely certain, that Pelagius includes physical death along with spiritual death when at 5.12 he says that "through the sin of Adam death entered" the world. Moreover, De Bruyn believes that it is important to acknowledge that Pelagius does treat ignorance and concupiscence in his comments on chapter 7. Nevertheless, De Bruyn concludes:

> But neither physical death nor ignorance nor concupiscence are significant elements of his discussion of Rm. 5:12–21, and, when he does treat the latter two, he emphasizes that they are the consequence of deliberate sin in the course of a human life. In short, in his comments on Romans, Pelagius concentrates on deliberate sin to the exclusion of any inherited consequences of the fall, unlike Origen, who, though he ultimately focuses on deliberate sin, nevertheless includes inherited consequences in his scope.[80]

De Bruyn further shows how Pelagius's one-sided and truncated appropriation of Origen stands out all the more tellingly when one compares it with that of the anonymous commentator on Romans, writing around 400, who used the Greek text of Origen's *CRm*.[81] Whereas Pelagius had excluded any discussion of the inherited effects of the fall passed on from one generation to the next, such as physical death, ignorance, and concupiscence, the anonymous commentator touches on all of these effects, and borrows heavily from Origen's *CRm* (in its Greek version) to do so.[82] This demonstrates that Pelagius's appropriation of Origen's *CRm* was not the only possible one.

In summation Origen seems to have been equally a source for Pelagius's stress on original sin as personal sin and deliberate imitation of Adam, as well as a source for the collective theory of original sin, which was expressed much later by Ambrosiaster and Augustine.[83] The orthodox writers would of course leave out Origen's theory of a prenatal fall. Nevertheless, the elements for the collective view of innate guilt that eventually prevailed in the Church also have roots in Origen's commentary. The fact that Pelagius omits this material and explains the passages in Paul that deal with original sin without making any reference to this traditional interpretation seems to confirm that Pelagius does not admit transmission of sin from Adam by propagation, even though he does not explicitly deny it in his commentary.[84]

Paul's Polemic Against "Works"

Pelagius's comments on Rom 3.20 and 3.28 contain important parallels to certain of Origen's remarks pertaining to Paul's definition of "works of the law." In a comment on Rom 3.20 Pelagius states: "By works of the law he means circumcision, the sabbath, and the other ceremonies, which had to do not so much with righteousness as with carnal pleasure."[85] These words reflect Origen's assertion:

> One should know that the works which Paul repudiates and frequently criticizes are not the works of righteousness which are commanded in the law, but those in which they boast who keep the law according to the flesh; that is, the circumcision of the flesh, the sacrificial rituals, the observance of Sabbaths and new moon festivals [cf. Col 2.18]. These and works of a similar nature are the works by which he says no one can be saved.[86]

It seems likely that Pelagius is depending directly on Origen for this insight; however, we should make clear that at least three other predecessors of

Pelagius on whom he drew, Victorinus, Ambrosiaster, and Augustine, interpreted the "works of the law" as referring to ceremonial acts. It is possible that they are equal sources for Pelagius.[87] Obviously the interpretation represents a broad consensus of patristic exegesis.

In a comment on Rom 3.28, Pelagius discusses a current abuse of Paul's text that is also reminiscent of Origen:

> Some misuse this verse to do away with works of righteousness [*operum iustitiae*], asserting that faith by itself can suffice [for one who has been baptized], although the same apostle says elsewhere: "And if I have complete faith, so that I move mountains, but do not have love, it profits me nothing" [1 Cor 13.2]; and in another place declares that in this love is contained the fullness of the law, when he says, "The fullness of the law is love" [Rom 13.10]. Now if these verses seem to contradict the sense of the other verses, what works should one suppose the apostle meant when he said that a person is justified through faith without works [of the law]? Clearly, the works of circumcision or the sabbath and others of this sort, and not without the works of righteousness [*iustitiae operibus*], about which the blessed James says: "Faith without works is dead" [Jas 2.26]. But in the verse we are treating he is speaking about the person who in coming to Christ is saved, when he first believes, by faith alone.[88]

Here Pelagius reports what he regards as a false interpretation of Paul that asserts that faith by itself can suffice for the baptized (*solam fidem [baptizato] posse sufficere adfirmantes*). It is well known that at the beginning of the fifth century, there existed in the Western Church a number of errors that presented salvation as more or less independent of good works. Pelagius does not specifically identify the source of these errors, but we learn from Augustine as well that they affected the Christian faithful.[89]

In the current passage, Pelagius repeats his conviction, which agrees with Origen, that when Paul says that we are justified by faith "without works of the law," the Apostle is referring to the works of circumcision or the sabbath and others of this sort (*Scilicet circumcisionis vel sabbati et ceterorum huius[ce]modi*). Paul does not mean without the postbaptismal works of righteousness, about which the blessed James says: "Faith without works is dead" (Jas 2.26) (*non absque iustitiae operibus, de quibus beatus Iacobus dicit: "fides sine operibus mortua est"*).

Origen had reported a similar erroneous interpretation of Paul in his commentary. Since Origen's comments on these matters were scattered in different locations, these borrowings prove that Pelagius does not always draw on Origen from the corresponding passage in the earlier commentary.[90] The verbal parallels here are striking and show the persistence of this kind of reading of Paul in the ancient Church, that is, one that asserts that faith alone is adequate for salvation and that the postbaptismal works of righteousness are not necessary for the Christian's salvation.

To review what Origen had written, we recall that Origen had exhorted believers to be edified by Paul's words in Rom 2.6 regarding the coming judgment according to works, "lest they think that the fact alone that they believe can suffice for them" (*ne putent sibi hoc solum sufficere posse quod credunt*).[91] Then, in 8.2 Origen had reported a false understanding of Paul which asserted that one can possess salvation by faith alone, without the advantages of good works and the obligation to pay heed to the virtues.[92] Both Origen and Pelagius find a fundamental harmony between Paul's doctrine of justification and the words of James 2.26; both have invoked Rom 13.10 and 1 Cor 13.2 as proof that love and postbaptismal works of justice are necessary for salvation.

Additional Pauline Themes

From the perspective of the subsequent controversies of the Protestant Reformation, we should also call attention to the paradoxical fact that, in spite of their strong repudiation of a heretical doctrine that asserts that salvation is by faith alone, both Origen and Pelagius still feel free to add the qualifying word "alone" to the Pauline formulation "justification by faith." Pelagius comments on Rom 4.5, "When an ungodly person converts, God justifies him by faith alone (*per solam fidem*), not for the good works he did not have. Otherwise he should have been punished for the works of ungodliness."[93] Precisely on this text Origen had used similar language: "The apostle says that *only* on the basis that he believes [*pro eo tantum quod credidit*] in him who justifies the ungodly, righteousness would be reckoned to a human being, even if he has not yet produced works of righteousness."[94] In these passages the qualifying words *alone* or *only* have been added to the Pauline text with the intention of excluding pre-baptismal works from making any contribution to salvation, whether they arise from natural law or from the law of Moses. Because of his repeated stress on *fides sola,* Eno hailed Pelagius's interpretations of the Pauline letters as being, "superficially at least," the "least objectionable" of the ancient commentators.[95] Eno seems correct when he essentially admits that his interpretation of Pelagius is only possible when Pelagius's statements are read in a superficial manner. Wiles speaks more reasonably when he says, "Pelagius does frequently use the words 'faith alone' without any qualification . . . but it is clear from his more detailed statements that he regards it as a first step which is of no value apart from the subsequent works."[96]

Further examples of parallels between Origen and Pelagius can be cited. On Rom 5.1 Origen had written, "By these words he is very openly inviting the one who has grasped what it means to be justified by faith and not by works to 'the peace of God which surpasses all understanding,' in which the sum of perfection consists."[97] Pelagius glosses the same verse, "He has discussed the point that none of them is justified by works, but all by faith . . . Now, having finished this argument, he urges them to be at peace, because none is saved by his own merit, but all are saved in the same way by God's grace."[98] The movement and progression of argument in Pelagius seems to reflect Origen's logical train of thought. A noteworthy parallel on the theme of the gratuity of divine grace is observable when Pelagius's text is compared with Origen's comment on Rom 6.23: " 'The wages of sin is death.' And he did not go on to say in similar fashion: but the wages of righteousness is eternal life. Instead he says, 'But the gift of God is eternal life,' in order [not only] to teach that the wages, which are assuredly comparable with a debt and reward, are a repayment of punishment and death, but to establish eternal life in grace alone."[99] Just above this Origen had explained Rom 4.4–5 with these words: This "seems to declare that in faith there is the gift of the one who justifies; in works, however, there is the righteousness of the one who repays."[100] These ideas are blended together in Pelagius on Rom 6.23: " 'For the wages of sin is death': He did not say in a similar manner: 'the wages of righteousness,' because there was no righteousness in us beforehand for him to repay: for it is not procured by our effort, but is presented as a gift of God."[101]

Once again, the unmerited, gratuitous nature of God's gift of salvation is stressed.

As a final example, we observe that the interpretations of Rom 8.1 are also noticeably similar. Both Origen and Pelagius understand the words "There is no condemnation" as applicable to those who deserve to be so described. Pelagius explains this text in these words: "There is nothing deserving of condemnation [*nihil in illis damnatione dignum est*] in those [who] have been crucified to the works of the flesh." Just prior to this comment he had glossed Rom 7.25 as follows: "The carnal person is, in a sense, made up of two persons and is divided within himself."[102] Now compare Origen on Rom 8.1–2:

Above he has shown what opposing forces exist in those who, as though placed in a type of combat, live indeed according to the law of God with the mind, but are led to the law of sin by the flesh. But now he is speaking of those who no longer are partly in the flesh and partly in the Spirit, but who are completely in Christ. He declares that there is nothing deserving of condemnation in them [*nihil esse in his damnatione dignum*] because "the law of the Spirit of life in Christ Jesus has set them free from the law of sin and death."[103]

The language used by Pelagius and Origen here is "almost identical"[104] and clearly reflects direct borrowing from Origen on Pelagius's part. Following Paul's text, "law" is placed by both Origen and Pelagius on the side of Christ and the Spirit. Those who are justified in Christ and not condemned are precisely those who, by Christ's liberating gift, do not deserve to be condemned, because they do not live according to the flesh. In them the law of the Spirit of life is really being fulfilled.

Summary and Conclusions

It is obvious that Pelagius read Romans under the tutelage of Origen. We have seen deep affinities between Origen and Pelagius in their commentaries on Romans. Not only are words and phrases from Origen incorporated directly into Pelagius's commentary, the logical structure of many of Pelagius's glosses seems to derive directly from Origen's train of thought.

Both men appear to be determined, as churchmen, to fight against the prevalent heresies of their day. For Origen the opponents are the heretics Marcion, Basilides, and Valentinus; for Pelagius they are principally Arius and the followers of Mani, though several other heretics are also mentioned.[105] Some form of determinism and predestinarianism is combated by both theologians.

Both Origen and Pelagius depict Paul as an arbiter between Jews and Gentiles who invites members of both groups to accept God's offer of gratuitous salvation through faith in Christ. In order for human beings to attain salvation, both theologians insist upon the absolute necessity of the objective redemptive work of Christ on the cross, since it is impossible for human beings to merit salvation by their works. Pelagius is clearly dependent upon Origen for his "anthropological optimism."[106] Bohlin states: "Pelagius appears to us to have found rich and central material for his doctrine of grace nowhere so much as in Origen's *CRm*."[107] His doctrines of free will, of predestination as foreknowledge of faith and merit, and of human sin as the cause of God's reprobation come substantially from Origen. Moreover, it appears that Origen is a key source for Pelagius's interpretation of Rom 5.12 in which it is understood that all human beings are condemned because they have actually sinned by following Adam's bad example, and not merely because they descend from Adam. This stress on actual sin as the cause of condemnation probably is due to the claims of Gnostic and Manichaean exegesis wherein sin is attributed to the human nature and flesh. Finally, both Pelagius and Origen have explicitly clarified that the works repudiated by Paul are the external works of Judaism, such as circumcision and sabbaths, and not the postbaptismal works of justice that the Christian needs in order to deserve to be justified. Both fight against the heresy that is present in the Church which asserts that justification is by faith alone.

There are also, however, important differences between Pelagius and Origen that must not be overlooked. Although I have not attempted to demonstrate this point from texts, Pelagius has explicitly repudiated Origen's theory of the pre-existence of human souls, a theory that is not very prominent in the latter's *CRm* in any case.[108] Pelagius has bypassed many of Origen's allegories and digressions. Perhaps most significantly, in his interpretation of Rom 5.12 Pelagius has concentrated on deliberate sin and excludes any inherited consequences of the fall. He passes over in silence interpretations given by Origen and others which state that human sin can be transmitted from Adam by propagation through his loins and not merely through imitation of his behavior. In addition, Pelagius overlooks Origen's claim that infants enter the world in a fallen condition and therefore need to be cleansed by baptism. These omissions betray a tendentious and one-sided appropriation of Origen.

In *De peccatorum meritis et remissione* 3.1.1, Augustine reports that he has just read Pelagius's *CRm*. Upon coming to the comments on Rom 5.12, he says, "Therein I found . . . an argument which is used by those who say that infants are not burdened with original sin."[109] In the light of what we have examined above, it seems that Augustine's suspicions of Pelagius's doctrine of the transmission of sin were well justified.

Chapter 3

Augustine's Reception of Origen's Exegesis of Romans

St. Augustine (354–430), a contemporary of Rufinus and Pelagius, established a great theological legacy in the Latin West by the way he synthesized theological topics into a coherent system of thought. Augustine's theology developed over time, the watershed being the Pelagian controversy. This means that the difference between the early and late Augustine is very pronounced. This chapter will investigate the possible influence of the Latin Origen's exegesis of Romans upon St. Augustine. To achieve this purpose I will consult a relevant sampling of Augustine's works in chronological order.

Augustine's Early Exegesis of Paul

Augustine's brief *Commentary on Certain Propositions from Paul's Letter to the Romans,* his *Unfinished Commentary on the Epistle to the Romans,* and his *Commentary on Galatians* appeared long before Rufinus's translation was published.[1] This excludes the possibility of any direct influence of the Latin Origen's *CRm* on Augustine's early exegesis of Paul, since Rufinus's translation appeared in 406. Gorday's conclusion, however, that "Augustine does not show any sign of knowing Rufinus' version of Origen's *Romans-Commentary*"[2] is true only of Augustine's exegesis of the years 394–96.[3] Augustine's later works do appear to show some direct influence of the Latin Origen's *CRm*. Moreover, indirect influence of Origen's Pauline interpretations upon the early Augustine could have occurred by way of St. Ambrose's sermons and writings, and by St. Jerome's Pauline commentaries, which are largely based on Origen.[4] However, this matter will not be explored here.

It is interesting to observe that Augustine's earlier exegesis of Romans repeats certain ideas found in Origen's *CRm*. For example, Augustine's concern to affirm the justice of the divine call and the suggestion that divine predestination is essentially divine foreknowledge of the most hidden merits of souls (*animarum occultissima merita*) is found in Origen.[5] Bammel noted that it is perhaps paradoxical that Augustine's thought was closest to Origen's in the period before he had direct access to Latin translations of Origen's works.[6] The reason for this, of course, is that the Pelagian controversy caused Augustine to reconsider many theological issues.

In a study that compares the interpretations of Romans made by Origen, Pelagius, and Augustine, Burns focuses on the watershed distinguishing the early and later Augustine. He observes that the difference between Augustine's analysis of the Epistle to the Romans in his early works and during the Pelagian controversy centers on the fifth, seventh, and ninth chapters. In Augustine's early period when he was in debate with the Manichaeans, he shares the assumptions about the power of human freedom and the limits of divine sovereignty which characterize the exposition of Pelagius and the Latin version of Origen's commentary. Even in explaining divine election, Augustine endeavored to retain a degree of individual responsibility. All this changed after his encounter with Pelagius. Burns explains:

> In the later controversy with Pelagius, he abandoned these principles to deny fallen humanity's power to elicit good desires or even to respond to divine teaching and exhortation. He asserted a universal sinfulness, which is prior to personal choice, an original guilt. This dramatic shift was caused, I have argued, by a recognition of the uniqueness of Christ as savior and the Church as the sole way to him. Pelagius and Rufinus' Origen accepted these premises but

refused to draw the conclusions Augustine asserted. I suspect that the controversy with the Donatists forced them into their central place in Augustine's later theology.[7]

It seems conclusive that the Pelagian crisis marked a turning point for Augustine's theology which caused him to abandon some of his earlier emphases. The implication is that the Latin Origen (and Pelagius) is closer to the early Augustine than to the later. Augustine's later focus on the fifth, seventh, and ninth chapters in Romans suggests that the doctrines of original sin (Rom 5.12), human powerlessness (Rom 7.14–25), and pre-destination (Rom 9.10–29) became central to this theology in a way that they were not at the beginning.[8]

Augustine's Later Exegesis of Paul

De peccatorum meritis et remissione and *De spiritu et littera*

The spade work for detecting the *direct* influence of the Latin Origen's Pauline exegesis upon St. Augustine was done by Hammond Bammel, the editor of the critical edition of Origen's *CRm*. One of her most valu-able contributions to this field of study has been her work with the manu-script tradition of the Origen-Rufinus *CRm*.[9] In a 1992 article, Hammond Bammel provides interesting evidence to show that Augustine or one of his allies used Origen's *CRm* during the Pelagian controversy. She reports on the earliest extant manuscript of the Origen-Rufinus commentary, which dates to the fifth century.[10] A contemporary reader has left mar-ginal notes at four significant points, the most striking of which reads, "Contra eos qui traducem negant peccati" (Against those who deny the propagation of sin).[11] The note directs attention to a passage in Origen's *CRm* on Rom 6.6 where Origen affirms the hereditary transmission of sin, and that newborn infants are already unclean at birth, for which rea-son the Church baptizes them.[12] These and other marginal notes suggest · that the fifth-century annotator of Origen's *CRm* was interested in Origen's views on original sin, the impossibility of obedience to the Mosaic law, and whether children can become guilty of sin before the age of reason. These are precisely the issues debated in the Pelagian controversy. It is evident that the annotator was not an adherent of Pelagianism himself. The fact that Augustine, in *De pecc. mer.*, apparently borrows thoughts and arguments from Origen precisely on the Origenian passages that were annotated by the fifth-century annotator suggests to Hammond Bammel the possibility that the annotator was Augustine himself.[13] While this possibility should not be ruled out, the more probable view that Hammond Bammel favors is that the annotator was some other early reader who was familiar with the issues discussed by Augustine and his opponents. At the least these marginal annotations show that the Catholic enemies of the Pelagians studied Origen's *CRm* carefully and were interested in what he had to say. Their consultation and appropriation of Origen on the themes of original sin and the necessity of infant baptism resembles that of the anonymous commentator mentioned in the previous chapter.

Also in 1992 Bammel published a path-breaking article entitled "Augustine, Origen and the Exegesis of St. Paul," which includes an appendix of parallel texts showing correspondences between Origen's *CRm* and Augustine's works *De pecc. mer.* and *De spiritu et littera*. Her aim was to demonstrate the likelihood that "Augustine did indeed read and react to Rufinus' translation of Origen's *Commentary on Romans* by about 411."[14] We should first recall that, ostensibly in *De pecc. mer.*, Augustine is repudiating *Pelagius's* interpretations of Paul. Augustine tells us in 3.1.1 that he has just read Pelagius's *Commentary on Romans*. He specifically reproaches Pelagius's interpretation of Rom 5.12. Upon reading it, Augustine responded, "There I found a new line of argument from those people who deny that little ones have original sin."[15] Book 3 of Augustine's *De pecc. mer.* was written, then, to counter Pelagius's interpretation of original sin.

The results of Bammel's analysis can be summarized as follows. Augustine's earliest anti-Pelagian treatise, *De pecc. mer.*, shows a positive influence of Origen in Augustine's adoption of certain new ideas of Origen and his incorporation of individual comments. However, Augustine's subsequent treatise, *De spiritu et littera*, gives evidence of a reaction against Origen's views.[16] An important example of a positive appropriation of Origen is from *De pecc. mer.* 1.9, where Augustine reports that his Pelagian opponents claim to believe that sin is transmitted from Adam not by propagation but merely by imitation. If this were correct, Augustine says, Paul in Rom 5.12 would have ascribed the origin of sin not to Adam, from whom the human race is propagated, but to the devil, whom humanity imitates in sinning. The very same argument is found in Origen's *CRm* on Rom 5.12.[17] This leads Bammel to conclude that Augustine is taking up arguments found in Origen's commentary.[18] Also, in *De pecc. mer.* 2.11, 15, and 38 Augustine has taken up Origen's exposition of "body of sin" in Rom 6.6, where Origen says that the impulse of concupiscence transmits the pollution of sin to those conceived by sexual intercourse and that Christ was free from this pollution by virtue of his virginal conception.[19] Another fairly clear example of borrowing is found in 1.65–66 of Augustine's work, where he adapts Origen's illustration of a young child who strikes his parents to illustrate that the sin remitted in infant baptism must be original sin, not actual sin, for such a child cannot have committed sin, since it lacks the capacity to reason.[20] These samples suggest that Augustine viewed Origen's *CRm* as a reservoir of Catholic exegesis that could be used as ammunition against the Pelagians.

Bammel has also documented what appears to be a reaction *against* some of Origen's interpretations in Augustine's work *De spiritu et littera*. In chapter 50, for example, Augustine dissents from a distinction found in Origen's text between salvation from faith (*ex fide*) and salvation through faith (*per fidem*).[21] Augustine claims that there is no real distinction between these phrases.[22] It is noteworthy that Pelagius had also explicitly rejected Origen's distinction.[23] Through these and other sets of parallel passages, Bammel has convincingly shown that Augustine probably had his own copy of Rufinus's translation and that he was directly influenced by it. Bammel concludes her study as follows:

> Origen's *Commentary on Romans*, even in the drastically reduced version of Rufinus, was a work of Pauline exegesis greatly superior to anything Augustine had so far had at his disposal. His engagement with it shows his openness to stimulation and his acceptance of some new ideas, but equally his exceptional independence of thought, his readiness to disagree and to argue ruthlessly, even perversely, for his own views, and above all his concentration on those insights which he had come to regard as central to the Christian message.[24]

While Augustine was open to Origen's views and could borrow them for various purposes, he was also capable of strong disagreement. His use of

Origen's work is somewhat myopic and riveted on texts that could supply him with ammunition against Pelagius.

One can find other texts in Augustine's anti-Pelagian works which Bammel left undiscussed. It is noticeable, for example, that Augustine strenuously argues *against* the idea that Paul's polemic against "works of the law" in Romans is delimited to the external and sacramental works of Judaism. Origen and Pelagius had argued that these external works were Paul's main concern when he excluded "works of the law" from justification. Moreover, Victorinus, Ambrosiaster, and even Augustine himself in his earlier *Commentary on Galatians* 19 (Gal 3.1) had made this the focus of his explanation of Paul's phrase "works of the law." In the *Commentary on Galatians*, which appeared in 394/395, Augustine divided the "works of the law" into two types: moral works and sacramental works. He says that sacramental works include circumcision of the flesh, sabbath, new moons, sacrifices, and so forth. Under moral works fall the Ten Commandments and the like. In *Expositio in epistulam ad Galatas* 3.1, Augustine says, the Apostle is primarily concerned with the sacramental works, although he sometimes includes moral works as well, as in Gal 5.13ff.[25] Bammel noticed that in this work Augustine shows "a much greater awareness of the historical context and far more readiness to make distinctions when speaking about law."[26] She attributes this in part to Augustine's reading of Jerome's *Commentary on Galatians*, which was largely based on Origen.

Augustine next passes through a transition in his theological development which is noticeable in *Ad Simplicianum de diversis quaestionibus* (397). He now assumes that Paul's purpose in the Epistle to the Romans is to prevent boasting and to show that the grace of the gospel is not given in return for merits. This affects his understanding of law in a decisive way. During the later anti-Pelagian period, Augustine stresses that Paul, when he says that we are justified by faith and not by works of the law, intends to include moral law and obedience to the Decalogue under the concept of law. In *De spiritu et littera*, he writes:

> We conclude that human beings are not justified by the commandments that teach us to live well [*praeceptis bonae vitae*], but only through faith in Jesus Christ, that is, not by the law of works, but by the law of faith, not by the letter, but by the Spirit, not by the merits of actions, but gratuitously by grace [*non factorum meritis, sed gratuita*

gratia]. The apostle seems to rebuke and correct those who were persuaded to receive circumcision in that by the term "law" he refers to circumcision and other such observances of the law. Christians do not now observe them, since they were foreshadowings of what was to come. And they now actually possess what was promised symbolically through those foreshadowings. The apostle, nonetheless, wanted us to understand that the law, by which he says that no one is justified, is found not only in those sacraments which they had as symbols of what was promised, but also in those works which amount to a righteous life for whoever does them. Among them we also find the commandment, You shall not desire [Ex 20.17]. And so that what we are saying may be made more clear, let us look at the Ten Commandments.[27]

Shortly after this, commenting on Rom 7.7ff., Augustine makes more explicit that Paul's polemic against "works" is not delimited to Jewish ceremonial law: "Consider the whole passage and see whether he says anything on account of circumcision or the Sabbath or any other foreshadowing sacred rite."[28] And then again in chapter 50, while commenting on Rom 10.4, "For the end of the law is Christ for righteousness for everyone who believes," Augustine writes along similar lines; however, this time he inserts a very important qualifying phrase:

> Are we still in doubt about which are the works of the law which do not justify human beings, *if they believe them to be their own without the help and gift of God that comes from faith in Jesus Christ?* Do we have in mind circumcision and other works of that sort, because in other passages we read some statements like this about these sacraments as well? But in this passage they certainly did not want to establish circumcision as their own righteousness, for God had by his command established it.[29]

In brief, Augustine's understanding of "works of the law" includes the moral law and is not delimited to the sacramental (external) law. This is an important difference between his interpretation of the Pauline term and Origen's. However, the qualifying words that I have placed in italics indicate that Augustine's main point in affirming this more comprehensive understanding of law is to assert the need for God's helping grace. The context is polemical and is clearly directed against the Pelagians.

In contrast with Augustine's interpretation, for Origen Paul was clearly not intending to include the moral law (the law of God) as embodied by the Decalogue, but rather he was aiming to exclude the external works of Judaism, that is, circumcision, sabbaths, festivals, and so forth. Pelagius had basically followed Origen. It seems that the difference is not that great when we observe that the interpretations are intending to make different points. Origen's point was anti-Gnostic: that Paul is not declaring Christians to be free from God's moral law or rejecting the necessity of the Christian's postbaptismal works of justice. Surely Augustine would not disagree with this point. In contrast, Augustine's point is anti-Pelagian: that justification from prebaptismal sins is completely independent of human works, not merely of the ceremonial works of the Mosaic law but also of its moral works. It appears that Origen would entirely agree with this point. As Grech has stated, Origen "cannot insist more persistently on the fact that both Jews and Gentiles come to salvation not through their own righteousness but through God's mercy."[30]

To continue our examination of Augustine's anti-Pelagian treatises, many of the distinctions Origen makes in Pauline theological terminology were not accepted by Augustine. Bammel suggests that much of Origen's exegesis must have seemed to distract from what Augustine considered the main point of Paul's letter:

> For Augustine justification by faith applies to the transition made from law to grace or from the letter to the spirit at the point of conversion or baptism, when the believer with no antecedent merits is received and justified by God's mercy. To suggest [as Origen does] that one needs a number of acts of faith or that one can count faith as one among other virtues does not fit with this picture.[31]

It seems in general that Origen understands Paul to be using terms such as *law* and *works* in a far more nuanced and complex manner than Augustine was prepared to concede. Origen thinks that the term *law*, for example, is used repeatedly in Paul but with divergent meanings. In

Bammel's view the problem is that Augustine has imposed a "forceful pattern on Paul's thought."[32] His theological preoccupations do not have room for many of Origen's complex and nuanced insights. Thus when Augustine identifies the relationship between works of the law and grace as the central message of Romans and stresses the contrast between these principles in order to refute the Pelagians, he has constructed a system of interpretation completely different from what Origen had followed.

Bammel explains that it is in their discussion of the Pauline term *law* that important differences between Origen and Augustine can be identified. Origen on repeated occasions offers detailed treatments of the term *law* and often suggests alternative explanations according to the different nuances of the word *law*. For Origen the Pauline term is complex: he distinguishes various kinds of law, including the law of Moses, which in its literal sense is superseded by the gospel, the written laws of other peoples, the natural law written in the heart of the human being, and the law of sin described by Paul as dwelling in his members. By way of contrast, Augustine does not raise this question but simply refers to the law without further qualification, both where the Mosaic law is clearly intended and where he is apparently speaking of law in general.[33] Bammel adds that Augustine, as a Pauline exegete, "takes virtually no interest in the historical situation in which Paul was writing," whereas Origen "had an unusually clear grasp of the problems Paul faced."[34] These are serious criticisms of Augustine with which I do not disagree.

Enarrationes in Psalmos 31

In the last published article before her death, Bammel compared Augustine's sermon on Ps 31, which was written in 411,[35] with Origen's Latin commentary. A major concern of Augustine's sermon is the interpretation of Rom 4 where Paul quotes from this psalm. Inspired by Schelkle's notice[36] that Augustine had followed the Latin Origen in certain points of this sermon, Bammel expanded the list of correspondences. The most obvious parallel concerns the explanation of Paul's logical argument respecting Abraham's glory and justification before God (Rom 4.1–8).[37] Bammel further noticed that when Augustine emphasizes the danger of supposing that faith alone without good works is sufficient and refers to the Epistle of James (Jas 2.21) as correcting a false interpretation of Paul, he appears to use phrases that derive directly from Origen-Rufinus. Augustine's aim is to demonstrate that the two apostles are in harmony with each other. In these passages it appears that Augustine read Origen appreciatively and with agreement. At II, 3 Augustine states:

> James dwells on an action performed by Abraham that we all know about: he offered his son to God as a sacrifice. That is a great work, but it proceeded from faith. I have nothing but praise for the superstructure of action, but I see the foundation of faith; I admire the good work as a fruit, but I recognize that it springs from the root of faith.[38]

Bammel noticed that both Augustine and Origen appeal to James as a means of correcting a false understanding of Paul. Using a metaphor that appears to derive directly from Origen's *CRm*, Augustine pictures faith as the foundation on which works are built. He also describes faith as the root that brings forth the fruit of good works.[39] Augustine says, "Laudo superaedificationem operis, sed video fidei fundamentum; laudo fructum boni operis, sed in fide agnosco radicem." Similarly, Origen had said that works that are not built on the foundation of faith ("supra fundamentum fidei") cannot justify the doer,[40] and that the root of righteousness does not grow out of works, but the fruit of works grows out of the root of righteousness ("Non ergo ex operibus radix iustitiae sed ex radice iustitiae fructus operum crescit").[41]

Also, in sections 5 and 6, Augustine provides citations from Paul which show the need for works after faith (Gal 5.6, "Faith working through love"). He stresses the centrality of love (Rom 13.10), or rather of faith, hope, and love (1 Cor 13.13). Like Augustine, Origen spoke of faith, hope, and love (1 Cor 13.13) as being respectively the beginning, advancement, and culmination of salvation.[42] Moreover, in section 7, Augustine considers Rom 4.4 and notes the contrast between grace and debt. Remission of sins is freely given, whereas works deserve condemnation, since all have sinned. In his discussion of this verse, Origen also contrasts grace and debt and states explicitly that debt should be taken in a negative sense, as the punishment deserved by sin.[43] Bammel concludes: "Augustine is clearly influenced by this negative understanding, though he doesn't agree entirely."[44]

In summary, the organic and architectural conceptions that illustrate the relation between faith and postbaptismal works run parallel in Origen and Augustine and may point to direct influence. This agrees with the observation of R. Eno, who said that in the area of grace and justification, Augustine does not seem to be that different from antecedent commentators, including Origen and Pelagius, "except that he stresses the ongoing dependence of the Christian in the post-baptismal justification process on God's gracious initiative and help. But this emphasis does not lead him to downplay the activity of the Christian in life. Another specific emphasis of his is the role of love."[45] Bammel concludes her study with this summary: "Augustine found much to agree with in his reading of Origen and picked up a number of ideas from him. He did not, however, treat Origen as an authority and he felt free to differ from his interpretations."[46] After citing a series of differences between these two interpreters, Bammel states that like his predecessors, Augustine read Origen critically and selectively and "seems to have looked at the particular parts which attracted his interest at the time, rather than studying the work right through."[47]

De fide et operibus

Bammel challenged scholars to pick up where she left off and look for traces of the Origen-Rufinus *CRm* in Augustine's later works.[48] Consequently, I would like to examine some passages in Augustine's work *De fide et operibus* (*On Faith and Works*). The subject matter of this later work of Augustine (413) fits the theme of this investigation, which is the legacy of Origen's Pauline exegesis in subsequent Christian thought, especially since I am aiming to give particular emphasis to the themes of justification, faith, and works. Since in this work Augustine comments on Paul's Letter to the Romans, a comparison between this work and Origen's *CRm* may be productive. The work was written immediately after *De spiritu et littera*, thus after Augustine would have had the chance to be exposed to Origen's Latin commentary.[49]

Augustine's stated aim in *De fide et operibus* is to refute those who were "convinced that one is able to attain eternal salvation, not without faith, of course, but without good works."[50] These people, Augustine tells us, are living in a treacherous false security and are in danger of losing their salvation. For they are under the illusion "that faith alone is sufficient for salvation, [even if] they neglect to live a good life and fail by good works to persevere in the way that leads to God."[51] Augustine rejects this doctrine and submits as a fundamental principle of pre- and postbaptismal catechesis that faith must be accompanied by works if final salvation is to be attained.[52] Augustine insists that "the only faith that justifies is that faith that is enlivened by charity."[53]

We have already seen that the claim that faith alone is sufficient for salvation was repudiated before, by both Origen and Pelagius. Origen had described and repudiated a current interpretation of Rom 10.9–10:

> For it will seem to some through this that even if the advantages of good works are lacking someone, even if he does not pay heed to the virtues, nevertheless, in this, that he has believed, he would not perish but would be saved and would possess salvation, even if he would be unable to have the glory of blessedness.[54]

Similarly, Pelagius had described a false interpretation of Rom 3.28 in these words:

> Some misuse this verse to do away with works of righteousness [*opera iustitiae*], asserting that faith by itself can suffice [for one who has been baptized], although the same apostle says elsewhere: "And if I have complete faith, so that I move mountains, but do not have love, it profits me nothing" [1 Cor 13.2]; and in another place declares that in this love is contained the fullness of the law, when he says, "The fullness of the law is love" [Rom 13.10].[55]

In parallel fashion but with the intention of making a different point in a different polemical context, in the current work Augustine asserts that a heresy that advocated the sufficiency of faith alone for salvation was represented in the days of the apostles by people who misunderstood the words of Paul and interpreted his statements as a license to sin.[56] Augustine clarifies his own understanding of the Apostle's doctrine of justification in words that are reminiscent of both Origen and Pelagius:

> When the Apostle says, then, that in his opinion a human being is justified through faith without the works of the Law, he does not

intend by this decision to express contempt for the commandments and the works of justice [*opera iustitiae*] by the profession of faith, but to inform anyone that he can be justified by faith even if he has not previously fulfilled the works of the Law; for they follow when one has been justified, and do not come before one is justified. There is no need, however, for further discussion of this problem in the present work, especially since I have published a detailed answer to the question in a book bearing the title, *The Letter and the Spirit*. Since this problem is by no means new and had already arisen at the time of the Apostles, other apostolic letters of Peter, John, James, and Jude are deliberately aimed against the argument I have been refut-ing and firmly uphold the doctrine that faith does not avail without good works [*ut vehementer astruant fidem sine operibus non prodesse*]. Paul himself also does not approve any kind of faith whatever as long as it achieves belief in God, but only that salutary and definitely evangelical faith from which good works proceed through love, for he says very plainly: "But faith which works through charity" [Gal 5.6]. That is why he claimed that the faith which seems to some suffi-cient for salvation is useless, so that he says: "and if I have all faith so as to remove mountains, yet do not have charity, I am nothing" [1 Cor 13.2]. It follows that where charity is operative in the Chris-tian, there is no doubt that he is living the right kind of life: "Love therefore is the fulfilment of the Law" [Rom 13.10].[57]

This passage shows Augustine clarifying Paul in a way that seems closer to Origen's exegesis and also recalls Pelagius's line of argument. It is notable that all three commentators introduce 1 Cor 13.2 and Rom 13.10 as crucial texts for grasping Paul's understanding of the inseparable and organic union between faith and postbaptismal love, obedience to God's law, and good works. All three agree that works antecedent to faith and baptism do not justify, but that subsequent good works are necessary for salvation. Augustine asserts that Paul's intention is not to condemn the necessity of postbaptismal works of righteousness (*opera iustitiae*). On the contrary, it is Augustine's firm conviction that the apostles insisted upon them and even in their own lifetimes refuted those who denied their necessity for salvation and who insisted that faith alone was adequate.[58]

Elsewhere, in *De fide et operibus* 23.42, Augustine appears to be specifically combating an interpretation of Rom 2.12 that derives solely from Origen. The Pauline text says, "For whosoever have sinned without the law shall perish without the law; and whosoever have sinned in the law shall be judged by the law." Origen had distinguished the meaning of *perish* and *judge*.[59] Augustine found this distinction unsatisfactory and writes, "There is no difference here, *as some might think,* between 'perish' and 'judged,' since both words mean the same thing."[60] Since it was Origen who had distinguished the meaning of these terms, it seems likely that this text provides further evidence that Augustine had a copy of the Origen-Rufinus text in his hands and was referring to it. It is noteworthy that Pelagius also rejected Origen's distinction.[61]

Augustine's Later Reflection on Origen's Principal Errors

De civitate Dei

Finally, in order to give a sample of Augustine's theological criticisms of Origen, two final Augustinian texts will be briefly consulted which count among Augustine's last works. In *The City of God* Augustine criticized Origen by name on two points: his cosmology and his eschatology. In 11.23 Augustine voices astonishment over the doctrine of creation Origen expounds in *Peri Archon,* according to which pre-existent human souls were consigned to material bodies as a result of their falling away from God in their previous existence. To Augustine's mind this theory is contrary to the plain meaning of the Scriptures, where it says, "And God saw that it was good."[62] Then in 21.17 Augustine faults Origen as the leader of those who denied that the punishment of hell would be eternal. Origen seems most compassionate, says Augustine, in his belief that even the devil and his angels will be rescued from their torments and brought into the company of angels. But his speculations lose even the appearance of compassion when they are analyzed, because in effect Origen is denying that the saints may experience the joy of everlasting good in genuine security, since they always stand in danger of falling away.

De haeresibus

Augustine's criticisms of Origen's errors were traditional, and in fact his own assessments are largely dependent on Jerome and Epiphanius. In fact, Augustine translated an epitome of Epiphanius's work on heresies in his own *De haeresibus*. In this latter work as well Augustine assessed Origen's principal errors, distinguishing among Epiphanius's accusations (namely, that Origen rejected the resurrection of the dead and that he taught that Christ and the Holy Spirit were creatures), the assertions of Origen's defenders and of those well versed in his works, and the teachings where there is no doubt concerning his heresy. Without giving formal support to Epiphanius's additional charges, Augustine makes clear the errors in Origen that he believes cannot be denied by any Catholic.

> But there are other teachings of this Origen which the Catholic Church does not accept at all. On these matters, she does not accuse him unwarrantably, and cannot herself be deceived by his defenders. Specifically, they are his teachings on purgation, liberation, and the return of all rational creation to the same trials after a long interval. Now what Catholic Christian, learned or otherwise, would not shrink in horror from what Origen calls the purgation of evils? According to him, even they who die in infamy, crime, sacrilege and the greatest possible impiety, and at last even the devil himself and his angels, though after very long periods of time, will be purged, liberated and restored to the kingdom of God and of light.[63]

Augustine then refers back to his recently written *City of God*, where he says he has discussed these matters thoroughly, and also Origen's error about the pre-existence of souls. It seems that Origen's doctrine of freedom, which entailed the hope of remission of mortal sins in the future life, was central to Augustine's criticisms of Origen's theology. It is a debated question whether Origen dogmatically held these condemned views, or tentatively put them forward for the sake of discussion as interpretive possibilities in an attempt to refute the arguments of his Gnostic opponents, with no intention of violating the Church's Rule of Faith. Some scholars even deny that Origen held these views in this form at all.[64] In any case, this citation gives us the heart of Augustine's theological criticism of Origen.

Conclusion

It is noteworthy that Augustine's repudiation of Origen's doctrines is not aimed primarily at Origen's exegesis of Romans but at his speculative work, *De principiis*. In *De pecc. mer.* Augustine borrowed arguments from Origen's *CRm* as ammunition to be used against the Pelagians and their faulty understanding of the transmission of sin. In his *Commentary on Ps 31* Augustine found Origen helpful to make the point that James and Paul do not contradict each other. In this case, Bammel claims that Augustine's very wording was influenced by the Origen-Rufinus *CRm*. From Origen, Augustine apparently derived the metaphors that faith is the beginning, root, and foundation of justification from which good works grow by means of divine grace. This manner of usage of Origen seems to confirm Rivière's thesis mentioned at the beginning of chapter 1, namely that Origen's *CRm* cleared a path for later theologians who would attempt to demonstrate the harmony between the notions of Paul and James, by showing the intimate and organic connection between faith and good works as the two complementary conditions of salvation that must not be separated. On the other hand, it seems undeniable that Augustine's conflict with Pelagius led him to occupy theological positions that are quite distinct and even adverse to Origen's interpretations of Paul, particularly in his interpretation of Romans 5, 7, and 9. The following chapter on William will illustrate some of these differences in a quite dramatic way.

Excursus on Bammel's Comparison of Origen and Augustine on Justification

In an important study, Bammel compared Augustine and Origen's "definitions" of justification by faith.[65] Her main conclusion is that Augustine had a faulty understanding of the Latin term *iustificare* which led him to misunderstand the Pauline term and interpret justification as a process of becoming righteous or "being made" righteous, a process that begins at baptism or conversion. In contrast with Augustine's "mistaken" understanding, Bammel asserts that Origen "defined" justification as a momentary event in which sins are forgiven and the new convert is accounted righteous before God. Origen's "definition" corresponds to what Bammel takes to be the true meaning of the Greek term δικαιοῦν which, she says, means "to count as just."[66] Bammel later qualifies her discussion by admitting that Augustine's "mistaken" understanding of the actual words *justification* and *justify* is less important than one might expect, since the context in which Paul speaks of justification also includes references to the remission of sins and to faith being counted for righteousness. She concludes from this that it is likely that "the concept of the believer being counted as righteous will often be touched on within the same complex of ideas."[67] She also nuances her description of Origen's understanding by saying that for him justification (i.e., one's faith being counted for righteousness) marks the beginning of a process of progress in justice and good works. Yet she seems to imply that Origen would not call this latter process "justification."

When Bammel asserts that δικαιοῦν means "to count as just," she does not cite from modern scholarship to support this contention. Evidently she assumes that the point is to be taken for granted. The assertion happens to agree with standard Protestant theology according to which Paul's term *justify* excludes the concept of human renewal and moral transformation. Many Protestants claim that the latter ideas (renewal and moral transformation) are termed by Paul "sanctification," a concept that is sharply and systematically distinguished from "justification."[68] Possibly Bammel is following the thesis of A. McGrath, who makes this exact claim and also faults Augustine for misunderstanding the term *justification*.[69]

McGrath's claim echoes the assertion of Martin Chemnitz (1522–86), a student of Melanchthon, who said that Augustine misrepresented the Greek word δικαιοῦν to refer to "making just" instead of "declaring just." Melanchthon himself made this very reproach of Augustine in a passage that will be cited and discussed in chapter 6. McGrath posits a radical dichotomy between the Greek and Latin conceptions of justification and claims that the initial transference of a Hebrew concept to a Greek concept to a Latin concept led to a fundamental alteration in the meaning of justification. On p. 15 he asserts the following:

> The Greek concept of justification had the primary sense of *to be considered or estimated as righteous*, whereas the Latin verb denotes *being righteous*. The shift in emphasis from righteousness before God to righteousness among men can be blamed on the Latin lan-

guage, which had a far greater influence on the development of doctrine than has been appreciated. The emphasis of the original Hebrew concept was not anthropocentric as was the Latin idea.

One can say in response to this that McGrath's assertion that δικαιοῦν does not mean "to make just" contradicts the proper meaning of Greek –όω verbs. M. J. Lagrange long ago observed, "First, we should note that verbs in όω mean to make whatever the root indicates. Thus δικαιόω should properly mean 'make just.'"[70] One recent author has convincingly shown that McGrath's linguistic analysis has read into history what his theology dictates, since in biblical usage δικαιοσύνη is understood as that which is inherent within both God and the human being due to the good they have done.[71] Moreover, McGrath's work is reproachable on other grounds: He purports to be writing a history of the doctrine of justification, and yet makes the astonishing claim "Justification was simply not a theological issue in the pre-Augustinian tradition."[72] McGrath appears to be completely unaware of Origen's *CRm*.

For our present purposes, it is sufficient to say that it is reasonable to question whether Origen is giving a "definition" of justification in the text that Bammel cites.[73] At the least this seems reductionistic and leaves a large number of texts out of consideration. It appears to me that both Origen and Augustine conceive justification as an interior process of "being-made just" through the transformative indwelling of Christ and the Trinity, a process that only begins at faith and baptism.

Chapter 4

William of St. Thierry's Reception of Origen's Exegesis of Romans

The Medieval Landscape

In the Middle Ages the stage was set for a favorable reception of Origen's Pauline exegesis, to begin with, when St. Jerome (d. 420) had sanctioned it by integrating a substantial portion of it into his own. This certainly applies to Jerome's commentaries on Ephesians,[1] Galatians, and Philemon.[2] Jerome never wrote a commentary on Romans, but it does not seem unjustified to suggest that a primary reason for this was that Rufinus's Latin translation of Origen's *CRm* left Jerome with little to say.[3] In addition to the example of Jerome, Cassiodorus (490–583), in his *Institutiones,* upon reaching the book of Romans, named Origen's *CRm* as the first work to be recommended for those for whom he is indicating the ecclesiastical authors who can provide the safest guidance for understanding the individual books of the Bible: "Of [the epistles of] Saint Paul the first of all and the one destined to be more admired is known as the one 'to the Romans,' which Origen clarified in twenty books in the Greek language; which however the above-mentioned Rufinus translated very eloquently into Latin, reducing it to ten books."[4] This recommendation is very significant, since it comes from a man who was a vigorous opponent of all heresies,[5] and who was enormously influential for subsequent monasticism.[6]

Theologians during the Middle Ages essentially followed Jerome's example and implemented Cassiodorus's advice. To give a few samples, Notker the Stammerer (840–912) wrote, "On the Epistle to the Romans, Origen wrote many wonderful things."[7] This was recorded in a work in which he compiled a catalogue of the main theologians, to which he gave the following title: "Observations on the illustrious men who made a careful exposition of Sacred Scripture and gave opportune explanations of certain decisions on the part of divine authority."[8] The *Glossa Ordinaria,* a twelfth-century compilation of scriptural glosses traditionally attributed to Walafrid Strabo, cites Origen's *CRm* on Rom 3.3, 4.15, and 8.3, though the influence is more extensive than these explicit citations.[9] Origen's work was also consulted by such Latin theologians as Peter Lombard, Bonaventure, and Thomas Aquinas.[10] It is woven into the fabric of Peter Abelard's *Commentary on Romans.*[11] And in his study of the history of interpretation of Rom 1.17, Denifle found it noteworthy and significant that the two Western Scripture scholars who used Origen's *CRm* very extensively were Sedulius Scottus (eighth–ninth centuries)[12] and Augustinus Favaroni of Rome (1360–1443).[13] This irenic usage of Origen's Pauline exegesis during the Middle Ages suggests that the clouds of suspicion that hung elsewhere over Origen's orthodoxy did not render suspect his *CRm.* As an exegete of Paul, he was normally cited as a Catholic authority of good faith.[14]

Introduction to William of St. Thierry's *Exposition on Romans*

This chapter will investigate in some detail the use of Origen's *CRm* in the *Exposition on Romans* written by William of St. Thierry (1085–1148).[15] William was a Cistercian[16] monk and former Benedictine abbot whose *Exposition* is the only surviving Cistercian commentary on Romans from the twelfth century.[17] The author became abbot of the monastery of St. Thierry at the age of thirty-four.[18] He began the commentary at St. Thierry and completed it at Signy.[19] William has been described as "one of the most attractive personalities of the twelfth century, one of its most profound and original spiritual thinkers, and perhaps its most outstanding theologian."[20] William borrows massively from the Origen-Rufinus commentary

in his own *Exposition on Romans,* in what amounts to copying, sum-
marizing, amplifying, adapting, and plagiarizing.[21] William was both an
admirer of Origen's exegetical abilities and a man completely committed
to the Augustinian doctrines of original sin, grace, and predestination. The
promise of this examination, then, is to offer a concrete example of how
a medieval Augustinian theologian was able to receive Origen's Pauline
exegesis.

William's *Exposition on Romans* has been described as a monastic text
from beginning to end. Anderson, the editor of the first English translation of this work, reminds us that William's aim is not refutation, dialectic, or scholastic disputation, but joy and delight: "His goal is humility of
heart and devotional purity. Fundamental to William's motivation is the
centrality of grace in the spiritual life. Only when man is in touch with
grace and its radical importance in his existence and in all that he accom-
plishes can growth occur."[22] Another prominent scholar of William has
said, "To sing the praises of grace is the single theme that dominates
William's writing and research."[23]

Use of Origen and Augustine

Scholars have depicted William's procedure in using his theological predecessors differently and even in contradictory terms. Bouyer described
William's singularly original achievement in his *Exposition on Romans*
as consisting in his ability to synthesize two great systems of thought,
that is, of grace and free will, which are allegedly the systems of Augustine and Origen respectively. In Bouyer's estimation, since these systems
almost diametrically oppose each other in their fundamental conceptions,
William indicates the measure of his stature as a theologian by combin-
ing the basic principles of these two thinkers and making their conceptions supplement each other.[24] Déchanet is in substantial agreement with
Bouyer's position. He notes that it is impossible to fail to be struck by
William's curious linking of St. Augustine with Origen.

In managing it when the two stand so far apart William has really
outdone himself. For although it is a mosaic, his *Exposition* hangs

together remarkably well. From beginning to end the thought works its way along, firm and smooth . . . No earlier compilation resembles it.[25]

The structure of William's work is indeed a coherent unity, centered on the theme of divine grace. Despite the contrasting materials William has used to construct his work, it seems accurate to describe the final product as a blending and synthesis of Augustine and Origen. For this is exactly what he does in a large number of texts pertaining to fundamental exegetical and theological themes of Romans. But this general picture needs to be qualified in many passages.

More recently, two scholars, Anderson and Cartwright, have shown more caution in their assessment of William's use of Origen. Both object to Bouyer's and Déchanet's depiction. Anderson claims that Bouyer's description of William's work as a synthesis of Origen and Augustine is not justified: "For the most part, William borrowed spiritual vignettes and passages [from Origen] which gave added dimension to the statements of Paul."[26] But in reality, it is simply not true, Anderson contends, that in William there is any blending of Augustinian and Origenian theology. On the contrary William is a thoroughgoing Augustinian. Cartwright concurs with Anderson and claims that William has simply used traditional monastic sources for his exegesis of Romans. It is not permissible, he says, to conclude from his dependence on Origen that William took a special interest in Origen or other Greek writers.[27]

Cartwright's comprehensive analysis of the use of patristic sources in William's commentary will be discussed in greater detail in the conclusion of this chapter. He has drawn the important conclusion that William's work is not merely a compilation of patristic citations but an original work presenting William's own thought. The heart of William's teaching is given in his comments on Rom 7 and 8 where he speaks with his own voice, under the primary influence of Augustine.[28] Tellingly, William bypasses direct citation of Origen in this section of his *Exposition on Romans*. Cartwright's analysis shows that no more than one fourth of William's commentary draws on patristic sources, a point that has been neglected by some secondary sources. The core insights here are that the originality of William's *Exposition* should not be overlooked and that

Augustine's influence on William is paramount. This seems to call into question Bouyer's and Déchanet's description of William's commentary as a synthesis of two systems of thought.

Many of the texts I have studied tend to support the view of Anderson and Cartwright, that William's *Exposition* offers a decidedly Augustinian interpretation of Romans. And yet, William assimilates so much of Origen's exegesis of Paul into his own that it does not seem unjust to describe his work as a blending and synthesis of Origen and Augustine. For this very accurately describes William's procedure in a large number of texts, especially throughout his explanation of Romans 1–6.

The "Troublesome Questions"

William begins his exposition with a disclaimer: his exposition does not profess originality. He tells the reader that he has combined certain opinions and statements of the holy fathers into a continuous commentary, but omitted troublesome questions in the former works (*suppressis, quae in ea sunt quaestionum molestiis*). In William's eyes the very lack of originality of his exposition is an important reason for its commendation. He states:

> [The resulting commentary] should be much more acceptable to the readers since it is not founded on novelty or vain presumption but is recommended by the profound authority of outstanding teachers, especially, as has been said, of blessed Augustine, and also Ambrose, Origen and some other doctors; and of certain other teachers of our time, who, we are certain, have not in any way transgressed the limits set by our Fathers. Therefore no one should accuse us of theft, since we have given ourselves away.[29]

William has thus admitted his reliance upon his predecessors, both the early Church Fathers, among whom he names Augustine, Ambrose, and Origen as the outstanding "doctors," and more recent "teachers," who he says have not transgressed the limits set by the "Fathers." Thus for William, Origen ranks among the Doctors of the Church as an interpreter of Romans. By admitting his dependence on these authorities, William wishes to avoid the charge of plagiarism and theological innovation.

William also admits that he has "suppressed the troublesome questions." Lubac has observed that it was precisely the pointed and scandal-filled questions (*quaestiones scrupulosas et plenas scandalis*) of Peter Abelard that led William to denounce him:

> Being as he was very aware himself of the "annoying questions" with which the Letter to the Romans abounds, he strove to "suppress" them somewhat too readily at times. The author of the *Disputatio altera adversus Abaelardum,* who is even more vehement, would like to dam up this torrential spate of questions, which are so "tempestuous," so "perilous," and which run the risk of leading to shipwreck.[30]

Thus the troublesome questions that William has suppressed in his predecessors, including Origen (some of which will be noted below), may bear directly on his conflict with Peter Abelard.[31] However, I will not pursue these connections further in this book.

Positive Appropriation of Origen

Definitions of Pauline Terms

The reader of William's *Exposition on Romans* notices immediately that William is fond of citing Greek textual readings. He has found these transliterated and discussed in Rufinus's version of Origen.[32] Verbatim copying from Origen is evident everywhere in the section covering Rom 1–6, and many examples could be given of William's taking over Origen's distinctions and definitions. On Rom 1.5 William explains the Apostle's words "grace and apostleship" with this gloss: "Gratiam ad laborum patientiam, apostolatum ad praedicationis auctoritatem."[33] Origen had said, "Gratia ad laborum patientiam referenda est, apostolatus ad praedicationis auctoritatem."[34] On Rom 1.10 where Paul describes his own prayers, William says, "Expectat tamen donec obsecrationibus imploret, non solum prosperum, iter sibi fieri, sed et in voluntate Dei prosperum."[35] Compare Origen: "Expectat donec obsecrationibus impetret non solum prosperum sibi iter fieri sed et in voluntate Dei prosperum fieri."[36] Similarly, on Rom

1.16b, "To Jew first and to Greek," William copies Origen word for word in discussing Paul's threefold division of the human race.[37] Such texts could be multiplied and plainly demonstrate that William has done exactly what he said he was going to do in the preface: He has not composed an innovative commentary but borrowed many of the thoughts of his exegetical predecessors, among whom Origen is outstanding.

Many of these borrowings pertain to key theological ideas. For example, on Rom 2.26–27 Origen had discussed the difference between perfecting/fulfilling the law and keeping/observing the law:

> And he has added well, "who perfects the law." For he who lives according to the letter is said to keep the law; but he who lives according to the Spirit perfects it. The perfection of the law takes place in Christ, who said, "I have not come to destroy the law but to fulfill it." Now to fulfill the law means to perfect the law.[38]

Although William's use of the Vulgate leads to a slight alteration in wording (*consummo* for *perficio*), while Rufinus's version was based on the Old Latin, it is evident that William is drawing directly from Origen in his explanation of Rom 2.26–27:

> The author did well to say "If they fulfill the law." One who lives according to the letter observes the law, but one who lives according to the spirit fulfills it. But perfection is in him who says, "I did not come to destroy the law, but to fulfill it."[39]

William's distinction between "fulfilling the law" and "perfecting the law" is taken from Origen along with the cross-reference to Mt 5.17. William follows Origen in seeing Christ as the fulfiller and not the destroyer of the law. He has also learned from the Alexandrian that the human being *can* fulfill the law by grace through Christ and the Spirit and has assimilated this insight into his own theology.

At this point it is worthwhile to point to Renna's observation about an essential difference between William's and Luther's theology, which will be more fully clarified in chapter 6. Renna notes that unlike Luther, William tells how one *can* fulfill the law and that grace does indeed move the will toward good acts. Renna conjectures that Luther would have been appalled at the presumptuous latitude William allows the will in cooperating and participating in grace:

> The Leitmotif in William's commentary is the progress the soul makes once it has become aware of its helplessness. He would have made little sense of Luther's idea of good works as sin. No doubt Luther would have considered William's ascetical doctrines Pelagian.[40]

Significantly, Renna's prediction about Luther's likely response to *William's* teaching anticipates conclusions I have actually reached of Melanchthon's and Luther's actual reception of *Origen's* interpretations, which they did indeed accuse of being "Pelagian."

Origen's discussion of "anger and indignation" (Rom 2.9) is clearly the source of William's explanation of these Pauline terms.[41] Another example of William's taking over Origenian definitions is found under the lemma to Rom 4.6 and pertains to Paul's citation of David's pronouncement concerning faith and works. William writes, "Videtur enim ostendere, quasi in fide quidem gratia sit iustificantis; in opere vero sonare videtur iustitia retribuentis."[42] Origen's definition appears in a comment on Rom 4.4–5: "Videtur ostendere quasi in fide quidem gratia sit iustificantis, in opere vero iustitia retribuentis."[43] Thus William adopts Origen's explanations of faith and grace, two fundamental concepts of Pauline theology. In a similar fashion, under the lemma to Rom 4.25 it is theologically significant that William largely copies Origen. William writes:

> Let no one therefore think that his faith in Christ will be reputed to him as justice, unless he puts off the old man with his acts, and puts on the new man, making himself conform to, and share in, his death and resurrection. Otherwise, there is not concord between justice and injustice.[44]

Origen had similarly written that faith cannot be reckoned as righteousness unless the new man is renewed in the knowledge of God (Col 3.9–10).[45] Also, on Rom 4.25, Origen had asked why Paul speaks of Abraham's God as the one "who raised the Lord from the dead," rather than as creator of heaven and earth, or some other designation. The answer, according to Origen, is that the raising of the dead is more glorifying to God than mere creating.[46] William repeats Origen's whole train of thought and in nearly the same words.[47] In such instances as these, none of which lacks serious theological significance, William adopts and assimilates what he must view as Origen's perceptive and accurate distinctions and explanations of Paul's theological terms. Origen's exegesis is received not because it is Origen's but because it is orthodox.

The Stages of Conversion

William's interpretation of Rom 4.7–8 is clearly taken from Origen and shows how near they are to each other on the important theological concepts of conversion, merit, forgiveness/covering/nonimputation of sins, perfection, and blessedness. William's patron theologian Augustine had taken Paul's three statements in these verses as equivalents; Augustine was aware of but did not follow Origen's idea of three stages.[48] In a rare example of (anonymous) disagreement with Augustine, William follows Origen instead. Origen had written:

> The distinction of this order is striking to us. He has said firstly, "Blessed are those whose iniquities are forgiven"; secondly, "whose sins are covered"; and thirdly, "to whom the Lord will not impute sin." Consider whether perhaps it is possible for this order to be recognized in one and the same soul. Thus, because the beginning of the soul's conversion is to abandon evil, on account of its doing so it would merit the forgiveness of iniquities. But when it begins to do good, as if covering over each of the evils it had previously committed with later good actions and introducing a quantity of goods more numerous than the evils which had existed, it may be said to cover its sins. But when a [soul] would forthwith come to perfection so that every root of evil is completely cut off from it to the point that no trace of evil can be found in it, at that point the summit of blessedness is promised to the one to whom the Lord would be able to impute no sin.[49]

Verfaillie comments on Origen's text, "Origen speaks as a moralist here, but his psychology leads to a theology."[50] In brief, Origen sees Rom 4.7–8 as describing the soul's conversion in a three-stage progression: remission, covering, and nonimputation of sins. The soul first detaches itself from evil; then it puts the good positively into practice; and finally it arrives at the "summit of blessedness." At the first stage the soul receives the remission of sins. At this stage one can scarcely imagine that sins continue to subsist. In the second stage, the soul covers them, that is to say, the evils disappear under the abundance of good works. Finally, when no vestige of sin remains, and God finds no ground for reproaching the soul, it has reached perfection.

William has taken over this moralistic scheme but makes some interesting alterations and additions to Origen, which I will place in italics. William writes as follows:

> Notice the different order: first, he says that iniquities are remitted, then sins are covered, and finally that sin is not imputed. The beginning of conversion is to leave aside evils, and this merits the remission of former evils. Then individual evils are covered by individual or even additional goods, and when the matter has come to perfection, *by the grace of God and zeal for a good life* the very affection for sin is radically removed from the depths of the heart by an affection for virtue. Sin is no longer imputed to have been committed before God; it has thus been amputated from the soul *now renewed by God's justification.*[51]

William follows Origen step by step through this passage. For both Origen and William the first stage of conversion entails the abandoning of evil, which *merits* the forgiveness of sins. William apparently has no objection to using the term *merit* in connection with the process of human salvation. But William has converted Origen's description of the second stage of conversion (the covering of sins) from the active to the passive voice. He turns Origen's statement "when it begins to do good, as if covering over each of the evils it had previously committed with later good actions and introducing a quantity of goods more numerous than the evils which had existed" into "individual evils are covered by individual or even additional goods." This change of voice from active to passive possibly enables William to stress the action of divine grace upon the soul, rather than the soul's initiative.

For the third stage in the process of conversion (the nonimputation of sins), William turns Origen's statement: "ubi vero iam ad perfectum venerit" (when [the soul] forthwith has come to perfection) into: "ubi vero ad perfectionem res venerit, gratia Dei et studio bonae conversationis" (when the *matter* forthwith has come to perfection, *by the grace of God and zeal for a good life*). William has inserted the ablative of means clause evidently in order to put a stronger stress on the necessity and instrumentality of the grace of God as the source of perfection. Yet by no means has William abandoned Origen's moralizing focus on the necessity of human effort for conversion. In fact William has even added words to this effect into his rewriting of Origen's text. He inserts "and zeal for a good life" and "by an affection for virtue." But in William's adaptation, the matter (*res*) is on center stage in the process and progressive stages of conversion, rather than the individual *soul*. This is done, evidently, in order to make God's actual renewing grace the chief agent in conversion, rather than the individual soul. Without denying that the soul *acts* and *cooperates* with grace, and even *merits* the forgiveness of sins by its action of abandoning evil, William evidently wishes to emphasize that the soul is simultaneously *acted upon* by grace and owes nothing to itself. Finally, William eliminates Origen's mention of the summit of blessedness reached by the soul to which God could impute no sin. He replaces this with the more general assertion that such a soul will have been renewed by God's justification.

Renna summarizes William's general tendencies in altering the text of Origen in these words:

> William inserts his idea of grace into Origen's descriptions of how the Spirit brings *gratia* to the obedient soul. There is probably nothing in William's notion of grace which Augustine and Origen would strongly oppose. The difference rather lies in William's emphasis on the function of grace in each step of the soul's climb up the ladder of perfection.[52]

William's practice agrees with the basic theme of his work, which was described above as "to sing the praises of grace." It seems correct to say with Renna that Origen might not oppose William's insertions pertaining to the need for helping grace in order for the soul to reach perfection, especially if Origen had been exposed to the Pelagian doctrine that denies the need for helping grace at each stage along the way.

It is also interesting to observe that Origen's trademark words "Consider whether perhaps" (*vide si forte*) are consistently dropped in William's adaptation. This indicates, on the one hand, that the very humble Origen was a pioneering exegete, with few if any predecessors, who conducted his exegesis in the manner of an investigator and explorer, rather than as a dogmatician. Furthermore, it shows that William has a thousand-year tradition to build upon for his more dogmatic presentation. It may also indicate William's theological conservatism, for it is also known that very early on in his *Disputatio adversus Petrum Abaelardum,* William criticized Abelard for using much the same terminology (*videtur nobis*).[53] To William this phrase indicated that Abelard's theology was too speculative, it contained too much opinion, and it was not firmly grounded in certain doctrine.[54]

Such texts demonstrate that many of William's exegetical and theological insights in his exposition on Romans 1–6 are taken word for word, thought for thought, from Origen. It seems clear that the use of Origen's commentary on Paul has in a sense saved work for William. Origen consistently supplies clear distinctions and useful definitions of key terms in Romans which William adopts, such as grace, apostleship, will of God, Jew, Greek, faith, works, mortification of the flesh, anger, fury, day of wrath, perfection of the law, law according to the letter, law according to the Spirit, stages of conversion, and so forth. On these and many other theological themes in Romans, Origen's insights were assimilated by William. Origen also offers the important biblical cross-references that need to be consulted in explanation of Paul's words in Romans. William adopts these as well. But in William's mind Origen's exegesis at times needs to be replaced altogether or supplemented and perfected by a greater stress on the initiative and continual assistance of divine grace as the true source of human activity leading toward salvation.

Origen's Questions, Augustine's Answers

By Faith, Through Faith

Sometimes William mentions but explicitly dissents from Origen's explanation, and instead follows Augustine. For example at Rom 3.30 William disagrees with Origen's distinction between justification "by faith" (*ex fide*) and justification "through faith" (*per fidem*). He writes: "The expressions 'by faith' and 'through faith' seem to be variations in wording only, not in meaning, because elsewhere he says that uncircumcision is justified by faith [*ex fide*] and circumcision through faith [*per fidem*]."[55] In this instance William has clearly taken Augustine's side in an exegetical debate, since Augustine had also mentioned and dismissed Origen's suggestion.[56] William's commitment to the interpretation of Augustine is anonymous here, but it is evident in such passages, as can be confirmed when we consult the original sources.

"God handed them over" (Romans 1.18ff.)

In some passages St. Augustine provides the answers to questions raised originally in Origen's *CRm* and answered differently by Origen. In certain cases William will appeal to the divine mysteries or will simply suppress theological inquiry in response to theological problems for which Origen had given a clear explanation. These texts illuminate William's settled Augustinian theological position. For example on Rom 1.24, "God handed them over to the desires of their hearts to impurity," Origen had observed that both Catholic and Marcionite theology had difficulties explaining these words of Paul. The followers of Marcion were perplexed with this text since it unambiguously refers to a punishing activity of the God in whom Paul professes to believe, and Marcion denied that Paul's God was a just judge. On the other hand Origen admits that ecclesiastical exegesis found these words problematic as well, because they seem to make God responsible for the evil conditions to which human beings are handed over. Origen first replies to the school of Marcion:

> Let us ask those who deny that the good God is also a just judge, what shall they say in response to these things which the Apostle says, namely that God "handed them over to the desires of their hearts to impurity, to the degrading of their bodies"? For in this not only will their system, once completely excluded, be forced out, but even our own explanation. For how shall it be just that whoever is handed over—granted that it is on account of their own sins that they are handed over—nonetheless are handed over to lusts and handed

over to this, to the devotion of their own bodies to impurities and lusts? For example, anyone who is handed over to the dungeon for punishment cannot be charged with the accusation that he is in darkness. Or, anyone handed over to fire cannot, for this very reason, be blamed for why he is burnt. Likewise in the case of those who are handed over to sinful desires and impurities so that they degrade their bodies, it will not seem fitting for them to be charged when, situated amongst lusts and impurities, they defile their bodies with degradations.[57]

Origen has raised these particular questions of and objections to the Pauline text. His explanation of the passage amounts to a defense of his own most cherished doctrine, the free choice of the will. Origen insists that "according to the faith of the Church" (*iuxta ecclesiae fidem*) the people referred to by Paul in Rom 1 have justly and deservedly earned God's abandonment of them for the reasons previously given for their guilt.[58] To solve the difficulty of God's "handing them over," Origen essentially interprets this as figurative language and introduces his well-known tripartite anthropology.[59] Human beings consist of spirit, body, and soul. The soul is placed in the middle between the spirit and the lusts of the flesh. If the soul assents to the desires of the spirit it becomes united with God and Rom 8.9 is fulfilled: "You are not in the flesh but in the Spirit." But if the soul chooses the lusts of the flesh, it becomes indwelt with the vices and Gn 6.3 is realized: "My Spirit shall no longer abide in these men, for they are flesh." But, Origen insists, the duty of choice is preserved in this matter. Human souls are not compelled to sin but have freely chosen it and have been handed over by God based upon this previous choice of theirs. Thus for Origen the souls under discussion have made their own previous decision about whether they wanted to choose life, that is, Christ, or to turn aside to death, the devil. They have chosen the latter, and God responded to their previous choice by "handing them over" to these impurities, that is by forsaking and abandoning them to the vices they have chosen.[60] Thus in Origen's explanation, antecedent human sin is the grounds for the divine handing over. Essentially this means that the handing over to impurities was a passive and permissive handing over, not active.

William's handling of this problematic text in Paul is clearly inspired by Origen's discussion and borrows heavily from it. This is evident in the questions that William raises about God's justice, in the tripartite anthropology he introduces and affirms, and in the scriptural texts he cites as a means of explanation, which include Rom 8.9 and Gn 6.3. However, William clearly introduces decidedly Augustinian elements at crucial points in the exposition which completely alter the spirit of Origen's exegesis. Like Origen William poses a question of the Pauline text related to the justice of God in handing human beings over to sins.

> The question is asked in regard to one who is handed over, although he is handed over to this concupiscence for his sins, whether his being under concupiscence is justly imputed to him. The same question could be asked about a man put in jail for his crimes, for no one could rightly attribute to him his being in darkness, because he is there unwillingly, though justly. But as the same Apostle says, man is said to be spirit and soul and body. Between the spirit and the flesh exists that familiar quarrel that everyone knows so well. *The man whom grace does not draw* is associated with the flesh and made one with it, and of that man it is said, "My spirit will not remain in him, because he is flesh" [Gn 6.3]. *The man whom grace attracts* is associated with the Spirit and is made one spirit with him, and it is said to him, "You, however, are not in the flesh, but in the Spirit" [Rom 8.9]. *To be drawn or not to be drawn is the same as to be handed over or not to be handed over, why this man is drawn and that one is not—these are the Son's secrets. Do not try to seek the answer to these questions if you do not wish to err. If you are not drawn, pray that you may be; and if you pray faithfully now, you will be drawn and not handed over. In those who are drawn and not handed over, it is the grace of God alone at work; in those who are handed over and are not drawn, God's blameless justice is at work.*[61]

The obvious differences between Origen's explanation and William's have been put in italics above and in the footnoted Latin text. William grants that these sinners are handed over *on account of their sins*. This is an important point of agreement with Origen's exegesis. But he has transformed Origen's assertion "[the soul that] joins itself to the flesh becomes one body with it in its lust and sinful desires" into: "*The man whom grace does not draw* is associated with the flesh and made one with it." What for Origen was the soul's active choice in joining itself to the flesh has become in William God's action, or rather inaction, in not drawing the person. This is a drastic change of focus. William has introduced predestination, or rather reprobation, into the explanation, while at the same time affirming antecedent human sin.

Likewise, Origen's words "but if it [the soul] should associate itself with the spirit it shall be one spirit with it" have become in William: "*The man whom grace attracts* is associated with the Spirit and is made one spirit with him." Origen's active verbs related to the free choice of the soul have become passive in William and related to God's predestining activity. In other words, William has significantly altered Origen's explanation of the soul's responsibility for being joined with the flesh. Where Origen had stressed real human merit as the cause both for the state of being in the Spirit and the state of being in sin, William, at these exact points, introduces the Augustinian doctrine of unmerited grace and divine determination as the causes of these situations. The result is a generalized and rather gloomy interpretation of Rom 1.18ff., in which humanity is divided into two classes: those who are secretly drawn by divine grace and not handed over, in whom the grace of God alone is at work, and those who are not drawn by grace and who are handed over, in whom God's blameless justice is at work. And in order to give this Pauline text such an accent, William is forced to reach far for a source of his appended explanation (the final italicized sentences in the above citation). In explanation of Paul's words in Rom 1.20–21, William paraphrases Augustine's repeated use of Jn 6.44.

In summary, in Origen's explanation of Rom 1.18ff., human beings are themselves actively and meritoriously responsible for being handed over or not handed over, in the Spirit or in the flesh. They are in these states because they deserve to be. For William God's secret predestination, that is, the secrets of the Son (*occulta Filii*), seems to be the ultimate explanation for these situations, even though he admits that it is an explanation that transcends human reason. William must regard Origen's explanation of Rom 1.24 as one of the "troublesome questions" that he wishes to suppress in his own exposition. Origen's stress on the soul's merit could imply for William that human beings initiate their own salvation apart from divine grace, or that they receive divine grace as a reward for their own antecedent merits (something Origen in some sense admits).

On questions of grace and predestination William has not so much syn-thesized Origen's standpoint with Augustine's as inserted Augustine's settled point of view into his plagiarisms of Origen's exegesis. This example seems to confirm the reading of William favored by Anderson and Cartwright. Origen's basic explanation has been overruled by Augus-tine's theology, while at the same time a great deal of Origen's exegesis has been assimilated.

From Origen's point of view, William's explanation would probably seem to make God responsible for humanity's sinful conditions. Even if we grant the radically different historical and theological circumstances under which Origen's *CRm* and William's *Exposition* were written, the con-flict between Origen and Augustine/William on the question of predesti-nation and reprobation does not seem unreal. This especially applies to William's generalized Augustinian description of those who have been handed over to lusts as "the man whom grace does not draw." For Origen this kind of explanation would utterly mistake Paul's point, which he takes to be the defense of human freedom. Chadwick summarizes the essential conflict between Origen and Augustine's theology as focused precisely on these sorts of issues. He says that it is simply not the case that Origen has absorbed more Platonism than Augustine. On the contrary, Origen is on the whole far more defensive toward the Platonic tradition and incorporates less of it in his theology than does Augustine. Rather, Chadwick states:

> The divergence lies in their notions of free choice, which, for Augus-tine, is a virtually unreal concept unless grace restores to the will the delight in righteousness that comes from the infusion of the Holy Spirit in the hearts of believers. Augustine thinks there is no bliss in a goodness that is not secure.[62]

Freedom seems to be a true locus of disagreement in the theological sys-tems of Origen and Augustine respectively.

A Universal Mass of Perdition

William's tendency to insert Augustinian sentiments in places where such thoughts are completely absent from Origen's work is evident elsewhere.

At Rom 3.23–24, for example, William invokes the help of Augustine's doctrine of the human race as a universal mass of perdition.

> The whole of the human race lay subject to punishment, and if the punishment of damnation which was due to all were rendered, without a doubt it would not have been done unjustly. Who therefore is so completely out of his mind that he does not give unspeakable thanks to him who mercifully liberated whom he willed, and who in no way could rightly be blamed for injustice if he completely condemned everyone? Since this is a most just conclusion, it is most evidently out of the question that anyone should glory in himself, or in the law, or in anything except the Lord.[63]

These are Augustinian themes.[64] The whole human race, infants included, is a mass of perdition that justly deserves eternal damnation.[65] God would be blameless if he were to damn everyone to hell without exception. But God's merciful predestination has elected to rescue some from this mass and leave the rest to their own deserts. All boasting on the part of humans is therefore excluded, since everyone deserves damnation. And all injustice on God's part is excluded for the same reason. William inserts these Augustinian thoughts into explanations that had been strictly dependent upon Origen's exegesis, both in what precedes and in what follows. This appears to confirm that, particularly on issues about which Augustine and Origen significantly differ, William regularly sides with Augustine.

Original Sin

Another such example occurs under the lemma to Rom 5.12, which is a key text for the Church's doctrine of original sin. William makes use of Origen but supplements him by Augustine. Origen had observed:

> If then Levi, who is born in the fourth generation after Abraham, is said to have been in the loins of Abraham, all the more were all men, those who are born and have been born in this world, in Adam's loins when he was still in paradise. And all men who were with him, or rather in him, were expelled from paradise when he was himself driven out from there.[66]

A careful comparison of this text with William's shows that William has adopted Origen's explanation, word for word, but he supplements it with a crucial addition from St. Augustine. William writes:

> If then Levi, who was born in the fourth generation after Abraham, is said to have been in the loins of Abraham, all the more were all men in the loins of Adam when *he sinned, and they sinned in him* and were expelled from paradise with him; and through him death passed into all those who were in his loins.[67]

William has added the italicized words into the middle of Origen's sentence. In chapter 2, we observed that in one of his interpretive possibilities, Origen had placed humanity in Adam's loins in the Garden of Eden. He had postulated that humanity "fell" with Adam, but he did not explicitly state that humanity "sinned" in Adam. William adds words precisely to this effect. Cartwright summarizes the significance of what William has done by his additions to Origen's text:

> Here William's alteration is most important: he has changed Origen's emphasis on the *presence* of all humanity in Adam to a more Augustinian emphasis on *humanity sinning* in Adam when he sinned. Origen's position was not strong enough for William. It provided phraseology sufficiently useful to quote, but did not sufficiently convey the notion of inherited guilt.[68] [italics added by Cartwright]

In other passages as well we have observed that Origen's position was not strong enough for William. On Rom 5.12 Origen's explanation was a useful starting point to this medieval exegete. Origen was on the road that led to Augustine and transmitted important elements and scripture passages (Heb 7.11) that would be used in the construction of the Church's doctrine of original sin. But for William Origen's explanation did not arrive at the destination. Therefore Origen needed supplementation from Augustine's fully orthodox doctrine. Anderson comments on the importance of the doctrine of original sin in William's commentary:

> Insistence on inherited guilt characterizes William's interpretation of Romans 5.12, and it was repeated time and again through William's commentary. This position separates William's reading of Romans

from anything that can be called Eastern or Greek. William's stance was diametrically opposed to that of the East wherein man suffers a weakening and inherits an inclination toward sin, but has no share in Adam's guilt. Consequently it is simply not true to suggest that in William we can hope to find a blend of Augustinian theology and Eastern Orthodox theology.[69]

As both Cartwright and Anderson correctly observe, William would hardly have made his additions to Origen's exegesis had he deemed it adequate as it stood. On the other hand, both of these scholars seem to have an inadequate understanding of Origen's doctrine of original sin, which does indeed embrace the idea of a "hard fall," even if he does not emphasize this aspect. This matter was discussed in chapter 2 of this book.

Jacob and Esau

William does not consult Origen's interpretations of Rom 7, 8, and 9, which is striking when we consider his heavy reliance upon Origen for the interpretation of chapters 1–6. Significantly, Cartwright observes that the heart of William's teaching is found precisely in his comments on Rom 7 and 8 where he speaks with his own voice, under the primary influence of Augustine.[70] This would help explain the absence of Origen from this section. It seems clear that William does not support Origen's understanding of predestination as being God's foreknowledge of future human merits. For example, Origen had claimed that "God loved Jacob" because he foresaw that Jacob would cleanse himself from sin. And in Origen's view, God "hated Esau" because he foreknew that Esau would not cleanse himself from these causes of reproach.[71] In dramatic contrast, William says that what God hated in Esau was his original sin, and in Jacob what God loved was nothing but the free gift of his own mercy.[72] For William, grace did not find merit but made merit.[73] These are clearly formulations derived from the late anti-Pelagian Augustine and are not present in Origen's interpretation of Paul.

Grace and the Free Choice of the Will

Later in the commentary, William resumes his practice of glossing Origen's words with clarifications from Augustine. Under the lemma to Rom

11.22–24 there is virtual verbatim copying of Origen in which William has made an insertion. Originally Origen was refuting the Gnostic doctrine of natures which he attributed to Basilides and Valentinus. It affirmed that there is a nature of souls that would always be saved and never perish and another nature of souls that would always perish and never be saved. Yet since Paul has stated in Rom 11.16–24 that branches were broken off on account of unbelief, Origen wrote:

> Just as all physical matter, since it, no doubt, consists of a single nature, through its inherent qualities produces various species of bodies or trees or plants, in the same way, since there is one nature for all rational beings, the choice of each—the liberty of the impulse of each is distributed equally—when summoned by the power of choice, and by guiding the soul subjected to them either toward virtue or toward evil desire, creates the species of a good tree or an evil tree. It may be called a good tree if, through its power of choice, it appoints good things; or it may be called evil if it should choose evil things. And in this way, each person, according to the impulses of his own purpose, will be designated either a good olive tree, if he travels down the road of virtue, or a wild olive tree, if he follows the opposite path. This, after all, is why even the Lord was saying in the gospel, "Either make the tree good and its fruit good; or make the tree evil and its fruit evil," in order to show that a tree, good or evil, is made, not born.[74]

Once again we can compare William's text with Origen's and observe both verbatim copying and explanatory insertions, which I will place in italics.

> Just as all physical matter, although undoubtedly of one nature, through accidental qualities produces different physical objects, such as men, animals, trees and grass; in just the same way, although all rational beings have one nature equally endowed with freedom of choice, yet each one's own movements, brought forth [*prolati*] [Migne: approved (*probati*)] by free choice, lead the soul subject to them either to virtue or to lust, and either form the soul to the beauty of a good tree (*according to the antecedent grace of God*) or else deform it into a bad tree through its own fault. Therefore, in order to show

that a tree becomes good and is not born good, the Lord says, "Either make the tree good and its fruit good, or make the tree evil and its fruit evil.[75]

While William has adopted the main features of Origen's explanation, there are also striking alterations and insertions. William agrees with Origen that all rational beings have one nature endowed with freedom of choice. Origen says that the form of the tree, good or evil, is created by this free choice, when the power of choice summons the soul to virtue or lust. William alters this only slightly to say that souls are formed into good or evil trees when each one's own movements are brought forth (Migne, "approved") by free choice and lead the soul subject to them either to virtue or to lust. The existence of free choice is thus a fundamental doctrine of both theologians.

But William makes an important insertion into Origen's text: "vel praeeunte gratia Dei" (by the antecedent grace of God). In other words, William stresses that God's grace must go before the person and anticipate the movement of the soul. To be sure the soul *chooses* the good and is led to the form of the good tree by this choice, but William adds that this is done with the assistance of the antecedent grace of God. Conversely, other souls choose lust and are formed into evil trees through their own fault. William, like Origen, excuses God from the responsibility of forming evil trees; but, unlike Origen, William expressly credits the prevenient grace of God as the cause of the creation of good trees, which Origen did not do. Evidently, for William Origen's text needed to be altered because, as it stood, it could be read to imply that human beings initiate the movement toward the good, apart from and independent of the antecedent grace of God. Although Origen had not explicitly denied the necessity of the antecedent grace of God, one can perhaps understand why his text could be taken that way under the new theological conditions in which William was writing. William wants to avoid such a troublesome Pelagian implication by inserting the words about God's prevenient grace. The changes William has made are consistent with his theology of redemption, which affirms human cooperation along with divine election.

Billy has summarized William's theology of salvation by suggesting that for William, one's return to God is indeed contingent on human cooperation, but it is always preceded by divine selection (elective grace), accompanied by a sense of the Spirit's absence (hidden grace). The latter, in time, is slowly transformed by illuminating grace into an overwhelming sense of union with God (divinizing grace). In short, William understands redemption as a gradual process of deification. Billy writes:

> A person, whose nature is imprinted with the divine image, slowly regains his or her lost resemblance to God. This movement from image (*imago*) to resemblance (*similitudo*) corresponds to an increase in self-knowledge and the supreme creaturely participation in the life of the Trinity. Resemblance to God is the whole of human perfection.[76]

Many of these elements have roots in Origen's thought, such as the idea of returning to God, the necessity of human cooperation, the progressive transformation of the soul through the gradual process of deification, the movement from image to likeness of God, and the creature's participation in the attributes of the Trinity. It seems clear that William has perfected Origen's ideas by an Augustinian stress on the constant need for divine grace.

Conclusion

In many respects this chapter has given a concrete exemplification of Lubac's claim that Origen was the "grand master" of exegesis during the Middle Ages.[77] The stress here should be placed on Origen's *exegesis* more than on Origen's *theology*. And yet, such a distinction is not really possible when we consider that William's assimilation of Origen's exegesis includes many themes of Pauline theology that are of fundamental theological importance. Origen has obviously aided William in that he has raised proper questions of the Pauline text and in many instances, particularly throughout Romans 1–6, has provided adequate solutions. Yet William is not an Origenist in the sense of being unconditionally committed to defending Origen's interpretations. Rather, his standpoint is that of a settled Augustinian. However important Origen was to William exegetically, Augustine clearly towered over him in theological authority.

Cartwright's comprehensive analysis of the patristic sources used in William's *Exposition* documents some important statistical facts about William's commentary. William quotes twice as much material from Augustine as from Origen. He draws from more than twenty of Augustine's works, and in the sheer volume of citations Origen takes a second place to Augustine.[78] He frequently cites Origen, to the near-total exclusion of Augustine, in his comments on 1.5–21, 2.5–9, 4.6–25, 6.3–17, and 14.13–19. Cartwright correctly observes that the topics covered by these citations, which include grace, justification and faith, and the new life of dying to sin and conformity to Christ, are all key to the Epistle to the Romans and to subsequent Christian doctrine. But he adds:

> William's use of Origen on grace and justification does not mean, though, that he is not Augustinian on these topics. He cites many passages of Augustine dealing with grace or justification in chapters three, five, seven and eight. At any rate, Origen and Augustine do not differ greatly on grace and justification, at least not in the passages cited. On these subjects, William uses Origen without being "Origenist."[79]

Cartwright goes on to indicate that on the topics of original sin, the Trinity, the sacraments, and predestination, William relies on Augustine, using almost no passages from Origen.[80] And yet this seems overstated, since above, in a text pertaining to Rom 5.12 and Levi's presence in Adam's loins, we saw William copying Origen word for word and then filling in the exegesis with Augustinian glosses. At the least this shows that Origen's text gave William a starting point for his Augustinian explanation of original sin.

Cartwright has also reached the important conclusion that William treats Origen's text differently from the way he does Augustine's. Not only has he borrowed more from Augustine's works than from the Origen-Rufinus commentary, he does not alter the essential wording of Augustine as he does when he paraphrases Origen. William changes only Augustine's voice (active to passive) and person (third to second), but with Origen he alters the wording of entire sentences and paragraphs and rewrites the formulation of key concepts.[81] Cartwright concludes that while Origen is important to William, he is not as important as Augustine is. William obtains significant moral teaching and hermeneutical guidance from Origen, but he scrupulously avoids anything from Origen that might be controversial. "Apparently aware of Origen's tainted reputation, he chooses only those passages of greatest benefit to his readers, and even then he alters them to ensure an Augustinian-based orthodoxy."[82] What is clear is that William has used Origen extensively and has capitalized on Origen's abilities as an exegete of Paul, but he has done so through the lens of Augustinian thought.

The changes William makes to Origen's exegesis certainly place greater stress on the necessary role of helping grace in each step of the soul's climb up the ladder of perfection. On the questions of prevenient grace, predestination, and original sin, William evidently feels that Origen's exegesis needs to be updated and glossed; as it stands it is no longer adequate. Possibly this is due to what he takes to be a resurgence of Pelagianism, which he finds in the thought of Abelard. Origen is undoubtedly recognized as a great and insightful exegete and a highly esteemed Doctor of the Church. Yet Origen's authority as an *exegete* needs to be completely subordinated to the *theology* of St. Augustine, at least on theological issues on which Origen and Augustine significantly differ.

Chapter 5

Erasmus's Reception of Origen's Exegesis of Romans

Introduction

In the twentieth century the Augustinian priest Erasmus of Rotterdam (1466–1536) was respected by an outstanding series of illustrious Catholic historians and theologians, beginning with Cardinal Gasquet, H. Grisar, R. Padberg, H. de Lubac, G. Chantraine, L. Bouyer, L. Halkin, J. Olin, R. DeMolen, and H. Pabel. The most formidable of these was perhaps Lubac, who displays a unique mastery of the total corpus of Erasmus's writings and finds Erasmus's Catholic orthodoxy to be both sincere and constant.[1] Lubac was particularly impressed with Erasmus's patristic scholarship. Indeed, the writings and personalities of the Church Fathers accompanied Erasmus of Rotterdam from his youth until the day of his death.[2] Alongside the New Testament, the Fathers played an essential role in Erasmus's program for renewing the Church and theology.[3] The learning and holiness of the Fathers and the superiority of their writings was so obvious to Erasmus that he was deeply tormented by the loss of so many of their works. He wrote, "I can scarcely refrain from tears as I read the lists of ancient authors and see what wealth we have lost. My grief increases when I compare the quality of our losses with what we now commonly read."[4] Proof of Erasmus's devotion to the Fathers is seen in what is perhaps his most staggering scholarly achievement: twelve published critical editions of the Greek and Latin writings of the Church Fathers.[5] Erasmus completed editions of the writings of Jerome (1516), Cyprian (1520), Arnobius (1522), Hilary (1523), John Chrysostom (1525), Irenaeus (1526), Athanasius (1527), Ambrose (1527), Augustine (1529), Gregory of Nazianzus (1531), Basil (1532), and Origen (1536).[6] Erasmus has rightly been described as "the great patrologist of the age."[7]

Before turning to the role that Origen's *CRm* played in Erasmus's program of *ressourcement,* I will briefly describe the context of Erasmus's theological mission, which involved him in conflicts on two principal fronts. On the one hand, his contemporary Catholic representatives of scholastic theology accused Erasmus of heresy and innovation and forced him to write apologies.[8] Though deeply wounded by these accusations from fellow Catholics, Erasmus refused to allow these disturbances to drive him into schism. He wrote the following to Archbishop Alfonso Fonseca on 25 March 1529:

> Stephen was struck down with stones only once, Sebastian was pierced with darts only once—I believe that their sufferings were lighter than mine. For very many years now I have been pierced by the tongues of men who have the poison of asps on their lips. I have been struck on all sides by insults hurled like stones. Their many assaults would draw me away from the orthodox party if for any reason I could be torn away from the pledge [*fide*] I once gave to the church, the Bride of Christ.[9]

Five days later, Erasmus once again looked back retrospectively on the lifetime of attacks he had endured from fellow Catholics. He assessed them in a letter to Louis Ber:

> It is not obscure for what frivolous reasons these people first rose up against me. To the great advantage of theology I cultivated languages and more polite literature, which they now pretend to support, although more than forty years ago they left no stone unturned to destroy and uproot them when they were just beginning to spring

up. And that was the seedbed of this present tragedy [the Protestant schisms]. I exhorted the theologians that, leaving aside their little questions which have more of ostentation than of piety, they should betake themselves to the very sources [*fontes*] of the Scriptures and to the ancient Fathers of the Church. Moreover, I did not wish that scholastic theology should be abolished, but that it should be purer and more serious. That, unless I am mistaken, is to support, not to hurt it.[10]

Such texts provide evidence against the allegation of Yves Congar, who said that Erasmus's theological program was not content to reform or complement scholasticism, but intended to replace and suppress it.[11] To be sure Erasmus reproached the form of scholastic theology that was then current, for distancing itself from Scripture and for its infidelity to the mind of the Fathers.[12] But Erasmus's aim was to renew, not destroy, the bond that had become too slack between exegesis and theology by a program of retrieving both the Greek New Testament and the Greek and Latin exegetical tradition. He located the authority of the Church Fathers in their closeness in time as well as in spirit to the divine source. "Their chief value lay in interpreting and helping us to understand the sacred text."[13]

On the other side, Erasmus carried on a prolonged battle against the newly arisen Protestants, above all Luther and Melanchthon, whom he accused of arrogance and betrayal of the Catholic theological tradition. Erasmus repeatedly said that the Protestant Reformation spoiled his life's work.[14] Among Erasmus's anti-Lutheran writings, *Hyperaspistes 1* and *2* (1527–28)[15] and *Epistola contra pseudevangelicos* (1530) make particularly clear that Erasmus rejected Protestantism in principle and sided decisively with the old "papist" Church.[16] By his having met with Luther's vehement condemnation, Erasmus said that he was not offended, but was, on the contrary, relieved. He wrote to Luther:

But in the end is it any affront to me to have you disparage my knowledge, since you have long since belittled the knowledge of every council and all bishops and popes and the Doctors of the church, whether ancient or modern, and finally of all the universities? Was anyone ever wise if he departed a hair's breadth, as they say, from your teachings?[17]

One of the core differences between Erasmus and the Lutherans was that Erasmus believed that both the ancient Fathers and the Middle Ages had preserved fundamental religious truth, even if distortions occurred in the age of scholasticism. Still, even the Middle Ages had prolonged the life of the Church in its age.[18] In contrast, the Lutherans accused both periods of propagating fundamental errors.[19]

Navigating between his extremist[20] Catholic scholastic critics on the one side and the Lutherans on the other, Erasmus understood his mission to be recalling theology to its scriptural and patristic sources without repudiating medieval Catholicism. Convinced that the way to build a new future was not to engage in wholesale rejection of the past, even of the medieval period, Erasmus endeavored instead to embrace the entire history of Western Christendom. He did this "in full awareness of all its shortcomings, in order to steer the future in a more desirable direction."[21]

Erasmus's Discovery of Origen and His Vow to St. Paul

Erasmus had become a passionate enthusiast for Origen's writings, and especially for his *CRm,* in part as a result of his encounter with a fellow priest and Franciscan monk named Jean Vitrier, a man whom Erasmus regarded as the holiest individual he had ever met and whose brief biography he composed in his *Ep* 1211.[22] It was Vitrier who had spoken to Erasmus of Origen in these terms: "There can be no doubt that the Holy Spirit dwelt in a heart that produced so many books with such learning and such fire."[23] During a retreat at Courtebourne in 1501, Erasmus read Origen's homilies and his *CRm.* One immediate result was the composition of the *Enchiridion,* Erasmus's first great essay in devotional literature, which was infused with citations from these particular works of Origen.[24] Eventually Erasmus would produce an edition of Origen's writings that was published posthumously. This edition will be described in an excursus at the end of this chapter.

This chapter will focus on Erasmus's use of Origen in his *Annotations on Romans* and *Paraphrase on Romans.* At the end of the *Enchiridion* (1503), Erasmus speaks of a commentary on Romans he has in preparation, which is based upon a thorough study of Origen, Ambrose, Augustine, and others, his goal being "to adorn the Lord's temple with rare treasures . . . so that by means of these treasures fine intellects could be kindled into a love for Holy Scripture."[25] This work was left unfinished until 1514. In that year, after sustaining a back injury, Erasmus made a vow to St. Paul to complete a commentary on Romans if he should be healed.[26] When in answer to this prayer, St. Paul obtained relief from the back pain, Erasmus fulfilled his vow and published his *Paraphrase* and *Annotations on Romans*.

Godin has demonstrated that in these commentaries of Erasmus, Origen's exegesis is "omnipresent."[27] In the *Annotations on Romans* found in the last edition of Erasmus's New Testament (1535), there are 139 explicit citations from Origen's *CRm*, compared with 124 from Chrysostom, 113 from Theophylact, 106 from Ambrose, 67 from Augustine, 48 from Jerome, and 14 from Valla.[28] Of course, explicit citations only scratch the surface of the deeper assimilation of Origen. I will endeavor to build on Godin's research by giving a special focus to some of the Origenian themes articulated throughout the course of this book. After first identifying some of the fundamental structures of Erasmus's reception of Origen, as these are revealed in his *Annotations on Romans,* I will then turn to Erasmus's *Paraphrase on Romans* to compare his interpretation of Paul with Origen's interpretations in the *CRm*. At the end of the chapter, I will include an excursus on Origen's legacy during the age of Erasmus and a survey of the first printed editions of Origen's writings.

Origen as a Revealer of Theology's Wellsprings

In a letter written to John Colet in 1504, Erasmus reports, "I have gone through a good part of Origen's works; under his guidance I think I have achieved worthwhile results, for he reveals some of the well-springs, as it were, and demonstrates some of the basic principles, of the science of theology."[29] Godin assesses the modes of Erasmus's appropriation of Origen in these terms:

As regards piety and biblical-theological knowledge, it is to Origen, his "praeceptor," that Erasmus is indebted for the fundamental methodological principles which are at the source, at the origin [*fons*] of his *ars*, of his exegetical and spiritual knowledge.[30]

Origen reveals the wellsprings (*fontes*) and basic principles (*rationes*) of the science of theology above all in his *Commentary on the Epistle to the Romans*. According to Godin, he does so in three principal ways: first, Origen's text is a witness to the original text of Scripture, which for Erasmus is the heart and soul of theology; second, Origen has the ability to untangle grammatical and terminological difficulties in the Pauline text; and third, Origen's exegesis was literally the source of much of the Eastern and Western exegetical tradition. Let us investigate each of these structures individually.

As a Witness to the Original Text of Scripture

Erasmus noticed that Origen was extremely well acquainted with scriptural details in both the OT and the NT. For example, in the *CRm* Origen detected a discrepancy in Paul's citation from Genesis. This is an observation that could only have been made by a man who possessed a word-perfect knowledge of Scripture. In Rom 4.3 Paul quotes Gn 15.6 and refers to "Abraham"; and yet, until Gn 17 Scripture speaks of Abram, not Abraham. Erasmus commends Origen's attentiveness: "I certainly praise the man's diligence, and am ashamed of my own slackness."[31] Also inspirational to Erasmus was Origen's typical exegetical method, which was to explain the text he is interpreting by consulting other scriptural passages. A character in Erasmus's colloquy "The Godly Feast" says to someone who has just offered a good interpretation of Scripture, "You explain the matter admirably by comparing passages, an excellent method of biblical study." Erasmus asserted this strength of Origen's exegesis in a question posed to Luther: "Is there anyone at all who is more careful than Origen in linking up parts of Scripture or in noting the origin, the progress, the outcome of the Spirit?"[32]

Indeed, Godin has documented that the first level on which Erasmus situated the authority of Origen's exegesis of Romans was that, in view of Origen's antiquity and his incomparable knowledge of the Scriptures, Origen is a good witness to the original Greek text.[33] As the first editor of the published Greek NT in 1516, Erasmus was acutely concerned to explain and defend both his Greek text and his new Latin translation.[34] His *Annotations* are, therefore, in the first instance, "a roll-call of witnesses, one after another, to the readings of the text."[35] Obviously, then, Origen, as a Greek, and as the oldest surviving commentator on Paul's Letter to the Romans, is going to play an important role in establishing the original Pauline text, in spite of the fact that his commentary survives only in Rufinus's Latin translation.

As a Gifted Commentator on Paul's Text

Secondly, Godin observes, Origen reveals the wellsprings of theology in that he supplies helpful grammatical arguments to explain Paul's text. Origen is valuable for restoring the order of the discourse and, more generally, for clarifying the obscurity of the movements and directions of Paul's discourse.[36] In other words, Origen is a gifted commentator on Scripture. In his *Ratio Verae Theologiae*, "Method of True Theology," which was published in conjunction with his New Testament (1516), Erasmus praised Origen as incomparably the greatest among the ancient commentators on Paul,

> among whom Origen is outstanding, having raised the morning star so high that no one after him dared to set a hand [to the task]. . . . I am not saying this because I wish to be the patron to anyone who would lay claim to or even hunt for the knowledge of Holy Scripture from the past commentaries of the ancients. Rather, let the effort of the ancients take away part of our labor; let us receive help from their commentaries, provided only that we first select the best of them, such as Origen, who is so much the first that no one can be compared with him.[37]

Origen's exegetical achievement in commenting on Romans is incomparable and has virtually rendered superfluous the need for subsequent writers to comment on Paul's text. Yet for Erasmus there is no question of Origen's having done our work of studying Scripture for us, but his effort should be allowed to assist ours. In his annotation to Lk 22.38 Erasmus called Origen "without question the most learned among the theologians of old." And in a famous exchange with John Eck, Erasmus confessed that he learned more theology, which he terms "Christian philosophy," from a single page of Origen than from ten of Augustine.[38] It should be noted that the context of this oft-quoted statement is controversy over the interpretation of Romans. Erasmus was almost certainly referring Eck to

Origen's extensive *CRm*, which far surpasses in breadth and detail anything Augustine has left behind as commentary on Romans. In a similar
statement to Martin Luther, Erasmus admitted, "For my part, Augustine is
a man to whom anyone may grant as high a status as he likes; but I would
never attribute so much to him as to think he sees further in Paul's epistles
than the Greek interpreters."[39] When we recall that much of Augustine's
exegesis of Paul is embedded in polemical tracts directed against Pelagius, whereas Origen and other Greeks (e.g., Chrysostom) have left behind
full-blown commentaries on the Pauline text, Erasmus's preference for
the Greek interpreters seems justifiable from an exegetical perspective.[40]

In his *Annotations on Romans,* abundant examples can be found of
Erasmus's learning from Origen's philological and theological insights.
These especially pertain to passages where Origen shows his gift for recognizing distinctions that reflect not only an elegance of mind but deep
knowledge of scriptural word usage. Origen's gift in this regard, according to Sider, was a chief reason for Erasmus's esteem for Origen's Pauline
exegesis.[41] For example, Erasmus praises the way Origen suggests a fancy
distinction between *predestination* and *destination:* the first word can be
used of one who does not yet exist (i.e., a human being); the second, of
one who already does exist (i.e., the eternal Christ).[42] Or, again, Origen
distinguishes the various meanings of πρόγνωσις (Rom. 8.29): we can
"foreknow" in the sense of "predestine"—God foreknew even those who
were to perish—or in the sense (customary to Hebrew idiom) of "embracing with affection."[43] Erasmus is clearly pleased with the "elegant" manner in which Origen defines the distinction intended in Rom 5.14 between
Adam and Christ, which implies at once both a parallel and a contrast:

> The type is similar in genus but contrary in species. . . . Similar in
> genus in that, just as something is diffused to very many men from
> the one Adam, so also something is diffused to very many men
> from the one Christ. But the species is contrary because the trans-
> gression which began with Adam "made the many sinners," whereas
> by Christ's obedience "many will be made righteous."[44]

In Erasmus's judgment Origen's ability to make "elegant" distinctions like
this that are based on a thorough knowledge of scriptural word usage indicates that Origen had seen far into the mind of Paul.

As the Fountainhead of Subsequent Exegesis

Third, Origen reveals the wellsprings of theology in that an acquaintance with his writings, not least his *CRm,* will show us the source of many of the thoughts of subsequent orthodox exegetes. For Erasmus one of Origen's greatest achievements was in his supplying an abundance of material that was received with approval in later exegesis.[45] Origen was an important source from which Greek writers, such as Chrysostom, Theophylact, Basil, and Gregory of Nazianzus, and Latins such as Pelagius, Ambrose, Hilary, and Jerome[46] drew their chief exegetical ideas. Moreover, Latin commentators during the Middle Ages, with whom Erasmus is also familiar, repeated this pattern of assimilating Origen.[47] Erasmus perceptively observes that Origen stands in a relation to the Greek and Latin exegetical tradition in a way that is analogous to the relation of Greek and Latin poets to Homer: as a principal source and fountainhead from which they drew many of their thoughts.[48] Origen's relation to the Greek tradition was analogous to Tertullian's relation to the Latin tradition.[49] This widespread use of Origen's exegesis demonstrates Origen's substantial orthodoxy as a Pauline exegete.

Erasmus makes this point explicit to Luther in response to a passage in *De Servo Arbitrio* where Luther attacked Origen's explanation of the causes of the hardening of Pharaoh's heart (Rom 9) as residing in the Pharaoh's free will. Origen had observed that the text of Rom 9.17 does not exclude Pharaoh's free will as the antecedent cause of God's judgment, since the Scripture says, "For this very purpose I have *raised you up,*" not "For this very purpose I have *made you.*" Otherwise, Pharaoh would not have been wicked, if God had made him like that.[50] In his *Discourse on the Free Will* (1524), Erasmus had cited Origen's interpretation with approval. Luther replied to this by saying that no ecclesiastical writers have handled the Divine Scripture more ineptly and absurdly than Origen and Jerome.[51] Then, in the *Hyperaspistes 2,* which was Erasmus's response to Luther's *De Servo Arbitrio,* Erasmus replies to Luther's accusation: "The Church has approved of this gloss of Origen; Jerome, together with orthodox teachers, follows it."[52] The principle that is involved here is a programmatic one: Erasmus tends to follow Origen particularly where Origen was himself followed by other writers whom Church tradition recognizes as orthodox. Conversely, Erasmus's distrust of Luther's theological judgment is focused precisely on the fact that Luther tends to attack those aspects of the Catholic exegetical tradition that had always received broad approval.

A similar reaction is found in response to a passage in which Luther raged against Jerome's interpretation of Gal 3.19. Erasmus writes:

> How hatefully he [Luther] fumes against a man whose memory has been held sacred by God's church for so many centuries! Why is Jerome said to be dreaming about this passage when he is fol-lowing, or rather translating, so many Greek Fathers? Why do not Chrysostom, Theophylact, and Ambrose also share in the beating, since they give the same interpretation?[53]

Origen is not mentioned here, but it is well known that Jerome had adopted Origen's exegesis throughout his Pauline commentaries.[54] Eras-mus's point seems to be that for Luther to express such contempt for an interpretation that is represented by a broad consensus of ancient Chris-tian exegesis, both Latin and Greek, is not only arrogant, but reflective of a mind that has departed from the Church. Erasmus prefers to be "wrong" with such a consensus, than "right" with Luther and Luther's adherents.

Erasmus makes a similar point in a dim reflection on Melanchthon's *Commentary on Romans* (1532), a work that will be analyzed in some detail in the next chapter. In a letter to Boniface Amerbach, Erasmus complained that Melanchthon "distorts many things, he arrogantly rejects Origen and Augustine, he skips over not a few things."[55] A short time after this, in a letter to Jacob Sadoleto, Erasmus says of the same commentary:

> I have sent the *Commentary* of Melanchthon, not that you should imitate it (for he does not twist the Scripture anywhere more than where he has professed a "marvelous simplicity"), but, since the various opinions of many [exegetes] are recorded there, I knew that your prudence would excerpt from there whatever contributes to the understanding of the mind of Paul.[56]

Wengert summarizes Erasmus's point very well: "Erasmus proposed that Sadoleto use Melanchthon according to the rules of Erasmus's own *consen-sus patristicus,* as a kind of flawed *Catena aurea* of sources."[57] The key point is that it is in the consensual interpretation of ancient patristic exegetes of Paul that Erasmus hears the mind of Paul being truly expounded. From this point of view, Protestants like Luther and Melanchthon who arrogantly dismiss ancient Christian exegesis deserve to have their own exegesis ignored.

The Influence of Origen in Erasmus's *Paraphrase on Romans*

General Theme

Now let us turn to Erasmus's *Paraphrase on Romans* to compare his understanding of Paul's letter with Origen's. First of all we should call attention to the fact that the very method of paraphrasing Paul's text can be traced in part to Origen, who does this extensively.[58] For example, in an expansive paraphrase of Rom 13.8–9 ("He who loves his neighbor has fulfilled the law"), Origen writes:

> Can the one who loves his neighbor murder him? Certainly no one would kill the one he loves. Love, therefore, is the means by which what is commanded, "You shall not murder," is fulfilled. And again, does a man who loves his neighbor commit adultery with his wife? . . . In a similar way as well the one who loves his neighbor does not steal his possessions; . . . [or] bear false testimony against him.[59]

Notice how closely Erasmus follows Origen's method and wording in his paraphrase of the same verses from Romans:

> Will the one who loves commit murder? Or will someone lie with the wife of another man when he loves that man as much as he loves himself? Will he pillage someone by theft when he is prepared to help him even with his own riches? Will he ruin another by false testimony whom he would be willing to save even at his own risk?[60]

The very technique of paraphrasing Paul's text to make the meaning clearer is a method Erasmus has adopted in imitation of Origen, who had done this extensively.

In Erasmus's section explaining the argument of Paul's letter, the reader is immediately reminded of Origen. Erasmus depicts Paul's role in this epistle as that of an arbiter between Jews and Gentiles. Erasmus writes on p. 9:

> This unique craftsman [Paul] aims his message at both Jews and gentiles in his eagerness to entice everyone to Christ through every possible means. He wishes that, if possible, no mortal at all should be lost to the commander under whom he is serving. Thus, now he rebukes one group, now the other, now again he encourages and supports them. He checks the arrogance of the gentiles, showing them that neither the law of nature nor the philosophy by whose profession they are swollen up is of any use in preventing them from falling into every kind of disgraceful crime. On the other hand, he restrains the arrogance of the Jews, who by trust in the law, had destroyed the chief point of the law, namely, faith in Jesus Christ.

These fundamental structures for understanding Paul's theological strategy in Romans are thoroughly Origenian. Origen had compared Paul to a military recruiting officer of a commander (God) who has been sent out to enlist soldiers in the ruler's army.[61] The ruler does not want to destroy but to liberate his soldiers, for they are the ruler's own men, even though they are presently serving in a tyrant's army.[62] Origen also depicts Paul as an arbiter between Jews and Gentiles who is inviting both groups to salvation:

> In this letter Paul, like an arbiter sitting between the Jews and the Greeks, i.e. believing Gentiles, summons and invites both groups to faith in Christ in such a way as to not offend the Jews completely by destroying the Jewish ceremonies nor to cause despair in the Gentiles by affirming the observance of the law and of the letter. And whether he is recalling the promises or the punishments, he apportions the word to each people.[63]

Then at 3.2, Origen writes:

> Paul always tempers and balances his discourse as a kind of arbiter between those who had believed from the circumcision and those

who believed from the Gentiles, so that sometimes he seems to accuse the one group of certain things, sometimes the other group. Next he openly encourages specific groups with the sure hope in the promise.[64]

These Origenian passages appear to be the background, if not the direct source, of Erasmus's very similar depiction of Paul's method and form of argument.

In this same introductory section, Erasmus makes no secret of his belief that Paul's Letter to the Romans is difficult to understand. He posits three reasons for this: the order of speech is confused; Paul is speaking about obscure things; and Paul frequently and suddenly changes his persona. Origen had explicitly indicated all three of these reasons for the difficulty of Romans.[65] Then Erasmus quotes a passage from Origen's *CRm* that he particularly admires in which Origen illustrates the difficulties of Paul's language:

> Origen, in my opinion not less truly than elegantly, compares Paul to a man who leads a stranger into some very powerful ruler's palace: a confusing place, owing to various kinds of winding passageways and to the recesses from the rooms. However, from afar he displays certain things from a most abundant treasury of wealth; he brings some things closer, but is unwilling that others be seen. Often, moreover, after having entered in through one door, he exits through another, so that the stranger himself wonders where he has come from, where he is, or what way he should go out.[66]

In this passage Erasmus has paraphrased Origen's *CRm* 5.1.[67] The point of Origen's illustration is that Paul has been given a mission to reveal the mysteries of God.[68] The very nature of this task means that there are certain things that will be hard to comprehend in the Pauline letter which the unlearned could easily distort to their own ruin (cf. 2 Pt 3.16). For example, the different entrances and exits to the inner chambers can indicate Paul's custom of using a single word to designate different things, such as law, Jew, death, circumcision, and so forth.[69] Erasmus seems to have admired the way Origen, first of all, recognizes the mysterious and awesome nature of the theological discipline, which causes linguistic difficulties to arise. This corresponds well with what Chantraine assessed as an important general theme of Erasmus's theological method:

> At the heart of Scripture, as its sanctuary, lies the mystery. The Holy Spirit alone is able to penetrate it; submissiveness to the Holy Spirit alone prepares one to understand Scripture. To be submissive is to have one's heart pure and one's soul at peace, to have the mind thirsting after understanding alone; it is to venerate the mysteries without succumbing to "impious curiosity"; it is to have no other purpose, no other wish, no other action than to be entranced, inspired, transformed by what one is comprehending.[70]

I would suggest that Erasmus viewed Origen as an exemplary role model of one who embodied these theological ideals. Evidence for this is found in what Erasmus tells us in his *Ratio Verae Theologiae,* namely that a great part of theological learning depends on the piety of the individual. For this statement, Erasmus was criticized by Jacob Latomus. Erasmus explained his meaning in these words:

> Piety does not automatically make a man a theologian in the sense that we use that word: but one who does not love what he reads and says cannot truly be a theologian [*sed quod vere Theologus non sit, nisi qui quod legit ac loquitur, amet quoque*]. As Plato says: "A man who is on fire with the love of wisdom is neither totally without wisdom, nor completely in control of it." Long before our time Augustine taught us to approach the study of sacred literature with a mind as pure and as free from vice as it could possibly be. Paul numbers that power of prophecy which enables us to expound the Scriptures and their mysteries as one of the gifts of the Holy Spirit. Understanding the mystic texts with your mind is not enough: you must understand them with your soul as well.[71]

In his *Edition of Origen* (1536), Erasmus states explicitly that Origen "loved what he spoke about" (*amabat quae loquebatur*).[72] This echo suggests that in Erasmus's estimation, Origen was in possession of this absolutely essential qualification of a theologian, namely piety.

Romans 1 and 2

Now we turn to specific samples of Erasmus's exegesis of the epistle which seem to reflect Origen's influence. In his New Testament, Erasmus had correctly translated παρέδωκεν of Rom 1.18 as *tradidit*, "gave up" or "handed over." Yet in his paraphrase, Erasmus renders this verb by *passus est*, "allowed."[73] Erasmus evidently wishes to avoid making God the author of sin. In this interpretation Erasmus has followed Origen,[74] along with Chrysostom and Ambrosiaster.[75] The divine handing over is a permissive and not a causative reality. This calls attention to an important conclusion reached by R. Sider, in his path-breaking article on Erasmus's interpretation of Romans. In language that seems deliberately to contrast Erasmus's approach to Paul with Luther's, Sider writes:

> The sense betrayed by the Paraphrases is not that of a man who trembles before the impossible demands of the divine justice, but of a man who protests—perhaps too much—against the critic and the unbeliever; who feels a need incessantly to defend the divine justice; a man absorbed by the task of justifying the ways of God to men.[76]

This emphasis will be found below in other parts of Erasmus's *Paraphrase*. It is noteworthy that the same theological emphasis, that is, that of a man defending the justice of God over against the charges of critics, heretics, and unbelievers, is found in Origen's *CRm*.

An addition made in 1532 to his paraphrase of Rom 2.6 ("For he will render to everyone according to his works") shows Origen's influence. Erasmus supplies to his text "through faith."[77] In the original paraphrase of 1517 Erasmus interprets Paul as meaning here in 2.6–13 that good works are necessary in order to receive the eternal reward. He sees no contradiction between this passage and 3.20 ("For no human being will be justified in his sight by works of the law"). The addition of 1532 shows that Erasmus has adopted the exegesis of Origen and Chrysostom, which applies the verses to Christians who are judged on the basis not only of faith but of works.[78] These sorts of late additions to his text also indicate that Erasmus made the engagement of Origen's exegesis a lifelong endeavor. They also confirm the Erasmian tendency to follow Origen when other Fathers also represented Origen's interpretation.

Also, Erasmus's paraphrase of Rom 2.29 ("He is a Jew who is one in secret, and circumcision is a matter of the heart, in the spirit and not the letter") reflects Origen's explanation. Erasmus writes, "For one whose flesh alone has been circumcised can indeed boast among men that he is a Jew; but one becomes a true Jew *only when his mind has been purged from sin* and is inclined toward Christ."[79] Compare Origen: "For it is not that circumcision, which is outward in the flesh, that purifies the soul, but the circumcision of the heart, which is in secret, that *purifies the mind* and cuts away the stains of the vices."[80] The *CWE* editors describe this as "allegorizing and moralizing"[81] exegesis. Whatever name one gives it, the point is that Erasmus has received direct assistance from Origen for his interpretation of Paul's text.

Law (Romans 3 and 4)

Erasmus follows Origen, Ambrosiaster, and Pelagius in interpreting the law that is negated by faith in Christ (Rom 3.21–22) to be the ceremonial law. Godin writes, "On the central problem of justification by faith apart from works, Erasmus, less radically than Luther, thinks that Paul does not exclude all works of the law, but only the ceremonial laws."[82] This is certainly an Origenian point of view, as has been seen in chapter 1 earlier, but it is also an interpretation that has broad representation in both the Greek and Latin patristic tradition. Reasoner has recently indicated that it is an interpretation that has been largely recovered in modern times in the "new perspective" in Pauline interpretation.[83]

Erasmus writes in his paraphrase of Rom 3.21–22:

> Righteousness, I say, not of the law but of God, and this not through circumcision or through ceremonies of the Jews but through faith and trust in Jesus Christ, through whom alone true righteousness is conferred, not only upon the Jews, or upon this or that nation, but without distinction upon each and every one who has faith in him . . . Justification . . . is certainly not paid back to us as a reward earned through the observance of the Mosaic law or even through the observance of the law of nature. Rather it is given freely by the

divine goodness, not through Moses but through Jesus Christ by whose blood we have been redeemed from the tyranny of sin.[84]

Erasmus reflects direct Origenian influence here.[85] He stresses that Paul's negation of law is directed against the Jewish ceremonial law; that justification is not paid out as a reward for observance of the law, whether Mosaic or natural, but is given freely by the divine goodness; that Christ's blood delivers us from sin's tyranny; and that the description of Christ is as the true propitiatory, the antitype of Ex 25.17.

Payne has further observed that several additions made to the *Paraphrase on Romans* in 1532 underline that for Erasmus it is not the law as such, but the law when observed according to the flesh or according to the letter which is opposed to faith or justification. And since Erasmus has already identified the carnal law as the law dealing with ceremonies, Payne concludes, "The clear implication of these additions is that it is only the ceremonial law that is opposed to Christ."[86] The various distinctions of law that Erasmus uses (law of Moses, law of the flesh, law of the letter, law of the Spirit of life, and so forth) were first identified and discussed extensively in Origen's *CRm*.

On a related theme, Erasmus's explanation of Rom 3.31 ("Do we then destroy the law by this faith? By no means! On the contrary, we uphold the law") emphasizes that faith in Christ fulfills and does not destroy the law. This insight arises directly from Paul's text; however, the discussion seems to owe a lot to both Origen and Ambrosiaster. Erasmus writes:

> We are so far from abolishing or destroying the law that we are actually confirming and establishing it, preaching that what the law had promised for the future has now been accomplished, and announcing him towards whom the whole law pointed as its goal. For something is not abolished when it is restored to a better condition—no more than when fruit follows the blossoms that fall from the trees, or when a body takes the place of a shadow.

Compare Origen:

> Not even the Lord sets aside the law, but its temporal and transient glory is set aside and surpassed by the eternal and abiding glory. . . .

Not only is the law not set aside through the faith, it is established and confirmed through the apostles. For these very apostles are proclaiming that the Christ has now come, whom the law and the prophets predicted was coming; and it is assuredly a confirmation of prophecy and of the law when what was predicted is shown to be fulfilled.[87]

In general, Erasmus seems to follow Origen closely in his elucidation of the Pauline law/gospel distinction, which he interprets, like Origen, more in terms of shadow versus fulfillment, imperfect versus perfect religion, than in terms of contraries.

From Erasmus's other writings it is known that he strongly rejected Luther's categories for interpreting the law/gospel distinction. According to Luther, "law" has an exclusively condemnatory role, whereas the gospel contains no threats but only consolation for sincere Christians. In *Hyperaspistes* Erasmus formulates his response to Luther's articulation of his law/gospel distinction which Luther had given in *De Servo Arbitrio:*

Luther presents new laws for interpreting the threats of scripture when he says, "An expression of Law is directed only at those who do not feel or recognize their sins. So too, an expression of grace comes only to those who feel their sins, are afflicted by them, and are tempted to despair." We utterly reject those hyperbolic laws of his. Quite the contrary, the Law enlightens well-disposed people so that they do not fall into sin; and words of promise are very often spoken to a rebellious people who turn God's kindness to them into a license to sin. And the commandment "Love the Lord, your God," etc. does not indicate that we ought to perform something that we cannot do but rather admonishes us that God is to be preferred before all creatures and that we should always make progress in loving him— which is within the power of mankind with the help of grace.[88]

In refusing to support Luther's new interpretation of the relation of law and gospel, an interpretation that Luther himself later admitted was a theological novum,[89] Erasmus was heavily influenced not merely by clear texts in Paul and by common sense, but by ancient exegesis (Pelagius, Jerome, Ambrosiaster, Chrysostom) and especially by Origen, who also stressed that the essence of the New Covenant is the liberating gift of the "law of the Spirit of life" (Rom 8.2) that is infused into believers' hearts. The law does not have solely a condemnatory function, but in its new aspect it teaches believers to make progress in loving God and it gives them the power to do so.

In a remarkable concluding reflection to his recent study of the history of interpretation of Romans, M. Reasoner offers the following bold criticism of the "new perspective" of Pauline interpretation. The point made has relevance to the present discussion.

> The new perspective has not yet fully explained the antitheses of faith versus works of the law in [Romans] 3:27–28 and 9:30–10:13. Nor has it assimilated Paul's complex view of "law," for example, Paul's assertion that "the law of the Spirit of life" has delivered him from the law of sin and death (8:2, 4). Origen rightly saw that the historical Paul was capable of viewing the law as an instrument of deliverance, while modern interpreters continue to resist this point of view.[90]

It seems that the Erasmian/Origenian (i.e., the Catholic) perspective on Paul's doctrine of law may yet have a future in the field of modern biblical interpretation.

Necessity of Mortification and Moral Renewal (Romans 6)

The pervasive stress in Erasmus's theology on the necessity of moral regeneration as a constitutive aspect of human justification is partially derivative from Origen. Erasmus's final reflection on this theme is found in his "last will and testament,"[91] *De Amabili Ecclesiae Concordia,* "On Mending the Peace of the Church,"[92] where Erasmus writes, "Let us concede that the hearts of the faithful are justified, i.e. purified, by faith, provided that we admit that the works of love are necessary for attaining salvation. For true faith is not inoperative, since it is the font and seed-bed of all good works."[93] In short, salvation, for Erasmus, cannot be reduced to "faith alone" but it requires works of love for completion.

With respect to his exegesis of Romans, Rabil observed that the fact that Erasmus viewed *fides* and *fiducia* as interchangeable terms that describe the gate of salvation "precludes the idea of *sola fides* in Erasmus's thought and suggests that for him (as for Origen, Ambrosiaster, and Chrysostom among the Fathers, whom he often cites in his annotations), faith is not an entirely free gift but a merit in which free will has a role."[94] This judgment, as it stands, evinces Lutheran prejudices and draws a false inference. Rabil assumes that any theological position that adds complementary conditions to faith, such as human cooperation through free will, love, and meritorious good works, fails to conceive of faith as an "entirely free gift." However, even if Rabil has wrongly concluded that Erasmus denies that faith is an "entirely free gift," he has at least correctly assessed Erasmus's stance against the *sola fide* doctrine.

It is noteworthy that in his paraphrase of Romans 3.1, Erasmus goes so far as to place "the pious life and innocent habits" ahead of "faith in Christ" as the basis of salvation.[95] Rabil comments: "The order reveals where his emphasis lies."[96] Rabil also records that, in response to a criticism from Beda of his addition "of works" to Gal 5.2, Erasmus replies that he is not rejecting all merits of faith working through love, but only the merits of works that precede faith and love, especially the ceremonies of the law.[97] This is of course traditional Augustinian theology.

For Erasmus justification is a process that embraces, and does not exclude, the mortification of the flesh, the renewal of the moral life, and the fruitful reception of God's grace. In the paraphrase on Rom 4.25, Erasmus makes this point in a way that seems to have Origen's interpretation directly in its background. Erasmus writes:

> He died, I say, in order that he might slay sin in us, and he rose from the dead so that we who once died through him to our former sins, and were then raised again along with him and through him to a new life, might live henceforth for righteousness, a righteousness we have received through his kindness.[98]

The editorial comment on this text seems to be seriously understated: "Like Origen and other Fathers, Erasmus understands Paul as viewing very seriously post-baptismal sins."[99] As Sider has indicated, for Erasmus the innocence that is given in baptism must be retained, since postbaptismal sin destroys the Christian's friendship with God and makes him subject once more to eternal punishment.[100] This is clearly a perspective that put

Erasmus in strong opposition to Luther, who had claimed that even if he wished, the baptized Christian "could not lose his salvation, however often he sinned, save only if he refused to believe."[101] In his *Exposition of Psalm 85*, Erasmus anonymously criticizes Luther's doctrine of *justificatio sola fide*:

> But let no one allow this wicked thought to suggest itself: "I have God to protect my soul; once I have entrusted it to him, with such a guardian it cannot come to any harm. I can live free from anxieties and there is no reason for me to torture myself with good works." Alas, what a preposterous idea! We hear such remarks nowadays tossed off by certain people who boast of their confidence in God—based on what I have no idea! They seem to believe that living faith is to be found in the company of wicked deeds. These people are undoubtedly pitifully deceiving themselves. God does indeed protect souls, but only of those who are themselves also keeping watch as best they can. That is why Solomon advises us to protect our heart with all vigilance, for from it life proceeds. It is pointless for you to keep watch if the Lord does not protect your soul, but he will not protect it unless you take care of it to the best of your ability. His protection is a result of his kindness, but your vigilance is a question of duty. Assist the poor, instruct the ignorant, encourage those who doubt, console those who suffer, forgive those who do wrong, wear down your body by fasting, and amidst all this, cry out: "Preserve my soul."[102]

There seems to be no great mystery about Erasmus's insistence on the necessity of postbaptismal good works for salvation. The same stress is found in other Fathers, including Origen, who, for his part, in his comment on this Pauline text (Rom 4.25), goes so far as to say:

> If we have not yet laid aside the old man with his deeds, but we live in unrighteousness, I dare say that to us Christ has not yet been resurrected for justification nor has he been handed over on account of our sins. . . . Christ justifies only those who have received the new life in the pattern of his resurrection and who reject the old garments of unrighteousness and iniquity as if they were the cause of death.[103]

The necessity of moral renewal through the voluntary conformity with Christ's death and resurrection is stressed elsewhere. One notices that Erasmus's interpretation of Rom 6.4 is strikingly similar to Origen's. Erasmus writes:

> Dead to our former sins and living now the new life, let us follow in the footsteps of piety, always progressing from virtue to greater virtue. . . . We shall henceforth live together with the living Christ if our conduct is innocent and blameless, and we shall so live that we shall never again fall back into death. And in so doing, we shall reproduce the image of Christ as far as possible.[104]

Compare Origen:

> So then let us walk in newness of life, showing ourselves daily to him who raised us with Christ as new persons and, so to speak, as increasingly more beautiful people, uniting the beauty of our face with Christ, as in a mirror and, beholding the Lord's glory, let us be transformed into the same image by which Christ, rising from the dead, has ascended from earthly lowliness to the glory of the Father's majesty.[105]

The need for moral renewal is a favorite theme for both theologians.

Likewise Erasmus's interpretation of Rom 6.11 seems to reflect direct borrowing from Origen. Erasmus emphasizes that new life in Christ is an interior renewal of the virtues: "No one lives to God except one who is alive to piety, righteousness, and all the other virtues."[106] Origen had said the same thing:

> "Alive to God in Christ Jesus" . . . is just as if he had said: "alive to God in wisdom, in peace, in righteousness, in sanctification," all of which are Christ. . . . But if no one is alive to God without righteousness, without peace, without sanctification and without the rest of the virtues, it is certain that no one may live to God except in Christ Jesus.[107]

It is also noteworthy that Erasmus stresses that we leave the tyranny of the devil and give ourselves into the command of Christ (Rom 6.16–17) *freely.* We present our bodies to the service of righteousness (Rom 6.18) *voluntarily.*[108] No one is compelled to live a virtuous life. No one lives to God who does not will it. These exact emphases are found in the commentaries of Chrysostom and Origen respectively.[109] Also, Erasmus's paraphrase of Rom 6.23 as "The reward of the devil is death, with which he repays a foul and miserable servitude" is traceable to Origen, who had connected sin here to the devil.[110]

Like Origen, Erasmus stresses the importance of moral endeavor and pious zeal for Rom 8.1 ("there will be no condemnation") to be realized: "But if there still remain some remnants of former servitude in some Christians, they will overcome these by a pious zeal and will not be dragged against their will into any serious sin for which those deserve to be condemned who, through faith and baptism, have once been incorporated into Jesus Christ."[111] The human being himself is culpable for serious sin, which brings condemnation, even for those who have once been justified. By committing sin, believers will incur again the sentence of condemnation from which they had been pardoned in baptism. Origen says this as well.[112]

Also, the way Erasmus immediately divides the law into two parts, the fleshly and the spiritual, is an insight taken from Origen.[113] Erasmus paraphrases Rom 8.9 ("But you are not in the flesh, but in the Spirit, if the Spirit really dwells in you") as "provided you so live that the Spirit of God sees fit to dwell in your heart."[114] This is almost identical with the paraphrase of Origen, who writes, "Provided your deeds and manner of life are such that you should deserve to have the Spirit of God in you."[115] In both theologians the Christian's voluntary manner of life is the condition of their sanctification by the Spirit.

The Meaning of Divine Election

Rabil claims that Erasmus's subsequent editions of his *Paraphrase* make a "startling change in the direction of asserting predestination." The paraphrase of Rom 9.16 ("So it depends not upon man's will or exercise, but upon God's mercy") read in the 1517 edition: "And yet some part of it depends on our own will and effort, although this part is so minor that it seems like nothing at all in comparison with the free kindness of God."[116] But in the 1532 revision, Erasmus removed this sentence and substituted

"However, it does not follow that God is unjust to anyone, but that he is merciful toward many."[117] Rabil thinks that Erasmus was attempting to accommodate Protestant views and soften the antagonisms. While this conjecture may not be completely lacking merit, it seems more likely that Erasmus is "accommodating" Augustinian, not Protestant, views. The fact that Erasmus left so many other passages unchanged argues against Rabil's suggestion.

In general one can see a great deal of common ground between Erasmus and Origen, who both deny that divine election is arbitrary and irresistible. This is a perspective that is flatly contradictory to Luther's theology.[118] Both Erasmus and Origen explain election in a way that is not destructive of free will and human responsibility. For Origen, election is essentially divine foreknowledge of those who would conform themselves into the likeness of Christ. Erasmus likewise rejects arbitrariness on God's part and any thought that divine foreknowledge imposes necessity on the human will. Yet, as Rabil noticed above, Erasmus puts a stronger emphasis on the divine determination than Origen had done. This is seen in Erasmus's paraphrase of Rom 8.29:

> Those whom God has chosen have not been chosen at random. He knew those who belong to him long before he called them. He not only knew those whom he called, but by an unalterable decision, he had determined that they would be grafted into the body of Jesus his Son and be transformed into his likeness.[119]

As with Origen, for Erasmus those who are called and determined by God are chosen to be grafted into Christ's body and transformed into Christ's likeness. There is no thought of divine reprobation. Origen also stresses that God's election is a positive determination and applies to the good. Origen writes:

> For if it is those whom he foreknew he also predestined to be conformed to the image of his Son, and yet no evil man can be conformed to the image of the Son of God, then it is obvious that he is only speaking of the good, "whom he foreknew and predestined to be conformed to the image of his Son."[120]

For Origen, as Grech states, "both call and election are graces conferred freely, but only to those who God foreknows will prove themselves worthy of such an election. Paul himself confesses that he submitted his own body to servitude lest he be lost."[121] Erasmus follows Origen's direction, even while being aware that the late Augustine excluded foreknown merits as the reason for election (i.e., why Jacob was chosen and Esau rejected), and that Augustine's interpretation makes original sin the cause of God's "hatred" of Esau. But Erasmus also recognized that Augustine stood alone and against the whole Greek tradition of exegesis, and much of the Latin tradition, in this interpretation.[122]

Erasmus follows Origen in understanding Rom 9.14–16 as the objection of an imagined opponent, not Paul's own point of view.[123] In fact the whole section, which interprets the "hardening of Pharaoh's heart" as figurative speech follows Origen closely.[124] Paraphrasing Rom 9.19ff., Erasmus admits that no one resists the will of God, but nevertheless the will of God is not the cause of destruction. The human being, not God, is responsible for sin. Human beings perish through their own fault, not God's. Thus, God hardened Pharaoh's heart in the sense that he postponed his destruction after patiently enduring his wickedness.

> He did not harden the heart of Pharaoh in such a way that he himself caused Pharaoh's stubbornness, but although he knew the tyrant's arrogance was worthy of sudden destruction, nevertheless little by little he used heavier punishments against him by which Pharaoh might have been corrected if he had not resisted by his own ill will.[125]

Erasmus continues, "For God does not harden human minds to hinder them from believing in the gospel of Christ; but to illuminate the magnitude of his kindness and to reveal the glory of his power, God uses the stubbornness of those who, through their own obduracy, refuse to believe."[126] On this same theme, Origen writes:

> The heart of Pharaoh was hardened in this manner: God was unwilling to inflict immediate and total revenge upon him. For although he was a man of consummate malice, nevertheless God, in his

patience, had not barred the capacity for conversion; and therefore he uses lighter punishments on him at first, then he gradually increased their severity. But because God bore with patience, he was hardened from this leading to greater contempt, storing up such wrath for himself . . . It is not, therefore, that God hardens whom he wants, but the one who is unwilling to comply with patience is hardened.[127]

While recognizing Erasmus's close dependence on Origen in this chapter, Payne has observed that Erasmus avoids some of Origen's speculations that extend God's patient care and therapeutic cure into the ages to come. Erasmus does not suggest, as does Origen, that God's providential care for Pharaoh continued beyond this life and drowning in the Red Sea.[128] Rather, Erasmus "underlines the goodness of God's creation, the responsibility of the human will, Pharaoh's own guilt, and God's intentional use of Pharaoh's malice to bring about the salvation of his people."[129] Moreover, Payne notes that Erasmus's exegesis of Rom 9, which stresses that Paul's language does not nullify human free choice, follows not merely Origen but also Jerome, Ambrosiaster, Pelagius, and Chrysostom.[130] In other words, it is not Origen's isolated interpretation that Erasmus is retrieving, but the broader consensus of orthodox Fathers, both Greek and Latin.

Once again, a fundamental difference between the exegesis of Erasmus and Martin Luther is observable in their respective interpretations of Rom 9. In brief, Erasmus does not believe that the point of the Pauline text has to do with the question of eternal predestination and damnation of individuals, but rather with the corporate rejection of the Jews and the election of the Gentiles. Moreover, Erasmus takes Paul's words about God's choice of Jacob and "hatred" of Esau as referring to temporal advantages, not eternal salvation. In *Hyperaspistes,* Erasmus defends his interpretation to Luther, namely that Paul's point in Romans 9 is to show that the pre-eminence of the gospel was transferred corporately from the Jews to the Gentiles.

Why not, since God once did the same thing with Jacob and Esau? The same God acted in both cases, bestowing the pre-eminence on whomever he wishes and taking it away from whomever he wishes.

These events did not happen by chance: they were done according to God's secret plan.[131]

In contrast, Luther was convinced that what is at stake in Rom 9 is the doctrine of irresistible grace and a supralapsarian double predestination of individuals to heaven and hell. Luther writes against Erasmus's interpretation:

> God's love toward men is eternal and immutable, and his hatred is eternal, being prior to the creation of the world, and not only to the merit and work of free choice; and everything takes place by necessity in us, according as he either loves or does not love us from all eternity, so that not only God's love but also the manner of his loving imposes necessity on us.[132]

Thus for Luther, God's eternal decision to save and damn individuals imposes an irresistible necessity on the human will. Luther goes so far as to deny human responsibility altogether, even in damnation. He claims that it would be pointless for Paul to bring in murmurers against God as potter, if the guilt is seen to lie with the vessels and not the potter: "For who would murmur if he hears that someone worthy of damnation is damned?"[133] In short, Luther so repudiates the concept of merit and demerit that for him not even the damned deserve the damnation they receive.[134]

Erasmus disagrees fundamentally with Luther's interpretation, not only on the basis of the Pauline context, but by an appeal to the consensus of ancient exegesis. He shows clearly that Origen's resistance to such a predestinarian interpretation of Paul was broadly supported by subsequent exegetes. For instance, in *Hyperaspistes 2,* Erasmus refers back to his *Discussion of Free Will* in which he had reported the interpretations of Origen and Jerome on Romans 9, interpretations that Luther had scathingly dismissed in *De Servo Arbitrio.* And so, Erasmus adopts a different strategy and asks, What will Luther say if Erasmus demonstrates that Chrysostom, Augustine, and Ambrose agree with Erasmus's interpretation? He then accurately sets down the words of Chrysostom in explanation of Romans 9 by translating a long section from Greek.[135] Erasmus says:

These are not the words of Origen, that "inept scriptural exegete," nor do they come from the "sacrilegious mouth of Jerome," but from the golden mouth of Chrysostom. And you can see that in this passage he completely disagrees with Luther. Luther says that the purpose of the whole epistle is to show that mankind can do nothing at all, either for good or for evil, but that everything is borne along by sheer necessity and is accomplished at God's pleasure. Chrysostom completely rejects this purpose. Luther excludes all merit; Chrysostom posits two kinds: a character and mind capable of grace; and second, the merit of using grace well when it arrives. The rewards were destined and predicted for them before they were born, but this was done by one who knew what they would be like. Then Luther says that here the difficulty is resolved; Chrysostom denies this, saying that the difficulty is brought in here to check the arrogance of an objector and to render him more docile.[136]

Erasmus then adds Ambrose's interpretation, which stands in fundamental agreement with Chrysostom's.[137] Such texts show that it is wrongheaded to describe Erasmus's exegesis of Paul as "Origenist." It is rather a question of his retrieving patristic consensus. In this instance Chrysostom and Ambrose agree with Origen and Jerome that Rom 9.14–19 is not Paul's own words, that Paul's theology does not altogether exclude the contribution of human merit from salvation, and that the divine foreknowledge does not impose irresistible necessity on the human will.

Romans 12.1–2

Origen had introduced the parenetic section of Romans (chaps. 12ff.) with a summary, in the form of antitheses, of the principal ideas covered in the first eleven chapters of Paul's letter. He described how the essence of religion had been transferred (*religionis summa translata sit*) from the Jews to the Gentiles, from circumcision to faith, from the letter to the Spirit, from shadow to truth, from fleshly observance to spiritual observance, in accordance with the prophecies.[138] Now, in Rom 12.1ff., Origen says that Paul "sets about to establish the moral conduct and practices of this spiritual observance, to which, he teaches, the services of the worship of God have been transferred [*translatum*]."[139] Erasmus's summary paraphrase at the beginning of chapter 12 seems to be based directly on Origen's ideas.[140] He writes:

> Therefore, now that by the gift of God you have been brought over from your former superstition to the true religion [*ad veram Religionem*] and are free from the burden of the Mosaic law, I beg and implore you, brethren, through these mercies of God which he has already bestowed on you in many ways and continues now to bestow (to whose freely given goodness you owe your entire happiness [*cujus gratuitae bonitati summam vestrae felicitatis debetis*]), that henceforth you sacrifice victims to him worthy of this profession . . . namely, that you offer your own bodies to him.[141]

Erasmus's reliance on Origen here at the end of the epistle, or rather, at the beginning of the parenetic section of Paul's letter, shows that generally Erasmus is reading Paul's epistle under Origen's tutelage. For both at the beginning section of his *Paraphrase* where Paul's argument is articulated, as well as here at the end, Erasmus consults Origen and receives assistance from him. This applies to the explanation of both the major ideas and the particular details.

Concluding Summary

As a result of his encounter with a living saint, the Franciscan priest Jean Vitrier, the Augustinian priest Erasmus of Rotterdam came to the conviction that a great part of theological learning depended on the piety of the individual. Both Vitrier and Erasmus believed that Origen had embodied that ideal, as his writings attest. In the *Annotations* and *Paraphrase on Romans,* Erasmus finds Origen's *CRm* to be a good witness to Paul's original text. He adopts many of Origen's insights regarding Paul's basic theological strategy as an arbiter between Jews and Gentiles and as a revealer of the divine mysteries. Erasmus finds Origen to be appropriately tentative in his treatment of the divine mysteries that Paul has been summoned to reveal in part. Origen discusses religious truth with the reverence that is appropriate to one who is treading on holy ground, or rather who is touring the palace of the divine king. Erasmus supports Origen's stress on freedom of will insofar as Origen interprets Paul's letter in a way that is not destructive of human cooperation in salvation. Erasmus also admires Origen's nuanced interpretation of Paul's term *law*, and he stresses with Origen the positive function of law as that which cultivates the faith of the justified. Erasmus reflects Origen's views on the necessity of moral renewal in the virtues and follows important aspects of Origen's interpretation of Rom 9, according to which God's election does not nullify human cooperation and human responsibility.

Admittedly, for many of the parallels I have found between Erasmus and Origen, there are other intermediate sources that could also be attributed as sources of Erasmus's exegesis. But this situation illustrates the exact point I wish to emphasize in this chapter: Erasmus's reception, adoption, and adaptation of Origen's exegesis of Romans is controlled by his awareness that on the vast majority of theological issues that are at stake, Origen represents a broad consensus of patristic interpretation, both Greek and Latin. To Erasmus this fact strengthens the authority of "Origen's" interpretations, which are the oldest among the intermediate sources and the nearest to the fountainhead of the apostles. In short, there is no question of Erasmus's being some sort of "Origenist" interpreter of Paul, as he is often depicted, or of his being a "sworn adherent of Origen's philosophy."[142] It is rather a question of Erasmus's electing to follow the broad consensus of the Greek and Latin patristic interpretation of Paul.

Excursus on Origen's Legacy in the Age of Erasmus and the First Printed Editions of His Writings

One of the aims of this excursus is to help clear up misunderstandings about the nature of Erasmus's "Origenism," which has sometimes been overstated or misrepresented in modern scholarship. I will endeavor to do this by comparing and contrasting Erasmus's reception of Origen with that of his immediate predecessors and contemporaries. The chief result of this survey is the finding that Erasmus was the heir of an Origen renaissance and not the author of it. His support for Origen was mild compared with that of some of his contemporaries, and unlike others he never denied the presence of serious errors in Origen's writings. I will also shed light on the rebirth of patristic studies that was occurring from 1480 to

1520. A spectacular theological renaissance was under way prior to the Protestant Reformation, a renaissance that had the support of some of the Catholic Church's leading scholars. Far from being a period of sheer darkness and ignorance, as Protestant historiography has often attempted to assert, the years prior to the advent of Luther were actually an age of scholarly enlightenment and liberal-minded openness.

Cristoforo Persona, Marsilio Ficino

The first printed edition of a work of Origen appeared in 1481, a Latin translation of Origen's *Contra Celsum* by Cristoforo Persona (1416–85).[143] This was the first new Latin translation of Origen since antiquity and was dedicated to Pope Sixtus IV. Persona's translation made available to the Latin West that writing of Origen that constitutes alongside Augustine's *City of God* the most important Christian apologetic work of antiquity. The edition was well received and had a decisive influence.[144] It was reprinted in Venice (1514) and became established through the Merlin (1512) and Erasmus (1536) editions of Origen's writings.

The great Italian philosopher Marsilio Ficino (1433–99) had enumerated Origen's virtues and praised his doctrine in chapter 35 of *De Christiana Religione* in 1477.[145] Ficino was drawn to Origen's Platonism rather than Aristotelianism. "He cherished the idea of man's ontological position in the center of the great chain of being, thus sharing in material and spiritual creation. Ficino knew that Origen was deeply committed to all these."[146] Ficino clearly paved the way for the staunch and learned support of Origen by Pico della Mirandola (1463–93), the philosopher who was so admired by Erasmus's close friend Thomas More.

Pico della Mirandola

Pico was himself one of the central figures of the Italian Renaissance.[147] In 1486 Pico published 900 Theses and attached an introduction to them entitled *A Speech About the Dignity of Man*, in which he postulated among other things that the creation of humanity in the image of God is the source of human dignity. Because the human being possesses free will, he has the capacity for divinization through contemplation. One of Pico's theses stated: "It is more reasonable to believe that Origen is saved than damned."

Pico's work was one of the first books to be placed on the Index. Thirteen of the theses were declared heretical including the one just cited. Pico then wrote an *Apology* for his condemned theses entitled *A Disputation About Origen's Salvation*. Pico's opponents argued that it was not permissible to hope for the salvation of Origen because the Church had already condemned him, and the Church is incapable of error; nor is it permissible to question the rightness of the act of condemnation, since just as when the Church canonizes someone it declares that he or she has been received in heaven, so when it condemns someone as a heretic it declares that he is in hell. On 31 March 1487 Pico countered this argument with a full defense of his thirteen theses.

Pico's *Apology* was dedicated to his patron, Lorenzo de' Medici. Far from raising a scandal, it was received very favorably in religious circles.[148] Some of Pico's arguments may be summarized here.[149] The theologians of the pontifical commission who condemned Pico's theses have said that Pico's conclusion, that it is more reasonable to believe Origen saved than to believe him damned, is "rash and blameworthy, that it smells of heresy, and that it goes against the decision of the universal Church." Pico aims to show that their judgment is mistaken and that his thesis is not contrary to the decision of the Church. Pico knew that doctrines deriving from Origen had been condemned by two early Church councils. Of the Synod of Alexandria (400), which included Origen's name in a list of anathemas, Pico said that it had the authority of a regional council but not that of the universal Church. In any case it was theologically suspect because of its entanglement in regional politics. Of the Second Council of Constantinople (553), Pico sensed that it seems to have had in view teachings loosely attributed to Origen which were the real target of condemnation.

Turning to specific issues, Pico said that except on the doctrine of the pre-existence of souls, highly esteemed Church Fathers and the writings of Origen himself unanimously testify that Origen neither believed nor wrote heretical views. Disputed passages should be viewed as heretical interpolations. (Here Pico was following Rufinus's theory described in the preface to his Latin translation of *De Principiis*, to the effect that heretics had inserted interpolations into Origen's writings.) Moreover, Pico continued, no guilt accrues to Origen for the error on the doctrine of the soul's pre-existence, since up to the time of St. Augustine there was no clarity on the

Church's position regarding the origin of souls.[150] Pico went on to say that even if Origen had represented heretical views that contradicted subsequent Church teaching, he did not do this by way of dogmatic assertion, but always hesitantly, as one conducting scientific research (*neque dogmatice neque assertive sed dubitative semper et inquisitive*). Pico added, even if Origen had taught errors, this was no mortal sin, for there was no malicious or perverse intent and will, but mere intellectual error. And many saints taught errors, that is, doctrines that were later condemned by the Church as heretical, and yet they were still canonized. Not even Jerome accused Origen of malicious or heretical intentions. Pico continued, assuming that Origen had committed mortal sin, there were indications that he repented before his death, and therefore he cannot be conclusively damned.[151] Moreover, even if nothing were known of his repentance, it would still be pious and reasonable to hope for his redemption. For, while it is true that the Church condemned the doctrines attributed to Origen and also Origen as a teacher, it has never issued a decree concerning the damnation or redemption of his soul, nor is the Church qualified to do so. For it is God alone who judges the living and the dead. Further, even if the Church did teach the damnation of Origen's soul, we are not obligated to believe the same. For such matters are not essential for salvation and do not touch the substance of the faith.

Pico's defense of Origen is not completely original, but various elements of it were advocated by Eusebius, Pamphilus, Jerome, Didymus, Rufinus, and even Athanasius, all of whom Pico cited as authorities.[152] Schär credits Pico with establishing the "Origen renaissance" in Italy and with making a significant contribution to the requirement of tolerance for later ages.[153] Yet Schär seems to exaggerate the originality of Pico and, more generally, the newness of this revival of Origen under Pico. Schär does not seem sufficiently aware of the extent of Origen's popularity throughout the Middle Ages and early Renaissance. Nodes has observed, "It seems that Schär overstates the limitations of Origen's revival when he writes that with the condemnation of Pico's thesis, and in the heat of the Savonarolan austerity campaign, the newly opened Origen revival suddenly stops." In any case Pico was an influential authority and many of his arguments used in defense of Origen would be picked up by Aldus Manutius and Jacques Merlin and to a more limited extent by Erasmus.[154]

Aldus Manutius's Edition of Origen's Homilies (1503)

Some of Pico's views were assimilated into the edition of Origen's *Homilies on the Heptateuch* published by Aldus Manutius (Venice, 1503).[155] Aldus Manutius (1452–1515) was perhaps the most famous Venetian printer and was known intimately by Erasmus, who had stayed at his house in 1507. His edition was dedicated to Fra Egidio (Giles) da Viterbo (1469–1532), the famous humanist, outstanding Augustinian-Eremite preacher, and later cardinal of the Catholic Church. Egidio delivered the famous opening address to the Fifth Lateran Council on 3 May 1512.[156] Aldus's edition confined itself to Origen's homilies on the Old Testament. Aldus gave his edition two prefaces, one of which is signed by him and quotes several times from Pico's *Apology for Origen*.[157] Here he adopted the commonplace assessment of Origen derived from St. Jerome, "Ubi bene dixit, nemo melius; ubi male, nemo peius," "When Origen spoke well, no one has ever said it better, when he spoke badly, no one has ever spoken worse." Thus the attraction to Origen was complex and involved the use of caution.[158]

The second preface of Aldus's edition was anonymous but has been reasonably attributed to Jerome Aleander (1480–1542),[159] the brilliant young humanist scholar who later became the papal legate to the Diet of Worms (1521), which condemned Martin Luther. Aleander would eventually become a cardinal. He was also a one-time friend and colleague of Erasmus but later a bitter enemy. In this second preface the twenty-three-year-old Aleander invites the reader to drink deeply from Origen, "the supreme fountain of saving wisdom." Aleander adds a passionate eulogy of Origen addressed to the Christian reader:

> Whoever thou art, faithful soul, who desirest to be built together for the heavenly Jerusalem that rises with living stones [cf. 1 Pt 2.5]: enter these sacred grounds . . . where there is the well of living waters flowing flowing from the heights of Lebanon, irrigating all the surface of the earth and issuing into life eternal . . . Let me speak with daring: for many things have I read, yet nothing, in my opinion, was I ever granted to see which was so noble, so mysterious, so profound, so perfect, so suited to every age, condition and degree. But I better be silent about this than say little; for if I had a hundred tongues for praise, I would not yet be able to touch the lowest hem

of his [Origen's] garment. For if you will come close and unfold and see for yourself—you, too, will say with the Queen of Sheba [cf. 1 Kgs 10.6–7]: True is what I heard in my own country about these sayings and about this wisdom great in the extreme; and I did not believe those who told me of it until I came myself and saw with my own eyes, and found that the better part of it had not been reported to me: for greater is this wisdom than the renown of it, which I heard. Truly, to have come here is sufficient. And for us too it is time to sound the retreat. Let Origen himself, setting out from the shore, offer the sails to the winds and lead us seaward.[160]

Whereas the first preface by Aldus was characterized by caution, here we encounter an enthusiasm for Origen that is virtually boundless. With intense and passionate emotion, the future cardinal Aleander promotes Origen as a Christian writer and homiletician.

Egidio da Viterbo

Egidio (Giles) da Viterbo, under whose patronage Aldus hoped to place Origen, had himself expressed an opinion about Origen in his *Historia Viginti Saeculorum*. On the one hand, Giles could repeat Jerome's view that Origen was a "heretic." Yet Giles could also speak very highly of Origen's person, and he confessed that he was impressed by the virtues and insights of those whom the Church had condemned.

When we study the writings of the ancient heretics, would it not seem that nothing could be more saintly, more chaste, more sacred than they, except for the one or two points on which they differed from other right believers? For to speak alone of Origen, whom Jerome and the Church condemn, what could be chaster, what purer, what more exalted in the rejection of human frailty, what more inspiring, more forceful and more felicitous in desiring, observing and revealing things divine? So that Jerome said he was unique after the Apostles and deserved, and should receive, a place before all mortals.[161]

Clearly the author of these words is no stranger to the writings of Origen. Egidio admits that Jerome and the Church condemn Origen, but this applies to only a few points of his teaching. The greater part of Origen is received and venerated by the Church. Let us now turn to a survey of the first published editions of Origen's *CRm*.

Theophilus Salodianus (Venice, 1506)

The *Editio Princeps* of Origen's *CRm* was printed in Venice in 1506 by the printer Simon de Lueres (Simone da Lovere).[162] The editor was a friar named Theophilus Salodianus (of Salò, Italy), who was a member of a mendicant order devoted to St. Jerome. His dedicatee is a patron, "the very brilliant knight Alexander," for whom Theophilus provides what Hammond has described as a "charming description"[163] of his joy at the discovery of the manuscript in a monastic library in the city of Fiesole (Italy) and of his painstaking effort to restore and correct the manuscript.

> As I was diligently combing through our monastic library in Fiesole, excellent Alexander, and inspecting individual manuscripts very carefully, I was hoping that I might by chance find some writings of my holy father Jerome, which had been ruined through the teeth of time and the disfavor of the years. Instead, I found these ten books of the highly learned man, Origen Adamantius, on the Epistle of Paul to the Romans. They were so gnawed by moths and worms that many words were missing on a number of pages. Moreover, through the ignorance and neglect of the librarian, some of the chapters were so deformed and stained by blemishes that in many passages not even the sense could be elicited. I really think that our predecessors allowed them to become run-down with neglect and dust for no other reason but that, when they saw them so excessively corrupted, they judged them to be beyond repair, so that they had to be passed over. Wherefore, I, who at first sight had jumped for joy at the discovery of such a great treasure, began to be overwhelmed with grief. For I was in a state of despair over ever being able to remove the blemishes and restore the books completely. But encouragement from my friends breathed new life into me, and their prayers to God gave me the help I needed. And so I set my hand to the task. After a great and ceaseless effort, I have at last restored our Origen, polished and corrected, to his ancient elegance and to his original dignity.[164]

As a monk dedicated to St. Jerome, it was fitting that Theophilus was searching for manuscripts of Jerome. He mistakenly attributes the current translation to Jerome rather to Rufinus, due to the corruption of the end of the manuscript, which is the only place where Rufinus's name originally appeared. In fact many manuscripts substituted Jerome's name for Rufinus's. Theophilus's complaint about the lack of attention of past generations, who had allowed the text to decay to its present condition, captures well the spirit of Christian humanism during the Renaissance, which sought to restore and correct the monuments of Christian and classical antiquity. Theophilus's text of Origen's *CRm* was adopted in both the Merlin (1512) and Erasmus (1536) editions.

Jacques Merlin (Paris, 1512)

In 1512 under the editorship of Jacques Merlin (1490–1541), who was assisted by Josse Bade and John Parvus, appeared a four-volume complete Latin edition of Origen's works. This was not only the first French printing of Origen's works but the first complete edition of the writings of Origen that were available in Latin translation.[165] Jacques Merlin had acquired the degree of doctor in theology at the Sorbonne in 1510. Afterward he became a member of the theological faculty and was active in the diocese of Paris. He was known as an outstanding preacher and later became a staunch opponent of French "Lutherans." Next to his Origen edition, his most important publication was a collection of council acts and papal decrees.[166] From 1522 to 1528 Merlin was engaged in a bitter dispute with Noël Béda, a theologian of the Sorbonne, over the *Apologia* for Origen, which appeared in Merlin's edition of Origen's works. The dispute was intensified when Merlin publicly ridiculed Béda for attempting to stifle the works of Erasmus. Eventually the case was allowed to drop.[167] A firsthand account of its outcome, in which Béda was suppressed, is preserved.[168]

Merlin's edition of Origen is dedicated to Michael Boudet (d. 1529), the bishop of Langres. It begins with an impassioned panegyric of Origen, in which the twenty-two-year-old Merlin praises the Alexandrian highly as a teacher of the Church. Origen is said to hold the same place among philosophical theologians (*inter theosophos*) as the sun among the stars, the eagle among birds, and Atlas among the giants. Origen is pre-eminent, just as Pythagoras, Socrates, Plato, and Aristotle stand out among the philosophers; Homer, Vergil, Menander, and Terence among the poets; Sallust, Herodotus, and Livy among the historians; Lysias, Gracchus, Demosthenes, and Cicero among the orators. Merlin exclaims that no one was holier, more scholarly, more eloquent, and more universally learned than Origen.

> You, O my Adamantius, have restored the best seed of Christianity in moistened ground. By your splendor of doctrine the entire world receives an unfailing illumination. You tear down the intricate curtain of the tabernacle and separate the linen from the purple. You reveal the feet and countenance of the Cherubim and you untangle their wings. You lead out wheel from wheel. You are eyes for the blind, feet for the lame. In short, the service Abraham offered to the angels, Joseph to the Egyptians, Moses to the Israelites, Job to those who are suffering, Daniel to the captives, you perform for the worshipers of Christ.[169]

Merlin's preface resembles Aleander's (cited above). It is remarkable for its Ciceronian eloquence, its biblicism, and its passionate enthusiasm for Origen.

Merlin praises the apologetic achievement of Origen as displayed in his work *Contra Celsum:* "No one who approached him went away uninstructed; no one who came to him with the intention of fighting against the truth departed the victor."[170] He extols the good fortune of Greece in possessing such a great star. But the Greeks were blind, he says, referring to the harassment Origen faced in his lifetime and his subsequent condemnation; for they charged with innumerable errors the one God had sent. Mistreated and abused by the Greeks, Origen fell into the hands of robbers. Instead of embracing him they sent him into exile. In Origen Merlin sees the traveler in the parable of the Good Samaritan whom the Levite and the priest pass by. Merlin wants to be like the Good Samaritan to Origen, to bind his wounds and restore him. He requests that his patron bishop, Michael Boudet, do the same.[171]

The unique feature of Merlin's edition is the defense of Origen's orthodoxy that Merlin mounts in these prefaces. This aspect of his edition distinguishes it from Erasmus's later edition. Merlin named this part of his edition the "Apology,"[172] and it caused him immediate difficulties with

Catholic authorities. In the "Apology" Merlin reveals a detailed knowledge of the history of the Origenist controversy in the ancient Church. He asserts that Pope Gelasius (492–96) had prematurely and unfairly condemned both Rufinus and Origen based on Jerome's testimony alone.[173] Merlin argues that it is illicit to condemn a man (whether Origen or Rufinus) based on the testimony of one witness. Therefore the pope was obligated to listen to a series of sworn witnesses. "For a judgment which affects everyone requires the approval of everyone."[174] By this statement, Merlin means that a sentence of condemnation by a pope demands the agreement of the entire Church. This reflects a thesis of conciliarism, which was still a burning issue at the beginning of the sixteenth century. Schär has observed that in making these statements, Merlin is clearly placing the council over the pope. Nor is this really surprising when we recall that Merlin himself was the first editor of the texts of the councils.[175]

Merlin defends Origen's orthodoxy on the question of Origen's alleged assertion of a universal restoration of all rational creatures. Invoking numerous citations from Origen's homilies and from the *CRm*, Merlin tries to prove that Origen's eschatological views were incontestably orthodox.[176] According to Merlin, Origen did not teach that the devil would be restored nor did he assert that the fire of hell would be of limited duration. Merlin followed Rufinus's claim in asserting that the errors found in *De Principiis* were heretical interpolations. He also repeated Pico della Mirandola's line of defense, that Origen had spoken hesitantly and inquisitively. Like Pico, Merlin encouraged his readers to think well on the subject of Origen's eternal salvation.[177]

Startlingly, Merlin's "Apologia" for Origen totally absolves Origen of error, even on the question of the pre-existence of souls. In contrast with Pico, Origen's great fifteenth-century defender, who conceded that Origen taught error in his doctrine of the soul's pre-existence, Merlin defends Origen even on this point. Moreover, it is surprising that Merlin is completely silent about the condemnation of Origen in 553 at the Fifth Ecumenical Council. Schär conjectures that Merlin's faith in the authority of the councils over that of the pope resounds in this silence. For whereas Merlin consistently expresses doubt about the binding authority of papal decisions, conciliar decisions are sacrosanct for him, since they are an expression of the general will of the Church. Thus for Merlin to report the condemnation of Origenism at the Fifth Ecumenical Council in 553 would be to undermine the legitimacy of his own edition of Origen's writings.[178] This was not entirely candid of him, and he was judged as an imprudent scholar by later generations. Lubac says of Merlin, "Intending to exalt Origen, he expressed himself, as Huet would say, 'without sufficient prudence' concerning Pope Gelasius as well as Saint Jerome and his language was not the product of a considered theologian."[179] We recall that Merlin was a mere twenty-two-year-old when he wrote this "Apology." This may excuse him in part for his defensive and pretentious outpourings.

Merlin concludes his preface with the wish that Origen "may rise like a morning star for the entire Church" and that this edition "may soon be turned by the hands of many."[180] Insofar as his edition became standard for scholars north of the Alps, this wish was fulfilled. No fewer than six reprints appeared before 1536.[181] This is the edition that Catholic theologians and the Protestant Reformers would have used until it was replaced and superseded by Erasmus's edition of 1536.

Erasmus (Basel, 1536)

Erasmus's edition of Origen's writings was not merely his last edition of a Church Father but his very last work. It was published posthumously by Froben Press two months after Erasmus's death in Basel on 12 July 1536.[182] Erasmus's edition was based upon the Merlin edition of 1512, but it differs from Merlin in many important respects. For one thing there is no apology for Origen in Erasmus's edition. Moreover, Erasmus mercilessly censured Origen's translator, Rufinus. Erasmus was the first to identify Rufinus, rather than Jerome, as the translator of Origen's *CRm*. He describes the process that led to this detection in an addition made to his annotation to Rom 3.5 in 1535.[183] In other passages Erasmus had faulted Rufinus's translations for inserting statements that are diametrically opposed to the views of the real Origen.[184] For example, Erasmus said that Rufinus, in his translation of Origen's *CRm*, had altered Origen's text in order to make Origen fight against the Arians.[185] This is almost certainly true,[186] and it shows how far Erasmus was ahead of his time as a critical editor. In general, Erasmus's negative view of Rufinus strongly contrasts with the high esteem in which Merlin held him. Erasmus is probably referring to Jacques Merlin's defense of Rufinus when he writes the following in his edition of St. Jerome:

There are some who allow some merit to Rufinus. I however not only find his learning inadequate, but I scent a character, I think, that is venomous and sly and by no means open. Surely when Jerome paints him in such colors, always ridiculing and attacking the lack of eloquence, the inexperience, and the stupidity of the man, we must either admit that Rufinus was such a person or make Jerome a slanderer.[187]

However highly Erasmus may have thought of the scholarship of Jacques Merlin, he disagreed strongly with Merlin's high regard for Origen's translator, Rufinus. Erasmus's lifelong concern had been with restoring ancient texts to their pristine form. Rufinus has always been a persona non grata to editors like Erasmus, since Rufinus's paraphrastic and lacunar translation method was rendered suspect. On the other hand, Erasmus's attacks on Rufinus's character and orthodoxy are unjust. They reflect prejudices that stem from his partisanship of St. Jerome.

Erasmus's Reflections on Origen's Orthodoxy

Erasmus has been described as Origen's "most avid sixteenth-century supporter."[188] A comparison of the respective prefaces to their editions of Origen shows that, if anyone, it is the twenty-two-year-old Jacques Merlin who truly deserves to be so described. Erasmus's presentation of Origen is significantly different from Merlin's in that he never attempted to present Origen as totally orthodox, as Merlin did. Elsewhere, Erasmus freely admitted that Origen taught some errors. For example, in his *Apology to Latomus* (1518), Erasmus reports that Latomus had criticized his preference for Origen in his *Annotations on Romans*. Latomus was scarcely prepared to allow even a seasoned theologian to read that Father's works. To this Erasmus replies:

Yet everyone, without exception, recognizes that Origen had the profoundest knowledge of the Scriptures and there are very few passages in his surviving books which are suspect. . . . If anyone was prepared to do the arithmetic exactly, he would perhaps find more mistakes in the works of Peter Lombard than in those of Origen which have come down to us.[189]

Erasmus goes on to say that Origen has none of that feigned effusiveness that makes us look fearfully for the hidden trap. His language is entirely straightforward and churchmanlike. Moreover, none of Origen's heretical doctrines are extant except in Jerome, "who made it his business to see that the world knew about Origen's errors, but not about the sound points he made."[190] Erasmus clarifies this point further in his *Explanation of the Creed,* where he explains the added words "of whose kingdom there will be no end" with this remark:

> It has been added because of some who have foolishly uttered cer-
> tain outlandish blasphemies about the Platonic cycles. It was from
> this source that Origen drew his erroneous teaching (if indeed he
> really believed what he reported rather than asserted in his writ-
> ings) that after many thousands of years the demons would become
> angels and the angels would become demons; that those condemned
> to hell would sometime or other be freed from suffering and return
> purified to a state of happiness; that, finally, Christ would be crucified
> again, and in this way the kingdom that Christ prepared for himself
> by his death would sometime come to an end. This blasphemy is
> too senseless to be refuted.[191]

The views described here are reported to be Origen's by Jerome in *Ep* 124 and by Augustine in *De haeresibus.* Erasmus stands then with both Jerome and Augustine in rejecting such views, though, unlike Augustine, Erasmus expressly wonders whether Origen really intended to assert these opinions dogmatically.

Generally, Erasmus's stance toward Origen's errors was that when he did go astray he ought to be and in fact is pardoned for two reasons: "First, because he wrote to investigate such things, not to define them; and then because he wrote at an early period when it was legitimate to have doubts about many points which cannot now legitimately be considered ambiguous."[192] These words were directed to Martin Luther, who had reviled Origen. Erasmus's statement here repeats an idea found in his dedicatory epistle to his edition of Origen's *Commentary on Matthew,* where he said, "There are many things about which today it would be the height of impiety to doubt, though once upon a time in Origen's day it was a matter of religious diligence to inquire into these same things."[193] In other words, Erasmus noticed that many Fathers had expressed heterodox ideas, in particular during the early period. There is no reason to make a fuss about this, he says, for we can admire authors without sharing all their ideas. Moreover, no author, ancient or modern, can escape the charge of heresy from an overzealous critic. Erasmus stresses that we must understand the Fathers in light of the opinions and customs prevailing in their own century, rather than measuring them by modern standards.[194]

In an important discussion of heresy that is based on a figurative interpretation of Ps 33 (34), Erasmus makes the point that in the determination of who is a heretic, emotional attachment to a heresy is of far greater importance than intellectual error. Although he does not name Origen in this passage, the text still seems relevant to the present discussion.

> Irenaeus became a chiliast, Cyprian thought that those baptized by heretics were in need of rebaptism, while St. Jerome condemned as heretical the opinion that a bishop who, once baptized, remarried after the death of a wife he had married before his baptism should be removed from office. Augustine constantly proclaims that unless baptized children have received the Lord's body and blood they are lost eternally, their baptism benefiting them not at all, and it is clear that almost the whole western church was of this opinion, and probably the eastern church as well. Now if these men were saints, why did the Lord not "guard all their bones"? And if they were not saints, why does the church honor them as such? A wounded or dislocated bone is one thing, but a broken bone quite another. A wounded bone can be healed, a bone out of joint can be put back in place, but a broken bone is scarcely curable. There are very few examples of a confirmed heretic's return to the church. But those whose error is a merely intellectual one and whose emotions have not been seduced are easily brought back to the path. This was the case with Paul, and so when he received a warning he at once returned to the path. Consequently, if the church had admonished those devout men, they would immediately have rejected their erroneous beliefs.[195]

The distinction Erasmus makes here between merely intellectual error and emotional/inner disposition is important. It seems that Erasmus assessed Origen's errors as being primarily intellectual mistakes and did not detect in him any emotional attachment to heresy or malicious intent. On the contrary, Erasmus rated Origen very highly in terms of the emotional/inner disposition that is displayed in his writings.

Evidence for this is to be found in abundance in the preface to Erasmus's printed edition of Origen's writings. Here Erasmus does not discuss the question of Origen's orthodoxy. Instead, he includes a *Life of Origen* and essays on Origen's education, written works, style of preaching, and a survey of Origen's individual works. These essays display a deep sympathy for and admiration of Origen's emotional disposition. He treats Origen as a pious churchman and an "outstanding doctor of the Catholic Church," whose life, scholarship, and service to the Catholic Church are worthy of emulation. Erasmus explicitly contrasts Origen with Tertullian, who left the Catholic Church, and with Arius, who split it down the middle. Origen "did not even contend with his detractors in embittered writing, but he shut the mouths of his accusers by doing good, which is a far more beautiful kind of victory, according to St. Peter."[196] In Origen Erasmus observes the same combination of literary erudition and sanctity of life that he also found in the other Fathers of the Church and in a few of the great men of his generation, such as Thomas More, John Colet, John Fisher, and above all Jean Vitrier.[197] One can conclude from this treatment that Erasmus believed that Origen's spirit was Catholic and that he would have immediately rejected his erroneous beliefs and would have been brought back to the right path had he lived to receive admonition from the Church.

Conclusion

It appears that several of the leading Christian scholars of Erasmus's epoch, some of whom would one day occupy high offices in the Catholic Church, were enthusiastic advocates of Origen's legacy and were endeavoring to make Origen's writings productive to their contemporaries. Thus Erasmus should not be interpreted as an isolated figure. On the contrary he was an active member of a small group of men who advanced the cause of learning in the German world, taking Italy as their model. More generally, Christian humanism was not a movement that Erasmus initiated, not even in his own country. The rebirth of ancient literary culture, including patristic studies and the Origen renaissance, was in full stride when Erasmus came into his prime. Erasmus went along with existing tendencies, and he energetically tried to support and develop these patterns in a favorable climate.[198]

Chapter 6

Luther and Melanchthon's Reception of Origen's Exegesis of Romans

Grech wondered how the Reformers would have received Origen's exegesis of Paul.[1] This chapter will endeavor to answer that question by examining the reception of Origen's doctrine of justification by Martin Luther (1483–1546) and Philipp Melanchthon (1497–1560). Melanchthon, a Greek scholar, was Martin Luther's most important theological colleague. At the age of twenty-four he became the first systematizer of Luther's thought in his work *Loci Communes* (1521). As the author of Lutheranism's confession of faith (the *Augsburg Confession*, 1530) and the *Apology* for the same, the architect of Lutheranism's pedagogy, and a very important source for the theology of John Calvin,[2] Melanchthon as a magisterial Protestant needs no defending. Melanchthon is an appealing theologian for the current investigation because of the clarity of his attitude toward Origen's exegesis of Romans. Also, he makes Origen's doctrine of justification an integral part of his decadence theory of Church history—a fact previously unnoticed in scholarship.

Luther's Postconversion Alienation from the Fathers

In order to understand Melanchthon's criticism of Origen properly, it will first be necessary to introduce Luther's attitude toward the Fathers, since Luther's views seem determinative for Melanchthon's positions. In his article "Martin Luther and the Church Fathers," M. Schulze rightly recognizes that Luther was not a historian, that patristics was not his concern, and that he did not produce editions of the Fathers like Erasmus of Rotterdam, "who was well-versed in their languages and familiar with their works, and made the Fathers of Christian antiquity accessible to the early modern age."[3] Yet Schulze makes several erroneous judgments. While admitting that Luther was biased in his reading of Augustine, Schulze formulates a ludicrous generalization when he says that "most of the Scholastics ranked Augustine among the embarrassments of church history."[4] Moreover, Schulze's summary of Luther's reception of the patristic tradition is seriously flawed. He concludes his essay by saying that Luther rendered an "inestimable scholarly service to the church, to theology, and to historiography by freeing the Fathers from tradition. At long last it was possible for them to be mistaken."[5]

In reality, no Christian theologian has ever denied that the Fathers were capable of being mistaken. Thus Luther's "service" to the Church is not located here. Rather, the originality of Luther appears to be that he was the first to accuse the Fathers of being in fundamental error on several doctrines that he regarded as constituting the essence of Paul's gospel. Luther is the source for the theory that the exegetical blindness of the Fathers caused Christ to be absent from the visible Church for fourteen centuries.[6]

Luther's railing indictments of the Church Fathers included serious criticisms of Augustine, though this is seldom mentioned in modern scholarship. In a recent volume dedicated to the thought of Augustine, P. D. Krey's article on Luther does not mention a single passage in which Luther sharply criticized Augustine's understanding of Paul.[7] Schulze's article cited above also overlooks these clear texts where Luther claims that after his religious conversion he could no longer accept Augustine's basic interpretation of Paul. It is true that Luther made contradictory statements about the subject of Augustine's fidelity to Paul's understanding of the "gospel," as did Melanchthon, and I will attempt to analyze these contradictions below. But it would not be right to neglect the passages in Luther where Augustine is rejected, especially since these texts bear directly on the Lutheran criticism of Origen.

Luther seems to have come to his conviction about Augustine's departure from Paul as a result of his conversion experience. He describes his own conversion in the *Preface to His Latin Writings:*

> At last, by the mercy of God, meditating day and night, I gave heed to the context of the words, namely, "In it the righteousness of God is revealed, as it is written, 'He who through faith is righteous shall live.'" There I began to understand that the righteousness of God is that by which the righteous lives by a gift of God, namely, by faith. And this is the meaning: the righteousness of God is revealed by the gospel, namely, the passive righteousness with which merciful God justifies us by faith, as it is written, "He who through faith is righteous shall live." Here I felt that I was altogether born again and had entered paradise itself through open gates. There a totally other face of the entire Scripture showed itself to me.[8]

He goes on to say that subsequently he read Augustine's work *Spirit and Letter* and found his new understanding confirmed. Notice that the discovery of justification by faith does not originate with his study of Augustine; only by way of an afterthought, after Luther knew what he desired to know, does he admit to finding in the Fathers what they had not been able to teach him previously.[9]

The center of Luther's experience seems to have been an enlightened understanding of Paul's doctrine of justification by faith that is expressed in Rom 1.17. Luther's new insight instilled in him the conviction that a defection from the "gospel," that is, the authentic understanding of Paul, occurred at a very early date in Christian history. Luther says that he subsequently regarded the study of the Fathers as a waste of time by comparison with direct attention to the Scriptures.

> Ever since I came to an understanding of Paul, I have not been able to think well of any doctor [of the Church]. They have become of little value to me. At first I devoured, not merely read, Augustine. But when the door was opened for me in Paul, so that I understood what justification by faith is, it was all over with Augustine.[10]

Grisar's assessment of this passage is that, in spite of Luther's claim to once have "devoured Augustine," he "certainly did not allow himself sufficient time to appreciate properly the profound teachings of this, the greatest Father of the Church, and best authority on grace and justification."[11] It seems certain that Luther's attitude toward the Fathers, including Augustine, was decisively altered after his "Tower experience." For Luther expresses similar sentiments in his didactic writings. In a sermon on the second book of Moses, for example, he said, "In my studies, I wasted and lost much time on Jerome, Origen, Cyprian, and Augustine."[12] The Fathers as a whole have now become estranged from Luther's mind because they have failed to apprehend the doctrine of justification. In a programmatic statement, Luther asserts that the article of justification by faith alone constitutes the "head and cornerstone" of the Church of God, without which the Church cannot exist for an hour. "Therefore anyone who does not safeguard justification by faith cannot teach anything that is right in the church."[13] For Luther this means:

> Jerome can be read for the sake of history, but he has nothing at all to say about faith and the teaching of true religion. Origen I have already banned. I have no use for Chrysostom either, for he is only a gossip. Basil doesn't amount to anything; he was a monk after all, and I wouldn't give a penny for him.[14]

In a sermon preached in 1530, Luther said, "Neither Jerome nor Cyprian nor Origen nor any of them preached Christ."[15] By "preaching Christ," Luther obviously means teaching in accordance with his own doctrine of justification.[16]

Luther often links Jerome and Origen together in his denunciations. One of his clearest statements about them is found in his *Exposition of the Prophet Amos:*

> I have consequently been the more frequently amazed, almost indignantly, about what earned for Jerome the title of a *Doctor Ecclesiae* and for Origen that of a *Magister Ecclesiarum* . . . although it is hard to find three lines in them which teach the doctrine of justification, and although one cannot make anyone a Christian on the basis of any of their writings, as they come sweeping in so arrogantly with

their allegories or allow themselves to be entrapped by the showi-ness of works. The same thing would have happened to Augustine if the Pelagians had not eventually exercised his full attention (*exercitium*) [*sic*] and driven him to the righteousness that is of faith. A *Doctor Ecclesiae* is really the product of such a controversy and such practical experience (*exercitium*) [*sic*] and Augustine is almost the only one after the age of the Apostles and that of the earliest Church Fathers.[17]

Although Luther mentions that he is repulsed by the "arrogant allegories" of Jerome and Origen, it does not appear that allegorical exegesis is the heart of his criticism. At any rate this method applies chiefly to the interpretation of the OT and not to their exegesis of Paul's writings. The core issue seems to be that Jerome and Origen did not teach Luther's crucial doctrine of justification by faith alone. And in spite of his claim here that his doctrine agrees with Augustine, the evidence cited above suggests that Augustine is necessarily included in the Lutheran criticism of the Church's traditional understanding of justification. In other words, Luther's alleged endorsement of Augustine here does not deserve to be taken seriously in light of his other statements. Moreover, the emphatic effort made by Melanchthon and Luther in 1530 to prove that the heritage of the ancient Church, which had been abandoned by medieval Catholicism, was restored in the *Confessio Augustana,* is betrayed by Luther and Melanchthon's own explicit criticisms of Augustine's doctrine of justification. This matter will be examined more fully below.

Melanchthon's Decadence Theory of Church History

We now turn to Melanchthon, who seems to be a perpetuator of Luther's views on these matters. In his *Funeral Oration* for Luther (1546), Melanchthon elaborates a theory of ecclesiastical decadence in which his now-deceased colleague is depicted as the bearer of God's word in the early sixteenth century and a holy prophet of God, on par with Isaiah, John the Baptist, Paul, and Augustine.[18] In the published form of this oration, *The History of the Life and Acts of Martin Luther* (1548), Melanchthon discusses not only Luther's prophetic role in the history of the Church, but the disastrously negative significance of the teaching of the ancient Church and of Origen.[19] Luther is described as the rescuer and restorer of Christianity from fourteen centuries of previous darkness and decadence. His principal achievement is said to be his epoch-making explanation of the Epistle to the Romans and the lectures on the Psalms. Melanchthon describes Luther's key insight on justification as the voice of God revealing the truth to humanity. He writes:

> He [Luther] so illuminated these writings that, as light after a long, dark night, so new doctrine seemed to appear, by the judgment of all pious and prudent men. Here he pointed out the essential point of the Law and the Gospel [*monstravit Legis et Evangelii discrimen*], there he refuted the error, which held sway at the time in the Schools and in debates, which taught that men merited forgiveness of sins by their own works, and that men were justified before God by discipline, as the Pharisees taught. Accordingly Luther called the minds of men back to the Son of God, and, like the Baptist, he showed that the lamb of God, who took away our sins, freely forgives sins on account of the Son of God, and therefore this favor must be accepted by faith.[20]

Melanchthon's narration exalts Luther to more than prophetic stature. Before Luther there was darkness in the Church. The essential distinction between law and gospel was not grasped. Error held sway in the schools and monasteries, and men were taught a form of Judaism, not Christianity. But with the coming of Luther, a light dawned.

Grisar described Melanchthon's depiction of Luther's lectures in this short sketch of Luther's life as "pompous."[21] Some modern Protestants tend to agree. M. Wiles, for example, asserts that the theory that the thought of Paul was totally lost in the obscurity of a dark Pelagian world until the shining of the great Augustinian light "is one deserving to be dismissed to that very limbo of outworn ideas in which it would itself seek to place the early patristic commentaries on the writings of the divine apostle."[22] Likewise, McGrath admits that the Lutheran accusations of a Pelagian darkness of the early Church are false.[23] In any case there seems to be no questioning Melanchthon's sincerity. At the end of this same work, Melanchthon trumpets Luther's Reformation with this devotional outpouring:

> Therefore let us give thanks to God the eternal Father of our Lord Jesus Christ, who wanted the dirt and poisons to be driven out again from the Gospel sources by his servant Martin Luther, and he restored the pure doctrine of the Church, wherefore it is proper for all pious thinking men in the whole world to join prayers and lamentations together and to beg with burning hearts that God strengthen that which he has done among us on account of his holy temple.[24]

Like a new Nehemiah rebuilding the walls of Jerusalem, and a new Hercules cleansing the stables of Augeas, Luther has cleansed the gospel sources and restored the "pure doctrine of the Church." Melanchthon laments Luther's death and describes him as the charioteer and chariot of Israel, who guided the Church in this last age of the world. "For the doctrine of the remission of sins and the pledge of the Son of God was not apprehended by human sagacity. It was revealed by God through this man, Whom we saw was roused [*excitatum*] even by God."[25]

Aetas Origenica: The Age of Origen

In this same writing, Melanchthon depicts the history of the Church as consisting of four periods subsequent to the age of the apostles: those of Origen, Augustine, monasticism/scholasticism, and Luther. After an initial period of truth and purity during the first age, which was coextensive with the lifetime of the apostles, Melanchthon claims that "four prominent changes of doctrine seem to have followed."[26] The second age (the first after the apostles) saw the first corruption introduced and was called the "age of Origen."[27] Melanchthon says that this age "nearly totally lost the essential distinction of Law and Gospel."[28] The proper distinction between law and gospel was the exact point that he had earlier said Luther had recovered. I will analyze the meaning Melanchthon assigned to these terms more fully below. Origen's age was followed by the third age, which was that of Augustine. Melanchthon asserts that it was in order to oppose Origen's errors, which were perpetuated by Pelagius, that God roused up (*excitavit*) Augustine, who "moderately cleansed the sources again."[29] Thus Augustine is depicted as a proto-Luther figure who conducted a sort of dress rehearsal for the Reformation. Both men were "roused up" (*excito*) by God to oppose Origen's interpretation of Paul. Melanchthon admits, though, that even Augustine's age allowed the seeds of superstition and idolatry to remain. Melanchthon claims that Origen was the source of Pelagius's errors, but he does not define "Pelagianism." Below, I will show that Melanchthon's conception of this heresy differs essentially from its historical definition.

According to Melanchthon, Augustine's age was followed by the fourth age of monasticism and scholasticism. The Dominican and Franciscan movements tried to set up a simpler way of life, but achieved nothing except to shut men up "as if in jails of discipline." Then the scholastics, led by "Albert and those like him," "began to transform the doctrine of the Church into philosophy" (*transformare Ecclesiae doctrinam in philosophiam coeperunt*). This fourth age "poured not only mud but moreover poisons into the Gospel's sources."[30] Finally, in the fifth age (fourth after the apostolic era), God revealed the doctrine of remission of sins to Martin Luther, who restored the pure doctrine of the Church and inaugurated the last age of the world.[31] Grisar's assessment of Melanchthon's decadence theory does not seem entirely unjust, for in this sketch of Church history, Melanchthon manifests "his entire unacquaintance with the old Church and the truths for which she stood."[32]

Comparison of Melanchthon's Periodization Theory with the *Centuries of Magdeburg*

In a recent examination of the authority attributed to the early Church in the Lutheran *Centuries of Magdeburg* (1559–74), E. Norelli finds that the unique and guiding idea of the writers of this first major Lutheran history of the Church is that *doctrine* is the distinctive element of the Church. According to the writers, the Lutheran Church equals the true Church. "The Centuriators wrote their History in order to present to their readers all those who conformed to the pure (or the Lutheran) doctrine throughout the centuries."[33] According to this schema, the historical process has no positive function: the history of the Church could develop only in a negative direction.

This perspective, according to Norelli, is not the same as the humanist idea of recovering truths that were present in ancient times and then obscured and deformed. For unlike the Lutheran historians, the humanist perspective does not set the whole question in the framework of doctrine. For the Centuriators, what matters is to bring back to light the apostolic doctrine in its integrity, which is something Luther is alleged to have done. The way of living of the early Church and the structural and organizational aspects of the early Church are not of central importance.[34] The aim of the *Centuries of Magdeburg* is thus to show that the true Church survived in the Church of Luther. The heavenly doctrine is identical with Lutheran theology.[35] A perfect state of doctrine existed in apostolic times. Every subsequent age represents a degeneration in pure doctrine, which was restored by the prophet Martin Luther. After Luther's death, decadence reappeared and the period of the Centuriators seems similar to the second century.

It appears to me that the writers of the *Centuries* are describing Luther's status in terms strikingly reminiscent of Melanchthon's *Funeral Oration*. The Centuriators claimed:

> As a matter of fact, the time of the German prophet Martin Luther, thanks to whose voice and ministry the light of the Gospel was, so to say, brought back from the darkness of Egypt, corresponds roughly to the age of the Apostles. However, now that he has been carried away, (the word *sublato* means literally "elevated," allusion to an ascension almost like that of Christ), we have undoubtedly entered another age of the Gospel, in which numerous fanaticisms begin to multiply and little by little to reign.[36]

This perspective appears to be a replication of the dogmatically based decadence/restoration theory first formulated by Melanchthon. Norelli makes no such linkage, but there seems to be one.

Origen's Decadence

According to Melanchthon, Luther's Reformation consisted in a cleansing of the contamination of Church doctrine that had been introduced by Origen. Previous scholarship has not noticed that his whole accusation turns on Origen's *CRm*. Melanchthon says:

> Origen . . . turned the gospel into philosophy in the minds of many, pouring out his conviction that moderate mental training earns forgiveness of sins, and that this is the righteousness about which the verse "The righteous will live by his faith" speaks. This age almost completely lost the essential point of the Law and the Gospel and gave up the Apostolic teaching. For it did not keep the natural meaning in the words "letter," "spirit," "righteousness," "faith." And having lost the peculiar nature of words which are the signs of things, it is necessary to fabricate other things. Pelagius's error, which spread widely, arose from these seeds and since the Apostle had given the pure doctrine or the pellucid and most health-giving sources of the Church, Origen filled the sources with a great deal of mud.[37]

Just as Melanchthon had heralded Luther's principal achievement to be that of introducing a purer understanding of Pauline theology and a recovery of the Pauline distinction between law and gospel, so conversely his repudiation of Origen focuses explicitly on Origen's allegedly corrupt Pauline exegesis. Romans 1.17 is explicitly cited, and he mentions Origen's failure to apprehend "apostolic teaching" concerning the proper distinction between law and gospel, along with the other Pauline terms such as *letter, spirit, righteousness,* and *faith.* As he said of the age of monasticism and scholasticism, Melanchthon charges Origen with teaching that moderate mental training earns the forgiveness of sins. Origen has likewise filled the sources with mud. Melanchthon claims that "Pelagius's error" has its source in Origen, and yet he offers no substantiation of this or any definition of "Pelagius's error," though his text implies that Pelagius's error was related to the proper distinction between law and gospel. Certainly it would be historically inaccurate and contrary to Augustine to suggest that this was Pelagius's error.

Fraenkel's general summary of Melanchthon's assessment of the Church Fathers applies with heightened intensity when directed against Origen: "Melanchthon left his contemporaries in no doubt about his conviction that the Fathers had erred at what was for him the very center of the faith: the understanding of justification according to the Epistle to the Romans."[38] The significance of Melanchthon's periodization theory respecting the *Aetas Origenica* is assessed as follows:

Here for the first time a great teacher of the Church has not contributed to the distinction of truth and error but has seriously confused them in his own teaching. A new doctrinal situation is thus created. Even at the very earliest stage of his theological career Melanchthon had warned his readers to read Origen "with care," since much that he wrote is in conflict with Apostolic teaching. But his criticism of Origen in no way abated in later years.[39]

We should not be misled by Fraenkel's qualification "here for the first time." Except for the apostles, Melanchthon has not discussed any Christian theologians prior to Origen. Moreover, Origen was the first churchman to write a commentary on Romans. In other words, for Melanchthon there does not seem to have been a time after the age of the apostles when the Church's understanding of Paul was anything but corrupt. This claim complements and agrees with Luther's declaration to Melanchthon: "No one has expounded St. Paul better than you, Philipp [Melanchthon]. The commentaries of St. Jerome and Origen are the merest trash in comparison with your annotations [on Romans and Corinthians]. Be humble if you like, but at least let me be proud of you. Be content that you come so near to St. Paul himself."[40] For all their disdain for ancient patristic exegesis, Luther and Melanchthon seem to have held one another's understanding of Paul in extremely high esteem.

Melanchthon's Essay *Concerning the Errors of the Fathers* (1539)

Melanchthon's criticisms of the Fathers are systematized in his essay originally entitled: *De Autoritate Ecclesiae et Erroribus Patrum,* "Concerning the Authority of the Church and the Errors of the Fathers" (1539).[41] This essay was published under a slightly different title, *De Ecclesia et de Autoritate Verbi Dei,* "Regarding the Church and the Authority of the Word of God." Melanchthon appended an edited version of this essay (with important omissions) to his *Commentary on Romans* (1540), which makes the latter a very convenient source for analyzing Melanchthon's doctrine and his attitude toward the ancient Church.[42] The essay's original title, which was announced in the letter of dedication to Duke Albert,[43] accurately depicts what Melanchthon sets out to do in this essay. For in *De*

Erroribus Patrum, Melanchthon discusses the fallibility of the Church Fathers and attempts to define the nature and limits of their authority. R. Keen describes the significance of Melanchthon's essay in these terms: "Few texts of the Reformation period state so clearly the principles according to which the Fathers and the councils of the church may be considered authentic sources for Christian doctrine."[44]

The essay begins with a rather shocking story taken from Herodotus which sets the defiant tone for the rest of the work.[45] Melanchthon reports that Astyages, king of Medes, enraged with his prince Harpagus for not killing the infant Cyrus, fed the prince's own son to him. When Harpagus recognized the limbs of his own child on the platter, the king asked him whether he was satisfied with the feast. Prince Harpagus replied: "Whatever the king does is indeed pleasing to me." Melanchthon draws the lesson: "So the pope and his satellites have carried on tyranny for many centuries and demand that the people without any discrimination approve of all their decrees."[46] His exposure of the errors of the Fathers is intended, then, to show exactly why the Lutherans will not submit to the Roman Church, namely because of the grave theological errors and abuses that have abounded in the Church since the death of the apostles. R. Keen writes, "That Melanchthon saw Luther and himself as fulfilling the same theological function as the Fathers is incontestable."[47]

Fraenkel points out that Melanchthon's basic theological presupposition is that Christ was the fountainhead of a teaching or message, right from the time of his first conversation with Adam, when he promised a Redeemer (Gn 3.15). The validity of what the Church says today depends directly on its being a restatement of the gospel as originally given.[48] This appears to be the same "doctrinal" reading of Church history that is found in the *Centuries of Magdeburg,* according to which the sole value of the Church as an institution depends on its fidelity to this "gospel" (as interpreted by Melanchthon and Luther). Thus for Melanchthon, the aim of critical study of the Fathers is to find in their teaching the one unimpaired faith of the "Church."

In contrast, for Melanchthon's Catholic adversaries, Christ had founded a hierarchical institution and entrusted it with teaching authority. The value of the Church's teaching depends on its institutional legitimacy. Roman Catholics like Erasmus thought in terms of dogmatic progress according to which God willed that certain parts of the original revelation be understood with increasing comprehension over time. As Fraenkel points out, "Nothing could be further from Melanchthon's mind than such an idea." In other words Melanchthon does not seem to know the idea of development or progress in theology. Fraenkel writes:

> In his eyes the Scripture-Foundation contains the whole faith, and not merely the "seeds" of doctrine that the doctors of the Church have later to develop . . . when Melanchthon speaks of the building activity of the doctors of the Church as adding something to the Scripture-Foundation, he does not think in terms of historical growth of doctrine, but rather of presenting and applying what that Foundation itself contains, in the form of such Christian teaching and life as is in harmony with it, as opposed to "opinions" or "ceremonies" that do not fulfill this condition.[49]

A sample of Melanchthon's exposé of the ancient Fathers shows that they are all equally subjected to doctrinal criticisms that are distinctively "Lutheran." For example, Melanchthon attacks Tertullian for approving of offerings for the dead; Cyprian for defending canonical penalties for sinners and making forgiveness depend on them, and for "blustering vehemently about celibacy"; Irenaeus for calling the Mass a sacrifice; Basil for instituting monasticism; Gregory of Nazianzus for supporting the invocation of saints; Chrysostom for praising pilgrimages, prayers for the dead, and monasticism; Ambrose for foolish statements about the Mass and for supporting the Church's right to legislate a forty-day fast; Jerome for defending celibacy and abstinence from meat and wine; and Augustine for supporting religious vows, the doctrine of purgatory, and prayers for the dead. Melanchthon's criticism of Origen focuses on his exegesis of Paul.[50] Before turning to a deeper analysis of Melanchthon's critique of Origen, I want to mention briefly the reaction that Melanchthon's essay provoked among his Catholic and Protestant contemporaries.

Contemporary Reception of Melanchthon's Essay

The severe censures found in Melanchthon's essay *On the Errors of the Fathers* were offensive to many of his contemporaries, both Catholic and Protestant. Erasmus of Rotterdam had anticipated many of these criticisms in his *Epistola contra pseudevangelicos* (1530), in which he accused the Lutherans of fighting against "what the progeny of the church during so many centuries taught, venerated, accepted and still accept with great consensus as divine oracles." Erasmus asserted that the Lutherans lack a historical sense and fail to understand the irreversible character of historical development. To reduce the Church to its first origins was therefore no less absurd than to put an adult back into the cradle.[51]

Among the later Catholic apologists, Caspar Ulenbergius (1549–1617), rector of the University of Cologne, in his *History of the Reformers* said that Melanchthon's writing was so evil that surely Luther had poured his poison into the pen of Melanchthon.[52] Similarly, Fridericus Staphylus (1512–64) reproached the "laughable education" of Melanchthon, "who punishes all theologians with his rod" and "thinks that he himself is the one who excels all the doctors."[53] Along similar lines, in his fifth *Phillipic,* John Cochlaeus (1479–1552) said that authority to distinguish true doctrines from false is bestowed on the Church, not on any private person. "What else is Philip doing than making himself by his own will the supreme judge over the Pope, the Emperor, and every dignitary no matter how elevated, who has condemned Luther?"[54] Cochlaeus was stunned that Melanchthon, who wants to seem the most humane and gentle of men, and who is held by all to be more modest than Luther, would slander all the Catholic doctors of the past in this way.[55] The most extensive criticism from the Catholic side came from Jacobus Latomus,[56] who attacked Melanchthon's claim that Christ had abandoned his Church in fatal theological error on such fundamental doctrines as faith, works, merit, and justification. Latomus also reproached the Reformation Scripture principle, according to which nothing is to be received "which is not proven by the Scriptures expressly."[57] As a final sample, John Fabri, bishop of Vienna, wrote to Sadoleto:

> Would that Melanchthon had pursued his studies on the lines indicated by his teacher Reuchlin! Would that he had but remained content with the rhetoric and grammar of the ancients instead of allowing his youthful ardor to carry him away, to turn the true religion into a tragedy. But alas, . . . when barely eighteen years of age he began to teach the simple, and, by his soft speeches, he has disturbed the whole Church beyond measure. And even after so many

years he is still unable to see his error or to desist from the doctrines once imbibed and from furthering such lamentable disorders.[58]

Thus the contemporary Catholic assessment of Melanchthon's skills in patrology was extremely dim.

Yet extensive criticism of Melanchthon's essay also arose from his fellow Protestants, many of whom were equally scandalized by his censures. Melanchthon's first biographer, Camerarius, reports that Melanchthon's patrology created quite a stir among his Protestant cobelligerents. Fraenkel points out the significance of this:

> In passing we would also draw attention to the fact that Camerarius' account plays havoc with the conventional theory that Melanchthon differed from his fellow-reformers by his particular "traditionalism"; for according to Camerarius not only were Melanchthon's adversaries shocked by this Patrology and its censures, as indeed we know that they were; but also his friends and allies in the Reformation cause found fault with the Preceptor's Patrology. Yet what disappointed them was not its over-estimation of the Fathers, but rather the severity of the criticisms it contained.[59]

Melanchthon has found a modern defender in J. Van den Brink, who claims that the Catholic rejection of the Protestant principle of *sola scriptura* which is evidenced by the Catholic response to Melanchthon's essay is the important basis for the construction of a completely uncritical ecclesiology.[60] It is significant that Van den Brink, in spite of the title of his article, makes no mention whatsoever of the negative Protestant reactions to Melanchthon's essay. For Van den Brink, to challenge the validity of Melanchthon's assessments of the Church Fathers is equivalent to attacking the *vox coelestis* itself. Likewise, Wengert defends Melanchthon as a superior and more careful patrologist than Erasmus.[61] Neither of these modern scholars seems completely objective in his assessment.

Meijering's Assessment of Melanchthon as Patrologist

In his recent study of Melanchthon's use of the Fathers, Meijering concludes that the Fathers did not really influence Melanchthon, but rather

he used the Fathers as supporters of dogmatic views that he already held.
Melanchthon had a stockpile of quotations from the Fathers that he had
either found himself in their writings or to which contemporaries drew
his attention. He used these passages wherever it suited him, and he
merely ignored what did not suit him.

> Not seldom he—consciously or unconsciously—twisted his quo-
> tations in such a way that they suited him even more. When in the
> course of his life there was a development in his thought on various
> matters he obviously looked for more and other quotations from the
> Fathers which could support his views.[62]

Meijering has also observed that as Melanchthon's theological views
changed over time, correspondingly his assessment and criticisms of the
Fathers also evolved. What he attacked as "unscriptural speculation" at
one stage in his career, he later embraced and defended. At the same time
he always expressed explicit opposition to "speculation." Meijering interprets this to mean that Melanchthon did not change in his rejection of
speculation, but he did change his view on what actually is speculation.
The reason for this is that in his controversies with his Roman opponents
he could simply not afford to make any concessions in his theological
principle that Scripture is the exclusive norm of theology (*sola scriptura*).
Meijering assesses Melanchthon's evolution as seemingly arbitrary:

> But from our point of view it must be called arbitrary to reject specu-
> lation about the person of Christ at one stage and to engage in
> such speculation at a later stage and to accuse those who do not
> agree with these speculations of being speculative in an unscriptural
> way—or to reject the affirmation of free will as unscriptural specu-
> lation at one stage and to reject the negation of free will as unscrip-
> tural speculation at a later stage. Such an attitude can now receive
> approval from different corners at the same time.[63]

My intent in this brief digression on Melanchthon's assessment of the
Fathers is to show that his radical theories about the errors of the Fathers
provoked a strong negative reaction from both his Catholic and Protestant
contemporaries. It can hardly be considered unecumenical to criticize
Melanchthon's censures of the Fathers. Moreover, recent scholarship shows

that, in any case, Melanchthon's assessments constantly evolved in a seemingly arbitrary fashion. If it is true that Melanchthon "accepts the Fathers and simultaneously criticizes them on the basis of the biblical 'primum et verum' [what is first and true],"[64] it is equally true that Melanchthon's definition of what constitutes the "first and true" constantly evolved. Doctrines listed in his catalogue of "unscriptural speculation" in the *Loci* 1521 were asserted by Melanchthon himself in the *Loci* 1555.

Melanchthon's Understanding of the Pauline Gospel

In his essay on the errors of the Fathers, Melanchthon focuses his criticism of Origen on Origen's exegesis of Romans. In Melanchthon's view this is the book of the Bible that contains the core of the gospel message. For Melanchthon the hinge texts for a proper understanding of Romans are 3.24 and 3.28. Rom 3.24 says, "They are justified by his grace as a gift [*gratis*], through the redemption which is in Christ Jesus." Melanchthon defines justification in these terms:

> [Justification] means to be accounted just by God on account of Christ when we believe. And the word *iustitia* does not signify the righteousness of the Law, or universal obedience, or our qualities. . . . It signifies the imputation of *iustitia,* or acceptance. And *iustus* is in this way understood relationally as acceptance to eternal life.[65]

In Melanchthon's understanding, to be just does not properly mean to be intrinsically just through infused divine grace. In fact he denies that the grace that makes us righteous is in any sense a quality or a *habitus*. Melanchthon leaves no justifying grace actually inherent in the human being but merely sees in God a gracious willingness not to regard us as sinners. Melanchthon calls the remission of sins the "formal principle of justification."[66] Justification refers to God's acceptance of the unclean and unworthy through mercy on account of Christ.[67]

The Law/Gospel Distinction

Melanchthon refers often to his contemporary Catholic opponents in his commentary. He observes that they have not denied that justification embraces the remission of sins in baptism, but they have objected to the Lutheran reduction and delimitation of justification to the remission of sins. Catholics had advanced certain passages in which everlasting life is promised to those who keep the law and where love of God with the whole heart rather than faith alone is represented as the true source of righteousness and salvation. For example, Melanchthon's opponents quote Rom 2.6, which says, "God will pay back each one according to his works." They also appeal to Jesus' words in Mt 19.17, "If you wish to enter into life, keep the commandments"; and they rely on Jas 2.24, which declares explicitly that Abraham was justified by his works and not by faith alone. Melanchthon's answer to his critics appeals to the "law/gospel" distinction that became emblematic of Lutheran thought:

> The entire divine Scripture sets forth the Law in some places, in others the Gospel, so some of its statements are statements of the Law, and some of its statements are statements of the Gospel. Nevertheless, the Gospel is the light and interpretation of the Law. This is a phrase of the Law: "He will reward everyone according to his works." The meaning is: "He will give rewards to the righteous, and the unjust he will punish." Neither is there any doubt that the explanation of who the righteous are and what works please God must be added from the Gospel. For the pronouncements of the Law without the Gospel produce despair. Never can a conscience in the midst of true terrors declare that it has works worthy of the forgiveness of sins or eternal life. Thus when Christ says, "If you wish to enter into life, keep the commandments" [Mt 19.17], it is necessary to mitigate what is said by adding the interpretation of the Gospel. For no one satisfies the Law.[68]

In Melanchthon's view Christ's teaching in the gospels about the necessity to keep God's commands as a precondition for eternal life needs to be "mitigated." Melanchthon claims that Christ did not come in order to bring a law, nor is he a new Moses.[69] He did not come to make us uncertain about the worthiness of our works. On the contrary Christ is the mediator, propitiator, and sacrificial victim for sin who came to console our consciences.[70] As such, Christ does not threaten, he consoles. According to these categories, law refers to everything in the nature of a precept binding on the Christian, the infringement of which involves him in guilt. Law is that which speaks to us of our sins and of God's wrath. The gospel is the contrary of law, namely the soothing message of consolation whereby grace and forgiveness of sins are offered. And Jesus is conceived to be a proclaimer of the "gospel," not of law. The "righteous" are those who are labeled righteous by imputation.

Justification by Faith Is Not Synecdoche

It is essential to keep in mind the Lutheran law/gospel categories in order to understand Melanchthon's exact criticism of Origen, since he accuses Origen of failing to understand the distinction between them. Melanchthon's criticism makes repeated use of the term *synecdoche,* a rhetorical figure that also recurs in Melanchthon's polemics with his contemporary Roman Catholic adversaries. This term provides a very helpful key to understanding Melanchthon's doctrine of justification. It will be appropriate to begin this discussion by citing Quintilian's description of the meaning of synecdoche, since both Melanchthon and his Catholic opponents were immersed in ancient rhetoric. Quintilian defines the term as follows:

> *Synecdoche* has the power to give variety to our language by making us realize many things from one, the whole from a part, the *genus* from a *species,* things which follow from things which have preceded; or, on the other hand, the whole procedure may be reversed. It may, however, be more freely employed by poets than by orators. For while in prose it is perfectly correct to use *mucro,* the point, for the whole sword, the *tectum,* roof, for a whole house, we may not employ *puppis,* stern, to describe a ship, nor *abies,* fir, to describe planks; and again, though *ferrum,* the steel, may be used to indicate a sword, *quadrupes* cannot be used in the sense of horse. It is where numbers are concerned that *synecdoche* can be most freely employed in prose. For example, Livy frequently says, "The Roman won the day," when he means that the *Romans* were victorious; on the other hand, Cicero in a letter to Brutus says, "We have imposed on the people and are regarded as orators," when he is speaking of himself alone.[71]

In brief, synecdoche is an ambiguous figure of speech in that it can mean part for the whole or whole for the part. Melanchthon normally uses it to mean part for the whole. We shall see that this term is mentioned repeatedly in Melanchthon's explanations of his understanding of the Pauline gospel.

The Error Melanchthon Finds in His Catholic Critics

Melanchthon repeatedly condemns his Catholic opponents (of any epoch) for their synecdochical interpretation of the biblical texts that speak of justification by faith (Rom 3.28). Conversely, Melanchthon consistently interprets as synecdoche texts that place other conditions on salvation in addition to faith, such as love, fear, obedience, good works, and virtues. Let me first cite some passages in his *Commentary on Romans* where this figure of speech is discussed. Then I will come to his discussion of Origen's exegesis of Paul where the same accusations are made. My aim is to show that the alleged corruption that Melanchthon finds in Origen's Pauline exegesis is hardly unique to Origen. The same blemish stains the exegesis of all of Melanchthon's Catholic adversaries, including not only his contemporaries but also St. Thomas and even St. Augustine.

Commenting on Rom 4.9, "Abraham believed God and it was counted for him as righteousness," Melanchthon says, "It was counted for righteousness to Abraham that he believed. Therefore we also are justified by faith, not on account of our works or by the Law."[72] Then he refers to his Catholic adversaries:

> Some mock this argument in many ways. Some say it is a synecdoche. Believing, they say, is a work signifying obedience as such. Abraham believed, that is, he obeyed God (according to a synecdoche) because obedience must follow faith. Therefore, they say, obedience, as such, is signified by faith.[73]

The Catholic explanation of Rom 4.9 is synecdochical in the sense of part for the whole. It aims to establish harmony between Paul and the rest of Scripture, especially James, the Psalms, and the gospels. In this particular instance, Catholic interpreters argue that Abraham was justified by faith

(Paul) *and* by his obedience to God (James). In other words, the condition of faith demanded by Paul is synecdochical (*pars pro toto*) and can thus embrace the obedience demanded by James. Melanchthon opposes this tactic in these words:

> The meaning is "he believed," that is, he was sure he had a gracious God, although he felt that he was unworthy, and in this confidence he expected help and the promised Seed, etc. Thus he was justified by faith, that is, he was pleasing *gratis*, through mercy, not on account of his own worthiness. . . . Therefore we must not invent the synecdoche: Abraham was justified on account of his knowledge of the Word, *and* on account of his morals that agreed with his teaching and profession. Faith does not rest on the worthiness of one's own virtues, but only looks at mercy.[74] [Italics added]

Belief is defined here as certainty that one has attained grace from God, and this understanding of faith is projected onto the historical Abraham.[75] For Melanchthon, faith is a confident apprehension that looks away from one's worthiness and seizes hold of Christ's mercy. Justification, then, excludes the idea of an intrinsic renewal in virtue. Shortly after this, Melanchthon attacks "Sadoleto and others" who have interpreted justification by faith as synecdoche.[76] He paraphrases them as saying, "'We are justified by faith,' that is, by faith we acquire virtues; on account of that we please God. But these men are imagining. Paul excludes this merit and says that we are sinners in the sight of God, and so are accounted righteous by the remission of sins."[77] Once again, an essential incompatibility is posited between faith and interior virtue and the obedience of good works, even when these interior qualities are viewed as infused gifts of divine grace. Melanchthon reports that his Catholic adversaries mock his interpretation of this passage in this manner, saying:

> But other passages ascribe blessedness to works: [For example] "Blessed is the man who fears the Lord" [Ps 112.1]; "Blessed are the merciful" [Mt 5.7]; etc. Therefore, [they say,] we can argue similarly that we are justified on account of our works, as Paul argues on the basis of a Psalm that we are justified by the remission of sins.[78]

Once again, according to the Catholic viewpoint, the necessity of faith for justification is assumed, but it is not interpreted as being exclusive of the necessity of obedience, fear, mercy, love, and the other virtues. On the contrary, faith embraces these things as well, by synecdoche (part for the whole), and this is how the totality of Scripture is harmonized. In other words, for the Catholic interpreters it is not permissible to isolate texts in Paul and make them incompatible with other scriptural texts that place conditions upon human salvation in addition to the condition of faith that Paul demands. Melanchthon answers this "cavil" by denying the conclusion. He states:

> In all passages about works there must be included the passage: "Blessed are those whose sins are forgiven" [Ps 32.1], because works are not pleasing except in a believer or a righteous person. Therefore Paul cites this passage most correctly, since it speaks about the remission of sins which is gratuitous.[79]

Strangely, Melanchthon interprets the Bible passages that deal with works performed under grace as really referring to faith, again by means of synecdoche. When he says here, "Works are not pleasing except in a believer or righteous person," he means that Christians who keep the law are certainly just, but not by any means owing to their fulfillment of the law, for they were already just beforehand by virtue of the gospel. That is to say, they have been labeled "just" by mere imputation. They neither are nor ever will be *really* just, nor will they ever *really* keep the law. Instead, since God for the sake of Christ has forgiven them, they are gratuitously *labeled* just and gratuitously reckoned as those who satisfy the law.

Melanchthon reports that his opponents counter his explanatory tactic by asking him, "Why do you make a synecdoche in passages about works and not in passages about faith?" Melanchthon's answer is given in these words:

> Because works are not pleasing except in a believer or a righteous person. Therefore in passages about works we include faith. In passages about faith there is no synecdoche, because it receives remission of sins through mercy and does not rest on the worthiness of works. Instead, it would become uncertain and be driven out if it

depended on the worthiness of works or on merit. Therefore it is *gratis* in order that the promise may be firm.[80]

Once again, the discussion focuses on the concept of synecdoche. Essentially, Melanchthon's exegesis turns on the question of whether justice is merely imputed to faith or is infused and internal. He firmly denies that the grace that constitutes us just is in any sense an infused interior quality. If it were, it would not be *gratis*. Melanchthon understands the Christian's justice to be external to the human being. It consists merely in God's gracious disposition not to regard us as sinners. No change occurs in the human being with the acceptance of divine righteousness. For there can be no justifying grace actually inherent in us, for that would imply the unacceptable concept of merit and would render our justification uncertain.[81]

The Error Melanchthon Finds in Origen

We have attempted to describe the basic structures of Melanchthon's understanding of "the gospel." Now we turn to his critique of Origen. In his essay *De Erroribus Patrum,* Melanchthon finds Origen as well guilty of seeing a synecdoche in Paul's doctrine of justification by faith. In fact, his criticism of Origen is riveted on this point. Melanchthon strongly objects to Origen's interpretation of Rom 3.28, "We are justified by faith, not by works":

> [Origen] understands it according to a synecdoche: "we are just by faith, that is, by perfect faith which embraces all virtues." He explains this by saying that the same could be said about other virtues. We are saved through mercy, namely, perfect mercy that embraces the other virtues. This is saying nothing except that people have forgiveness of sins and are righteous on account of works and virtues. And since he pays no attention to what Paul is saying, what Paul calls faith, what the exclusive phrase means: "not of works," he adds confused and intricate explanations and is not consistent with himself.[82]

Notice that the reproach of seeing a synecdoche in Rom 3.28 is again made. Melanchthon accuses Origen of understanding justification as a reality that includes the interior possession of infused virtues. Melanchthon's critique of Origen, then, exactly corresponds with the criticism he had leveled against his contemporary Catholic adversaries, in particular "Sadoleto and others." Melanchthon was himself aware of this connection between Origen and other Catholic writers. In his *Commentary on Romans* he says:

> Now I must reprove the sophistry of Origen, of the monks, and of many others who think that "We are justified by faith" is spoken according to a figure of speech called synecdoche, that is, on account of professing [the faith] and other virtues or that we are righteous on account of general obedience. This is how they understand faith, and they think that professing is praised by Paul because, although the profession is made also by criminal persons, nevertheless, without it the other virtues, as is the case with Turks, would not please God. Thus this synecdoche transforms the Gospel into Law, transfers the glory of Christ to our virtues, destroys the comfort of consciences, and does away with the true doctrine about faith, that is, trust in mercy. . . . Therefore I shall refute this synecdoche, which militates against the entire disputation of Paul.[83]

The heart of this criticism is directed against all who understand justifying grace as actually inherent in the human being. Melanchthon explicitly links Origen, the monks, and his contemporary Catholic opponents as teachers who have transformed the gospel into law, the gospel into philosophy, who have transferred Christ's glory into our virtues. For Melanchthon, Christ cannot be glorified unless his righteousness remains something external and alien to the believer. Christ's justice is *imputed* to faith; it is not *infused* into the soul. Wengert has adequately summed up Melanchthon's forensic understanding of justification in these words:

> Justification is a matter of pronouncement, not a matter of an inner change of virtues, or, as he put it, it is to be understood not "proprie" but "relative." It is directly connected to the actions "in foro," in the court of law . . . It is a matter of divine acceptation.[84]

For Melanchthon, everything rests on the entirely outward covering over of the human being by Christ's merits received through faith, or rather, through confidence in one's justification. Christian perfection consists solely in one's readiness, whenever oppressed by a sense of guilt, to find consolation by wrapping oneself up in the righteousness of Christ. Because this purely mechanical conception of justification is absent from Origen's exegesis of Paul, and from Melanchthon's contemporary Catholic opponents, he accuses them all of being great enemies of the gospel.[85]

On the other hand, Melanchthon concedes that Origen, occasionally, "pours out some tolerable statement." He has no objection to the way Origen reported that the Churches received from the apostles the teaching that infants should be baptized. For Melanchthon this is a proper and correct way to quote the authority of the Church.[86] Origen is also a useful witness for posterity about a number of the articles of faith: the Trinity, the two natures in Christ, original sin, the use of the Lord's Supper, and certain others.[87] Several of Melanchthon's judgments here turn upside down the traditional Catholic assessment of Origen's doctrine. In particular, Origen's teaching on the Trinity and original sin were seen as inadequate. The fact that Melanchthon can explicitly endorse Origen's doctrine of original sin suggests once again that his dispute with Origen does not center on issues traditionally associated with Pelagianism. The dispute, rather, focuses on the doctrine that Melanchthon and Luther view as the central dogma of the Christian religion, that is, justification by faith alone. This is why Melanchthon immediately adds that whatever good statements Origen makes in his *CRm*, "soon afterward he ruins them."[88]

For Melanchthon, a "tolerable statement" of Origen on justification is his comment on Rom 4 where Origen says, "The root of righteousness is not from works. Rather, the fruit of works grows from the root of righteousness."[89] Melanchthon approves of this statement and interprets it as Origen's admission that works grow from the root of faith-righteousness, which Melanchthon also affirms. He also says that Origen seems closer to the meaning of Paul (*videtur iam propior esse Paulinae sententiae*) in his comment on Rom 3.27, where Origen "admits the exclusive [phrase]" (*admittit exclusivam*), that men are justified solely by faith. Origen had indeed said that the good thief and the sinful woman mentioned in Luke 7.48 were (exceptional) scriptural examples of persons justified "by faith alone."[90] For Melanchthon this is and indeed has to be the normative situation. The decisive issue for him is admitting the exclusive phrase *sola fide* and renouncing synecdoche. Melanchthon goes on to say, however, that Origen has ruined his own good interpretation immediately thereafter:

> But afterward, when he explains these things, he seems to want to say that man *in the beginning* receives remission of sins solely by faith, but afterward *is righteous* through other virtues, as he himself says afterward: "Faith is counted for righteousness to him who is converted, but afterward righteousness is counted for righteousness." Moreover, there is a strange variety and confusion in his explanation, although he grants that man in the beginning receives remission solely by faith. Nevertheless, if afterward he imagines that the converted are without sin, that they satisfy the Law and are righteous on account of other virtues, he disagrees with Paul and with the other divine Scriptures.[91] [Italics added]

For Melanchthon the *sola* in *iustificatio sola fide* must be interpreted in a sense that excludes all interior conditions of worthiness in the human being. For if justifying righteousness were intrinsic, it would necessarily mean, according to Melanchthon, that the converted are sinless, that they perfectly satisfy the law, and that they are just on account of their own virtues. Melanchthon repudiates the thought that faith is the beginning of justification but not the sum total of it.

The Error Melanchthon Finds in Thomas and Augustine

Melanchthon repudiates the heart of Origen's Pauline exegesis and explicitly links it with that of his Catholic adversaries Sadoleto, Cochlaeus, Eck, and Erasmus.[92] Similarly, Melanchthon attacked Thomas Aquinas's doctrine of justification, according to which justification takes place through faith that has been formed by the theological virtues, especially love. According to Aquinas, it is precisely by love that faith justifies.[93] Melanchthon's judgment upon this is that it would mean that the human being is in fact "justified through his own virtues."[94] This assessment once again exactly corresponds to Melanchthon's accusation of Origen's doctrine of justification cited above. Meijering noticed that Melanchthon's attitude toward Thomas is comparable with his view on Origen. Origen was his most important target in his criticism of the corruption of the truth, which began in the early Church. "Thomas Aquinas is his most important target when he attacks the almost total corruption of the truth in Scholastic theology. But in both he finds also statements which suit him and to which he freely draws attention."[95]

Melanchthon's repudiation of scholastic theology is well known. What is less well known is that Melanchthon published reproaches of St. Augustine's doctrine of justification as well, which turn on these exact same issues.[96] There is confusion about this because of the contradictory ways in which Melanchthon spoke of Augustine in public and in private. In his essay *On the Errors of the Fathers,* Melanchthon states that Augustine was a proto-Lutheran: "Such statements which one meets here and there in Augustine show sufficiently clearly that he thinks the same about grace and about faith as we teach."[97] Moreover, in the *Augsburg Confession* of 1530, Melanchthon had the courage to appeal publicly to Augustine as the most prominent and clearest witness to the Lutheran view of faith and justification.[98] But even as the *Confession* was being printed, Melanchthon wrote a confidential letter to Johann Brenz in which he endeavored to explain why he had ventured to claim Augustine as being in entire agreement with the Lutherans when, in fact, he knew that this was not the case. Melanchthon essentially admits to Brenz that he had recourse to dissimulation, because Augustine was held in such high esteem, and that he feared the calumnies of his opponents that would arise were he to admit publicly that the Lutherans dissent from Augustine.[99]

In his confidential letter to Brenz (May 1531), Melanchthon articulates his criticism of Augustine and accuses Brenz of adhering to a "fancy" of St. Augustine:

> You are still cleaving to Augustine's fancy, which he arrived at when he went so far as to deny that the justice of reason is reputed before God for justice; and he thinks rightly. From there he imagines that we are reputed just on account of this fulfilling of the law, which the Holy Spirit effects in us. Thus do you imagine that men are justified by faith, because by faith we receive the Holy Spirit, and afterward we can be just by the fulfilling of the law, which the Holy Spirit effects in us. This fancy locates justice in our fulfilling, in our cleanness or perfection, even though this renovation ought to follow faith. But turn your eyes entirely away from this renovation and from the

law to the promise and Christ, that we are just for the sake of Christ, that is, we are accepted before God and we find peace of conscience, and not on account of that renovation. For this very newness does not suffice. The reason we are just by faith alone is not because [faith] is a root, as you write, but because [faith] apprehends Christ on account of whom we are accepted, whatever that newness is, even though it ought necessarily to follow, but it does not pacify the conscience. Therefore, love, which is the fulfillment of the law, does not justify, but faith alone, not because it is a certain perfection in us, but only because it apprehends Christ; we are just, not for the sake of love, not for the sake of fulfillment of the law, not for the sake of our newness, even though they are gifts of the Holy Spirit, but for the sake of Christ, and we apprehend him only by faith. Augustine does not satisfy the thought of Paul, even if he makes a nearer approach than the Scholastics.[100]

Melanchthon correctly recognizes that Augustine places our righteousness in the fulfillment of the (new) law (of Christ). Its root is faith, but its branches are our works of justice done through divine grace. This is a conception that is very near to Origen's, as we have seen above. Melanchthon's response to such a view is spoken openly to Brenz: "Avert your eyes from such a regeneration of man and from the Law and look only to the promises and to Christ. . . . Augustine is not in agreement with the doctrine of Paul."[101] Melanchthon thus associates the new command of love and the renovation of human nature through divine grace with the "law."

A short time after this, in the 1532 edition of his *Commentary on Romans*, Melanchthon again rejects Augustine's theology of justification that implies the beginning of the human being's renewal. He writes:

The fancy of others is also to be repudiated, who think that the reason we are justified by faith is because faith is the beginning of renovation. They imagine that we are just on account of our newness and quality. And they virtually have their fill of this persuasion out of Augustine.[102]

The term *synecdoche* is not invoked in these passages, but the criticisms of Augustine are riveted on this concept. Melanchthon recognizes that in

Augustine's view justification by faith means that faith is the beginning of a renovation of human nature through divine grace. Melanchthon calls this a "fancy" that must be repudiated. Melanchthon is essentially admitting that Augustine's doctrine of justification differs fundamentally from the Lutheran understanding. Again the thought seems to trace directly to Luther. In fact, Luther had entirely approved Melanchthon's earlier confidential letter to Johann Brenz and even appended the following words to it:

> My dear Brenz, in order to grasp this matter more clearly, I am accustomed to imagine the following: In the stead of every "qualitas" in myself, whether termed faith or love, I simply set Jesus Christ and say: This is my righteousness, this is my *qualitas* and my *formalis iustitia* (as they call it), so that thus I free myself and extricate myself from observance of the law and of works, or rather, from the observance of that "objective" Christ, who is understood either as a teacher or a giver of gifts. But I want him to be my gift or doctrine through himself, so that I have all things in him. Thus he says: "I am the way, the truth and the life." He does not say: I give to you the way, the truth, the life, as if he who was placed outside of me worked such things in me. He himself must remain, live and speak in me, not through me or in me, so that we are the justice of God in him, not in love or in the subsequent gifts.[103]

Luther does not speak explicitly of Augustine in this passage, but it is obvious that the text represents his own repudiation of Augustine's doctrine of justification, since these are Luther's words appended to a letter of Melanchthon, the theme of which is Augustine's defective understanding of justification. For Luther there is no mutual mediation between God, or Christ, and the human being, as there is in St. Augustine. The Christian's spiritual life collapses into the ever new beginning of the sinner's justification, a constant return to the spiritual *creation ex nihilo*. Far from being amenable to human voluntary cooperation, Luther's doctrine contradicts Augustine's by rendering the person entirely passive and thus excluding any freedom of human will in matters of religion.

Grisar observes of those appended words to Brenz that Luther "could not have expressed more strongly the purely mechanical conception of justification, nor have rejected more emphatically every human work, even man's co-operation under grace." Trueman rightly cites this passage as "crucial evidence" that shows that Luther and Melanchthon were fundamentally unified in their forensic understanding of justification. As Luther's appended words indicate, there is no hint of a disagreement about anything of substance between them, since Luther expresses his satisfaction with the approach of Melanchthon. Both men concur in opposing Brenz's [sc. Augustine's] notion that justification is primarily transformation by the Holy Spirit. Trueman claims, consequently, that any attempt to drive a wedge between Melanchthon and Luther on justification, as is done by Karl Holl, as well as by the Finnish school, is historically flawed; moreover, the many modern attempts to isolate statements made by the early Luther and set them in opposition to his own confessional trajectory is methodologically flawed, in light of the communal nature of Luther's development; it is also ecumenically irrelevant, since true ecumenism places at the center confessional documents of the churches involved, not isolated texts by individuals.[104]

McGrath has recently confirmed that Melanchthon's view of justification, at least, which reduces the concept to mere imputation, mere acceptance, without any change in the human being, differs radically from Augustine's conception.

> The simple fact remains that Melanchthon appears quite unaware of the fact that his interpretation of the Pauline concept of imputed righteousness, as expressed in his doctrine of forensic justification, is itself an innovation, in that it is not merely absent from the writings of the patristic era (*including* those of Augustine), but is actually excluded by those writings (*especially* those of Augustine) [emphasis McGrath's]. By his own criterion, Melanchthon has made the Lutheran Church guilty of schism.[105]

McGrath is certainly right that the Lutheran conception of justification is estranged from that of St. Augustine. But ironically, McGrath does not seem aware that Melanchthon knew that his interpretation of justification was an innovation. It is just that he was not forthcoming in admitting this publicly. It is worthwhile to recall that in chapter 3 of this book we saw that, according to Bammel, Augustine's conception of faith as the root of justice and the foundation and beginning of justification was a view that he expressed with language borrowed directly from the Latin Origen.[106] And this is exactly the view that Melanchthon and Luther condemn as a betrayal of Paul's mind.[107]

Conclusion

Luther's religious conversion spawned a conviction in his mind that a doctrinal defection from the "gospel" occurred immediately after the age of the apostles. He consequently assesses the commentaries of the early Fathers as being the "merest trash," and he repeatedly accuses Origen and Jerome of a defective doctrine of justification. Luther is clearly the principal source for Melanchthon's similar assessments of the Fathers and of his specific charge against Origen. It is noteworthy that Melanchthon's criticism of Origen turns on Origen's understanding of the nature of justification as an intrinsic renewal in virtue and of faith as the beginning of this process. The criticism is not focused on Origen's practice of allegorical exegesis, his doctrine of grace, or of original sin. In fact, Melanchthon praises the latter doctrine in Origen's *CRm*. A significant and original result of this examination is that Melanchthon accuses his Catholic opponents, as well as St. Thomas and St. Augustine, in the very terms in which he accuses Origen, namely for their understanding of justification by faith as synecdoche, which implies the beginning of an interior renewal in virtue. This is a view that Melanchthon cannot accept.

Evidence produced in this chapter does not support the theories of certain members of the "Lortzian" school of Catholic Luther-interpretation according to whom Luther's "fundamental and essential battle" was solely with what these scholars allege to be an "Ockhamist perversion" of the Catholic doctrine of justification;[108] or an allegedly rampant Pelagianism, or semi-Pelagianism, that had infected the pre-Reformation Church, both head and members.[109] On the contrary, Luther and Melanchthon would hardly have attacked the Catholic exegetical tradition including Augustine in the way they did, or have endeavored to detach their wavering disciples from *Augustine's* doctrine of justification, if their "fundamental and essential battle" was solely directed against Ockham and Biel.[110] The idea toward which the evidence clearly points is that the German Reformers vindicated their "Reformation," that is, schism from the Catholic Church, by an appeal to the allegedly faulty understanding of justification that is found equally in St. Augustine and Origen.

Recently, in a striking and unexpected way, a leading Protestant theologian has confirmed the chief results of my investigation into Luther and Melanchthon. R. Zachman states quite bluntly that the "Reformation," far from being a recovery of Augustine's theology, represents the first major challenge to an Augustinian reading of Paul in the Latin West.[111] The "Evangelicals" broke sharply from the Augustinian reading of Paul as a whole, even that reading that stresses the grace and mercy of God over and above any and all human striving. Zachman claims that "the Augustinian reading of Paul failed to meet the spiritual needs of many readers of Paul, beginning with but not limited to Martin Luther."[112] Zachman correctly recognizes that Luther and his followers had become convinced that the Church of Rome was preaching a false gospel, precisely because they (the Reformers) thought that the teaching that the gift of the Holy Spirit gave us the ability to fulfill the law of love had replaced Paul's teaching of justification by faith with justification by works.[113] According to Zachman, Catholic theologians, for their part, rightly saw that Luther was departing from the Augustinian reading of Paul. The Roman theologians "rightly detected that the Evangelicals were replacing the Augustinian narrative that had framed the interpretation of Paul for over a thousand years with a new narrative that first emerged from Luther's experience of a terrified conscience." Oddly enough, Zachman claims that such an admission does not imperil the validity of Luther's interpretation of Paul, since Luther's divergent reading of Paul was allegedly still based on Pauline texts. It does speak volumes, however, about Luther's ego and the role he assigned himself in salvation history, as well as about Luther and Melanchthon's effrontery in privately anathematizing Augustine's interpretation of Paul and then claiming publicly that their teaching was the same as Augustine's.

Chapter 7

Post-Reformation Controversies over Origen's Exegesis of Romans

Late Sixteenth-Century Protestants

Luther and Melanchthon appear to have found a more receptive audience for their repudiation of Origen's doctrine of justification among the Calvinists than among their immediate successors in the Lutheran Church. Theodore Beza (1519–1605), Calvin's successor at Geneva, wrote, "I condemn none of the ancients more bitterly than one Origen, whom I am so distant from that, although I ought with Erasmus to place him ahead of all the ancients, on the contrary, I freely confess that no writer seems to me to be more defiled."[1] We recall that in his *Method of True Theology*, it was not as a theologian, but as an exegete of the text of Romans, that Erasmus had placed Origen "ahead of all the ancients." This suggests that Beza's animosity is directed against Origen's exegesis of Romans. As for Calvin himself, it appears that his antipathy for Origen was as deep as it was dilettantish. Calvin attempted to perpetuate the legacy of Luther's work *De Servo Arbitrio* by defending the doctrines of total human depravity, the irresistibility of grace, and double predestination. Calvin's unconditional allegiance to Luther's doctrines is displayed most clearly in his dispute with the Roman Catholic theologian Albert Pighius.[2] In the footsteps of Erasmus's *Hyperaspistes,* Pighius had referred to a whole series of early Church Fathers, including Origen, as ancient witnesses to the Church's belief in human cooperation in the process of salvation. Calvin replied with the self-defeating assertion that "the authority of Origen's opinions should be left to Jerome to decide."[3] Calvin was apparently unaware that St. Jerome, even at the height of his anti-Origenist period, had endorsed and recommended Origen's defense of the free choice of the will. Indeed, Jerome attributed to Origen very great authority on this point.[4] Although Calvin does not interact with Origen in his own *Commentary on Romans,* it appears that on the question of justification by faith, Calvin's doctrine of imputation places him in profound agreement with Luther and Melanchthon as to the allegedly anti-Christian orientation of Origen's understanding of Paul.

Interestingly, however, the fate of Origen within Lutheranism in its second generation was less condemnatory. The Lutheran Church historian Flacius Illyricus depicted Origen as a representative of the Lutheran doctrine of justification by faith alone apart from works.[5] Likewise, Martin Chemnitz cited Origen's *CRm* favorably in his attack on the Council of Trent. In one passage he quotes the text from *CRm* 3.9 to substantiate Paul's claim to boast not in his own purity but in the cross alone.[6]

If we turn to other Protestant traditions, Thomas Cranmer, the archbishop of Canterbury from 1533 to 1556 and Marian martyr, cited Origen frequently in his *Notes on Justification* (1553?). Cranmer invoked Origen's authority in defense of justification by faith alone, referring twice to Origen's *CRm.*[7] In a manner similar to Cranmer, the Swiss Reformer Heinrich Bullinger (1504–75), disciple and successor of Ulrich Zwingli, cited from Origen's *CRm* 3.9 in which Origen affirmed justification by faith alone and offered the example of the thief on the cross as scriptural proof.[8] Bullinger's works were translated into English and exerted significant influence among English Protestants of the Elizabethan era.[9]

John Heigham and Richard Montagu

Origen's Pauline exegesis was engaged in an interesting exchange between the Jesuit-influenced Catholic lay apologist John Heigham (1568–1631?) and

the Church of England bishop Richard Montagu (1577–1641). The English-
man Heigham was a convert from Protestantism.[10] His best-known work
was the anonymous *The Gagge of the Reformed Gospel* (1623).[11] Heigham's
apologetics, influenced by the Jesuits, criticized the English Church and
associated it with many of the doctrines of Calvinism. The table of con-
tents of the second edition of Heigham's work contains fifty-three points
of doctrine on which he accuses the Church of England of being in error
and of breaking the Rule of Faith. Each is refuted principally from texts of
Scripture. These are uniformly introduced by the words "Contrary to the
express words of their own Bible . . ." Heigham also appeals to the ancient
Fathers as witnesses to the Catholic Rule of Faith. He specifically cites
Origen's *CRm* to support the Catholic doctrine that good works are absolutely necessary to salvation and that faith alone is not sufficient. The
precise charge leveled against the Protestants by Heigham is that they say
"that faith alone justifies; and that good works are not absolutely necessary
to salvation."[12] After citing a string of scriptures to refute this teaching,
Heigham then appeals to the Fathers who affirmed the absolute necessity
of good works. His most important witness is Augustine's *On Faith and
Works*. However, he also mentions "Origen on Romans 5." From Montagu's response, it is clear that Heigham intends Origen's comment on
Rom 4.23–25:

> For it is not possible that righteousness can be reckoned to a person
> who has any unrighteousness dwelling in him, even if he believes
> in him who raised the Lord Jesus from the dead. For unrighteous-
> ness cannot have anything in common with righteousness; nor can
> light with darkness, nor life with death. So also then to those who
> believe in Christ but do not lay aside the old man with his unright-
> eous deeds, faith cannot be reckoned as righteousness.[13]

To Heigham, Origen's text was clear evidence that the "Rule of Faith," as
witnessed to by Origen, insisted on these two points: (1) the absolute
necessity of good works for salvation; and (2) the denial that faith alone
is sufficient, since Origen says that righteousness cannot be reckoned to
one who has any unrighteousness dwelling within him. Heigham believed
the Protestants denied both of these theses by their slogan "justification
by faith alone."

A point-by-point response to Heigham's work was written in 1624 by Richard Montagu, the future bishop of Chichester and Norwich. Montagu was an Anglican historian, theologian, scholar, and eventually bishop who possessed great knowledge of classical and patristic antiquity.[14] In 1610–13 he had edited the works of St. Gregory of Nazianzus and St. John Chrysostom.[15] He believed that the Anglican positions in which he had been raised were derived from ancient sources.

Montagu was strongly opposed to the distinctive doctrines of credal Calvinism, especially as they had been formulated at the Synod of Dort in 1618. His abhorrence of Calvinism is revealed in a manuscript comment where he speaks of the "execrable impiety" of "Calvin's opinion concerning the antecedent immutable decree of predestination."[16] When Heigham attributed the doctrines of Calvinism to the Church of England, Montagu replied by dismissing Calvinism as "Puritanism." This provoked the fury of the Anglican Calvinists, who produced at least five books directed against Montagu in the course of the 1626 Parliament.[17] Montagu was labeled an Arminian, after James Arminius (1560–1609), the Dutch Reformed theologian who had rejected Calvin's doctrine of predestination. Montagu's Calvinist foes depicted Arminianism as a menacing Trojan horse that threatened to overthrow the Church of England.[18] These attacks led Montagu to compose a self-defense, *Appello Caesarem. A just appeale from two unjust informers* (1625), in which Montagu tried to vindicate himself against the charges of his fellow Protestants.

Montagu was appointed bishop of Chichester in 1628 and then transferred to the bishopric of Norwich in 1638.[19] His entire career was characterized by conflict with the Puritans inside the Church of England. Montagu's appointment to a bishopric was the most flagrant example of the promotion of Arminians to clerical leadership. This led to intense political frustration on the side of the Calvinists.[20] The Calvinists succeeded in having *Appello Caesarem* suppressed by royal proclamation in 1629.[21]

Montagu's answer to Heigham's *Gagge*, entitled *A New Gagg for an Old Goose*, had a dual purpose: to counter local missionary activity in Montagu's parish of Stanford Rivers in Essex by Catholic friars who were using Heigham's latest Catholic apologetic to gain converts;[22] and to give Montagu an occasion for attacking predestinarian Calvinism on the ground that this was no part of the teaching enshrined in the Thirty-nine Articles.[23]

Tyacke has examined the background circumstances of Montagu's reply to Heigham and believes that Montagu was a sort of "stalking horse for a court-based faction of leading clergy, who sought not merely to counteract the effects of Dort but fundamentally to alter the doctrinal stance of the English Church concerning predestination and much else."[24] Montagu wanted to dissociate the Church of England from the doctrines of the Calvinists.[25] Tyacke describes Montagu's *New Gagg* as a work "without precedent" in that previous English polemicists against Roman Catholicism had assumed a Calvinist consensus among members of the Church of England. This consensus was destroyed by Montagu's work and represented a test case for the Arminian reaction.[26]

Montagu's Use of Origen

In the context of refuting Heigham's "lying imputation" that the Church of England rejects the necessity of good works for salvation, Montagu appeals to Origen. Heigham had cited Jas 2.14 to show that faith without works cannot save. In response to this, Montagu denies that the faith in question was "real." It was a faith *boasted of* but not *had*, "only supposed, presumed, and in opinion."[27] He writes:

> For the Faith of the Protestants (general or special, I dispute not now) is a Faith wrought and infused by God, through the Grace of Christ: Living: lively: active: fruitful: declaring the root by the good fruit: they never separate them in their Doctrine. And your men doe blame them, because they never separate, the Spring and watercourse, Faith and good works, but they profess it must and doth work by Love. And therefore it is a lying imputation, that good works are not necessary to Salvation.[28]

While Montagu seems to have accepted the doctrine of justification by faith alone as an authentic position of the Anglican Church, he plainly repudiates Heigham's charge that the Church of England denies that good works are absolutely necessary for salvation. He calls this a "lying imputation" and affirms the necessity of good works *for salvation*. This position plainly contradicts the standpoint of Luther and Melanchthon, who refused to accept the formulation that good works are necessary "for salvation," claiming that it implied something merited.[29]

The discussion of Origen's *CRm* occurs precisely in this context. Montagu claims that Origen represents the Anglican doctrine exactly and on both points: that is, that justification is by faith alone, *and* that good works are absolutely necessary for salvation. First he appeals to the *CRm* 3.9 where Origen states that there were some, such as the thief on the cross, who were justified by faith alone, without any works at all.[30] Montagu is aware, however, that Origen had cited this example as an exceptional case and that his Catholic opponents will therefore claim that such a special and extraordinary case may not be cited for common use. Montagu replies to this objection as follows:

> Therefore in Rom. 3 he [Origen] speaks plainly, in general, not with that limitation of some. *Justification of Faith alone suffices: albeit a man hath not done any works.*[31] As direct a Protestant as ever wrote, Calvin, or Chemnitz could say no more.[32]

Thus Origen is represented as teaching that justification by faith alone is adequate for salvation and has spoken as well as Calvin and Chemnitz on the subject. Moroever, the Anglican Church follows Origen's doctrine.

As for Heigham's appeal to Origen's words in *CRm* 4.7 to the effect that faith cannot be reputed unto justice to those who believe in Christ but do not put off the old man with his deeds, Montagu retorts:

> Do Protestants say it can be? We distinguish historical, and justifying Faith. You do difference Faith in Degree, if in nothing else. Belief, may be before, without Justification; a general assent, without application, or adhesion. Origen is in this also, a perfect Protestant. It is their Doctrine, *That there is a Faith which justifies not.* It is Origen's Doctrine absolutely. Origen saith; *Which believes Christ:* He does not say, *Which believes in Christ.* Thus *per omnia*, in all points he sides with the Protestants in their Faith, concerning Faith as you propose it.[33]

Montagu thus receives Origen as the "perfect Protestant" in his distinction between different kinds of faith. Montagu distinguishes Origen's statements about believing Christ, and believing in Christ. Only the latter kind of faith justifies. The former is merely "historical faith." For Montagu, the Protestant understanding is "Origen's doctrine absolutely."

On both sides of the Catholic/Protestant divide, one would have to say that the exploitation of Origen is naive in that it assumes that Origen can be made to fit neatly into the polemical categories of the early seventeenth century. In any case such debates confirm the thesis that Origen's legacy in the West as an interpreter of Paul remained substantial even after the Reformation.

Cornelius Jansen

One final example of Origen's legacy in the West as an exegete of Romans will be explored which is nearly contemporaneous with the Heigham-Montagu exchange. Cornelius Jansen (1585–1638) was bishop of Ypres and the source of Jansenism, a doctrine interpreted to be an attempt to introduce Calvinism into the Catholic Church. Jansen's posthumously published work *Augustinus* was censured in general terms by the Holy Office on 1 August 1641 and placed on the Index. The following year Pope Urban VIII (1623–44) renewed the condemnation and interdiction in his bull *In Eminenti*. Scholars have only recently noticed that Jansen's work contains an indictment of Origen that specifically charges his *CRm* with being the main fountainhead of Pelagianism.[34] Jansen's work sets out to defend the authority of Augustine against Jesuit theologians like Vázquez, Molina, Lessius, and Suarez, who, allegedly, do not want Augustine to be the sole authority in faith and morals.[35] Jansen links these Jesuits with Pelagianism. He says that Suarez "hallucinates gravely" about Pelagianism on the one hand, and smells of semi-Pelagianism himself.[36] Jansen accuses Molina of turning the chief principles of Augustine's doctrine against the Pelagians upside down.[37] Vázquez, says Jansen, rejects Augustine's teaching on human nature and the propagation of original sin and behaves like a Pelagian.[38] Finally, on the subject of grace, Jansen asserts that Lessius hallucinates more enormously than the semi-Pelagians ever did.[39] Thus for Jansen, the accusation of Pelagianism or semi-Pelagianism[40] is one that is ready at hand and applies equally to these reputed Jesuit theologians.

Election *Post Praevisa Merita*

Jansen doles out accusations of "Pelagianism" quite liberally, both to the
Jesuits and to Origen. Because his accusations are focused on the interpretation of Rom 9 and the doctrine of election *post praevisa merita*, we
should first introduce the Jesuit theories on predestination that received
the brunt of Jansen's criticism. For this background material I have largely
followed the discussion of F. Clark. The aim of Clark's study was to defend
Gabriel Biel against the accusation made by H. Oberman to the effect that
Biel's doctrine was "essentially Pelagian."[41] Clark observes that Oberman
never defines what he means by "Pelagian." He seems to assume that any
doctrine of election that includes God's foreknowledge of human merits
in the scheme of predestination must be Pelagian, when in fact Biel's doctrine was not as superficial as Oberman thinks. Clark indicates that the
Church has never condemned Biel's theory or the Molinist theory of election that derives from it.

Clark points out that the problem of harmonizing the doctrine of predestination with belief in God's equity and in humanity's freedom and
moral responsibility has always been and remains a *crux theologorum*.[42]
The Church has not explicitly defined this mystery, and "within the fron-
tiers of orthodoxy much latitude is here allowable."[43] What is required is
that theologians hold that God is the first author and supreme master
of the whole economy of salvation; that it is his eternal predilection for
each and for all who are saved that brings them securely and infallibly to
their final end.

For Catholic orthodoxy, there is no predestination to damnation except
post praevisa demerita. This means that the first reason for divine reprobation is the freely chosen evil of the sinner himself. But the converse is not
true: those who are predestined to life do not owe the primacy in salvation
to themselves but to God's love. Within these structures, various theological theories have been formed. Clark indicates that for Augustine, God
exercises the primacy in salvation and infallibly achieves his purpose of
predestination by means of an intrinsic influence or predestining force by
which he steers the sinner to conversion and the just to final perseverance,
while not depriving them of personal free will in the process. Clark points
out that Catholic theologians have never been obligated to postulate the
existence of this special intrinsic force as the only means of ensuring that

one reaches his predestined end. The Molinists of the post-Tridentine era, for example, appealed to the hypothesis of middle knowledge according to which the execution of God's predestinating decrees is not achieved *ab intrinseco*, by some special energy or supernatural influx inserted into the human being's free will, but *ab extrinseco*, that is, by the transcendent factor of God's antecedently omniscient and omnipotent control of the whole existential order in which human responsibility operates. Clark writes:

> Accordingly thoroughgoing Molinists were able to affirm boldly that predestination was *post praevisa merita* (i.e. *merita futurabilia*), and yet to remain staunchly orthodox in holding that the absolute primacy in the salvation of the elect belonged to God's eternal predilection, which had chosen to actuate, out of numberless alternatives, this particular existential order in which their merits could be crowned.[44]

The roots of this completely orthodox position trace to the medieval period, to Gabriel Biel, who advocated a theory of predestination *post praevisa merita*, which Clark claims is more accurately described as predestination, *cum praevisis meritis*. Clark summarizes the debt that the Molinist school owes to Biel as follows:

> For Biel, as for Molina, the absolute and infallible control by God of predestination and salvation comes not from any steering force or transient influx inserted into the created system, but from his antecedent and transcendent mastery of the whole existential order of creation. Like all Catholic theologians, Biel held firmly to the need of the ever-present divine causality (*auxilium generale*) to maintain in being and in act all created causality; and likewise he affirmed strongly as revealed truth the necessity of man's possessing the intrinsic *habitus* of sanctifying grace for the attaining of salvation. But he saw neither of these two factors as a predetermining cause or means for the infallible execution of predestination.[45]

In short, predestination *post praevisa merita*, while certainly not an Augustinian concept, at least not the late Augustine, is nevertheless neither Pelagian nor heretical. Thus, Clark argues, Oberman is in error in accusing

Biel on this point, as a foil for his subsequent depiction of Martin Luther, who is viewed, consequently, as someone who is rightly reacting to a decadent form of theology. Clark contends, on the contrary, that Biel's medieval theory cast a shadow in the post-Tridentine Molinist school, and it is a view that has never been censured by the Church.

This background information has been given in order to inform Jansen's criticisms of the theology of both Origen and the Jesuits. For Jansen's accusations against both Origen and the Jesuits focus on the interpretation of Rom 9 and the theme of predestination, especially the matter of the hardening of Pharaoh's heart.[46] For Origen, there was no question of predestination by God here, only of his foreknowledge. Jansen was aware of Pelagius's dependence on Origen for his interpretation of this passage and also that the Greeks generally disliked predestination. Jansen interprets the view that understands predestination as foreknowledge to be a Pelagian error and accuses Origen of being the origin of Pelagianism.[47] He writes:

> Among all those who preceded Pelagius I found no abler architect of the whole Pelagian heresy than Origen, who was of much use to the ancient interpreters of the holy Scriptures and defenders of the faith, not because of his productive genius, but because his unbridled freedom of reasoning severely damaged the purity of the doctrine of the Church.[48]

Jansen focuses on Origen's work *Peri Archon* (On First Principles) as a "cesspit of errors." He goes on to say that it is not at all easy to find a single dogma that Pelagius and Julian hurled at the Church and no single interpretation of Scripture which supports the Pelagian heresy that Origen has not given its initial shape.[49] Jansen realizes that this seems incredible to many people, evidently referring to his Jesuit adversaries. He focuses the critique of Origen on five issues: (1) The free will and its natural possibility; (2) the law of nature and that of Moses; (3) on grace and merit; (4) on predestination; and (5) on the corruption of Scripture.[50]

Supported by statements from *Peri Archon* and Origen's *CRm,* Jansen argues that Origen's admiration of the philosophical concept of freedom caused him to determine that grace is given to human acts that precede. Only those who are worthy receive the sanctifying grace of the Spirit. The source of Origen's error which Pelagius followed is pagan philosophy. Origen's second error, that free will is the source of virtue, also stems from pagan philosophy, as do his errors on original sin and pure nature.[51] After a long quotation from *CRm* 7.8, Jansen vehemently attacks Origen's doctrine of predestination and complains that Origen "makes election depend 'ex praevisis hominum meritis' and vocation proceed 'secundum propositum hominis non Dei.'" Huet replied that the first proposition is still open in the Catholic Church, and that the second was maintained by Chrysostom and Theodoret.[52]

Parmentier observes that Jansen's principal source for his understanding of Pelagius is Augustine. "He had his own dossier of quotations, mostly from Augustine, but hardly from other church fathers—certainly not of Greek fathers."[53] The fact that Jansen critiqued Origen as the source of Pelagianism in terms that seem to replicate his criticism of the Jesuit theologians Vázquez, Molina, Lessius, and Suarez suggests that his definition of Pelagianism is broader than that of the Catholic Church. He defines as Pelagian the interpretation of Rom 9 that views predestination as divine foreknowledge of merits. This definition goes beyond the doctrines of Pelagius condemned in 417–18, and the fact that the Church censured Jansen's book suggests that the Church's understanding of what constitutes Pelagianism is not as broad as Jansen's.

Conclusion

Origen's legacy as an interpreter of Paul continued in the post-Reformation controversies of the late sixteenth and early seventeenth centuries. This demonstrates that his *CRm* continued to be studied and engaged, even if not always in a friendly manner. Whereas Calvinists like Beza perpetuated the decadence theory of Luther and Melanchthon as it concerned Origen's interpretation of Paul, second- and third-generation Lutherans and Anglicans sought to retrieve the patristic tradition to some extent, including Origen's doctrine of justification. Post-Tridentine Catholic apologetics, as exemplified by the Jesuit-influenced Heigham, made capital use of the Church Fathers in their efforts to defend the faith of the Church. In this context, Origen's *CRm* was appealed to for the defense of the Catholic understanding of justification by faith. Likewise, anti-Calvinist Anglicans

like Bishop Montagu treated the first five hundred years of Church history as sacrosanct. In this atmosphere, Origen was embraced as an interpreter of Paul, even if he was somewhat naively labeled "the perfect
Protestant." With Jansen, we encounter an extreme Augustinianism that
has little room for Greek theology in general, and Origen in particular.
Yet the mere fact that Origen became the focal point of Jansen's theory
about the sources of Pelagianism confirms the view that Origen's legacy
in this period continued to be substantive.

Conclusion: Origen and Modern Exegesis

J. Lienhard recently observed, "The study that traces the full extent of Origen's influence on the church's exegetical tradition is still to be written."[1] This book does not pretend to have filled this lacuna in scholarship, which in any case is beyond the capacities of a single scholar or a single study. Yet it is my hope that this study will at least make a small contribution. I have examined the content of one particular work of Origen and then explored the legacy of that work in a limited number of subsequent Christian theologians.

Rivière had observed that Origen's discussions of justification cleared a path for later theologians who would attempt to demonstrate harmony between the ideas of Paul and James on justification by faith and post-baptismal good works. By showing the organic connection of faith and good works as the two inseparable and complementary conditions of salvation, Origen helped make it possible for subsequent theologians to reconcile the diverse statements of Scripture. This book has essentially confirmed Rivière's thesis. My second main result has been to establish Origen's immense influence on the Catholic exegetical tradition. For the period investigated in this study, it does not seem entirely misleading to describe Catholic exegesis of Romans as "footnotes to Origen." This receptivity to Origen is found among both high Augustinians such as William of St. Thierry, and scholars like Erasmus, who attempted to assimilate the Greek and Latin exegetical tradition and give less emphasis to the peculiarly Augustinian categories for interpreting Paul.

Before concluding this investigation, I wish to attempt to move the discussion into the modern period. In her important monograph on Origen's interpretation of Romans, T. Heither endeavors to introduce the modern guild of Scripture scholars to Origen's understanding of Paul. Yet in her fine study of Origen's commentary, which builds on the scholarship of

F. Cocchini, Heither claims that Origen's interpretation of Paul was without subsequent influence in the Church.[2] The context suggests that Heither meant that Origen's central interpretation of Paul's message was ignored by later interpreters. My investigation has shown that this judgment stands in need of correction, especially if we consider the Catholic (and Protestant) exegetical tradition throughout the centuries. However, if we limit the discussion to modern Scripture scholarship, which is really the focus of Heither's comment in any case, Heither's claim seems to be true: modern scholars who engage Paul (both Catholic and Protestant) have shown no interest whatsoever in Origen's interpretation. The programmatic statement for the American guild was made in 1967 by R. E. Brown, who judged as a failure the attempts by Henri Cardinal de Lubac and Jean Cardinal Daniélou to give great value to patristic exegesis *as exegesis* and declared confidently: "I think we must recognize that the exegetical method of the Fathers is irrelevant to the study of the Bible today."[3] Brown's statement is eerily reminiscent of Luther. Once Brown had "silenced the Pharisees" in this way, no guild member, Catholic or Protestant, dared ask any more questions—for the next forty years. Brown's standpoint prevailed in the *Jerome Biblical Commentary*—a paradoxical title—since he was the editor of that work, and it became the default position of post–Vatican II Catholic New Testament studies.

However, hopeful signs are now emerging. Recently, a leading Protestant Pauline scholar has challenged his colleagues to consider Origen's exegesis of Romans.[4] Reasoner offers a succinct diachronic survey of the history of interpretation of Romans which centers around twelve theological "loci" or themes. The group of interpreters whose views are summarized include Origen, Augustine, Abelard, Aquinas, Luther, Erasmus, Calvin, Barth, the post-Barthian "new perspective" (Sanders, Dunn), and narrative-based approaches (N. T. Wright, Grieb). Reasoner is emphatic in his endorsement of his "hero" Origen's interpretation of Romans as one that he believes makes a very near approach to the mind of Paul.

In a way that resembles Heither's main thesis, Reasoner concludes that in spite of, or rather precisely because of, the way Origen transcends the Augustine/Pelagius and Lutheran/Calvinist categories of interpretation, he deserves a careful hearing today. Reasoner's recurring thesis is that "Origen remains the unacknowledged ancestor in the two millennia of conversations that have occurred over Romans interpretation."[5] A subsidiary thesis, which Reasoner does not develop, is that Erasmus is the voice through whom Origen's ideas were carried into Renaissance biblical interpretation. Interestingly and provocatively, Reasoner argues that modern interpreters, with their adoption of a "new perspective" on Paul, have now (unbeknownst to themselves) returned "full circle" to insights and proposals that were first made by Origen. (Here as well Reasoner is following the path taken by T. Heither in the above-cited monograph.) This interpretive turn particularly applies to the following themes: Paul's role in the Epistle to the Romans as an arbiter between Jews and Gentiles, a corporate as opposed to an individualistic way of reading Romans, the complexity of Paul's view of "law," the future expectation of Israel's salvation, the complementarity and necessity of both faith and good works in salvation, the preservation of human freedom in the justification process, and the interpretation of predestination as divine foreknowledge of human response.

Unlike so many modern exegetes, Reasoner seems convinced that Origen was capable of penetrating deeply into the mind of Paul and even of uncovering interpretive insights that have escaped the notice of those whose categories of interpretation continue to be determined by the Reformation. These significant monographs by Cocchini, Heither, and Reasoner will, it is hoped, make it increasingly difficult for future Pauline scholars to neglect Origen's interpretation of Romans.

In a way, such scholars resemble that monk Theophilus Salodianus described in chapter 5 as the editor of the *Editio Princeps* of Origen's *Commentary on the Epistle to the Romans*. Exactly five hundred years ago, in the year 1506, Theophilus discovered Origen's commentary decaying on the shelves of his monastic library in Fiesole, Italy. He wondered how his contemporaries could have neglected such a work and allowed it to deteriorate into its present condition. Determined to restore the text, and aided by prayer and divine grace, he thereafter endeavored to make Origen's work as widely known as possible. The hope of this book is that a new generation will likewise rediscover Origen as an interpreter of Paul's Epistle to the Romans.

Abbreviations and
Short Titles of
Frequently Cited Works

N.B. All citations from Origen's *CRm* are from the critical edition by C. P. Hammond Bammel, *Der Römerbriefkommentar des Origenes. Kritische Ausgabe der Übersetzung Rufins*, 3 vols. (Freiburg im Breisgau: Herder, 1990–98). English translations are from Thomas P. Scheck, trans., *Origen: Commentary on the Epistle to the Romans*, 2 vols., FOTC 103, 104 (Washington: Catholic University of America Press, 2001–2). Scheck's translation is based on the critical edition. Migne (*PG* 14) column numbers appear in parentheses.

ASD	*Opera omnia Desiderii Erasmi Roterodami*. Amsterdam: North Holland, 1969–.
BDEC	*Bibliographical Dictionary of the English Catholics*. Ed. Joseph Gillow. New York: Burt Franklin, 1887. Originally published in London.
CCCM	Corpus Christianorum: Continuatio Mediaevalis 86. *Guillelmi a Sancto Theodorico. Opera Omnia, Pars I: Expositio super Epistolam ad Romanos*. Ed. Pauli Verdeyen. Turnholt, 1989.
CE	*Contemporaries of Erasmus. A Biographical Register of the Renaissance and Reformation*. 3 vols. Toronto: University of Toronto Press.
Cels	Origen, *Against Celsus* (*Contra Celsum*).
CH	*Church History*.
CJn	*Commentary on John*.
CR	*Corpus Reformatorum. Philippi Melanchthonis opera quae supersunt omnia*. Ed. C. G. Bretschneider and H. Bindseil.
CRm	*Commentary on the Epistle to the Romans*.

CSEL	*Corpus scriptorum ecclesiasticorum latinorum.* Leipzig: G. Freytag, 1890.
CWE	*Collected Works of Erasmus.* Toronto: University of Toronto Press, 1974–.
DCB	*A Dictionary of Christian Biography.* Ed. W. Smith and H. Wace. London: William Clowes and Sons, 1887.
De pecc. mer.	*De peccatorum meritis et remissione.*
DNB	*Dictionary of National Biography.* Oxford: Oxford University Press, 1939–.
DTC	*Dictionnaire de Théologie catholique.* Ed. A. Vacant, E. Mangenot, and E. Amann. Paris: Letouzey et Ané, 1909–50.
Eps	*Epistles*
FOTC	The Fathers of the Church. Washington, DC: Catholic University of America Press, 1947–.
Gagge	John Heigham, *The Gagge of the Reformed Gospell.* 2nd ed. Douai, 1623.
Haer	Epiphanius, *Haereses = The Panarion of Epiphanius of Salamis.* 2 vols. Trans. Frank Williams. Leiden: Brill, 1994.
HE	*Historia Ecclesiastica.*
Historia Vita	Philipp Melanchthon, *Historia de Vita et Actis Lutheri.*
JEH	*Journal of Ecclesiastical History.*
JTS	*Journal of Theological Studies.*
LB	*Desiderii Erasmi Roterodami Opera Omnia.* Ed. Jean Leclerc.
LCC	Library of Christian Classics. Philadelphia: Westminster, 1953–66.
LW	*Luther's Works.* Ed. J. Pelikan and H. T. Lehmann.
New Gagg	Richard Montagu, *A Gagg for the New Gospell? No: A New Gagg for an Old Goose* (London: Thomas Snodham for Matthew Lownes and William Barret, 1624). Facsimile edition: Amsterdam: Theatrum Orbis Terrarum, 1975.
NPNF	Nicene and Post-Nicene Fathers. First and second series.
Peri Archon	Origen, *On First Principles.*
PG	*Patrologiae Cursus Completus: Series Graeca.* Ed. J.-P. Migne. Paris, 1857–66.

PL	*Patrologiae Cursus Completus: Series Latina.* Ed. J.-P. Migne. Paris, 1878–90.
SA	*Melanchthons Werke in Auswahl. Studienausgabe.* Ed. R. Stupperich.
VC	*Vigiliae Christianae.*
WA	*Luthers Werke. Kritische Gesamtausgabe [Schriften].*

Notes

Introduction

1. Lubac (1998), p. 157.

2. Most of these calculations are found in Hammond (1977), pp. 428–29, who points out that these are very rough estimates owing to the nonuniform length of the additional material found in the footnotes of Migne. (For example, the figures for *On First Principles* are too generous.) Sometimes my independent estimates have differed significantly from Hammond's.

3. Crouzel (1988), p. 506. Recently, a prominent Pauline scholar admitted his own and his guild's ignorance of the history of Pauline exegesis: "Like too many New Testament scholars, I am largely ignorant of the Pauline exegesis of all but a few of the Fathers and Reformers. The Middle Ages, and the seventeenth and eighteenth centuries, had plenty to say about Paul, but I have not read it." N. T. Wright, *Paul in Fresh Perspective* (Minneapolis: Fortress, 2005), p. 13. Revealingly, the index of Wright's book lists "Gollum," but not "Origen." The recent 1140-page Hermeneia commentary *Romans*, by R. Jewett, refers to Origen's *CRm* a single time. Drawing his reference from a secondary work, on p. 5 Jewett mistranslates a text-critical remark of Origen, *CRm* 10.43 (*caput* means "chapter" or "section" here, not "person"). The modern NT guild's ignorance of Origen's Pauline exegesis seems to be nearly invincible.

4. In Blowers, ed. (2002), p. 147. On the other hand, the recent appearance of two works is a very encouraging sign. Reasoner (2005) gives a full and sympathetic treatment to Origen. Maureen Beyer Moser (2005) has studied an important single theme from Origen's *CRm*.

5. Wagner (1945), pp. 2–3.

6. Cf. A. Harnack (1958), vol. 2, pt. 2, p. 41.

7. See Hammond Bammel (1981).

8. For a brief discussion of this reference, see Scheck (2001–2), vol. 1, p. 17.

9. Cf. J. A. Robinson, ed., *The Philocalia* (Cambridge: Cambridge University Press, 1893).

10. See A. Ramsbotham (1912, 1913). Vol. 6 (1999) of Heither's edition has the Greek *Fragmenta*.

11. Cf. Scherer (1957), Chadwick (1959).

12. Cf. Bennett (1997), pp. 128, 154. Cf. ibid., "The Soiling of Sinful Flesh: Primordial Sin, Inherited Corruption and Moral Responsibility in Didymus the Blind and Origen," *Adamantius* 11 (2005), pp. 77–92.

13. Cf. Frede (1973, 1974). See also de Bruyn (1988).

14. On the other hand, this subject might be worth an investigation. For example, a recent glance at the *Commentary on Romans* by Theodoret of Cyrus suggested to me that it might have been influenced by Origen's. Cf. Cocchini (1996), pp. 313–36.

15. For a general survey of Origen's legacy in the West, see Schär (1979).

16. Heither (1990), p. 292. I will return briefly to this statement in the conclusion.

17. All citations from Origen's *CRm* are from the critical edition, C. P. Hammond Bammel, *Der Römerbriefkommentar des Origenes. Kritische Ausgabe der Übersetzung Rufins*, 3 vols. (1990–98). Migne (*PG* 14) column numbers appear in parentheses. All English translations are my own (FOTC 103, 104).

18. In Heither (1990).

19. Völker (1930), p. 274: "Von Rechtfertigung aus Glauben spricht Origenes nie, denn die Ausführungen im Römer-Co. sind schwerlich echt."

20. The Origen fragments from the Tura papyrus were published by Scherer (1957) and Heither (1999). See also the article by Chadwick (1959), who discusses and defends Rufinus's reliability.

21. Cf. Heither (1999) (Origenes, *Römerbriefkommentar 6 [Fragmente]*), p. 104: "ἔχομεν γοῦν παραστῆσαι τὸν ἐκ μόνης πίστεως χωρὶς ἔργων δικαιούμενον, . . ." This is followed by the reference to the good thief and the sinful woman of Lk 7, just as in Rufinus's translation.

22. Lubac (1998), p. 146.

23. Cf. Völker (1931), p. 11. Molland (1938), p. 172n11 criticizes Verfaillie in these words: "Verfaillie makes this doctrine [justification] far too central and also shows too great confidence in Rufinus's translation of *In Rom.*"

24. Roukema (1988), p. 86n40.

25. Oddly enough, Eno (1984), pp. 4–5, claims that the exact reverse of my preceding argument is true. Citing Nautin and Scherer for support, he writes, "The traditional view has been that Rufinus' translation 'abbreviated and adapted' the original but was basically faithful. But in recent decades a section of the Greek original was found among the Tura manuscripts, showing that the traditional view was overly optimistic." Contrast such a conclusion with Grech (1996), p. 337, who also cites Scherer for support: "Most scholars, however, particularly Jean Scherer who compared Rufinus' Latin with the extant Greek fragments, maintain that the commentary is substantially reliable."

Hammond Bammel (1985), pp. 44–45, states that Rufinus's readers "were at a lower intellectual level than Origen. The difficult concepts had to be explained and simplified for them. . . . Rufinus's aim was to edify his readers, not to show off his erudition; thus he often simplifies problems or covers over difficulties. Inevitably his standpoint was different from that of Origen."

26. Cf. *CWE* 56, pp. 137–61. By 1535 Erasmus's note on Rom 5.12 had reached the length of thirteen pages. Sider discusses how Erasmus's dissent from Augustine's interpretation of Rom 5.12 provoked a storm of controversy from Catholic critics. Sider also clarifies how Erasmus's completely orthodox interpretation carefully assimilates the patristic tradition of interpretation, including Origen.

27. Grech (1996), p. 338.

Chapter 1
Origen's Doctrine of Justification

1. Two of the most recent treatments from the Catholic side are those of Sungenis (1997) and White (1995). Sungenis's work is one of the few Catholic investigations that seriously engages the works of Evangelical Protestants. White's dissertation is valuable for the way it assesses Catholic contributions to the ecumenical discussion and particularly for how it identifies some of the flaws of Küng's treatment of justification (namely his failure to define it). Mention should also be made of the recent joint declaration on the doctrine of justification by the Roman Catholic Church and the Lutheran World Federation. This latter document has not assimilated the revolution in Pauline exegesis known as the "New Perspective."

2. Cf. Verfaillie (1926), p. 5.

3. It is seriously alarming, however, that Origen's work is completely overlooked by McGrath (1986) in a monograph purporting to be a history of the doctrine of justification. I will discuss McGrath's work in more detail in chapter 3 on Augustine and chapter 6 on Melanchthon.

4. In Rivière (1925), 8, c. 2086: "Le catholicisme des premiers siècles n'a reçu nulle part de meilleure et de plus complète expression."

5. Jean Rivière (1878–1946) was chair of fundamental theology at the University of Strasbourg (1919–46). His magnum opus was *Le Dogme de la Rédemption: Etude théologique* (Paris: J. Vrin, 1905). He also wrote the famous article on "Merit" in the *DTC*. See "In Memoriam Mgr Victor Martin et M. Jean Rivière," *Revue des sciences religieuses* 21 (1947), pp. 5–16.

6. Rivière (1925), 8, c. 2086: "Ce qui importe, c'est que ces deux conditions sont complémentaires et, par conséquent, ne doivent pas être séparées."

7. Hieracas's views are reported by Epiphanius, *Haer* 67.2 (*PG* 42:176); cited in Rivière (1925), c. 2086.

8. *Haer* 67.2.

9. Cf. 5.9.168–73 (1047).

10. Cf. 3.3(6).56–60 (939).

11. Cf. 5.2.112–15 (1024).

12. Verfaillie (1926).

13. Predictably, Godin (1982b), p. 386n101, describes Verfaillie's analyses of Origen's doctrine as "very forced." Godin does not comment as to whether he thinks that the Protestant exploitation of Origen that provoked Verfaillie's research was equally forced.

14. Verfaillie (1926), p. 119: "En effet, après une longue période de calme, le XVIe siècle devait allumer la grande controverse qui a provoqué les définitions de l'Eglise en matière de justification. Il suffit de se rapporter au décret du concile de Trente pour voir dans quelle large mesure Origène en a anticipé les principales affirmations. Déchéance originelle mais non cependant corruption totale de l'humanité, nécessité et efficacité de l'oeuvre rédemptrice, son application par le concours indivisible de Dieu et de l'homme, sanctification effective de l'âme par la grâce, valeur méritoire de ses actes en vue de la gloire: telles sont les doctrines opposées par l'Eglise à la Réforme. Or on les trouve toutes déjà nettement chez Origène."

15. Cf. Rivière (1925), c. 2085; Verfaillie (1926), p. 11. Both scholars cite Thomasius, *Christi Person und Werk* (Erlangen, 1888), as an example. In chapter 7 of this book, I will describe Anglican bishop Richard Montagu's defense of Origen as a "proto-Protestant."

16. The text read was 3.6(9).61–66 (953): "A man is justified through faith; the works of the law contribute nothing to his being justified. But where there is no faith which justifies the believer, even if one possesses works from the law, nevertheless because they have not been built upon the foundation of faith, although they might appear to be good things, nevertheless they are not able to justify the one doing them, because from them faith is absent, which is the sign of those who are justified." Cf. Ehses (1911), p. 729. Other passages from Origen's commentary were also consulted at the Council of Trent. Cf. Ehses (1911), pp. 182, 190, 583.

17. This will be examined in detail in chapter 6 on Melanchthon.

18. Molland (1938), pp. 171–72.

19. Osborn (1976), p. 20.

20. Molland (1938), p. 121.

21. Cf. Origen, *CRm* 6.1.120–28 (1059).

22. Seeberg (1977), pp. 158–59, referring to Origen, *CRm* 4.7.109–12 (986).

23. Seeberg cites Origen, *Homilies ou Leviticus* 7.3; 2.4; *Cels* 3.71; 8.10.

24. I will discuss Grech's and Bammel's important articles throughout the course of the book rather than separately here.

25. Wiles (1967), p. 111. This is an old complaint and is found with reference to Clement of Alexandria in Bigg, (1970), p. 88.

26. Wiles (1967), p. 29. It seems fair to say that the Revised Standard Version is guilty of the opposite charge, that is, of heightening Paul's "attack" upon the law. Three times in Rom 3.27 this Protestant version translates the Pauline term *nomos* (law) by the word *principle*.

27. 2.12.4 (900).

28. 3.6(9).22–24 (952); 2.4.141–42 (878).

29. Wiles (1967), p. 113.

30. Ibid., p. 114.

31. In a grave mistranslation, J. Trigg, "Origen and Origenism in the 1990s," *Religious Studies Review* 22.4 (1996), p. 303, summarizes the argument of Heither's monograph *Translatio Religionis* as: "She makes it clear at the outset that, unlike most earlier authors dealing with Origen's Pauline interpretation, she will not accept *a priori* that salvation [*Rechtfertigung*] by grace [*Glaube*] alone is the 'essential and exclusively essential' element in Pauline theology and therefore judge Origen wanting for not finding it so." Revealingly, Trigg has misread Heither's phrase "justification by faith alone" as "salvation by grace alone."

32. Grech's conclusion (1996), p. 359, is less favorable: "One may say, however, that applying modern hermeneutical insights to Origen, this Alexandrian writer may often have read Paul upside-down, but he certainly more often comes to the right theological conclusions because his hermeneutical principle is guided by the *regula fidei*."

33. Heither (1990), pp. 234–35.

34. 1.1.5–9 (833): "Haeretici astruere solent quod uniuscuiusque gestorum causa non ad propositum debeat sed naturae diversitatem referri, et ex paucis huius epistulae sermonibus totius scripturae sensum qui arbitrii libertatem concessam a Deo homini docet conantur evertere." The study of the heresies engaged by Origen is one of the essential concerns of Cocchini's monograph (1979).

35. 8.10.15–18 (1191): "Putent esse naturam animarum quae semper salva sit et numquam pereat; et aliam quae semper pereat et numquam salvetur."

36. 2.10.2 (894).

37. The above account is drawn from Irenaeus, *Against Heresies* 1.6; Tertullian, *Against the Valentinians* 29–30. Although the Nag Hammadi discoveries have increased our knowledge of these heretical groups, to the best of my knowledge the fidelity of Irenaeus's and Tertullian's depiction of Valentinus's system has not been conclusively disproved. Cf. M. van den Broek, "The Present State of Gnostic Studies," *VC* 37 (1983), pp. 47–71.

38. Grech (1996), p. 338.

39. Origen, *Peri Archon* 3.1.1; see also *Cels* 1.7: "Almost the whole world has come to know the preaching of Christians better than the opinions of philosophers . . . [Has not everyone heard of the Christian teaching about] Jesus' birth from a virgin, and of his crucifixion, and his resurrection and the proclamation of the judgment which punishes according to their deserts and pronounces the righteous worthy of reward?"

40. Cf. Jackson (1966), p. 13.

41. Origen is hardly the inventor of such views. In the second century, Justin Martyr wrote in his *First Apology*: "We have learned from the prophets and declare as the truth, that penalties and punishments and good rewards are given

according to the quality of each man's actions" (*Apologia* 43). For a discussion of these texts, see R. Wilken (1969).

42. By his all-pervasive stress on free will, it is generally acknowledged that Origen has at times assigned his own theological preoccupations to the mind of Paul. Cf. Verfaillie (1926), p. 37.

43. 8.10.23–26 (1191); 5.10.169 (1052).

44. 1.21(18).65–74 (866): "Sed ex utraque parte favoris disciplina servatur. Non enim vi res agitur neque necessitate in alteram partem anima declinatur; alioquin nec culpa ei nec virtus possit adscribi nec boni electio praemium nec declinatio mali supplicium mereretur; sed servatur ei in omnibus libertas arbitrii ut in quod voluerit ipsa declinet sicut scriptum est: 'ecce posui ante faciem tuam vitam et mortem ignem et aquam.' Vita ergo Christus est et mors novissimus inimicus qui est diabolus. Habet igitur in arbitrio suo anima si velit eligere vitam Christum aut in mortem diabolum declinare."

45. Cf. Mt 22.11–12. *CRm* 8.7.168–74 (1184): "Quibus utentes aulam sapientiae et thalamos filii regis intrare mereamur."

46. 6.12.119–20 (1096): "Si tamen actus vestri tales sint et conversatio ut spiritum Dei in vobis habere mereamini."

47. 6.13.83–86 (1100): "Unde mihi videtur quod et meritis conquiratur hoc donum et vitae innocentia conservetur et unicuique secundum profectum fidei augeatur et gratia, et quanto purior anima redditur tanto largior ei spiritus infundatur.

48. Grech (1996), p. 356.

49. 3.6(9).81–101 (954): "Talis ergo gloriatio quae veniebat e operibus legis excluditur, quia non habet humilitatem crucis Christi in qua qui gloriatur audi quid dicit: 'mihi autem absit gloriari nisi in cruce Domini mei Iesu Christi per quem mihi mundus crucifixus est et ego mundo.' . . . Sola igitur iusta gloriatio est in fide crucis Christi quae excludit omnem illam gloriationem quae descendit ex operibus legis." Schelkle (1954), p. 311, noted that subsequent Fathers did not adopt Origen's total repudiation of religious boasting.

50. 3.6(9)(954).

51. Cf. Rivière (1925), c. 2085.

52. Cf. Harnack (1924), pp. 25–27.

53. Cf. Tertullian, *On the Flesh of Christ* 2; *Against Marcion* 1.2.

54. Cf. Tertullian, *Against Marcion* 4.8.

55. Cf. Tertullian, *Against Marcion* 1.20; 4.2–7.

56. Cf. D. Balas (1992).

57. Cf. 2.10.2 (894).

58. Crouzel (1989), pp. 153–54, claims that the objections Origen makes to the trio Basilides-Valentinus-Marcion are "somewhat stereotyped and do not reflect a very deep first-hand knowledge of these teachers."

59. 1.21(18).15–16 (865): "Tamen requiramus ab his qui Deum bonum negant etiam iustum esse iudicem . . ."

60. Cf. Tertullian, *Prescription Against Heretics* 30; *Against Marcion* 1.1.29; 4.11.

61. Cf. Irenaeus, *Haer* 3.25.2.3. My discussion here has been informed by J. Lightfoot, *The Apostolic Fathers*, vol. 1, part 2, "Ignatius and Polycarp" (Peabody: Hendrickson, 1989), p. 587.

62. Cocchini (1979), p. 112n290: "Nella dottrina di Marcione qualunque giudizio proveniva dal Dio giusto mentre al Dio buono, appunto perché tale, era riconosciuta solo la misericordia, che egli donava a tutti, prescindendo dalle azioni più o meno meritevoli."

63. In 1.21(18).28–30 (865), Origen describes his opponents as "Marcion and all who spring forth from his school like a brood of vipers."

64. Farkasfalvy (1968), p. 328, observes the following about Irenaeus's theology: "The word 'consonare' used by Irenaeus repeatedly in exegetical context, sounds almost as a technical term of his exegesis. He considers it as the principal result of his explanations that the Scriptures could be proved to be in perfect harmony among themselves: 'omnis Scriptura a Deo nobis data consonans (symphonos) invenietur' (II, 41, 4: I, 352)." This strikes me as an exact anticipation of Origen's hermeneutical principle in the *CRm*.

65. 3.4(7).140–44 (945): "Vide autem quia manifestandae iustitiae Dei non unam posuit causam tantummodo fidei sed et legem sociat ac profetas, quia neque fides sola sine lege et profetis manifestat iustitiam Dei, neque rursus lex et profetae sine fide; alterum ergo haeret ex altero ut sit ex utroque perfectio. . . . Ita utrumque sibi adhaerens alterum ex altero consummatur." Cf. 3.7(10).81–82 (957).

66. *Fides* and *religio* are related in Origen's *CRm*. Cf. 1.9(11).4 (855).

67. Cf. 4.1.216–24 (965).

68. Cf. 1.21(18).15–16 (865). On this passage see Cocchini (1979), pp. 109–12.

69. 8.2.117–21 (1163): "Uidebitur enim quibusdam per hoc quia etiam si desint alicui boni operis priuilegia, etiam si uirtutibus operam non dederit, hoc ipso tamen quod credidit non pereat sed saluetur et habeat salutem etiam si beatitudinis gloriam habere non poterit."

70. Heither (1994), 4:206n10, observes: "Es ist nicht zu erkennen, wen Origenes hier meint. Wenn es um Gnostiker, z.B. die Valentinianer, ginge, hätte er die Ansicht heftiger bekämpft; wenn es um rechtgläubige Auslegung ginge, hätte er sie stehen lassen, er korrigiert sie aber im Folgenden."

71. This text will be discussed below.

72. 8.2.131–34 (1164): "Si in me ipso eum non habeam suscitatum ego, si non in nouitate uitae ambulo et uetustam peccandi consuetudinem fugio, nondum mihi Christus resurrexit a mortuis."

73. 4.8.41–46 (989).

74. 2.4.140–43 (878): "Secundo in loco aedificentur fideles ne putent sibi hoc solum sufficere posse quod credunt sed sciant iustum iudicium Dei reddere unicuique secundum opera sua." Heither (1990), 1:186n10, notes that Origen views Marcion, Valentinus, and Basilides as representatives of this teaching. Cf. *On First Principles* 3.1.6.

75. Cf. Verfaillie (1926), p. 115, and Cocchini (1979), p. 112n290. The passage under discussion is 2.4.140–43 (878).

76. Cf. 7.8.22–31 (1130).

77. 2.6(8).23–29 (890).

78. 7.5(3).134–41 (1117).

79. McSorley (1969), p. 61.

80. It is beyond the scope of this study to show that for Origen "eternal ruin" does not imply the impossibility of restoration to grace in a future age (the "Apokatastasis"). This is a view of Origen that the Church would later declare to be erroneous. See Denzinger (1954), 211: "If anyone says or holds that the punishment of the demons and of impious men is temporary, and that it will have an end at some time, that is to say, there will be a complete restoration of the demons or of impious men, let him be anathema."

81. Cf. Molland (1938), p. 121.

82. 3.11.87–90 (959).

83. 9.1 (1201–3): "Cum per omnem textum epistulae in superioribus docuisset apostolus quomodo a Iudaeis ad gentes a circumcisione ad fidem a littera ad spiritum ab umbra ad veritatem ab observantia carnali ad observantiam spiritalem religionis summa translata sit, et haec ita futura profeticis ostendisset vocibus designata."

84. Cf. Heither (1990), pp. 57–63.

85. 3.1.22–28 (923): "Per omnem namque epistulae huius textum docere vult quae fuerit vel ante adventum Christi salus secundum legem viventibus vel quomodo per salvatoris adventum rursum ex incredulitate Israhel salus gentibus conferatur et rursum quod neque ex integro gentes nisi qui crediderint veniant ad salutem neque ex integro abiciatur Israhel, sed reliquiae credentium salvae fiant."

86. Cf. Scherer (1957), p. 124, 6–10.

87. Bammel (1992), p. 352. Reasoner (2005), pp. xxv, 145–46, finds this theme to be one of the most attractive in Origen's exegesis and the one that most clearly anticipates the "new perspective" in Pauline interpretation.

88. 2.14 (914).

89. 3.2.12ff. (928). Cf. Gorday (1983), p. 58.

90. Gorday (1983), p. 85.

91. The aim of Gorday's study was to see if these three ancient Fathers, like some modern interpreters of Paul, completely divided Rom 9–11 from Rom 1–8. By doing a comparative survey of a part of their exegesis of Romans, Gorday found Origen to be the best of the three interpreters under investigation. Cohen (2005) confirms the strength of Origen's interpretation.

92. 3.2(2–5).22–25 (928).

93. Grech (1996), pp. 345–46. Cf. Rivière (1909), p. 158: "Whatever may have been Origen's theory on original sin, there can be no doubt that according to him all men are sinners and that they were unable to save themselves and that salvation came only through God's mercy."

94. 1.18(15).12–14 (861): "Iustitia Dei in evangelio revelatur per id quod ad salutem nullus excipitur sive Iudaeus sive Graecus sive barbarus veniat."

95. Cf. Denifle (1905), p. xv.

96. This term is Grech's (1996), p. 350.

97. Heither (1990), p. 233n33.

98. Verfaillie (1926), p. 110. "Evidemment Origène ne se pose pas la question de savoir si la justice est imputée ou inhérente; mais on voit que le réalisme spirituel de sa psychologie va dans le sens de la dernière conception."

99. Cf. Denifle (1905), p. xv.

100. Cf. 3.4(7).118–22 (944).

101. 1.21(28).84–116 (867–68). Moser (2005), pp. 92–99, has shown that in spite of some anachronistic terminology in Origen's *CRm*, his theology does involve the activity of Father, Son, and Holy Spirit.

102. Cf. 4.9.24–28 (993): "Fidem namque et spem consequitur caritas Dei quae omnium maior est, et non solum replet mentem nostram sed et abundat ac diffunditur in cordibus nostris, pro eo quod non humana nobis arte quaeritur, sed per gratiam Sancti Spiritus inundatur."

103. 4.9.192–98 (997).

104. Cf. 8.10.95–101 (1193).

105. 8.10.111–14 (1194).

106. Cf. 7.8.1–2 (1130) (Rom 8.33–34).

107. Cf. 3.6(9).48–51 (953).

108. 3.4(7).154–58 (945): "Idcirco iustitia Dei per fidem Iesu Christi ad omnes perveniens qui credunt, sive Iudaei sint sive Graeci, purgatos eos a prioribus sceleribus iustificat et capaces facit gloriae Dei; et hoc non pro meritis eorum nec pro operibus facit sed gratis gloriam credentibus praestat."

109. Cf. 3.6(9).56–60 (953).

110. 6.12.146–52 (1097): "Data enim nobis remissione peccatorum fugatum est et exterminatum de carne nostra peccatum et coepit in nobis iustificatio legis impleri."

111. 2.7(9).29–30 (892): "Sed secundum spiritum per quem solummodo impleri lex poterit."

112. Mt 5.17. Cf. 2.9(13).135–37(901): "Perfectio autem legis in Christo est qui dixit: 'non veni solvere legem sed adimplere.' Adimplere autem legem hoc est perficere legem."

113. 6.12.108 (1096): "Et spiritus vivificans quae vere lex Dei est."

114. It is noteworthy that the recent *Catechism of the Catholic Church* (1966) states something very similar: "The New Law is the grace of the Holy Spirit given to the faithful through faith in Christ." For a discussion of this in relation to recent ecumenical dialogues, see A. Dulles (2004), pp. 228–29.

115. 6.1.127–28 (1059): "Sine dubio dicet quod non simus sub lege litterae quae occidit sed sub lege spiritus qui vivificat, quam hic gratiam nominavit." On this passage, see Roukema (1988), pp. 54–55.

116. 3.8(11).20–25 (957).

117. Roukema (1988), p. 37.

118. 5.3.7–12 (1026): "Qui autem abundantiam gratiae et doni iustitiae accipiunt, non solum ultra non regnat in eis mors, quod et ipsum utique non paruae esset gratiae, sed et alia duo eis conferuntur bona, unum quod pro morte uita in eis regnat Christus Iesus, aliud quod etiam ipsi regnabunt per unum Iesum Christum."

119. 4.1.194 (964): "Quae fides tanta est ut iustificet etiam eum qui impius fuerit ut ultra iam non sit impius."

120. Grech (1996), p. 351.

121. 3.3(6).79–82 (939): "Et sicut ipse est iustitia ex qua iusti omnes fiunt, et ipse est veritas ex qua omnes in veritate consistunt et ipse est vita ex qua omnes vivunt, ita et ipse est lex ex qua omnes in lege sunt." For other references see the Index of Sacred Scripture under 1 Cor 1.30 in Hammond Bammel (1998), vol. 3.

122. 5.5.92–96 (1032): "Propterea enim et ipse oboediens factus est usque ad mortem ut qui oboedientiae eius sequuntur exemplum iusti constituantur ab ipsa iustitia sicut illi inoboedientiae forma sequentes constituti sunt peccatores."

123. 3.5(8).14–26 (946). For a discussion of this text, see J. Rivière (1909), pp. 158ff.

124. Cf. Rivière (1909), p. 160.

125. Codrus was a legendary king of Athens (eleventh century B.C.) who sacrificed his life to save his country. The oracle of Delphi said that the Dorian invasion of Attica would be successful if Codrus's life was spared. In response, Codrus went out disguised as a woodcutter and provoked a fight with Dorian soldiers, who killed him. Thus he saved his country.

126. Marcus Curtius was the hero of an aetiological myth invented to explain the name of lacus Curtius, a pond in the Roman forum. He was a brave young knight who, in obedience to an oracle, to save his country, leaped armed and on horseback into the chasm which suddenly opened in the forum.

127. Iphigeneia was the daughter of Agamemnon who was sacrificed at Aulis, in obedience to an oracle, in order to avert the bad weather that was preventing the Greek fleet from reaching Troy.

128. Alcestis was the wife of Admetus, king of Pherae in Thessaly, who volunteered to die in Admetus's place.

129. Cf. CJn 6.53ff.; 28.19; Cels 1.31.

130. 4.11.41–55 (1000). Cf. Clement of Rome, *Epistle to the Corinthians*, 55.

131. Rivière (1909), p. 162.

132. 4.1.216–24 (965). Cf. 4.1.95 (962).

133. 2.5.256–59 (887).

134. 2.5.(5–7).280–82 (887).

135. 3.6(9).61–71 (953–54).

136. Cf. Ehses (1911), p. 729.

137. 3.6(9).79–81 (954): "Talis ergo gloriatio quae veniebat ex operibus legis excluditur, quia non habet humilitatem crucis Christi."

138. 5.8.47–48 (1038).

139. 5.8.132–35 (1041).

140. Cf. Verfaillie (1926), pp. 81–82.

141. 3.6(9).56–60 (953): "Post iustificationem si iniuste quis agat sine dubio iustificationis gratiam sprevit."

142. Cf. 1.15(13).56–60 (859).

143. 4.1.70–72 (961): "Indicium igitur uerae fidei est ubi non delinquitur, sicut e contra ubi delinquitur infidelitatis indicium est."

144. Cf. 2.6(8).345–50 (889). In this latter passage, as Windisch (1908), p. 480, observes, it is difficult to determine whether Origen has Montanists or Novatians in mind. If the latter are in view, then the comment must have been reworked by Rufinus, since the Novatians lived after Origen.

145. 2.5(5–7).341–43 (889).

146. 3.6(9).22–24 (952): "Et dicit sufficere solius fidei iustificationem, ita ut credens quis tantummodo iustificetur etiamsi nihil ab eo operis fuerit expletum."

147. The Greek text of this passage survives. Cf. Heither (1999) (Origenes, *Römerbriefkommentar 6 [Fragmente]*), p. 104.

148. 3.6(9).30–39 (953): "Nec aliud quidquam describitur boni operis eius in euangeliis sed pro hac sola fide ait ei Iesus: 'amen dico tibi hodie mecum eris in paradiso.' . . . Per fidem enim iustificatus est hic latro sine operibus legis, quia super hoc Dominus non requisiuit, quid prius operatus esset, nec expectauit quid operis cum credidisset expleret, sed sola confessione iustificatum comitem sibi eum paradisum ingressurus assumsit."

149. Both Verfaillie (1926), p. 88, and Heither, *Römerbriefkommentar* (1992), 2.132n72, agree that the examples Origen invokes of persons justified by faith alone are given as exceptional cases, which are intended to support Paul's statement.

150. Cf. Verfaillie (1926), pp. 63–67.

151. Cf. Verfaillie (1926), p. 51.

152. 4.11.67–75 (1001).

153. Cf. Verfaillie (1926), p. 52.

154. Cf. Heither (1990), p. 253.

155. "Accordingly just as through the trespass of the one came condemnation to all men, so also through the righteousness of the one comes the justification of life to all men."

156. 5.4.3–8 (1029).

157. 4.8.76–89 (990).

158. 4.8.89–91 (990).

159. Cf. Verfaillie (1926), p. 70.

160. 2.13.407–14 (908).

161. 2.9(12–13).403–8 (908); 2.9(12–13).62–63 (900).

162. Cf. Heither (1990), p. 238: "Origenes sieht keinen Gegensatz zwischen beiden [faith and works], sondern ihre grundsätzliche Bezogenheit aufeinander."

163. 3.7(10).81–83 (957).

164. 4.5.3 (975).

165. 4.1.3 (960).

166. 4.1.10 (963).

167. Heither (1990), p. 238; citing H. J. Schoeps, *Paulus: Die Theologie des Apostels im Lichte der jüdischen Religionsgeschichte* (Tübingen: Mohr, 1959), p. 212.

168. 4.1.20 (965–66): "Ubi vero iam ad perfectum venerit, ita ut omnis de ea malitiae radix penitus amputetur, eo usque ut nullum in ea vestigium possit inveniri nequitiae, ibi iam summa perfectae beatitudinis promittitur, cum nullum possit Dominus imputare peccatum."

169. Verfaillie (1926), p. 110.

170. 4.1.216–24 (965): "Dicit apostolus quod homini iustitia reputetur licet nondum opera iustitiae egerit, sed pro eo tantum quod credidit in eum qui iustificat impium. Initium namque iustificari a Deo fides est quae credit in iustificantem. Et haec fides cum iustificata fuerit tamquam radix imbre suscepto haeret in animae solo ut cum per legem Dei excoli coeperit surgant ex ea rami qui fructus operum ferant. Non ergo ex operibus radix iustitiae sed ex radice iustitiae fructus operum crescit, illa scilicet radice iustitiae quam Deus accepto fert etiam sine operibus."

171. Heither (1990), p. 235: "Wie Origenes das Problem löst, ist klar: Der Glaube erlangt die Gerechtigkeit, aus der hinwiederum die Werke hervorgehen; und dieses Verhältnis ist nicht umkehrbar. Nur auf dem Weg des Glaubens erlangt der Mensch die Vergebung der Sünden, die Versöhnung mit Gott." Cf. Heither, *Origenes. Commentarii* (1992), 2:132n72: "Das sola fide ist bei Origenes klar ausgesprochen, auch durch den griechischen Urtext bezeugt . . . und doch haben die Werke eine große Bedeutung. . . . Origenes sucht die Synthese."

172. Heither (1990), p. 236.

173. 4.6.46–49 (981): "Et puto quod prima salutis initia et ipsa fundamenta fides est; profectus vero et augmenta aedificii spes est, perfectio autem et culmen totius operis caritas, et ideo maior omnium dicitur caritas."

174. 4.12.72–73 (1004). Cf. *initium iustificari a Deo* in 4.1.216–24 (965) above.

175. 4.12.67–71 (1004).

176. 4.8.41–46 (989).

177. 7.3.13–23 (1113).

178. 7.3.123–25 (1116).

179. "Sin boldly, believe more boldly." This was Luther's advice to Melanchthon in *Ep* 91, 1 August 1521, written from the Wartburg. Luther goes on to say in this passage, "No sin will separate us from the Lamb, even though we commit fornication and murder a thousand times a day." See *Luther's Works* 48, *Letters I*, ed. G. Krodel (Philadelphia: Fortress, 1963), pp. 281–82.

180. 8.7(6).111–26 (1178): "Sciendum est opera quae Paulus repudiat et frequenter uituperat non esse opera iustitiae quae mandantur in lege, sed ea in quibus

hi qui secundum carnem legem custodiunt gloriantur; id est uel circumcisio carnis uel sacrificiorum ritus uel obseruatio sabbatorum et numeniarum. Haec et
huiusmodi ergo sunt opera ex quibus dicit neminem potuisse saluari et de quibus
in praesenti loco dicit: 'quia non ex operibus; alioquin gratia iam non fit gratia.'
Si enim per haec quis iustificatur non gratis iustificatur. Qui autem per gratiam
iustificatur ista quidem opera ab eo minime quaeruntur sed observare debet ne
accepta gratia inanis fiat in eo . . . Non facit ergo inanem gratiam ille qui digna ei
opera subiungit et gratiae Dei non exsistit ingratus. Qui enim post consecutam
gratiam peccat ingratus fit ei qui praestitit gratiam." Cf. also 3.7(10).19–21 (955).

 181. Cf. Verfaillie (1926), p. 82.

 182. 2.6(8).23–29 (890).

 183. Reasoner (2005), p. 25.

 184. Cf. Grech (1996), p. 353: "Origen takes for granted the necessity of good
works after justification."

 185. 4.6.84–89 (982). For the scriptural grounding of such an interpretation,
consider Ps 106.31, which says that Phineas's zeal was reckoned as righteousness.

 186. 4.7.75–83 (986).

 187. 4.7.109–12 (986).

 188. 4.7.99–100 (986); 4.6.166–67 (984).

 189. Cocchini (1979), pp. 56–57: "Origene ha già detto che la risurrezione di
Cristo costituisce un esempio per i cristiani, e tale esempio è basato sulla 'nuova
vita' che realmente unisce il Cristo risorto a quanti credono in lui. La differenza
poi tra Cristo e i cristiani consiste, secondo Origene, nel fatto che, mentre per il
Cristo si tratta di una vita nuova nel senso più completo del termine—poiché si è
già anche totalmente manifestata come tale—per i cristiani si tratta di una vita che,
fin quando non risorgeranno, si può manifestare come 'nuova' soprattutto sotto
l'aspetto morale."

 190. Cf. 1 Cor 1.30; Eph 2.14; Origen, *CRm* 5.10.264–66 (1055): "Quod si sine
iustitia sine pace sine sanctificatione ceterisque uirtutibus nemo uiuit Deo certum est quod nemo uiuat Deo nisi in Christo Iesu."

 191. 5.9.27–30 (1043); 5.9.83–90 (1045): "Christus ergo . . . ipse est arbor
uitae . . . nouo quodam atque ammirabili Dei dono mors illius nobis uitae arbor
efficitur. . . . Puto autem quod grate hoc et de illo latrone dici possit qui simul in
cruce pependit cum Iesu et per confessionem suam qua dixit: 'memento mei
Domine cum ueneris in regnum tuum'; et alium blasfemantem corripuit, com-
plantari per haec uisus sit similitudini mortis eius; sed et resurrectioni eius
complantatus sit per hoc quod ei dicitur: 'hodie mecum eris in paradiso.' Digna
namque erat planta paradisi quae arbori uitae sociata est."

 192. Cf. 3.6(9).22–24 (952).

 193. Verfaillie (1926), p. 117: "Ce caractère méritoire de nos actes a sa source
dans la grâce de la justification et en achève le concept. Affranchie de la mort du
péché, l'âme chrétienne est unie au Christ, qui lui donne une nouvelle vie et, par
là-même, les moyens de porter des fruits agréables à Dieu."

194. Reasoner (2005), p. 25.

195. Cf. 1 Cor 3.9; Rom 2.6; 14.10; Phil 2.12.

196. For a nice study of these themes that seems very consonant with Origen's conceptions, see Quinn (1985).

197. My analysis is in substantial agreement with that of Wiles (1967), p. 114, who concludes that for Origen the connection between faith and works is a logically necessary one.

198. Cf. 4.1.941–45 (963).

199. Cf. Grech (1996), p. 350, referring to 1.21(28).84–116 (867–68).

200. Bammel (1996), pp. 223–35.

201. Ibid., p. 232.

202. D. Huet, *Origeniana*, Lib. II, c. II, qu. VIII, n. 13–14; *PG* 17.936–50; cited in Verfaillie (1926), p. 92.

203. Freppel, *Origène*, II:20; cited in Verfaillie (1926), p. 92.

204. See Denzinger (1954), 101–8.

205. Clark (1965), p. 742.

206. McCue (2001), p. 180n29: "If they are to have a label this seems more appropriate than the more familiar 'semi-Pelagian.' They were followers of Augustine."

207. Cf. Parmentier (2003), p. 151.

208. See Denzinger (1954), 173b–200.

209. Clark (1965), pp. 746–47.

210. 4.5.21-27 (974–75): "Etenim ubi enumerat dona spiritus quae dicit secundum mensuram fidei credentibus dari ibi inter cetera etiam donum fidei asserit per Sanctum Spiritum tribui; post multa namque ita etiam de hoc dicit: 'alii fides in eodem spiritu'; ut ostendat quia etiam fides per gratiam datur. Sed et alibi idem apostolus docet dicens: 'quia a Deo vobis datum est non solum ut credatis in Christum sed etiam ut patiamini pro illo.'"

211. Cf. Balthasar (1984), p. 193.

212. 9.2.150–63 (1212).

213. 9.3.24–25 (1213): "Secundum mensuram ergo fidei uniuscuiusque diversitates dari pronuntiat gratiarum, ut verbi causa accepta quis gratia illud vel illud membrum in Christi corpore fiat."

214. 9.3.31–33 (1213): "Et ex nobis in eo agi aliquid ostendat, plurimum tamen in Dei largitione consistere."

215. Verfaillie (1926), p. 105.

216. 7.6.19–20 (1125); 7.14.53–55 (1145).

217. Cf. Preface of Origen 3, 6; 1.3.3 (845–46).

218. 7.6.102–5 (1126); cf. 7.10.134–44 (1136–37).

219. Cf. 2.5.299–311 (888); 3.2(2–5).142–50 (931–32). These passages are discussed by Bammel (1996), p. 228.

220. Cf. 2.7.6–7 (888).

221. Cf. 2.5.256–59 (887).

222. Cf. 3.10 (957).

223. Cf. 7.8 (1125–26), 7.17 (1149).

224. Burns (1979), p. 48, referring to 2.7 (887–89), 2.13 (908).

225. This is the interpretation of Roukema (1988), p. 89n23.

226. Schelkle (1956), p. 77.

227. Eno (1984), p. 5. This doctrine will not be further discussed in this book, except to say that the doctrine has never been condemned by the Church. Clark, "A New Appraisal," pp. 749–51, has demonstrated that the doctrine is neither Pelagian nor semi-Pelagian.

228. Balthasar (1984), pp. 192–93. Grech (1996), p. 341, citing 9.3 (1215–16), says that for Origen the pagan's natural virtues "possess no value in themselves but may be useful to merit supernatural faith, wisdom and prophecy if used wisely and humbly."

229. Cf. Heither (1999) (Origenes, *Römerbriefkommentar 6 [Fragmente]*), pp. 123–25.

230. 4.1.157–63 (963–64): "Sed ego cum considero sermonis eminentiam quod dicit operanti secundum debitum reddi uix mihi suadeo quod possit ullum opus esse quod ex debito remunerationem Dei deposcat, cum etiam hoc ipsum quod agere aliquid possumus uel cogitare uel proloqui ipsius dono et largitione faciamus. Quod ergo erit debitum illius cuius erga nos faenus praecessit?"

231. Verfaillie (1926), p. 116.

232. Balthasar (1984), 197n1.

233. 4.1.177–82 (964).

234. Verfaillie (1926), p. 117.

235. 7.11 (1132); 9.40 (1240).

236. Grech (1996), p. 356.

237. Balthasar (1984), p. 193.

238. Wiles (1967), p. 118.

239. For a good discussion of these texts, see Quinn (1985), pp. 86–91.

240. Consider the use of ἄξιος in Prv 3.15; 8.11; Ws 1.16; 3.5; 6.16; 9.12; 12.26; 15.6; 16.9; 18.4; 19.4; 2 Mc 4.38; 6.27; 7.19–20; 7.29; 8.33; 15.21; and of καταξιῶμαι in 2 Mc 13.12. Cf. also Sir 10.28–29; 16.15; 38.17, discussed by Quinn (1985), p. 83.

241. Wiles (1967), pp. 118–19.

242. Grech (1996), p. 355.

243. Grech (1996), p. 359. In this chapter, I have not discussed any passages showing Origen's views of predestination "according to foreseen merits." This topic will be discussed, however, in the chapters on Pelagius, William, Erasmus, and Cornelius Jansen.

244. Wörter (1856), p. 244: "Zwischen der Bestimmung des Pelagius und der des Origenes besteht also der große Unterschied, daß jene die Gnade, diese die Nothwendigkeit ausschließt; daher sie auch nicht pelagianisch ist."

245. B. Drewery, *Origen and the Doctrine of Grace* (London: Epworth Press, 1960), pp. 163–64.

Chapter 2
Pelagius's Reception of Origen's Exegesis of Romans

1. Cf. Hammond (1977), pp. 401ff.

2. Souter (1922), p. 4.

3. In *De Peccatorum Meritis et Remissione* 3.1.1 = *CSEL* 60.129.2.6ff. Augustine speaks of Pelagius in a qualified but complimentary fashion, but objects to Pelagius's interpretation of Rom 5.12.

4. Hammond (1977), p. 427.

5. Hammond Bammel (1985), p. 45. Some of these texts will be discussed in the next chapter on Augustine.

6. Ibid.

7. All Latin citations of it are taken from Souter's edition (1922).

8. Ferguson (1956), p. 16.

9. Cf. Tauer (1994), p. 319.

10. *Annotations on Romans* (*CWE* 56:155n22).

11. De Bruyn (1993), p. 28.

12. See ibid., pp. 1–10.

13. Cf. ibid., p. 18.

14. Bohlin (1957), p. 40: "Mit der aus seinem Antimanichäismus herrühren-den Dialektic scheint Pelagius' System zu stehen und zu fallen."

15. Cf. S. Lieu, *Manichaeism in the Later Roman Empire and Medieval China: A Historical Survey* (Manchester: Manchester University Press, 1985).

16. In C. Kannengieser, *Handbook of Patristic Exegesis: The Bible in Ancient Christianity*, vol. 1 (Leiden: Brill, 2004), p. 658.

17. Cf. Bohlin (1957), p. 40.

18. Cf. De Bruyn (1993), pp. 15–16.

19. Cf. ibid., p. 16.

20. Ibid., pp. 71ff.

21. Ibid., p. 99.

22. Ibid., p. 107.

23. This task has been accomplished admirably by Dempsey, de Plinval, Evans, Rees, and Ferguson.

24. Several modern scholars deny the authenticity of this prologue and think that it was attached to Pelagius's commentary at an early stage of its transmission. Cf. De Bruyn (1993), p. 9. I follow Souter (1922), 1:115, in affirming that the authenticity of the prologue, arguments, and expositions hangs together.

25. De Bruyn (1993), p. 58.

26. Cf. Souter (1922), p. 188; Bohlin (1957), pp. 47–53, 58–59, 89–90.

27. De Bruyn (1993), p. 98. Souter (1926), 2:51: "Simul notandum quod homo membra sua cui velit parti exhibeat per arbitrii libertatem."

28. Origen, *CRm* 6.1.28–29 (1056): "Ostendens in nostra potestate situm ut non regnet in corpore nostro peccatum."

29. Origen, *CRm* 6.3.12–18 (1059–60): "Unusquisque in manu sua habet et in arbitrii potestate ut aut peccati servus sit aut iustitiae. Ad quamcumque enim partem inclinaverit oboedientiam et cuicumque parere voluerit haec sibi eum vindicat servum. In quo ut dixi absque ulla cunctatione in nobis esse ostendit arbitrii libertatem. In nobis namque est exhibere oboedientiam nostram vel iustitiae vel peccato."

30. Dempsey (1937), pp. 67–68.

31. Ibid., p. 76.

32. Smith (1919), p. 132.

33. De Bruyn (1993), p. 67. Souter (1926), 2:16: "Propter causas superius memoratas in his flagitiis sunt dimissi."

34. De Bruyn (1993), p. 66. Souter (1926), 2:15: " 'Tradere' in scripturis dicitur deus, cum non retinet delinquentes propter arbitrii libertatem."

35. Origen, *CRm* 1.21(18).65–69 (866): "Non enim vi res agitur neque necessitate in alteram partem anima declinatur; . . . sed servatur ei in omnibus libertas arbitrii."

36. Origen, *CRm* 1.22(19).66–68 (870): "Deus tradere dicitur eos quorum actus et animum a se declinantem et indulgentem vitiis abhorrescit ac deserit."

37. Cf. McCue (2001), pp. 169–70.

38. John Chrysostom's theology is strikingly similar. See Christopher Hall, "John Chrysostom," in *Reading Romans Through the Centuries: From the Early Church to Karl Barth* (Grand Rapids: Brazos, 2005), pp. 39–57.

39. Origen's interpretation is found in 7.14.20ff. (1144–45). Cf. De Bruyn (1993), p. 117; Schelkle (1956), pp. 342–43.

40. Origen, *CRm* 1.5.18–21 (845): "Ergo et Paulus quod segregatus in evangelium dicitur et segregatus a ventre matris suae causas in eo et merita quibus in hoc segregari debuerit vidit ille quem non latet mens."

41. De Bruyn (1993), p. 59. Souter (1926), 2:8: "Ita hic per fidele primum servitium meruit apostolatum."

42. Dempsey (1937), p. 74.

43. Smith (1919), p. 130.

44. De Bruyn (1993), p. 112. Souter (1926), 2:68: "Secundum quod proposuit sola fide salvare quos praescierat credituros, et quos gratis vocavit ad salutem multo magis glorificabit [ad salutem] operantes. . . . Praedestinare idem est quod praescire. Ergo quos praevidit conformes futuros in vita, voluit ut fierent conformes in gloria."

45. Origen, *CRm* 7.6.81–85 (1126): "Quod et si secundum propositum ad Deum referatur, hoc est ut secundum propositum Dei, qui sciens in eis religiosam mentem et salutis inesse desiderium, vocati dicantur non videbitur his quae exposuimus etiam hoc esse contrarium."

46. Smith (1919), p. 161.

47. Cf. McCue (2001), p. 172.

48. Cf. A. J. Smith, "The Latin Sources of the Commentary of Pelagius on the Epistle of St. Paul to the Romans," *JTS* 19 (1917–18), pp. 162–230; 20 (1918–19), pp. 55–65, 127–77.

49. Cf. Grech (1996), p. 359. This will be discussed more fully at the end of chapter 7. St. John Fisher cited Origen's text (7.8.5–6 [1126]) in his *Assertionis Lutheranae Confutatio* 694 in order to refute Martin Luther's doctrine of irresistible grace and absolute necessity.

50. Smith (1919), pp. 137–38.

51. De Bruyn (1993), p. 81n33.

52. De Bruyn (1993), p. 81. Souter (1926), 2:32–33: "Iustificati gratis per gratiam ipsius. Sine legis operibus per baptismum, quo omnibus non merentibus gratis peccata donavit."

53. Cf. Rivière (1946), p. 23.

54. Cf. ibid.

55. Cf. Eno (1984), p. 11: "Pelagius as well as the other commentators are perfectly orthodox in teaching that we are justified by Christ without any previous merits or works on our part. It is the situation of the Christian after baptism that demands works. The Christian must make progress. We must do good for charity's sake but not boast about it."

56. De Bruyn (1993), p. 82.

57. Origen, *CRm* 3.4(7).154–58 (945).

58. Origen, *CRm* 3.5(8).14–26 (946).

59. Cf. Smith (1919), p. 138.

60. Cf. De Bruyn (1993), p. 82n34.

61. Cassiodorus modified this gloss to read: "(peccatum intravit) traduce et exemplo" (Sin entered by propagation and by example [*PL* 68:440A]). Cf. Dempsey (1937), p. 30.

62. De Bruyn (1993), p. 95.

63. Cf. Dempsey (1937), p. 28.

64. Cf. De Bruyn (1993), p. 92n19.

65. Cf. Dempsey (1937), p. 31.

66. Origen, *CRm* 5.1.264–66 (1011).

67. Origen, *CRm* 5.1.177ff. (1009).

68. Origen, *CRm* 5.1.192ff. (1009–10).

69. Origen, *CRm* 5.4.23–32 (1029).

70. Origen, *CRm* 5.9.140ff. (1046).

71. Cf. Williams (1927), p. 228.

72. Reasoner (2005), p. 44.

73. Kelly (1978), p. 182.

74. Ibid., pp. 181–82.

75. Roukema (1988), pp. 46–47: "Since in the comment on Rm 5,12b there is no reference to Adam at all, it is clear that Origen understood it as a causal conjunction. However, it is striking that in his comment on Rm 5,12a Origen seems to represent the doctrine of original sin, as he writes that all men were in the loins of Adam when he was in paradise, so that all men have been driven away from it with him or in him, and death came to them too. But in fact, Origen only wanted

to solve the problem why Paul wrote 'through one man' and not 'through one woman.' He does not say expressly that all men have *sinned* in Adam, but only that they are liable to death because of Adam's sin. Instead of introducing a doctrine of original sin he argues that all men, even the saints, have sinned *personally.*" Italics added by Roukema.

76. Similarly, De Bruyn (1988), p. 33, says that Origen's allusion to the pre-existent fall of spiritual creatures "precludes" his consent to any doctrine that holds Adam's descendants accountable for Adam's sin.

77. Bammel (1989), p. 83.

78. De Bruyn (1988), p. 32.

79. Ibid.

80. Ibid., p. 34.

81. Frede (1973, 1974) has published the text of this anonymous commentator.

82. Cf. De Bruyn (1988), pp. 34–39.

83. For the demonstration that Augustine, *De peccatorum meritis ac remissione et de baptismo paruulorum* 1.9, written in 412, was directly dependent on Rufinus's translation of Origen's commentary to prove that sin is transmitted by propagation from Adam and not merely by imitation, see Hammond Bammel (1992), p. 135. This will be discussed in the next chapter.

84. Cf. Dempsey (1937), p. 38.

85. De Bruyn (1993), p. 81. Souter (1926), 2:32: "Opera legis circumcisionem dicit sabbatum et ceteras caeremonias, quae non tam ad iustitiam quam ad carnis laetitiam pertinebant."

86. Origen, *CRm* 8.6.111–18 (1178): "Sciendum est opera quae Paulus repudiat et frequenter uituperat non esse opera iustitiae quae mandantur in lege, sed ea in quibus hi qui secundum carnem legem custodiunt gloriantur; id est uel circumcisio carnis uel sacrificiorum ritus uel obseruatio sabbatorum et numeniarum. Haec et huiusmodi ergo sunt opera ex quibus dicit neminem potuisse saluari."

87. Cf. Ambrosiaster on Rom 3.21, 28; 9.31; Augustine, *Expositio in epistulam ad Galatas* 19 (Gal 3.1). Augustine later shifts the emphasis of this interpretation in *De Spiritu et Littera* 8.14. These references were found in Wiles (1967), p. 68. Augustine's views will be discussed in more detail in the next chapter.

88. De Bruyn (1993), p. 83. Souter (1926), 2:34: "Abutuntur quidam hoc loco ad destructionem operum iustitiae, solam fidem [baptizato] posse sufficere adfirmantes, cum idem alibi dicat apostolus 'et si habuero omnem fidem, ita ut montes transferam, caritatem autem non habeam, nihil mihi prodest,' in qua caritate alio loco legis adserit plenitudinem contineri, dicens: 'plenitudo legis est caritas.' Quod si haec eorum sensui videntur esse contraria, sine quibus operibus [legis] apostolus iustificari hominem per fidem dixisse credendus est? Scilicet circumcisionis vel sabbati et ceterorum huius[ce]modi, non absque iustitiae operibus, de quibus beatus Iacobus dicit: 'fides sine operibus mortua est.' Hic autem de illo dicit, qui ad Christum veniens sola, cum primum credit, fide salvatur."

89. Cf. Lombardo [Augustine] (1988), pp. 67–68.

90. Smith (1919), p. 138.

91. Origen, *CRm* 2.4.140–43 (878).

92. Origen, *CRm* 8.2.117–21 (1163).

93. De Bruyn (1993), p. 85. Souter (1926), 2:36: "Convertentem impium per solam fidem iustificat deus, non per opera bona quae non habuit: alioquin per impietatis opera fuerat puniendus."

94. Origen, *CRm* 4.1.216–18 (965): "Dicit apostolus quod homini iustitia reputetur licet nondum opera iustitiae egerit, sed pro eo tantum quod credidit in eum qui iustificat impium."

95. Eno (1984), pp. 10ff.

96. Wiles (1967), p. 112n7.

97. Origen, *CRm* 4.8.5–6 (988): "Apertissime per haec eum qui intellexit quid sit, ex fide et non ex operibus iustificari, ad pacem Dei quae superat omnem mentem in qua et summa perfectionis consistit invitat."

98. De Bruyn (1993), p. 89. Souter (1926), 2:41: "Pertractata causa quia nemo eorum ex operibus iustificatus sit, sed omnes ex fide . . . qua ratione conclusa, pacem eos habere hortatur, quia nemo suo merito, sed omnes aequaliter dei gratia sunt salvati."

99. Origen, *CRm* 4.1.177–82 (964): " 'Stipendia,' inquit 'peccati mors'; et non addidit ut similiter diceret: stipendia autem iustitiae vita aeterna; sed ait: 'gratia autem Dei vita aeterna'; ut stipendium quod utique debito et mercedi simile est retributionem poenae esse doceret et mortis, vitam vero aeternam soli gratiae consignaret."

100. Origen, *CRm* 4.1.156–57 (963): "Videtur ostendere quasi in fide quidem gratia sit iustificantis, in opere vero iustitia retribuentis."

101. De Bruyn (1993), p. 100. Souter (1926), 2:54: "Non dixit similiter: 'stipendia iustitiae,' quia non erat ante quam remuneraretur in nobis: non enim nostro labore quaesita est, sed dei munere condonata."

102. De Bruyn (1993), p. 105. Souter (1926), 2:60: "Homo carnalis duplex est quodam modo et in semet ipso divisus."

103. Origen, *CRm* 6.11.3–9 (1091): "Quae esset diversitas in his qui velut in quodam certamine positi mente quidem secundum Dei legem vivunt carnis vero desideriis aguntur lege peccati in superioribus docuit. Nunc vero de his dicit qui iam non ex parte in carne et ex parte in spiritu sed ex integro in Christo sunt; et pronuntiat nihil esse in his damnatione dignum, quia lex spiritus vitae in Christo Iesu liberavit eos a lege peccati et mortis."

104. Smith (1919), p. 155.

105. For a complete list of heretics refuted by Pelagius, see Souter (1922), intro., p. 67.

106. Grech (1996), p. 359.

107. Bohlin (1957), p. 103: "Pelagius scheint uns nirgends für seine Gnadenlehre so reiches und so zentrales Material gefunden zu haben wie gerade in Origenes-Rufinus' *Römerbriefkommentar*."

108. Pelagius calls Origen's theory of the pre-existent fall of the soul a solution to the problem of evil that "certain heretics have dreamt up." *Expositio in epistula ad Ephesos, PL* Suppl. 1:1289 = Souter (1931), 3:345. Hammond Bammel (1985), p. 52, observes: "Origen expressed himself more cautiously in the *Romans Commentary* than in the much earlier writing *De Principiis*, and in the meantime transferred the chief stress of his own interests."

109. Bonner (1966), pp. 357–58, expresses the opinion that the clue to Pelagius's orthodoxy or heresy lies not so much in his concept of grace as in the matter of the baptism of infants for the remission of sins.

Chapter 3
Augustine's Reception of Origen's Exegesis of Romans

1. Augustine's works *Expositio quarundam propositionum ex epistula ad Romanos* and *Epistolae ad Romanos: Inchoata expositio* were published in 394–96. Augustine's *Commentary on Galatians* appeared in 394–95.

2. Gorday (1983), p. 141.

3. Cf. Bammel (1992), p. 351n46.

4. See Bammel (1995), pp. 495–513; Heine (2002).

5. See also McCue (2001), pp. 172ff.

6. Bammel (1992), p. 342.

7. Burns (1979), p. 54.

8. McCue (2001), p. 169, argues that for fifteen years after he became a bishop, Augustine continued to preach and teach as though he had never heard of predestination. When it was forced back on his agenda, he only slowly came out clearly in favor of it.

9. See the *JTS* articles under Hammond (1965), (1978), (1979). These are distillations of her doctoral dissertation under Henry Chadwick (Cambridge, 1965).

10. See Hammond Bammel (1992), pp. 133ff.

11. Ibid., p. 133.

12. Cf. Origen, *CRm* 5.9.134–73 (1046–47).

13. Hammond Bammel (1992), p. 137.

14. Bammel (1992), p. 342.

15. *De pecc. mer.* 3.1.1, in Teske (1997).

16. Bammel (1992), p. 359.

17. Origen, *CRm* 5.1.177ff. (1009).

18. Bammel (1992), p. 359.

19. Ibid.

20. Cf. ibid., p. 361. The passage in Origen is 5.1.357–71 (1014).

21. Origen, *CRm* 3.7(10).22–25 (955).

22. Bammel (1992), pp. 367–68.

23. Cf. De Bruyn (1993), p. 84.

24. Bammel (1992), p. 363.

25. Cf. Plumer (2003), p. 153: "Nunc ergo de his operibus maxime tractat, quae sunt in sacramentis, quamquam et illa interdum se admiscere significet."

26. Bammel (1992), p. 353.

27. *De spiritu et littera* 22–23, in Teske (1997).

28. *De spiritu et littera* 25, in Teske (1997).

29. *De spiritu et littera* 50, in Teske (1997).

30. Grech (1996), pp. 345–46. Cf. Rivière (1909), p. 158: "Whatever may have been Origen's theory on original sin, there can be no doubt that according to him all men are sinners and that they were unable to save themselves and that salvation came only through God's mercy."

31. Bammel (1996), p. 231.

32. Bammel (1992), p. 351.

33. Ibid., p. 353.

34. Ibid.

35. *Enarratio ii in Ps. 31*, CCL 38:224–44.

36. Schelkle (1956), p. 124.

37. Bammel (1996), pp. 224–25.

38. Boulding (2000), p. 365. CCL 41:226 (*Enarratio in Ps. 31*, II, 3): "Dicit autem opus omnibus notum, Abraham filium suum immolandum Deo obtulit. Magnum opus, sed ex fide. Laudo superaedificationem operis, sed video fidei fundamentum; laudo fructum boni operis, sed in fide agnosco radicem."

39. Bammel (1996), p. 227.

40. Origen, *CRm* 3.6(9).64 (953).

41. Origen, *CRm* 4.1.216–24 (965).

42. In Origen, *CRm* 4.6.44–47 (981).

43. Origen, *CRm* 4.1.150–52 (963).

44. Bammel (1996), p. 229.

45. Eno (1984), p. 15.

46. Bammel (1996), pp. 229–30.

47. Bammel (1996), p. 235.

48. Bammel (1992), p. 362. Specifically she recommended Augustine's *Epistle* 157 to Hilary of Syracuse, written in 414, which discusses Romans and shows positive contacts with Origen. I have not found Augustine's discussion there to be directly relevant to my current investigation.

49. Di Berardino, in Quasten (1975), *Patrology* 4:370, dates the work to 413.

50. *Retractions* 2.64 (*PL* 32, 583–656).

51. *De fide et operibus* 14, in Liguori (1955). Zycha (1890), pp. 61–62: "Quamobrem iam illud videamus, quod excutiendum est a cordibus religiosis, ne mala securitate salutem suam perdant, si ad eam obtinendam sufficere fidem putaverint, bene autem vivere et bonis operibus viam dei tenere neglexerint."

52. Cf. Di Berardino, in Quasten (1975), *Patrology* 4:370.

53. Liguori (1955), 16.30; cf. Lombardo (1988), p. 3.

54. Origen, *CRm* 8.2.117–21 (1163).

55. De Bruyn (1993), p. 83.

56. Zycha (1890), pp. 61–62: "Nam etiam temporibus apostolorum non intellectis quibusdam sub obscuris sententiis apostoli Pauli hoc eum quidam arbitrati sunt dicere: faciamus mala, ut veniant bona, quia dixerat: lex subintravit, ut abundaret delictum; ubi autem abundavit delictum, superabundavit gratia."

57. Liguori (1955), 14.21. Zycha (1890), pp. 61–62: "Cum ergo dicit apostolus arbitrari se iustificari hominem per fidem sine operibus legis, non hoc agit, ut percepta ac professa fide opera iustitiae contemnantur, sed ut sciat se quisque per fidem posse iustificari, etiamsi legis opera non praecesserint. Sequuntur enim iustificatum, non praecedunt iustificandum. Unde in praesenti opere non opus est latius disputare, prasertim quia ex hac quaestione prolixum librum edidi, qui inscribitur 'De littera et spiritu.' Quoniam ergo haec opinio tunc fuerat exorta, aliae apostolicae epistulae, Petri, Iohannis, Iacobi, Iudae, contra eam dirigunt intentionem, ut vehementer astruant fidem sine operibus non prodesse: sicut etiam ipse Paulus non qualemlibet fidem, qua in deum creditur, sed eam salubrem planeque evangelicam definivit, cuius opera ex dilectione procedunt. Et fides, inquit, quae per dilectionem operatur. Unde illam fidem, quae sufficere ad salutem quibusdam videtur, ita nihil prodesse adseverat, ut dicat: si habeam omnem fidem, ita ut montes transferam, caritatem autem non habeam, nihil sum. Ubi autem fidelis caritas operatur, sine dubio bene vivitur; plenitude enim legis caritas."

58. McGrath (1986), vol. 1, p. 30, correctly observes: "It is unacceptable to summarize Augustine's doctrine of justification as *sola fide iustificamur*—if any such summary is acceptable, it is *sola caritate iustificamur* because he includes the process of sanctification in his doctrine of justification. It is fundamentally concerned with 'being made righteous.' It includes remission of sins, ethical and spiritual renewal through the inner operation of the Holy Spirit."

59. Cf. Origen, *CRm* 4.6(8).71–74 (982).

60. Lombardo (1988), p. 49.

61. Pelagius, *CRm* 2.12 (De Bruyn [1993], p. 72). For a survey of patristic views of this verse, see Schelkle (1956), pp. 79–80.

62. A reader of my manuscript informs me that Robert O'Connell, in his work *The Origin of the Soul in Augustine's Later Works* (New York: Fordham University Press, 1987), has identified Augustine's discovery of the significance of Rom 9.11 as being of crucial importance in his rejection of Origen's theory of fallen souls. The discovery took place at about the time of his work *De fide operibus*.

63. Augustine, *De haeresibus*, chap. 43 (Müller [1956]). Bammel (1992), p. 346, describes Augustine's general attitude displayed here as "marked by cautious restraint and avoidance of personal polemics; his interest is directed to the teachings in question rather than to the individual."

64. For example, Bammel (1992), p. 346n26, writes: "The teachings of Origen which Augustine denounces in his later works are in fact a travesty of Origen constructed by anti-Origenists. Augustine would not have found them in this form in

the exegetical works available to him in Latin translation, nor even unambiguously expressed as 'teachings' in Rufinus' translation of *De principiis*. Such denunciations no doubt partly have the function of a safeguard enabling the denouncer to retain the useful insights of Origen and continue reading him without risking being accused as an Origenist."

65. Bammel (1996), p. 226.

66. Ibid., p. 232. For Origen's definition, she cites the Greek text found in Scherer (1957), p. 162, lines 14–16.

67. Bammel (1996), p. 233.

68. For example, the Protestant view is articulated by C. Cranfield, *The Epistle to the Romans*, vol. 1 (Edinburgh: T. & T. Clark, 1975), p. 95: "There seems to us to be no doubt that δικαιοῦν, as used by Paul, means simply 'acquit,' 'confer a righteous status on,' and does not in itself contain any reference to moral transformation."

69. McGrath (1986), vol. 1, p. 6, says of Augustine's understanding of *iustificare* as "to make just": "While this may be an acceptable interpretation of *iustificare* considered in isolation, it is not an acceptable interpretation of the verb considered as the Latin equivalent of δικαιοῦν."

70. M. J. Lagrange, *La justification selon saint Paul, Revue biblique* (1914), p. 121; cited by Sungenis (1997), p. 300n1.

71. Cf. Sungenis (1997), pp. 615–17, who cites 2 Cor 9.9 (cf. Ps 112.9); Heb 1.9 (cf. Ps 45.7); 1 Pt 3.12; Heb 11.7 (cf. Gn 7.1).

72. McGrath (1986), p. 19.

73. She invokes a Greek fragment found in Scherer (1957), p. 162, lines 14–16.

Chapter 4
William of St. Thierry's Reception of Origen's Exegesis of Romans

1. See R. Heine, *The Commentaries of Origen and Jerome on St. Paul's Epistle to the Ephesians* (Oxford: Oxford University Press, 2002).

2. For a detailed examination of Jerome's reliance on Origen's Pauline exegesis, see Bammel (1995).

3. Hammond (1977), p. 404, elucidates Rufinus's intentions in the epilogue to his translation of Origen's *CRm*, where he says that it would not be right for him to steal the title from Origen, since Origen laid the foundations of the work and supplied the material for the construction of the building: "Rufinus' stand against such plagiarism . . . was an implied criticism of Jerome's methods in his biblical commentaries. The procedure that he [Rufinus] refuses here . . . is similar to that for which he had attacked Jerome and those like him earlier. By directly translating Origen, he himself will reveal to Latin readers the source of Jerome's vaunted learning as a biblical commentator."

4. *PL* 70:1120–21: "Sancti Pauli prima omnium et admirabilior destinata cognoscitur ad Romanos, quam Origenes viginti libris Graeco sermone declar-

avit; quos tamen supradictus Rufinus in decem libros redigens, adhuc copiose transtulit in Latinum."

5. These included Donatism, Pelagianism, Arianism, Nestorianism, Apollodorianism, Sabellianism, Manichaeanism, and Eutychianism. Cf. P. G. Walsh, trans. and ed., *Cassiodorus: Explanation of the Psalms*, vol. 1, *Psalms 1–51 (50)* (New York: Paulist Press, 1990), pp. 11–12.

6. Courcelle (1969), pp. 356, 359, discusses Cassiodorus's esteem for Origen's exegesis: "Cassiodorus rates Origen very highly and, without minimizing the dangers of the doctrine, he considers his contemporaries' severity too excessive, for they prohibit even the reading of his commentaries. Without mentioning any of his dogmatic works, he carefully collected all the texts and translations by Origen that he could find, protecting himself by following St. Jerome's example. . . . Although he possessed a number of Latin commentators, he did not lose sight of the quality of Origen's works. To him, Greek Christian literature seemed like an inexhaustible reservoir for Latin exegesis."

7. "In epistolam ad Romanos multa et mira scripsit Origenes," *De interpretibus divinarum Scripturarum (PL* 131:997c); cited in Lubac (1998), p. 388.

8. Cited by Lubac (1998), p. 28.

9. *PL* 114:477, 483, 495. Cf. Matter (1997), pp. 83–111.

10. For specific references, see the respective essays in Backus (1997).

11. Cf. Peter Abelard, *Expositio in Epistolam ad Romanos / Römerbriefkommentar*, 3 vols. (Freiburg: Herder, 2000).

12. *PL* 103. Cf. Lubac (1998), p. 167: "Sedulius Scottus appropriates large blocks of the commentary on the Letter to the Romans. He goes so far as to reproduce, word for word, a phrase in which Origen, speaking in the first person, gives the opinion that the Hermas mentioned by Saint Paul is the author of the *Pastor* and that this work is divinely inspired."

13. Denifle (1905), pp. xv, 11–12, 220–35. On Favaroni, see Toner (1957–58).

14. Cf. Verfaillie (1926), p. 8.

15. In this chapter, Latin citations from William's commentary are from the critical text, edited by Pauli Verdeyen, CCCM 86. The English translation of William's commentary by John Baptist Hasbrouck was based on the *PL* 180 text. When using Hasbrouck's translation, I have corrected it against the critical text.

16. The Cistercians, taking their name from Citeaux, France, were a Benedictine reform movement that desired stricter observance of the Rule of St. Benedict, including manual labor and a greater emphasis on poverty, simplicity, and personal spirituality.

17. Cf. Renna (1989), p. 50.

18. See Bouyer (1968), pp. 200–205; Déchanet (1972), pp. 1–41.

19. Verdeyen (1989), xxvii–xxviii, liv–lv.

20. Bouyer (1958), p. 67.

21. These terms are borrowed from Lubac (1998), p. 167.

22. Hasbrouck (1980), p. 3.

23. Cf. Déchanet (1972), p. 36.

24. Bouyer (1958), pp. 84–85. Elsewhere in this same work (p. 102), Bouyer asks whether anyone, prior to Völker and Father de Lubac, interpreted the great Alexandrian's teaching as accurately as did William.

25. Déchanet (1972), p. 36.

26. Anderson (1978), p. 142.

27. Cartwright (2001), p. 106; (2003), pp. 27–54. Cf. Anderson (1978), p. 142.

28. Cartwright (2001), p. 98.

29. Hasbrouck (1980), p. 15. Verdeyen (1989), 3.8–16 (M547): "Quae tanto debebit gratior esse lectoribus, quanto eam non novitatis vel vanitatis praesumptio adinvenit, sed magnorum doctorum magna commendat auctoritas, praecipue, sicut dictum est, beati Augustini, deinde vero Ambrosii, Origenis et nonnullorum aliorum doctorum; aliquorum etiam magistrorum nostri temporis, de quibus certum habemus non praeterisse eos in aliquo terminos quos posuerunt patres nostri. Nemo ergo furti nos arguat: ipsi nos prodimus."

30. Lubac (1998), pp. 64–65.

31. Abelard's "Pelagianizing" errors are listed in Denzinger (1954), 373.6: "Quod liberum arbitrium per se sufficiat [sufficit] ad aliquod bonum" (That free will is sufficient in itself for any good). 376.9: "Quod non contraximus culpam ex Adam, sed poenam tantum" (That we have not contracted guilt from Adam, but only punishment). 386.19: "Quod neque opus neque voluntas neque concupiscentia neque delectatio, quae [cum] movet eam, peccatum sit, nec debemus eam velle exstingui [velle eam exstinguere]" (That neither action nor will, neither concupiscence nor delight, when it moves it [the soul] is a sin, nor ought we to wish to extinguish [it]).

32. Verdeyen (1989), 8.70–73 (M550); Hasbrouck (1980), p. 21; cf. Origen, 1.7(5).4–12 (849). Verdeyen (1989), 45.457–60 (M578); cf. Origen, CRm 3.4(7). 108–16 (944).

33. Verdeyen (1989), 9.125–26 (M551); Hasbrouck (1980), p. 23: "grace to be patient in our labors, and apostleship to give authority to our preaching."

34. Origen, CRm 1.9(7).4–5 (852): "Grace must refer to the patience of labors, apostleship to the authority of preaching."

35. Verdeyen (1989), 13.267–69 (M554). Hasbrouck (1980), p. 28: "He nevertheless waits until he has implored with prayers not only that the journey be prosperous for him but that it be prosperous according to the will of God."

36. Origen, CRm 1.13(11).9–10 (857): "He waits until, by means of prayers, he procures not only a successful journey for himself but also a success that comes about by the will of God."

37. Verdeyen (1989), 16.377–84 (M557). Hasbrouck (1980), p. 31; Cf. Origen, CRm 1.17(14).1–11 (861).

38. Origen, CRm 2.9(12–13).133–37 (901): "Et bene addidit: 'legem perficiens.' Ille enim qui secundum litteram vivit custodire dicitur legem; iste vero qui secun-

dum spiritum perficere; perfectio autem legis in Christo est qui dixit: 'non veni solvere legem sed adimplere.' Adimplere autem legem hoc est perficere legem."

39. Hasbrouck (1980), p. 60. Verdeyen (1989), 38.208–11 (M573): "Et bene addidit, 'legem consummans.' Ille enim qui secundum litteram vivit, legem observat; qui secundum spiritum, consummat; perfectio vero in eo est qui dicit: Non veni legem solvere, sed adimplere."

40. Renna (1989), p. 66.

41. Origen, *CRm* 2.5(5–7).200–205 (885); cf. William, Verdeyen (1989), 31.919–23 (M568); Hasbrouck (1980), p. 47.

42. Verdeyen (1989), 52.718–19 (M583); Hasbrouck (1980), p. 77: "This passage seems to show that in faith lies the grace of him who justifies, but in works seems to resound the justice of him who punishes."

43. Origen, *CRm* 4.1.156–157 (963): "He seems to declare that in faith there is the gift of the one who justifies; in works, however, there is the righteousness of the one who repays."

44. Verdeyen (1989), 60.991–99 (M590); Hasbrouck (1980), p. 87.

45. Origen, *CRm* 4.7.71–112 (985–86).

46. Origen, *CRm* 4.7.16–34 (984).

47. Verdeyen (1989), 59.972–81 (M588–89); Hasbrouck (1980), p. 86.

48. *Enarrationes in Psalmos* 31.1–2a. Cf. Bammel (1996), p. 229.

49. Origen, *CRm* 4.1.234–44 (966): "Sed permovet nos ordinis ipsius differentia quod primo dixit: 'beati quorum remissae sunt iniquitates'; secundo: 'quorum tecta sunt peccata'; tertio: 'quibus non imputabit Dominus peccatum.' Et vide si forte potest iste ordo in anima una eademque intellegi; ut quia initium est conversionis animae mala derelinquere pro hoc iniquitatum remissionem mereatur accipere; cum autem coeperit bona facere velut singula quaeque quae praecesserant mala bonis recentibus obtegens et abundantiorem numerum bonorum introducens quam prius fuerat malorum tegere peccata dicatur; ubi vero iam ad perfectum venerit ita ut omnis de ea malitiae radix penitus amputetur eo usque ut nullum in ea vestigium possit inveniri nequitiae ibi iam summa perfectae beatitudinis promittatur cui nullum possit Dominus imputare peccatum."

50. Verfaillie (1926), p. 110.

51. Hasbrouck (1980), p. 77. Verdeyen (1989), 52.698–707 (M583): "Sed inspicienda est ordinis ipsius differentia, qua dixit primum remissas iniquitates, deinde tecta peccata, postmodum vero non imputandum peccatum. Initium enim est conversionis mala relinquere, quod malorum praeteritorum meretur remissionem; deinde singula mala singulis vel amplioribus bonis obtegere; ubi vero ad perfectionem *res* venerit, *gratia Dei et studio bonae conversationis* per virtutis affectum ipsum peccati affectum a cordis intimo radicitus exstirpare. Iam enim peccatum coram Deo nec imputatur factum, quod ab anima *iustificatione Dei innovata* sic fuerit amputatum."

52. Renna (1989), p. 59.

53. *PL* 180:249–50.

54. This was pointed out to me by Steven Cartwright in an e-mail message.

55. William, Verdeyen (1989), 49.630–33 (M581); Hasbrouck (1980), p. 74; cf. Origen, *CRm* 3.8(11).73–83 (957).

56. Augustine, *De spiritu et littera* 50, NPNF 5.104–5.

57. Origen, *CRm* 1.21(18).15–28 (865): "Tamen requiramus ab his qui Deum bonum negant etiam iustum esse iudicem quid respondeant de his quae dicit apostolus quod tradidit eos Deus in desideria cordis in immunditiam ut contumeliis afficiant corpora sua. Videbitur enim in hoc non solum ipsorum ratio quae penitus excluditur sed et nostra responsio coartari. Quomodo enim iustum erit eum qui traditur quamvis pro peccatis tradatur tamen ad concupiscentias tradi et ad hoc tradi ut immunditiis et concupiscentiis afficiat corpus suum? Sicut enim huic qui verbi causa tenebris traditur ad poenam imputari non potest quod in obscuro sit; et qui igni traditur culpari pro hoc ipso non potest cur uratur; ita his qui desideriis et immunditiis traduntur ut contumeliis afficiant corpora sua, non digne videbitur imputari si in desideriis et immunditiis positi corpora sua contumeliis maculent."

58. Origen, *CRm* 1.21(18).6–9(865): "Precedentibus culparum causis iure et merito deserantur a Deo."

59. See the excellent essay on this subject by H. de Lubac, "Tripartite Anthropology," in Lubac (1996), pp. 117–200.

60. Origen, *CRm* 1.21(18).71–74 (865).

61. Hasbrouck (1980), p. 40. Verdeyen (1989), 23–24.641–58 (M562): "Quaeritur autem, ei qui traditur, quamvis pro peccatis suis tradatur in concupiscentias, utrum iuste sit imputandum esse eum in concupiscentiis, sicut ei qui pro criminibus suis carceri deputatur, apte nullus imputare debeat, quod licet iuste, invitus tamen sit in tenebris. Sed sicut idem dicit apostolus, homo spiritus et anima et corpus esse dicitur. Inter spiritum vero et carnem familiaris illa rixa nimis omnibus nota est. *Quem non trahit gratia* carni sociatur et efficitur una caro, et dicitur de homine illo: Non permanebit spiritus meus in eo, quia caro est. *Quem vero trahit gratia,* sociatur spiritui, et unus cum eo spiritus efficitur, et dicitur ei: Vos autem non estis in carne, sed in spiritu. *Trahi ergo vel non trahi, hoc est tradi vel non tradi. Cur autem trahitur ille, ille non trahitur, haec occulta Filii sunt; noli velle quarere, si non vis errare. Si non traheris, ora ut traharis; et si iam fideliter oras, iam traheris nec traderis. In illis qui trahuntur nec traduntur, sola gratia Dei est; in eis vero qui traduntur nec trahuntur, irreprehensibilis eius iustitia est."*

62. Chadwick (1985), p. 230.

63. Hasbrouck (1980), p. 71. Verdeyen (1989), 47.523–30 (M579): "Universa massa poenas debebat; et si omnibus debitum damnationis supplicium redderetur, non iniuste procul dubio redderetur. Quis igitur usque adeo dementissime insaniat, ut non agat ineffabiles gratias misericordiae quos voluit liberantis, qui recte nullo modo posset culpare iustitiam universos omnino damnantis? Quod

cum iustissime sit conclusum, evidentissime ies exclusum, ut nemo in se, nemo in lege, nemo nisi in domino glorietur."

64. Cf. Burns (1985), pp. 345–48.

65. Anderson (1978), p. 144, writes of William, "Our author's understanding of original sin and Romans 5.12 is thoroughly Augustinian down to the damnation of unbaptized children."

66. Origen, *CRm* 5.1.196–201 (1009–10): "Si ergo Levi qui generatione quarta post Abraham nascitur in lumbis Abrahae fuisse perhibetur, multo magis omnes homines qui in hoc mundo nascuntur et nati sunt in lumbis erant Adae cum adhuc esset in paradiso et omnes homines cum ipso vel in ipso expulsi sunt de paradiso cum ipse inde depulsus est."

67. Hasbrouck (1980), p. 102. Verdeyen (1989), 70.340–44 (M596): "Si ergo Levi, qui generatione quarta post Abraham nascitur, in lumbis Abrahae fuisse perhibetur, multo magis omnes homines erant in lumbis Adae, cum *peccaret; et in ipso peccaverunt*, et cum ipso a paradiso expulsi sunt, et per ipsum mors in omnes pertransiit, qui in lumbis eius habebantur."

68. Cartwright (2001), p. 109. Cf. Hasbrouck (1980), p. 127.

69. Anderson (1978), pp. 144–45.

70. Cartwright (2001), p. 98.

71. Origen, *CRm* 7.15.73–80 (1149).

72. Verdeyen (1989), 134.893–905 (M646); Hasbrouck (1980), p. 186.

73. Verdeyen (1989), 150.515–16 (M659): "Gratia enim non invenit, sed efficit meritum."

74. Origen, *CRm* 8.10.29–43 (1191–92): "Sicut omnis materia corporalis cum sine dubio unius naturae sit per accidentes sibi qualitates diversas species profert vel corporum vel arborum vel herbarum; ita et cum omnium rationabilium una natura sit arbitrii proprii aequaliter libertate donata uniuscuiusque proprii motus ex arbitrii potestate prolati vel ad virtutem vel ad libidinem subiectam sibi animam perducentes vel in bonae eam vel in malae arboris speciem formant; ut aut bona dicatur arbor si per arbitrii potestatem delegerit bona aut mala dicatur si elegerit mala; et sic unusquisque secundum propositi sui motus aut bona oliva si iter virtutis incedat aut si contraria sectetur oleaster nominabitur. Inde denique et Dominus in evangelio dicebat: 'Aut facite arborem bonam et fructus eius bonos; aut facite arborem malam et fructus eius malos'; ut ostenderet arborem malam vel bonam non nasci sed fieri."

75. Hasbrouck (1980), p. 215. Verdeyen (1989), 155.700–712 (M663): "Sicut enim omnis materia corporalis, cum sine dubio unius naturae sit, per accidentes sibi qualitates diversas species profert corporum, sive in hominibus, sive in animalibus, sive in arboribus, sive in herbis, ita et cum omnium rationalium una natura sit, arbitrii proprii libertate aequaliter donata, uniuscuiusque motus proprii ex arbitrii libertate probati, vel ad virtutem, vel ad libidinem subjectam sibi animam perducentes, *vel praeeunte gratia Dei* in bonae eam arboris speciem formant, vel proprio vitio in malam arborem deformant. Unde et dominus, ut ostenderet

arborem bonam fieri, non nasci: 'Aut facite,' inquit, 'arborem bonam, et fructus eius bonos; aut facite arborem malam, et fructus eius malos.'"

76. Billy (1990), p. 178.

77. Lubac (1998), p. 159.

78. Cartwright (2001), pp. 100–105.

79. Ibid., pp. 106–7.

80. Ibid., p. 107.

81. Ibid., p. 110.

82. Ibid., p. 111.

Chapter 5
Erasmus's Reception of Origen's Exegesis of Romans

1. See H. de Lubac, *Exégèse médiévale: Les quatre sens de l'écriture*, 2nd pt., 2 (Paris: Aubier, 1964), pp. 427–87.

2. Cf. Boeft (1997), p. 537.

3. Cf. DeMolen (1987), p. xiv: "As the proponent and originator of a philosophy of renewal, he sought to bridge two worlds, those of patristic Christianity and sixteenth-century society, in order to effect a new and more humane world order."

4. *CWE, Ep* 676.32–35. Allen (1913), vol. 3, p. 99.

5. As Olin (1979), p. 35, has pointed out, it is quite incomprehensible that major biographers of Erasmus, such as A. Huizinga and P. Smith, virtually ignore Erasmus's patristic editions. The Catholic Joseph Lortz makes the same mistake in *The Reformation in Germany*, vol. 1, pp. 144–51. On Lortz, see R. Krieg, *Catholic Theologians in Nazi Germany* (New York: Continuum, 2004), pp. 56–82.

6. For a brief discussion of each, see Boeft (1997).

7. Schulze (1997), vol. 2, p. 625.

8. Some of these opponents included Edward Lee, Noel Beda, J. Stunica, J. Latomus. See E. Rummel, *Erasmus and His Catholic Critics*, 2 vols. (Nieuwkoop: De Graaf, 1989).

9. Erasmus, *Ep* 2134 (Allen [1934] vol. 8, pp. 113, 189–94).

10. *Ep* 2136, 30 March 1529 (Allen [1934] vol. 8, pp. 120–21, 185–97).

11. *A History of Theology*, trans. Hunter Guthrie (Garden City: Doubleday, 1968), p. 149. Congar acknowledges certain positive aspects of Erasmus's Christian humanism, but claims that in general "humanists" like Erasmus and John Colet, while Catholic in intention, no longer grasped the doctrinal ensemble of the faith, and therefore paved the way for Spinoza's religion without dogmas. It is unfortunate that the famous Dominican theologian's analysis of Erasmus not only bypasses any discussion of Erasmus's theological works, patristic editions, *Hyper-aspistes 1* and *2*, and his major *Catechism* of 1533, but depends almost entirely on Martin Luther's judgments in *De Servo Arbitrio* for the conclusion about Erasmus's alleged antidogmatism.

12. Cf. Lubac (1996), p. 46.

13. Olin (1979), p. 35.

14. Cf. Bejczy (2001), p. 118.

15. Unfortunately, this particular work of Erasmus, which H. Grisar called "the scholar's incisive and brilliant rejoinder to Luther's DSA," has been almost totally neglected in modern Erasmus (and Luther) scholarship. Its importance was recognized by John Cochlaeus (d. 1552), who called it a noteworthy and very thorough book in which Erasmus "so energetically and lucidly dissolved all of Luther's arguments about free will that neither Luther nor anyone else from the other sects has yet attempted to answer him." Cf. Vandiver (2002), p. 204. St. Thomas More penned a glowing response to his reading of part 1 of *Hyperaspistes* in his Letter 38 [148] to Erasmus (Allen [1926], vol. 6, p. 1770), where he encourages Erasmus to complete part two of the work: "You have displayed the false charges he made against you; you have stabbed him with the point of your pen; all that remains for you is a discussion of Scripture. . . . Luther . . . is fully conscious that his worthless comments, which laboriously obscure the most obvious passages of Scripture while being frigid enough in themselves, would become, under your criticism, a mass of sheer ice" (*St. Thomas More: Selected Letters*, ed. Elizabeth Frances Rogers [New Haven: Yale University Press, 1961], p. 163). Erasmus's work became one of the few truly effective works of early Catholic apologetics. It eventually led Luther's right-hand man, Melanchthon, to embrace the Catholic position on the issue of debate (free will) and to suppress Luther's doctrines of double predestination, total human depravity, and irresistible grace as "Manichaean and Stoical ravings." Cf. *CR* 9, p. 766; *Loci Communes* (1535).

16. In *Hyperaspistes 1*, he wrote to Luther: "From the Catholic Church I have never departed. I have never had the least inclination to enlist in your church—so little, in fact, that, though I have been very unlucky in many other ways, in one respect I consider myself lucky indeed, namely that I have steadfastly kept my distance from your league. I know that in the church which you call papistical there are many with whom I am not pleased, but I see such persons also in your church" (*CWE* 76:117). On 23 July 1532 Eramus wrote to Cardinal Cajetan: "If I had even a particle of heresy in my heart, I would have long ago grown furious with so much endless growling and would have transferred to the camp of the heretics. The fact is, I have never attached a single disciple to myself, and if I was able to tear anyone away from that camp, I handed them over to the Catholic Church, preferring that they be fellow disciples of the Church rather than my own." See *Ep* 2690 (Allen [1941], vol. 10, p. 67).

17. *Hyperaspistes 1, CWE* 76:108.

18. Cf. Bejczy (2001), p. 187.

19. These accusations will be explored in the next chapter on Luther and Melanchthon.

20. Erasmus always had papal support during his lifetime (Leo X, Adrian VI, Clement VII) and the support of moderate Catholic theologians such as John

Colet, John Eck, John Cochlaeus, Beatus Rhenanus, Albert Pighius, Jacob Sadoleto, Cajetan, Thomas More, John Fisher, Juan Luis Vives, Martin Dorp, and Stanislaus Hosius. See A. Flitner, *Erasmus im Urteil seiner Nachwelt* (Tübingen: Max Niemeyer Verlag, 1952).

21. Cf. Bejczy (2001), p. 153.

22. Cf. Godin (1982b), 21–32; A. Godin, *Erasmus, vie de Jean Vitrier et de John Colet, traduction et présentation* (Angers, 1982).

23. *Ep* 1211; *CWE* 8:227; Allen (1922), vol. 4, p. 908.

24. Cf. McConica (1991), pp. 36–37; Godin (1978, 1982a) has documented these citations.

25. Cf. *CWE* 66:127. John Dolan's lacunar and paraphrastic translation of this passage in *The Essential Erasmus* suppresses the specific reference to Erasmus's commentary in preparation.

26. *CWE* 3:9; *Ep* 301; Allen (1910), vol. 2, pp. 5–6.

27. Godin (1978), p. 17.

28. Ibid., p. 17n2.

29. *Ep* 181 (*CWE* 2:87, 45–48). Allen (1906), vol. 1, p. 405, 38–41: "Origenis operum bonam partem evolui; quo praeceptore mihi videor non nullum fecisse operaeprecium [*sic*]. Aperit enim quasi fontes quosdam et rationes indicat artis theologicae."

30. Godin (1982a), p. 79.

31. *Annotations on Romans* (*CWE* 56:107).

32. *Hyperaspistes 2* (*CWE* 77:484–85).

33. "Par son ancienneté, sa science incomparable des Ecritures, Origène est d'abord un bon témoin du texte grec original" (Godin [1978], pp. 22–23).

34. Cf. Sider (1994), *CWE* 56, xi. Contrary to what has often been asserted, it was not Erasmus's main intention to edit the Greek text, even though his 1516 edition actually contains the *editio princeps* of the Greek New Testament. Recent scholarship has demonstrated that Erasmus's principal aim was to bring out a revised Latin translation, sustained by a Greek text and annotations. See H. J. de Jong, "The Character of Erasmus's Translation of the New Testament as Reflected in His Translation of Hebrews 9," *Journal of Medieval and Renaissance Studies* 14 (1984), pp. 81–87; H. J. de Jong, "Novum Testamentum a Nobis Versum: The Essence of Erasmus' Edition of the New Testament," *JTS* 35 (1984), pp. 394–413.

35. Cf. Sider (1994), *CWE* 56, xi.

36. Cf. Godin (1978), pp. 22–23: "Enfin, il est précieux pour restituer l'ordre du discours et de façon plus générale pour tirer au clair l'obscurité des tournures pauliniennes."

37. Welzig (1990), 3:462–64: "Inter quos praecipuus est Origenes, sic hanc Venerem exorsus, ut nemo post illum ausit manus apponere. . . . Non haec dico, quod cuiquam auctor esse velim, ut praeteritis veterum commentariis divinae scripturae scientiam sibi vindicet aut etiam venetur. Immo partem laboris adimat nobis veterum labor, adiuvemur illorum commentariis, dummodo primum ex his

deligamus optimos, velut Origenem, qui sic est primus, ut nemo cum illo conferri possit."

38. Lubac (1996), p. 46, rightly indicates that by "Christian philosophy," Erasmus means the "Mystery of Christ" in all its depths. *Ep* 844; in Allen (1913), vol. 3, p. 337.

39. *Hyperaspistes 2* (*CWE* 77:535). *LB* 10:1435: "Solus Augustinus excludit etiam praevisa merita fuisse in causa, ut Jacob eligeretur, Esau rejiceretur, et odii causam interpretatur peccatum originis. Cui viro quantumlibet per me quidem licebit tribuere qui volet, nunquam tamen hoc illi tribuam, ut plus viderit in Paulinis Epistolis quam interpretes Graeci."

40. With respect to the theme of his article, Cohen (2005), p. 263, noticed that most other extant patristic commentaries on Romans "pale in comparison with Origen's—in the depth of their exposition of chapters 9–11, in the level of their commitment to grapple with exegetical problems inherent in the text, and in extent of their engagement by the issue of Israel's salvation."

41. Sider (2002), p. 127.

42. Origen, *CRm* 1:4 (849); Erasmus, *Annotations to Romans, CWE* 56:11.

43. Origen, *CRm* 7.8 (1127); Erasmus, *Annotations to Romans, CWE* 56:226–27.

44. Origen, *CRm* 5.2 (1022); Erasmus, *Annotations to Romans, CWE* 56:168.

45. *Ep* 1844 (Allen [1928], vol. 7, p. 102): "Origenes omnibus fere Graecis scriptoribus materiam suppeditavit." Cf. *In Psalmum 38* = *LB* 5, 432B–435B: "Origen was a great doctor of the Church from whose sources the minds of nearly all the Greeks were irrigated."

46. On Jerome's knowledge of Origen's Pauline exegesis, see Courcelle (1969), pp. 108–9.

47. The previous chapter on William of St. Thierry has illustrated this.

48. *Ep* 1844 (Allen [1928], vol. 7, p. 101).

49. Cf. *LB* 5, 432B–435B.

50. Origen, *CRm* 7.16.7 (1146).

51. Luther, *On the Bondage of the Will*, in *Luther and Erasmus: Free Will and Salvation*, ed. G. Rupp, *LCC* (Philadelphia: Westminster, 1969), p. 224.

52. *LB* 10:1392: "Hoc Origenis commentum approbavit Ecclesia, sequitur cum Orthodoxis Hieronymus."

53. *Hyperaspistes 2* (*CWE* 77:668).

54. Cf. Bammel (1995), pp. 495–513.

55. *Ep* 2818 (Allen [1941], vol. 10, p. 244): "Torquet multa, arroganter reiicit Origenem et Augustinum, non pauca transilit."

56. *Ep* 2971 (Allen [1947], vol. 11, p. 45): "Miseram Commentarios Melanchthonis, non ut illos imitareris (nec enim alibi magis torquet scripturam, utcumque miram professus simplicitatem), sed quum illic commemorantur variae multorum opiniones, sciebam tuam prudentiam illinc excerpturam quod ad mentis Paulinae faceret cognitionem."

57. Wengert (1998), p. 150.

58. In *CWE* 42:xi–xix, the editors discuss other precedents for Erasmus's method in Cicero and Quintilian. See also Rabil (1978).

59. Origen, *CRm* 9.31.1 (1231).

60. *CWE* 42:76.

61. Cf. Origen, *CRm* 5.1.10 (1008).

62. Cf. Origen, *CRm* 5.10.11 (1051).

63. Origen, *CRm* 2.14.1 (914).

64. Origen, *CRm* 3.2.2 (928).

65. Cf. Preface of Origen, Origen, *CRm* 2.11.2 (895).

66. *CWE* 42:13.

67. Origen, *CRm* 5.1.126–61 (1008).

68. Cf. Heither (1990), p. 43.

69. Cf. Ibid., p. 108.

70. G. Chantraine, "The *Ratio Verae Theologiae* (1518)," in *Essays on the Works of Erasmus,* ed. R. L. DeMolen (New Haven: Yale, 1978), p. 180.

71. "Apology Against Latomus," *CWE* 71:55; *LB* IX 89 E.

72. *LB* 8.438C.

73. *CWE* 42:18.

74. Cf. Origen, *CRm* 1.18.1–2 (865).

75. Cf. *CWE* 42:141n20.

76. Sider (1991), p. 14.

77. *CWE* 42:20.

78. *CWE* 42:142n6.

79. *CWE* 42:22.

80. Origen, *CRm* 2.13.18 (907).

81. *CWE* 42:142n14.

82. Cf. Godin (1982b), p. 386. Godin follows Schelkle (1956), p. 105, in saying that Augustine, in *De spiritu et littera* 8.14, "categorically" rejects this interpretation. In fact, Augustine's interpretation was more complex than that (cf. *Commentary on Galatians* 3, *Faith and Works*) as has been seen above.

83. Reasoner (2005), p. 25.

84. *CWE* 42:25.

85. *CWE* 42:143n13.

86. Payne (1978), p. 322.

87. Origen, *CRm* 3.11.4–5 (958–60).

88. *Hyperaspistes 2* (*CWE* 77:409–10).

89. In his *Commentary on Galatians* (Dillenberger [1961], pp. 144–45) Luther wrote: "Of this difference between the law and the Gospel there is nothing to be found in the books of the monks, canonists, school-divines; no, nor in the books of the ancient Fathers. Augustine did somewhat understand this difference, and shewed it. Jerome and others knew it not."

90. Reasoner (2005), p. 148.

91. J. Dolan, *The Essential Erasmus* (New York: New American Library, 1964), p. 327.

92. The Latin text is found in *LB* 5, 470–506.

93. *LB* 5, 500: "Concedamus fide justificari, hoc est, purificari corda credentium, modo fateamur ad consequendam salutem necessaria caritatis opera. Neque enim vera fides potest esse otiosa, quum sit fons & seminarium omnium bonorum operum."

94. Rabil (1978), p. 151.

95. *CWE* 42:22.

96. Rabil (1978), p. 158n38.

97. Ibid.

98. *CWE* 42:32.

99. *CWE* 42:146–47n17.

100. Sider (1991), p. 12.

101. *Pagan Servitude of the Church* (Dillenberger [1961], p. 295).

102. *CWE* 64:36.

103. Origen, *CRm* 4.7.8 (986).

104. *CWE* 42:37.

105. Origen, *CRm* 5.8.13 (1042).

106. *CWE* 42:38.

107. Origen, *CRm* 5.10.18 (1056).

108. *CWE* 42:39. Cf. Godin (1982b), p. 375.

109. *CWE* 42:149nn11, 12.

110. Origen, *CRm* 6.7.5 (1068).

111. *CWE* 42:45.

112. Cf. Origen, *CRm* 6.11.1–2 (1091–92).

113. *CWE* 42:45; 42:150; Origen, *CRm* 6.11.2 (1091–92); 6.12.12 (1094).

114. *CWE* 42:46.

115. Origen, *CRm* 6.12.8 (1096).

116. Rabil (1978), p. 151.

117. *CWE* 42:55.

118. In his *Assertion of All the Articles of Martin Luther, Article 36*, Luther writes: "For I misspoke when I said that free will before grace exists in name only; rather I should have simply said 'free will is a fiction among real things, a name with no reality.' For no one has it within his control to intend anything, good or evil, but rather, as was rightly taught by the article of Wyclif which was condemned at Constance, all things occur by absolute necessity. That was what the poet meant when he said, 'All things are settled by a fixed law.'" Cited in Erasmus, *Hyperaspistes 1, CWE* 76:306.

119. *CWE* 42:50.

120. Origen, *CRm* 7.7.5 (1123).

121. Grech (1996), p. 348, citing Origen, *CRm* 7.8 (1142–43).

122. *Hyperaspistes* 2 (*CWE* 77:535); *LB* 10:1435. Grech (1996), p. 349, states: "Origen obviously found difficulty reconciling free will and predestination. His stress lies on free will, as he is arguing against the gnostics, and, in a certain measure, binds God's free will to man's foreknown merits. The later Augustine chooses the other alternative, which adheres more closely to Paul's text but creates more serious theological problems."

123. *CWE* 42:55; Origen, *CRm* 7.16.1 (1143).

124. Cf. Payne (1990). Boyd (1966), p. 438, offers a Calvinist perspective on Origen's interpretation. He observes that Origen understands the words "God hardened" as describing the result and not the intention of God acting in perfect goodness. He says that Origen's statement "God does not harden whom he wills, but he who refuses to respond to his longsuffering becomes hardened," Origen, *CRm* 7. 16 (1147), "is the nearest that Origen gets to flat contradiciton of the apostle."

125. *CWE* 42:55.

126. Ibid.

127. Origen, *CRm* 7.16.8 (1147).

128. Payne (1990), p. 124. This interpretation of Origen is found in *Peri Archon,* but not in his *CRm.*

129. Payne (1990), p. 124.

130. Ibid., pp. 121, 130. Jerome interprets the hardening of Pharaoh's heart as postponement of punishment in *Commentarii in Isaiam prophetam* 17 on Is 63.18–19, *PL* 24, 619 B–C.

131. Cf. *CWE* 77:546.

132. Cf. Luther's *Bondage of the Will,* in *Luther and Erasmus: Free Will and Salvation,* ed. Rupp, p. 252.

133. Cf. *CWE* 77:556, 559.

134. McSorley (1969), pp. 347–48, writes: "Many times Luther asserts, 'God damns those who do not deserve or cannot avoid deserving damnation!' No Christian apologist prior to Luther has ever tried to defend as non-contradictory the truly contradictory assertion that God is just even though he condemns men who, according to the standard of reason illumined by grace, do not deserve condemnation."

135. Commenting on Rom 9–10 in his Homily 16 on Romans (NPNF1, 11.469–70), Chrysostom writes: "As then Pharaoh became a vessel of wrath by his own lawlessness, so did these become vessels of mercy by their own readiness to obey. For though the more part [*sic*] is of God, still they also have contributed themselves some little . . . he does not deprive us of free-will, but shows that all is not one's own, for that it requires grace from above. For it is binding on us to will, and also to run: but to confide not in our own labors, but in the love of God toward man. . . . Whence then are some vessels of wrath, and some of mercy? Of their own free choice. God, however, being very good, shows the same kindness to both. For it was not those in a state of salvation only to whom he showed mercy,

but also Pharaoh, as far as his part went. For of the same long-suffering, both they and he had the advantage. And if he was not saved, it was quite owing to his own will: since, as for what concerned God, he had as much done for him as they who were saved. . . . Do you see that he too does not say that all are to be saved, but that those that are worthy shall? For I regard not the multitude, he means, nor does a race diffused so far distress me, but those only do I save that yield themselves worthy of it. And he does not mention the 'sand of the sea' without a reason, but to remind them of the ancient promise whereof they had made themselves unworthy."

136. *CWE* 77:533–34.

137. See Hall (2005).

138. Origen, *CRm* 9.1. (1201–3).

139. Origen, *CRm* 9.1.1 (1203).

140. Cf. Godin (1982b), p. 392.

141. *CWE* 42:69.

142. This was Melanchthon's accusation against Erasmus's Pauline exegesis; cited, discussed, and repeated in Wengert (1998), p. 140.

143. *Origenis proaemium Contra Celsum et in fidei Christianae defensionem,* liber 1 (Rome: Georgius Herolt de Bamburga, 1481) (Ludwig Hain, Repertorium bibliographicum . . . usque ad annum MD. 4 vols. [Stuttgart and Paris, 1826–38; repr. Milan, 1966], 12078). Cf. Schär (1979), pp. 112–26.

144. Pico della Mirandola possessed it. Cf. Schär (1979), p. 126.

145. Cf. Schär (1979), pp. 109–11.

146. Cf. Nodes (1999), p. 54.

147. Cf. H. de Lubac, *Une controverse sur Origène à la Renaissance: Jean Pic de la Mirandole et Pedro Garcia* (Vrin, 1977); Lubac (1999), pp. 61–66; Schär (1979), pp. 126–43.

148. Cf. J. O'Malley, "Preaching for the Popes," in *The Pursuit of Holiness in Late Medieval and Renaissance Religion,* papers from the University of Michigan conference, ed. C. Trinkhaus with H. A. Oberman (Leiden: Brill, 1974), pp. 408–43.

149. They are found with Latin text in Schär (1979), pp. 132–34, and summarized by Nodes (1999), pp. 56–57; Lubac (1996), pp. 61–66.

150. This is a point that Rufinus makes in his *Apology to Anastasius* (NPNF 3:431).

151. For a detailed discussion of the dispute over Origen's supposed fall and repentance, see Lubac, "The Dispute in Modern Times About the Salvation of Origen," in Lubac (1996), pp. 57–116.

152. Referring to Pico's *Apology,* Schär (1979), p. 136, makes the interesting observation that Pico seldom cites Origen's works directly. Instead it is the voices of other ancient Fathers that are heaped up in Pico's work. Apart from the second-hand citations from Origen's *Letter to Certain Friends in Alexandria* (a letter that is cited by Rufinus and Jerome in their respectives *Apologies*), the sole source of

Origen's words of which Pico makes immediate and strikingly frequent use is Rufinus's translation of Origen's *Commentary on the Epistle to the Romans*. Schär counted eight citations from this work.

153. Schär (1979), p. 142.

154. Nodes (1999), p. 60. See Pusino (1927).

155. On this edition, see Schär (1979), pp. 143–52.

156. For an English translation, see John C. Olin, *Catholic Reform: From Cardinal Ximenes to the Council of Trent, 1495–1563* (New York: Fordham University Press, 1990), pp. 47–60.

157. Schär (1979), p. 145.

158. Cf. Nodes (1999), p. 53.

159. This is the suggestion of Wind (1954), p. 423, who provides the following evidence. The preface author envies Origen because St. *Jerome* (Aleander's namesake) had been his bard, just as *Alexander* (cf. *Aleander*) the Great, standing at the tomb of Achilles, had envied him because his fame had been sung by Homer. As early as 1499, Aleander had engaged in a public debate with the title: "De natura angelica" (Wind [1954], p. 423, citing E. Jovy, *François Tissard et Jérôme Aléandre* [1899], vol. 1, p. 139). Wind further observes that Aleander's youthful proficiency in Hebrew, Greek, and Latin was extolled by Aldus in his dedication of the Homer (1504), and in 1521, in his oration at the Diet of Worms, Aleander protested against a comparison of Luther to Origen.

160. Wind (1954), p. 423. The last sentence alludes to Jerome's *Preface* to his translation of Origen's *Homilies on Ezekiel* and Rufinus's preface to Origen's *CRm*.

161. Wind (1954), p. 416. Jerome said this in the *Preface* to his translation of Origen's *Homilies on Ezekiel*.

162. See Schär (1979), pp. 153–60.

163. Hammond (1965), p. 356.

164. Schär (1979), p. 154n446.

165. J. Merlin, *Operum Origenis Adamantii tomi duo priores, cum tabula et indice generali. Venumdatur cum duobus reliquiis eorumdem tomis in edibus Joannis Parvi et Jodocii Badii Ascensii* (Paris, 1512); cf. Schär (1979), pp. 193ff.

166. Cf. Schär (1979), p. 194.

167. See Farge's article on Merlin in *CE*.

168. Cf. Erasmus, *Ep* 1763, Allen (1926), vol. 6, p. 429 (*CWE* 12). For a recent assessment of Beda, see Mark Crane, "Competing Visions of Christian Reform: Noel Beda and Erasmus," *Erasmus of Rotterdam Society Yearbook* 25 (2005), pp. 39–57.

169. Schär (1979), p. 198n169.

170. Ibid., p. 198n170.

171. Ibid., p. 198.

172. Ibid., p. 200.

173. Pope Gelasius, at a council at Rome in 494, drew up a list of books to be received in the Church, in which he said of Origen's translator Rufinus: "He was a religious man, and wrote many books of use to the Church, and many commentaries on the Scriptures; but since the most blessed Jerome defamed him on certain points, we take part with him [Jerome] in this and in all cases in which he has pronounced a condemnation." Cited by Fremantle, NPNF2, 3:410. The pope's judgment was taken by many to be an official endorsement of the late Jerome's condemnation of Origen.

174. Schär (1979), p. 202.

175. Ibid., p. 203.

176. Ibid.

177. Ibid., p. 204n211.

178. Ibid., p. 205.

179. Lubac (1996), p. 68.

180. Schär (1979), p. 204n211.

181. Ibid., p. 204.

182. It was published in September 1536 in two volumes under the title *Origenis Adamantii eximii scriptuarum interpretis opera, quae quidem extant omnia, per Des. Erasmum Roterodamum, partim versa, partim vigilanter recognita, cum praefatione de Vita, Phrasi, Docendi ratione, et Operibus illius, adiectis epistola Beati Rhenani nuncupatoria, quae pleraque de vita obituque ipsius Erasmi cognitu dicta continet, et indice copiosissimo.*

183. *CWE* 56:94–96.

184. Cf. *Annotations on Romans* 3.5 (*CWE* 56:94).

185. *Annotations on Romans, CWE* 56:244.

186. Cf. Cocchini (1979).

187. *CWE* 61:44.

188. Cf. Wengert (1998), p. 59.

189. *CWE* 71:72.

190. *CWE* 71:73.

191. *CWE* 70:316.

192. *Hyperaspistes 2* (*CWE* 77:449).

193. *Ep* 1844 (Allen [1928], vol. 7, p. 102): "Multa sunt de quibus hodie dubitare summa sit impietas, quum de iisdem olim inquirere religiosa fuerit diligentia."

194. This is discussed by Bejczy (2001), pp. 29–30.

195. *CWE* 64:367–68. The editor indicates that a fuller treatment is given by Erasmus in *In Psalmum 38, LB* V, 432B–435B; cf. *In Psalmum 22*, 185n399; *CWE* 63, intro., p. xxxii.

196. *LB* 8, c. 428; cf. 1 Pt 3.9–17.

197. Cf. Boeft (1997), p. 537.

198. Cf. Bejczy (2001), p. 106.

Chapter 6
Luther and Melanchthon's Reception of Origen's Exegesis of Romans

1. Grech (1996), p. 338.
2. See Ganoczy (1987), pp. 146–51.
3. Schulze (1997), vol. 2, p. 625.
4. Ibid.
5. Schulze (1997), p. 625.
6. In his *Assertion of All the Articles of Martin Luther,* Article 36, Luther writes: "[The Gospel] has been repressed and extinguished . . . by almost all teachers in the schools for more than thirteen hundred years. For on this point everyone writes against grace, not for it . . ." Cited in *CWE* 76:309–10.
7. "Luther," in *Augustine Through the Ages: An Encyclopedia,* ed. A. D. Fitzgerald (Grand Rapids: Eerdmans, 1999), pp. 516–18.
8. Dillenberger (1961), p. 11.
9. Cf. Schulze (1997), p. 612.
10. Luther, *Table Talk, LW* 54:49. *WA* Tischreden 1:140, no. 347: "Sind ich Paulum verstanden hab, so hab ich keinen Doctor konnen achten. Sie sind mir gar gering worden. Principio Augustinum vorabam, non legebam, sed da mir in Paulo die thur auffgieng, das ich wußte, was iustificatio fidei ward, da ward es aus mit ihm."
11. Grisar (1914), vol. 1, p. 305.
12. *WA* 16:67: "Wir habens uns gelegt auff Hieronymum, Origenem, Cyprianum, Augustinum, in his studuimus et perdidimus tempus."
13. Preface to *In prophetam Amos Iohannis Brentii expositio* (1530), *WA* 30:2, 650, 17–20.
14. *LW* 54:33–34; *WA* Tischreden 1:106, no. 252: "Hieronymus potest legi propter historias, nam de fide et doctrina verae religionis ne verbum quidem habet. Origenem hab ich schon in bann gethan. Chrisostomus gillt bei mir auch nichts, ist nur ein wesscher. Basilius taug gar nichts, der ist gar ein munch; ich wolt nit ein heller umb ihn geben."
15. *Predigten des Jahres 1530, WA* 32, 241, 28–31: "Hieronymus, Ciprianus, Origines et omnes non praedicavit Christum."
16. Cf. Wiles (1967), pp. 134–35: "When Luther said 'in toto Origene non est verbum unum de Christo,' what no doubt he really meant was that Origen did not teach the same doctrine of justification by faith alone which he found in the writings of Paul. That is what many later Protestant writers have really meant when they have complained of the unpauline character of Origen and other patristic writers."
17. Schulze (1997) 2:611. Preface to *In prophetam Amos Iohannis Brentii expositio* (1530), *WA* 30:2, 650, 24–33: "Quo circa saepius et pene cum indignatione admiror, Quomodo D. Hieronymus nomen Doctoris Ecclesiae et Origenes Magistri Ecclesiarum post Apostolos meruerint, cum in utroque autore non facile tres

versus invenias de fidei iusticia docentes Neque Christianum ullum facere queas ex universis utriusque scriptis; ita vagantur allegoriis rerum gestarum aut capiuntur pompis operum. Neque alius fuisset S. Augustinus, nisi Pelagiani eum tandem exercuissent et ad fidei iusticiam impulissent. Qua lucta et exercitio evasis vere Doctor Ecclesiae, ac pene solus post Apostolos et primos patres Ecclesiae."

18. Cf. *CR* 11:728: "Fuerint sane magni viri Solon, Themistocles, Scipio, Augustus, et similes, qui magna imperia vel constituerunt, vel rexerunt: tamen longe inferiores sunt his nostris ducibus Iesaia, Baptista, Paulo, Augustino, Luthero."

19. All citations from *Historia Vita* are from Frazel's translation in the new edition by Vandiver (2002). The Latin text is from *Historia Vita* (1548), which has never been published in a modern edition. This work does not appear in either the *CR* or the *SA* editions of Melanchthon's works. T. Frazel has made available to me a facsimile edition of the Latin text which forms the basis of his translation.

20. *Historia Vita*, Vandiver (2002), p. 18.

21. Grisar (1914), vol. 1, p. 303.

22. Wiles (1967), p. 139.

23. McGrath (1986), vol. 2, p. 10.

24. *Historia Vita*, Vandiver (2002), p. 24.

25. Ibid., pp. 38–39: "Ach!, Obiit Auriga et currus Israel, qui rexit Ecclesiam in hac ultima senecta mundi: Neque enim humana sagacitate depraehensa est doctrine de Remissione peccatorum, et de fiducia Filli Dei, Se a Deo per hunc virum patefacta, Quem etiam a Deo excitatum vidimus fuisse."

26. Ibid., pp. 22–23: "Post primam puritatem secutae videntur mutationes doctrinae insignes quatuor."

27. In this section, Melanchthon hides his attack on Origen behind the authority of St. Methodius (d. 311), whom he "singles out" as an ancient theologian who allegedly was correct to condemn Origen. However, Melanchthon does not inform his readers of the doctrines for which Methodius had criticized Origen. These were Origen's speculations about the pre-existence of souls, the nature of the resurrection body, and his excessively allegorical interpretation of Genesis. (The martyr Pamphilus of Caesarea had defended Origen against Methodius's charges in his *Apology for Origen*. See Quasten [1975], 2:129–37.) Consequently, Melanchthon's appeal to the name of St. Methodius in his own idiosyncratic attack on Origen's interpretation of Romans is misleading.

28. "Haec aetas pene totum amisit discrimen Legis et Evangelii."

29. *Historia vita*, Vandiver (2002), p. 23.

30. Ibid., p. 24. "Et non tantum coenum, sed insuper venena, id est, opiniones probantes manifesta Idola in fontes Evangelicos infudit."

31. Ibid., pp. 38–39.

32. Grisar (1914), vol. 1, p. 303.

33. Norelli (1997), p. 749.

34. Ibid., pp. 753–54.

35. Ibid., p. 751.

36. *Centuries of Magdeburg* (Cent. II. Praef. Aa 3v); cited by Norelli (1997), p. 752n23.

37. *Historia vita,* Vandiver (2002), p. 23.

38. Fraenkel (1961), p. 298.

39. Ibid., p. 86. He goes on to report that in *Cario's Chronicle* Melanchthon depicted Origen as the corrupter of later generations. He also blamed Chrysostom for having opposed the condemnation of Origen's writings and approved Epiphanius and others for the criticism of him, "since there is no doubt that his books contain 'tremendous errors.'"

40. *WA* 10, 2, pp. 309–10: "Scilicet neminem scripsisse melius in S. Paulum, tibi vere tribuo. . . . Quin amplius irritare volo nasutos istos et dico Hieronymi et Origenis commentaria esse meras nugas et ineptias, si tuis annotationibus comparentur. . . . Esto, sis humilis: sines tamen me in te superbire. . . . Sufficit te proximum Paulo esse."

41. *CR* 3:922.

42. *SA* 1:323–86; *CR* 15:733ff.

43. 8 January 1540 (*CR* 3:922).

44. Keen (1996), p. 1.

45. The story is taken from Herodotus 1.107–19 and was deleted from the version published in Melanchthon's *Commentary on Romans* of 1540. It appears in *SA* 1:324.

46. *SA* 1:324: "Talem in Ecclesia tyrannidem multis saeculis pontifices et eorum satellites gerunt. Postulant, ut sine discrimine populus omnia decreta, etiam aperte impia, omnes abusus, omnia monachorum deliramenta comprobet et tanquam coelestia oracula suspiciat."

47. Keen (1996), p. 3. For supporting evidence Keen cites *Declamatio de puritate doctrinae* (1537), *CR* 11:273; Melanchthon to Bernhard von Hagen, 24 March 1539, *CR* 3:667, no. 1786.

48. Cf. Fraenkel (1961), p. 178.

49. Ibid., p. 359.

50. Cf. *SA* 1:350, 351–52, 353, 354, 355–56, 356–57, 357–58, 365–66, and 345–47.

51. Cf. Erasmus, *ASD* IX-I, p. 291: 211–13. See Bejczy (2001), pp. 180ff.

52. Van den Brink (1969), p. 99.

53. Ibid.

54. Ibid., p. 101.

55. Ibid.

56. Jacobus Latomus or Masson (c. 1475–1544) was a theologian from Louvain who began to write against the Reformers in 1520. Luther regarded him as far superior to all his other opponents. He said of him in the *Tischreden* (*LW* 54:77), "Only Latomus wrote against Luther; all the rest, even Erasmus, were croaking toads." See E. Amann, *DTC* 8.2.2626–28.

57. Van den Brink (1969), p. 104.

58. Quoted in Grisar (1916), vol. 5, p. 266.

59. Fraenkel (1961), p. 307.

60. Van den Brink (1969), p. 104.

61. Wengert (1999), p. 119, thinks that even as a twenty-two-year-old, Melanchthon outdistanced the fifty-three-year-old Erasmus as a patristic scholar. Yet by this time Erasmus had already edited his annotated Greek NT and his edition of St. Jerome's writings. Wengert calls Meijering's criticism of Melanchthon's patristic knowledge "weak."

62. Meijering (1983), p. 139.

63. Ibid., p. 141.

64. Wengert (1999), p. 118, citing Fraenkel.

65. Kramer (1992), p. 25. *CR* 15:510–11: "Est ergo, Fide iustificamur, idem quod reputamur iusti a Deo propter Christum cum credimus. Et vocabulum, Iusticia, non hic significat iusticiam legis, seu obedientiam universalem, seu nostras qualitates, cum dicitur: Fide donatur nobis iusticia, sed significat imputationem iusticiae, seu acceptationem. Et iustus hoc modo relative intelligatur, pro accepto ad vitam aeternam."

66. Kramer (1992), p. 102. *CR* 15:590: "Ita ponit definitionem, et ut ita dicam, formale iustificationis."

67. *CR* 15:590: "Est itaque iustificatio iustos reputari, non propter nostras virtutes, sed Deo remittente peccata, et immundos et indignos acceptante, per misericordiam propter Christum."

68. Kramer (1992), p. 88. *CR* 15:576: "Ut enim tota scriptura divina alias legem proponit, alias Evangelium, ita sunt sua quaedam dicta legis, et sua quaedam Evangelii. Et tamen Evangelium est lumen et interpretatio legis. Haec est phrasis legis: Reddet unicuique iuxta opera sua. Estque sententia: Tribuet iustis praemia, et iniustos puniet. Nec dubium est ex Evangelio addendam esse enarrationem, qui sint iusti, et quae opera Deo placeant. Nam dicta legis sine Evangelio pariunt desperationem. Nunquam conscientia in veris pavoribus statuere potest, se opera habere digna remissione peccatorum, aut vita aeterna. Ut cum ait Christus: Si vis in vitam ingredi, serva mandata. Hic necesse est τὸ ῥητὸν mitigari addita interpretatione ex Evangelio. Nemo enim legi satisfacit."

69. *CR* 15:586–87: "Hic error eximendus est animis: Nam Christus non venit, ut legem ferret, nec Moises est, nec Solon, sed habet aliud multo maius officium, Est victima pro peccato, et gratis donat nobis remissionem peccatorum."

70. *CR* 15:589: "Nos e contra recte intelligamus, Christum semper manere mediatorem, et applicandum esse fide, id est, statuendum quod placeamus, non propter nostram dignitatem, aut impletionem legis, sed propter Christum. Non debemus opponere iudicio Dei nostras virtutes, sed victimam et propiciatorem Christum."

71. Quintilian, *Institutio oratoria* 8.6.19–20; Loeb edition, trans. H. E. Butler (New York: G. P. Putnam's Sons, 1921), pp. 311–13.

72. Kramer (1992), p. 107. *CR* 15:596: "Abrahae imputatum est ad iusticiam, quod credidit, Ergo et nos iustificamur fide, non propter nostra opera aut legem."

73. Kramer (1992), p. 108. *CR* 15:596: "Sed hoc argumentum cavillantur aliqui multis modis. Alii dicunt esse synecdochen. Et credere, dicunt esse opus, et significare universalem obedientiam, Abraham credidit, id est, obedivit Deo iuxta synecdochen, quia fidem debet sequi obedientia, Ideo fide aiunt significari universalem obedientiam."

74. Kramer (1992), p. 108. *CR* 15:596–97: "Est ergo sententia, credidit, id est, statuit se habere Deum propicium, quamvis sentiebat se indignum esse, et hac fiducia expectabat auxilium et promissum semen, etc. Ita fide iustificatus est, id est, placuit per misericordiam gratis, non propter propriam dignitatem . . . Quare non est affingenda synecdoche, Abraham est iustificatus propter noticiam verbi, et suos mores convenientes doctrinae et professioni. Quia fides non nititur dignitate virtutum propriarum, sed intuetur tantum misericordiam."

75. Hacker (1970, 1970a) argues convincingly that such an interpretation does violence to the text of the New Testament passage. It is undoubtedly an innovative interpretation in the history of exegesis.

76. Sadoleto's *Commentary on Romans* was in fact judged to be heterodox by Catholic authorities in the sixteenth century. It was censured by the Sorbonne, as Erasmus had foreseen. See R. M. Douglas, *Jacobo Sadoleto 1477–1547, Humanist and Reformer* (Cambridge: Harvard University Press, 1959), pp. 81–89. Significantly, however, the dogmatic issue for which Sadoleto was faulted was not that which Melanchthon reproaches here. On the contrary, Catholic authorities charged that Sadoleto, in his effort to reaffirm the capacity for free assent in man's response to God, came too near to Pelagius, having failed to examine later scholastics and having neglected prevenient grace in his treatment of the nature of justification. In short, according to Catholic authorities, the problem with Sadoleto's *Commentary on Romans* had nothing to do with what Melanchthon here identifies, namely his interpretation that Paul's insistence on the necessity of faith does not exclude the necessity of good works in human justification. This again confirms that Melanchthon's litmus test for the orthodoxy of the Catholic exegetical tradition was riveted on his own and Luther's forensic doctrine of justification by faith alone, which excludes interior renewal in good works from the constitution of justification. Melanchthon was not concerned primarily with the Augustinian theme of the necessity of prevenient grace.

77. Kramer (1992), p. 110. *CR* 15:599: "Nam Sadoletus et alii imaginantur synecdochen: Fide iustificamur, id est, fide consequimur virtutes, propter harum dignitatem placemus Deo. Sic illi imaginantur. Ad Paulus excludit hoc meritum, et dicit nos coram Deo peccatores esse, et ita iustos reputari, scilicet remissione peccatorum."

78. Kramer (1992), p. 111. *CR* 15:599: "Sed cavillantur hunc locum adversarii hoc modo. Alii loci tribuunt beatitudinem operibus: Beatus vir qui timet Dominum: Beati misericordes etc. Ergo simili modo possumus argumentari, quod iustifice-

mur propter opera, sicut Paulus argumentatur ex Psalmo, Quod iustificemur remissione peccatorum."

79. *CR* 15:599–600: "Respondeo: Neganda est consequentia, quia in omnibus locis de operibus debet includi locus: Beati quorum remissae sunt iniquitates, quia opera non placent, nisi in credente seu iusto. Ideo Paulus rectissime citat hunc locum, cum de remissione peccatorum loquitur, quae est gratuita."

80. Kramer (1992), p. 111. *CR* 15:600: "Quare facis synecdochen in locis operum, et non in locis fidei? Respondeo: Quia opera non placent, nisi in credente seu iusto. Ideo in locis operum includimus fidem. In locis de fide non est synecdoche, quia accipit remissionem per misericordiam, nec nititur, dignitate operum, imo fieret incerta et excuteretur, si penderet ex dignitate operum seu merito. Ideo gratis, ut sit firma promissio."

81. It appears to me that Erasmus had a keen perception of what is wrong with the Lutheran conception of divine grace. In *Hyperaspistes 1*, he writes: "When they say that those who have been justified by faith do nothing but sin, so that by loving and trusting God we become worthy of his hatred, are they not making God's grace extremely miserly? Grace justifies man by faith in such a way that he is still nothing but sin!" (*CWE* 76:84).

82. Kramer (1992), pp. 253–54. *CR* 15:749 (*SA* 1:346): "In Rom. tractans hanc propositionem: Fide iustificamur, non ex operibus, intelligit eam κατὰ συνεκδοχὴν, fide sumus iusti, id est, perfecta fide complectente omnes virtutes. Idque declarat, dicit idem posse dici de caeteris virtutibus. Misericordia sumus iusti, scilicet perfecta, complectente caeteras virtutes. Hoc nihil aliud est dicere, quam homines propter opera et propter virtutes suas habere remissionem peccatorum et iustos esse. Cumque non attendat, quid agat Paulus, quid vocet fidem, quid sibi velit illa exclusiva: Non ex operibus, addit enarrationes confusas et perplexas, nec sibi constat."

83. Kramer (1992), pp. 34–35. *CR* 15:520–21: "Nunc reprehendenda est sophistica Origenis, Monachorum, et multorum aliorum, qui κατὰ συνεκδοχὴν dici arbitrantur: Fide iustificamur, id est, propter noticiam historiae de Christo, seu professionem et caeteras virtutes, seu universalem obedientiam sumus iusti. Sic intelligunt fidem, et laudari professionem a Paulo arbitrantur, quia etsi communis est professio cum flagitiosis, tamen sine ea caeterae virtutes, ut in Turcis, non placerent Deo. Ita haec synecdoche transformat Evangelium in legem, transfert gloriam Christi ad nostras virtutes, delet consolationem conscientiarum, abolet doctrinam veram de fide, id est, fiducia misericordiae . . . igitur refutabo hanc synecdochen, pugnantem cum tota disputatione Pauli."

84. Wengert (1997), p. 179.

85. On 2 November 1540, Melanchthon wrote to Camerarius (*CR* 3:1126): "You see what thick darkness envelops the commentaries of the ancients and the whole doctrine of our opponents, how utterly ignorant they are of what sin really is, of the purpose of the law, of the blessings of the Gospel, of prayer, and of man's refuge when assailed by mental terrors."

86. Kramer (1992), p. 240.

87. Ibid., p. 253.

88. CR 15:749: "Interdum enim effundit aliquod tolerabile dictum, sed id postea mox corrumpit."

89. The passage is Origen, CRm 4.1 (965).

90. Cf. Origen, CRm 3.6(9).30–39 (953).

91. Kramer (1992), p. 254. CR 15:749–50: "Sed postea declarans illa, videtur hoc velle, hominem initio consequi remissionem peccatorum sola fide, postea iustum esse caeteris virtutibus, sicut ipse postea inquit: Fides reputatur ad iusticiam, ei qui convertitur, sed postea iusticia reputatur ad iusticiam. Porro mira varietas et perplexitas est enarrationis, etiamsi largitur hominem initio sola fide consequi remissionem, tamen si postea imaginatur, conversos sine peccato esse, satisfacere legi, et iustos esse propter caeteras virtutes, dissentit a Pauol et a reliquis scripturis divinis."

92. For Melanchthon's linkage of Erasmus and Origen, see Wengert (1998), p. 140.

93. Summa Theologica II-II (XV Faith), Art. 1, Q. 4, aa. 3–4.

94. Loci Communes (1521), SA 2:89.

95. Meijering (1983), p. 108.

96. Grisar (1916), vol. 3, pp. 333ff.; (1917), vol. 4, pp. 459ff. discusses Melanchthon's inconsistency and disingenuousness in dealing with Augustine's doctrine.

97. Kramer (1992), p. 267.

98. In the authentic version of the Augsburg Confession, Melanchthon's words were: "That concerning the doctrine of faith, no new interpretation had been introduced, could be proved from Augustine, who treats diligently of this matter and teaches that we obtain grace and are justified before God by faith in Christ, and not by works, as his whole book De Spiritu et littera proves."

99. Grisar (1916), vol. 3, p. 333, says that Melanchthon's morality is in question in this entire situation. J. Döllinger, in Die Reformation, accused Melanchthon of palpable self-contradiction and intentional and bare-faced deception. See Die Reformation: Ihre innere Entwicklung und ihre Wirkungen im Umfange des Lutherische Bekenntnisses (Frankfurt: Minerva, 1962).

100. Luther's Briefwechsel, WA 6:99–100; cf. CR 2:501ff., which is cited in SA 5:100n5. "Tu adhuc haeres in Augustini imaginatione, qui [SA, quo] eo pervenit, ut neget rationis iustitiam coram Deo reputari pro iustitia; et recte sentit. Deinde imaginatur nos iustos reputari propter hanc impletionem legis, quam efficit in nobis spiritus sanctus. Sic tu imaginaris fide iustificari homines, quia fide accipiamus spiritum sanctum, et postea iusti esse possimus impletione legis, quam efficit [in nobis] spiritus sanctus Haec imagination collocate iustitiam in nostra impletione, in nostra munditie seu perfectione, etsi fidem sequi debet haec renovation. Sed tu reiice oculos ab ista renovatione et a lege in totum ad promissionem et Christum, et sentias, quod propter Christum iusti, hoc est, accepti coram Deo

simus et pacem conscientiae inveniamus, et non propeter illam renovationem. Nam haec ipsa novitas non sufficit. Ideo sola fide sumus iusti, non quia sit radix, ut tu scribis, sed quia apprehendit Christum propter quem sumus accepti, qualisqualis sit illa novitas, etsi necessario sequi debet, sed non pacificat conscientiam. Ideo non dilectio, quae est impletio legis, iustificat, sed sola fides, non, quia est perfectio quaedam in nobis, sed tantum, quia apprehendit Christum; iusti sumus non propter dilectionem, non propter legis impletionem, non propter novitatem nostram, etsi sint dona Spiritus sancti, sed propter Christum, et hunc tantum fide apprehendimus. Augustinus non satisfacit Pauli sententiae, etsi propius accedit quam scholastici."

101. Wengert (1997), p. 180, admits that Melanchthon defined his own doctrine *against* that of St. Augustine: "Brenz's letter at the time the Apology was being published alerted Melanchthon to the danger of Augustine's (and Brenz's) misinterpretation of justification and led him to stress our acceptation by Christ . . . Brenz's position was rejected not only implicitly in the argumentum to the commentary on Romans, but also explicitly in comments on Romans 3:21f."

102. SA 5:100: "Repudianda est et imaginatio aliorum, qui ideo putant nos fide iustificari, quia fides sit initium renovationis. Hi fingunt nos iustos esse propter nostram novitatem et qualitatem. Ac propemodum ex Augustino hanc persuasionem hauriunt."

103. Luther's *Briefwechsel, WA* 9:100–101: "Et ego soleo, mi Brenti, ut hanc rem melius capiam, sic imaginari, quasi nulla sit in corde meo qualitas, quae fides vel charitas vocetur, sed in loco ipsorum pono Iesum Christum, et dico: Haec est iustitia mea, ipse est qualitas et formalis (ut vocant) iustitia mea, ut sic me liberem et expediam ab intuitu legis et operum, imo et ab intuitu obiectivi illius Christi, qui vel doctor vel donator intelligitur. Sed volo ipsum mihi esse donum vel doctrinam per se, ut omnia in ipso habeam. Sic dicit: Ego sum via, veritas et vita; non dicit: ego do tibi viam, veritatem et vitam, quasi extra me positus operetur in me talia. In me debet esse, manere, vivere, loqui, non per me aut in me etc. ut essemus iustitia Dei in illo, non in dilectione aut donis sequentibus."

104. Grisar (1917), vol. 4, p. 460. Trueman (2006), pp. 91, 92.

105. McGrath (1982), p. 235.

106. See p. 95.

107. Meijering (1983), p. 28, observes: "When he [Melanchthon] lists Augustine amongst the true proclaimers of the Gospel, as he often does, then it is because of Augustine's doctrine of grace. Yet throughout his life Melanchthon opposed Augustine's doctrine that the justification implies the beginning of man's renewal."

108. K. Adam, *The Roots of the Reformation* (New York: Sheed & Ward, 1951), p. 66, claims that Ockham's doctrine was an abuse within the Church that was never accepted by the Church. He cites as evidence for this the fact that Ockham himself was arraigned before a court of the Holy Office at Avignon and kept in custody. Adam does not inform the reader that Ockham's arraignment had nothing to do with his doctrine of justification!

109. McSorley (1969), p. 273, goes so far as to say that even the popes of Luther's time did not teach that we are saved solely by the grace of Christ.

110. Long ago, Rivière, "Mérite," *DTC* 10:705, defended the orthodoxy of Ockham and Biel's doctrine of justification. More recently, Clark (1965) has convincingly refuted Oberman's assertion that Biel's doctrine is "Pelagian," which, Clark notes, Oberman never defines.

111. "Medieval and Reformation Readings of Paul," in Aune (2006), p. 169.

112. Ibid., p. 179. Zachman claims that the reasons the Augustinian reading of Paul failed to meet Luther's spiritual needs "ultimately elude historical investigation." This seems an odd judgment for an academic researcher to make. Zachman seems to want to close off the topic to further research. In fact, as my colleague Bret Sunnerville has suggested to me, there does not seem to be any great or elusive mystery here. Karl Adam has shown that Luther's theology was based on his own subjective need for "assurance of salvation." It provided a mechanism for him to deal with his own scrupulosity, to break away from the Church tradition and authority, and to assuage his troubled psyche. In these connections, the "Augustinian" reading of Paul provided no help.

113. "Medieval and Reformation Readings of Paul," in Aune (2006), p. 186.

Chapter 7
Post-Reformation Controversies over Origen's Exegesis of Romans

1. "Neminem acerbius reprehendi praeter unum ex veteribus Origenem, quem quidem tantum abest ut cum Erasmo veteribus omnibus anteponam, ut contra libere profitear nullum mihi magis impurum scriptorem videri" (*Correspondance de Théodore de Bèze* [Geneva: Droz, 1962], 2:229).

2. Cf. Calvin (1996).

3. Cf. Calvin (1996), p. 84. In this same work (p. 85), Calvin says of John Chrysostom, "I have always acknowledged [that he] was excessive in his praise of human powers . . . the ancients unjustifiably exalted free choice, the Greeks especially and among them particularly Chrysostom. But I added that they themselves spoke in such confusion or obscurity or with such variety that it is not easy to deduce anything certain from their writings."

4. Cf. Jerome's *Ep* 85 to Paulinus (NPNF 2, 6:181–82).

5. In *Centuriae Magdeburgeneses seu Historia Ecclesiastica* 2:2.

6. *Examination of the Council of Trent:* 2 vols., trans. F. Kramer (St. Louis: Concordia, 1971, 1986), 2:505.

7. *Miscellaneous Writings and Letters of Thomas Cranmer, Archbishop of Canterbury*, edited for the Parker Society by John Edmund Cox (Cambridge: The University Press, 1846), pp. 205, 211.

8. *Third Decade*, in *The Decades of Henry Bullinger*, trans. T. Harding (Cambridge: The University Press, 1849).

9. H. J. Hillerbrand, *The Oxford Encylopedia of the Reformation*, 4 vols. (New York: Oxford University Press, 1996), 1:228–29.

10. Heigham's biographical outline is given in Allison (1957–58). He gives his own autobiographical account of the anti-Catholic zeal of his Protestant days in *Via Vere Tuta* (1631).

11. It was attributed to Matthew Kellison (1560–1642), the president of Douai College, until well into the twentieth century. Allison (1957–58), p. 237, has only recently exposed this misattribution.

12. *Gagge* (1623), p. 71.

13. Origen, *CRm* 4.7.75–77 (986).

14. *DNB*, p. 713.

15. Lambert (1989), p. 43.

16. Cited in Tyacke (2001), p. 187.

17. Tyacke (1987), p. 155.

18. Tyacke (1987), pp. 134ff.

19. *DNB*, pp. 715–16.

20. Tyacke (1987), p. 161.

21. In *Via Vere Tuta* (1631), Heigham cites this as an example of how Protestants, too, had an *Index Prohibitorum Librorum*.

22. Tyacke (1987), p. 125.

23. Tyacke (2001), p. 143.

24. Ibid., p. 187.

25. Tyacke (1987), p. 126.

26. Tyacke (2001), p. 165.

27. *A New Gagg* (1624), p. 148.

28. Ibid.

29. *WA* 39, I, 256, 23ff.; cited in Iserloh, Glazik, and Jedin (1980), p. 348.

30. *A New Gagg* (1624), p. 149.

31. Cf. 3.6(9).21–24 (952).

32. *A New Gagg* (1624), p. 150.

33. Ibid.

34. The present section relies heavily on Parmentier (2003).

35. Parmentier (2003), p. 151.

36. C. Jansenius, *Augustinus*, Rothomagi 1643, I, 208; cited in Parmentier (2003), p. 151.

37. C. Jansenius, *Augustinus*, Rothomagi 1643, II, 34; cited in Parmentier (2003), p. 151.

38. C. Jansenius, *Augustinus*, Rothomagi 1643, II, 15, 77, 85, 91–93; cited in Parmentier (2003), p. 151.

39. C. Jansenius, *Augustinus*, Rothomagi 1643, III, 88; cited in Parmentier (2003), p. 151.

40. The term *semi-Pelagian* is first found in the Lutheran Formula of Concord of 1577. It is defined as the teaching that "man by his own powers can make a

beginning of his conversion, but without the grace of the Holy Spirit cannot complete it." This term of Lutheran origin was adopted in the Catholic camp as well. Cf. Parmentier (2003), p. 151.

41. Likewise, McGrath (1986), vol. 1, p. 139, rejects Oberman's analysis of Gabriel Biel's supposed Pelagianism. On p. 229n77 McGrath says that Oberman labors under the mistaken apprehension that Augustine's most characteristic teaching on predestination is "double predestination."

42. Clark (1965), p. 752.

43. Ibid.

44. Ibid., p. 754.

45. Ibid.

46. For a Calvinist attack on Origen's view, see: W. J. P. Boyd, "Origen on Pharaoh's Hardened Heart," TU 92, SP 7.1 (Berlin, 1966), pp. 434–42.

47. C. Jansenius, *Augustinus,* Rothomagi 1643, I, 45, 46, 48, 63, 75, 83 (Origenes totius erroris fons); cited in Parmentier (2003), p. 152.

48. C. Jansenius, *Augustinus,* Rothomagi 1643, I, 149; cited in Parmentier (2003), p. 153.

49. Parmentier (2003), p. 153.

50. Ibid.

51. Ibid., p. 154.

52. *Origeniana* ii.7; cited by Bigg (1970), p. 201n1. Bigg adds, "But neither Huet nor Jansen appears to grasp the full scope of Origen's teaching."

53. Parmentier (2003), p. 157.

Conclusion

1. Lienhard (2000), p. 361.

2. Heither (1990), p. 292; Cocchini (1979), (1992).

3. "The Problems of the *Sensus Plenior,*" *Ephemerides Theologica Lovanienses* 43 (1967), p. 463.

4. Reasoner (2005).

5. Ibid., p. 145.

Bibliography

Primary Texts and Translations

Augustine

Boulding, M. 2000. *Exposition of the Psalms 1–32*. The Works of Saint Augustine: A Translation for the 21st Century. Hyde Park: New City Press.

Deferrari, R. J. 1955. *Saint Augustine: Treatises on Marriage and Other Subjects.* FOTC 27. Washington, DC: Catholic University of America Press.

Dekkers, D., and J. Fraipont. 1996. *Sancti Aurelii Augustini: Enarrationes in Psalmos I–L*. CCL 38. Turnholt: Brepols.

Fredriksen Landes, Paula. 1982. *Augustine on Romans: Propositions from the Epistle to the Romans, Unfinished Commentary on the Epistle to the Romans*. Chico, CA: Scholars Press.

Liguori, Marie, trans. 1955. *Faith and Works (De fide et operibus)*. In *Saint Augustine: Treatises on Marriage and Other Subjects*. FOTC 27. Ed. R. J. Deferrari. New York: Cima Publishing Co. Pp. 213–82.

Lombardo, G. J. 1988. *St. Augustine: On Faith and Works*. Ancient Christian Writers 48. New York: Newman.

Müller, L. G. 1956. *The 'De haeresibus' of St. Augustine*. Patristic Studies 90. Ed. R. Deferrari. Washington, DC: Catholic University Press.

Plumer, E. 2003. *Augustine's Commentary on Galatians*. Oxford: Oxford University Press.

Teske, R. J. 1997. *Answer to the Pelagians*. The Works of Saint Augustine: A Translation for the 21st Century. Hyde Park: New City Press.

Zycha, Joseph. 1890. *Sancti Aureli Augustini*. CSEL 41. Leipzig: G. Freytag.

Erasmus

Allen, P. S. 1906–47. *Opus epistolarum Desiderii. Erasmi Roterodami*. Ed. P. S. Allen, H. M. Allen, and H. W. Garrod. Oxford: Oxford University Press. 11 vols., plus index vol. by B. Flower and E. Rosenbaum. 1958. Oxford: Oxford University Press.

ASD. 1969–. *Opera omnia Desiderii Erasmi Roterodami*. Amsterdam: North Holland.
CWE. 1974–. *Collected Works of Erasmus*. Toronto: University of Toronto Press.
Hyperaspistes 1. In C. Trinkhaus, ed. 1999. *Controversies: De libero arbitrio. Hyperaspistes 1*. Trans. Peter Macardle and Clarence H. Miller. Toronto: University of Toronto Press. (*CWE* 76).
Hyperaspistes 2. In C. Trinkhaus, ed. 2000. *Controversies: Hyperaspistes 2*. Trans. Clarence H. Miller. Toronto: University of Toronto Press. (*CWE* 77).
LB. Leclerc, Jean. 1703–6. *Desiderii Erasmi Roterodami Opera Omnia*. 10 vols. Leiden; repr. Hildesheim 1961–62.
Sider, R. 1984. *New Testament Scholarship: Paraphrases on Romans and Galatians*. Trans. and annotated by John B. Payne, Albert Rabil, Jr., and Warren S. Smith, Jr. Toronto: University of Toronto Press. (*CWE* 42.)
Sider, R. 1994. *New Testament Scholarship: Annotations on Romans*. Trans. and annotated by John B. Payne, Albert Rabil, Jr., Robert D. Sider, and Warren S. Smith, Jr. Toronto: University of Toronto Press. (*CWE* 56.)
Welzig, W. 1990. *Erasmus von Rotterdam: Ausgewählte Schriften*. 8 vols. Darmstadt: Wissenschaftliche Buchgesellschaft.

Heigham, John

The Gagge of the Reformed Gospell. 1623. 2nd ed. Douai.
Via Vere Tuta, or the truly safe way. 1631. Vol. 275 of *St. Omers. English Recusant Literature, 1558–1640*. Ed. D. M. Rogers. 1975. London: Scolar Press.

Luther

Dillenberger, J., ed. 1961. *Martin Luther: Selections from His Writings*. New York: Doubleday.
LW. Luther's Works. 1955–86. Ed. J. Pelikan and H. T. Lehmann. Philadelphia: Muhlenberg.
WA. Luthers Werke. Kritische Gesamtausgabe [Schriften]. 1930–85. 65 vols. Weimar: H. Böhlau.

Melanchthon

CR. Corpus Reformatorum. Philippi Melanchthonis opera quae supersunt omnia. 1834–60. 28 vols. Ed. C. G. Bretschneider and H. Bindseil. Halle: A. Schwetschke and Sons.
Frazel, Thomas D., trans. 2002. *History of the Life and Acts of Dr. Martin Luther*. In Vandiver (2002). Pp. 14–39. (Cf. *CR* 6.155–70; *CR* 11.783–88).
Hill, Charles Leander, trans. 1962. *Melanchthon, Selected Writings*. Minneapolis: Augsburg. Contains a full translation of *The Church and the Authority of the Word*, 1539.

Historia de Vita et Actis Lutheri. 1548. Heidelberg. Transcribed from the original by Dr. Steve Sohmer, 1996.

Kramer, F., trans. 1992. *Commentary on Romans (1540)*. St. Louis: Concordia. (*CR* 15.)

Preus, J. A. O., trans. 1992. *Loci Communes 1543*. St. Louis: Concordia.

SA. Studienausgabe. 1951–75. Ed. R. Stupperich. *Melanchthons Werke in Auswahl*. 7 vols. Gütersloh: Gerd Mohn.

Smith, P., trans. and ed. 1913. *Luther's Correspondence and Other Contemporary Letters*. 2 vols. Philadelphia: The Lutheran Publication Society.

Vandiver, E., ed. 2002. *Luther's Lives: Two Contemporary Accounts of Martin Luther*. Trans. and annotated by Elizabeth Vandiver, Ralph Keen, and Thomas D. Frazel. Manchester: Manchester University Press.

Montagu, Richard

Appello Caesarem. A Just Appeale from Two Unjust Informers. 1625. London: Matthew Lownes. Facsimile ed.: Amsterdam: Theatrum Orbis Terrarum, 1975.

A Gagg for the New Gospell? No: A New Gagg for an Old Goose. 1624. London: Thomas Snodham for Matthew Lownes and William Barret. Facsimile ed.: Amsterdam: Theatrum Orbis Terrarum, 1975.

Origen

Balthasar, H. Urs von. 1984. *Origen: Spirit and Fire. A Thematic Anthology of His Writings*. Trans. R. J. Daly. Washington, DC: Catholic University of America Press.

Chadwick, H., trans. 1954. *Dialogue with Heraclides*. In *Alexandrian Christianity: Selected Translations of Clement and Origen*. Ed. H. Chadwick and J. E. L. Oulton. LCC 2. Philadelphia: Westminster.

Heine, R. 2002. *The Commentaries of Origen and Jerome on St Paul's Epistle to the Ephesians*. Oxford: Oxford University Press.

Scheck, T. P., trans. 2001–2. *Origen: Commentary on the Epistle to the Romans*. 2 vols. FOTC 103, 104. Washington, DC: Catholic University of America Press.

Origenes

Hammond Bammel, C. P. 1990. *Der Römerbriefkommentar des Origenes: Kritische Ausgabe der Übersetzung Rufins*. Buch 1–3. AGLB 16. Freiburg im Breisgau: Herder.

Hammond Bammel, C. P. 1997. *Der Römerbriefkommentar des Origenes: Kritische Ausgabe der Übersetzung Rufins*. Buch 4–6. Prepared and set for the press by H. J. Frede and H. Stanjek. AGLB 33. Freiburg im Breisgau: Herder.

Hammond Bammel, C. P. 1998. *Der Römerbriefkommentar des Origenes: Kritische Ausgabe der Übersetzung Rufins*. Buch 7–10. Published posthumously by H. J. Frede and H. Stanjek. AGLB 34. Freiburg im Breisgau: Herder.

Heither, Theresia. 1990–99. *Commentarii in epistulam ad Romanos / Römerbrief-kommentar.* 6 vols. Fontes Christiani 2 (1–6). Freiburg im Breisgau: Herder.

Jenkins, C. "Origen on I Corinthians." *JTS* 9 (1907–8), pp. 232–47; 353–72; 500–514; *JTS* 10 (1908–9), pp. 29–51.

Ramsbotham, A. "The Commentary of Origen on the Epistle to the Romans." *JTS* 13 (1912), pp. 209–24, 357–68; *JTS* 14 (1913), pp. 10–22.

Scherer, J., ed. 1957. *Le Commentaire d'Origène sur Rom. III.5–V.7, d'après les extraits du Papyrus no. 88748 du Musée du Caire et les fragments de la Philocalie et du Vaticanus graecus 762. Essai de reconstitution du texte et de la pensée des tomes V et VI du "Commentaire sur l'Épître aux Romains."* Cairo: Institut français d'archéologie orientale, Bibliothèque d'Étude 27.

Pelagius

De Bruyn, T., trans. 1993. *Pelagius's Commentary on St. Paul's Epistle to the Romans.* Oxford: Clarendon Press.

Souter, A. 1922–31. *Pelagius's Expositions of Thirteen Epistles of St. Paul.* Texts and Studies 9. Cambridge: Cambridge University Press. 3 vols. 1. *Introduction* (1922); 2. *Text and Critical Apparatus* (1926); 3. *Pseudo-Jerome Interpolations* (1931).

Tertullian

Tertullian. 1989. *On the Flesh of Christ. Against Marcion. Prescription Against Heretics.* In *Ante-Nicene Fathers* 3. Grand Rapids: Eerdmans Reprint.

William of St. Thierry

Hasbrouck, John Baptist, trans. 1980. *William of St. Thierry. Exposition on the Epistle to the Romans.* Ed. and introd. John D. Anderson. Kalamazoo: Cistercian Publications.

Migne, J.-P. 1878–90. *Patrologiae Cursus Completus: Series Latina.* Paris. (*PL* 180.)

Verdeyen, Pauli. 1989. Corpus Christianorum: Continuatio Mediaevalis 86. *Guillelmi a Sancto Theodorico, Opera Omnia, Pars I: Expositio super Epistolam ad Romanos.* Turnholt: Brepols. [CCCM 86.]

Secondary Works

Allison, A. F. 1957–58. "John Heigham of S. Omer (c. 1568–c. 1632)." *Recusant History* 4. Pp. 226–42.

Altaner, B. 1951. "Augustinus und Origenes: Eine quellenkritische Untersuchung." *Historisches Jahrbuch* 70. Pp. 15–41.

————. 1952. "Augustinus und die griechische Patristik." *Revue Bénédictine* 62. Pp. 201–15.

Anderson, H. George, T. Austin Murphy, and Joseph A. Burgess. 1985. *Justification by Faith: Lutherans and Catholics in Dialogue VII*. Minneapolis: Augsburg Publishing House.

Anderson, John D. 1978. "William of Saint Thierry's Exposition on the Epistle to the Romans." In *Cistercian Ideals and Reality*. Ed. John R. Sommerfeldt. Kalamazoo: Cistercian Publications.

Aune, David E., ed. 2006. *Rereading Paul Together: Protestant and Catholic Perspectives on Justification*. Grand Rapids: Baker.

Backus, I., ed. 1997. *The Reception of the Church Fathers in the West: From the Carolingians to the Maurists*. 2 vols. Leiden: Brill.

Balas, D. 1980. "Marcion Revisited: A 'Post-Harnack' Perspective." In *Texts and Testaments: Critical Essays on the Bible and Early Church Fathers*. Ed. W. E. March. San Antonio: Trinity University Press. Pp. 95–108.

————. 1992. "The Use and Interpretation of Paul in Irenaeus's Five Books Adversus Haereses." *The Second Century* 9. Pp. 27–39.

Bammel, C. P. 1989. "Adam in Origen." In *The Making of Orthodoxy: Essays in Honour of Henry Chadwick*. Ed. R. Williams. Cambridge: Cambridge University Press. Pp. 62–93.

————. 1992. "Augustine, Origen and the Exegesis of St. Paul." *Augustinianum* 32. Pp. 341–68.

————. 1995. "Origen's Pauline Prefaces." In Dorival and Le Boulluec (1995). Pp. 495–513.

————. 1996. "Justification by Faith in Augustine and Origen." *JEH* 47. Pp. 223–35.

Bardenhewer, O. 1908. *Patrology: The Lives and Works of the Fathers of the Church*. Trans. T. J. Shahan. Freiburg im Breisgau: Herder.

Bejczy, Istvan. 2001. *Erasmus and the Middle Ages: The Historical Consciousness of a Christian Humanist*. Leiden: Brill.

Bennett, J. B. 1997. "The Origen of Evil: Didymus the Blind's "Contra Manichaeos" and Its Debt to Origen's Theology and Exegesis." Ph.D. diss., University of Toronto.

Benoît, A. 1961. *L'actualité des Pères de l'Eglise*. Neuchâtel: Éditions Delachaux & Niestlé.

Bigg, C. 1970. *The Christian Platonists of Alexandria*. Oxford: Clarendon Press, 1886; repr. New York: AMS Press.

Billy, D. J. 1990. "The Retrieval of Perfection: William of Saint-Thierry's Theology of Conversion." *The Downside Review* 108. Pp. 175–87.

Blic, J. de. 1936. "L'date du sermon de saint Augustin 'in psalmum 31.' (ML 36, 257–75.)" *Gregorianum* 17. Pp. 407–12.

Blowers, Paul M., et al., eds. 2002. *Dominico Eloquio—In Lordly Eloquence: Essays on Patristic Exegesis in Honor of Robert Louis Wilken*. Grand Rapids: Eerdmans.

Boeft, Jan den. 1997. "Erasmus and the Church Fathers." In Backus (1997). Pp. 537–72.

Bohlin, T. 1957. *Die Theologie des Pelagius und ihre Genesis*. Uppsala: Almqvist & Wiksells.

Bonner, Gerald. 1966. *How Pelagian was Pelagius? An Examination of the Contentions of Torgny Bohlin*. Texte und Untersuchungen zur Geschichte der altchristlichen Literatur 94. Berlin: Akademie Verlag. Pp. 350–58.

Bostock, G. 1999. "The Influence of Origen on Pelagius and Western Monasticism." In *Origeniana Septima*. Ed. W. A. Bienert and U. Kühneweg. Leuven: Leuven University Press. Pp. 381–96.

Bouyer, L. 1958. *The Cistercian Heritage*. Trans. Elizabeth A. Livingstone. London: A. R. Mowbray.

———. 1968. *A History of Christian Spirituality*. 3 vols. Vol. 2: *The Spirituality of the Middle Ages*. New York: Seabury.

Boyd, W. J. P. 1966. "Origen on Pharaoh's Hardened Heart: A Study of Justification and Election in St. Paul and Origen." *Studia Patristica* 7, part 1. Texte und Untersuchungen 92. Ed. F. L. Cross. Pp. 434–42.

Brautigam, D. 2003. "Prelates and Politics: Uses of 'Puritan,' 1625–40." In Knoppers (2003). Pp. 49–66.

Brown, P. 1970. "The Patrons of Pelagius: The Roman Aristocracy Between East and West." *JTS* 21. Pp. 56–72.

Burnett, C. C. 1998. "God's Self-Revelation in the Theology of Pelagius." Ph.D. diss., Catholic University of America, Washington, DC.

Burns, J. P. 1979. "The Interpretation of Romans in the Pelagian Controversy." *Augustinian Studies* 10. Pp. 43–54.

———. 1985. "Grace: The Augustinian Foundation." In *Christian Spirituality: Origins to the Twelfth Century*. Ed. B. McGinn and J. Meyendorff. New York: Cross Road. Pp. 331–49.

Calvin, John. 1996. *The Bondage and Liberation of the Will: A Defense of the Orthodox Doctrine of Human Choice Against Pighius*. Trans. G. I. Davies. Grand Rapids: Baker.

Cartwright, Steven R. 2001. "The Romans Commentaries of William of St. Thierry and Peter Abelard: A Theological and Methodological Comparison." Ph.D. diss., Western Michigan University, Kalamazoo.

———. 2003. "William of St. Thierry's Use of Patristic Sources in His Exposition on Romans." *Cîteaux* 54:1–2. Pp. 27–54.

Catechism of the Catholic Church. 1994. Liguori, MO: Liguori Publications.

Chadwick, H. 1959. "Rufinus and the Tura Papyrus of Origen's Commentary on Romans." *JTS* n.s. 10. Pp. 10–42.

———. 1985. "Christian Platonism in Origen and in Augustine." In *Origeniana Tertia*. Ed. R. Hanson and H. Crouzel. Rome: Edizioni dell'ateneo. Pp. 217–30.

Clark, F. 1965. "A New Appraisal of Late-Medieval Theology." *Gregorianum* 46. Pp. 733–65.

Cocchini, F. 1979. *Origene: Commento alla Lettera ai Romani. Annuncio Pasquale, Polemica antieretica.* L'Aquila : Japadre Editore.

————. 1992. *Il Paolo di Origene: Constributo alla storia della recezione delle epistole Paoline nel III secolo.* Rome: Edizione Studium.

————. 1996. "I commentary di Origene e di Teodoreto di Cirro alla lettera ai Romani: Continuità e novità nella storia della recezione di Paolo." *Augustinianum* 36. Pp. 316–36.

Cochlaeus, J. See Keen (1995–96).

Cohen, Jeremy. 2005. "The Mystery of Israel's Salvation: Romans 11:25–26 in Patristic and Medieval Exegesis." *Harvard Theological Review* 98:3. Pp. 247–81.

Courcelle, P. 1969. *Late Latin Writers and Their Greek Sources.* Trans. H. E. Wedeck. Cambridge: Harvard University Press.

Crouzel, H. 1988. "The Literature on Origen 1970–1988." *JTS* 49. Pp. 499–516.

————. 1989. *Origen: The Life and Thought of the First Great Theologian.* San Francisco: Harper & Row.

De Bruyn, Theodore S. 1988. "Pelagius's Interpretation of Rom. 5:12–21: Exegesis Within the Limits of Polemic." *Toronto Journal of Theology* 4. Pp. 30–43.

Déchanet, Jean Marie. 1972. *William of St. Thierry: The Man and His Work.* Trans. Richard Strachan. Spencer, MA: Cistercian Publications.

DeMolen, Richard L. 1987. *The Spirituality of Erasmus of Rotterdam.* Nieuwkoop: De Graaf Publishers.

Dempsey, John J. 1937. "Pelagius's Commentary on Saint Paul: A Theological Study." Ph.D. diss., Pontificia Universitas Gregoriana, Rome.

Denifle, H. 1905. *Die abendländischen Schriftausleger bis Luther über Justitia Dei (Rom. 1, 17) und Justificatio.* Mainz: Franz Kirchheim.

Denzinger, Henricus. 1954. *The Sources of Catholic Dogma.* Trans. R. Deferrari from the 13th ed., Henry Denzinger, *Enchiridion Symbolorum.* Fitzwilliam, NH: Loretto.

————. 1963. *Enchiridion Symbolorum: Definitionum et Declarationum de Rebus Fidei et Morum.* 32nd ed. Freiburg: Herder.

Dolan, J. 1965. *History of the Reformation: A Conciliatory Assessment of Opposite Views.* New York: Desclee.

Dorival, G., and A. Le Boulluec, eds. 1995. *Origeniana Sexta: Origène et la Bible/ Origen and the Bible.* Leuven: Leuven University Press.

Dulles, A. 2004. "A Roman Catholic View of Justification in Light of the Dialogues." In *By Faith Alone: Essays on Justification in Honor of Gerhard O. Forde.* Ed. J. A. Burgess and M. Kolden. Grand Rapids: Eerdmans.

Ehses, S. 1911. *Concilium Tridentinum V, Actorum Pars Altera.* Freiburg im Breisgau: Herder.

Eno, Robert B. 1984. "Some Patristic Views on the Relationship of Faith and Works in Justification." *Recherches Augustiniennes* 19. Pp. 3–27.

Epiphanius. 1994. *The Panarion of Epiphanius of Salamis.* 2 vols. Trans. Frank Williams. Leiden: Brill.

Esser, H. H. 1963. "Thesen und Anmerkungen zum Exegetischen Paulusverständnis des Pelagius." In *Zwischenstation: Festschrift für Karl Kupisch zum 60. Geburtstag.* Ed. Ernst Wolf. Munich: Kaiser Verlag. Pp. 27–42.

Evans, G. R. 1987. "Augustine on Justification." *Studia Ephemeridis Augustinianum* 26. Pp. 275–84.

Evans, Robert F. 1968. *Pelagius: Inquiries and Reappraisals.* New York: Seabury.

Farge, James K. 1986. "Jacques Merlin." In *Contemporaries of Erasmus: A Biographical Register of the Renaissance and Reformation.* 3 vols. Toronto: University of Toronto Press. 2:435–36.

Farkasfalvy, D. 1968. "Theology of Scripture in St. Irenaeus." *Revue Bénédictine* 78. Pp. 318–33.

Feld, H. 1973. "Lutherus Apostolus. Kirchliches Amt und apostolische Verantwortung in der Galaterbrief-Auslegung Martin Luthers." In *Wort Gottes in der Zeit. Festschrift für Karl Hermann Schelkle zum 65. Geburtstag.* Ed. Helmut Feld and Josef Nolte. Düsseldorf: Patmos. Pp. 288–304.

Ferguson, John. 1956. *Pelagius: A Historical and Theological Study.* Cambridge: W. Heffer & Sons.

Fisher, John. 1967. *Ioannis Fischerii Opera Omnia.* Farnborough: Gregg Press.

Fraenkel, P. 1961. *Testimonia Patrum: The Function of the Patristic Argument in the Theology of Philip Melanchthon.* Geneva: Droz.

Frede, H. J. 1973. *Ein Neuer Paulustext und Kommentar. Band I: Untersuchungen.* Aus der Geschichte der Lateinischen Bibel 7. Freiburg: Herder.

———. 1974. *Ein Neuer Paulustext und Kommentar. Band II: Die Texte.* Aus der Geschichte der Lateinischen Bibel 8. Freiburg: Herder.

Fremantle, W. F. 1887. "Rufinus." In *DCB* 4:555–561.

Freundorfer, J. 1927. *Erbsünde und Erbtod beim Apostel Pauls. Eine religionsgeschichtliche und exegetische Untersuchung über Römerbrief 5, 12–31.* Neutestamentliche Abhandlungen 13, 1–2. Münster.

Gager, J. 1972. "Marcion and Philosophy." *VC* 26. Pp. 53–59.

Ganoczy, A. 1987. *The Young Calvin.* Trans. D. Foxgrover and W. Provo. Philadelphia: Westminster Press.

Godin, A. 1978. "Fonction d'Origène dans la pratique exégètique d'Erasme: Les Annotations sur l'Épitre aux Romains." In *Histoire de l'exégèse au XVIe siècle.* Ed. O. Fatio and P. Fraenkel. Geneva: Libraire Droz. Pp. 17–44.

———. 1982a. "The Enchiridion Militis Christiani: The Modes of an Origenian Appropriation." Trans. H. Gibaud. *Erasmus of Rotterdam Society Yearbook* 2. Pp. 47–79.

———. 1982b. *Erasme lecteur d'Origène.* Geneva: Libraire Droz.

Gorce, D. 1957. "La Patristique dans la Réforme d'Erasme." In *Festgabe Joseph Lortz.* Vol. 1, *Reformation Schicksal und Auftrag.* Ed. E. Iserloh and P. Manns. Baden-Baden: Grimm. Pp. 233–76.

Gorday, P. 1983. *Principles of Patristic Exegesis: Romans 9–11 in Origen, John Chrysostom, and Augustine.* Studies in the Bible and Early Christianity 4. New York: Edwin Mellen Press.

Grech, P. 1996. "Justification by Faith in Origen's Commentary on Romans." *Augustinianum* 36. Pp. 337–59.

Grisar, H. 1914–17. *Luther.* Authorized trans. from the German by E. M. Lamond. Ed. Luigi Cappadelta. 6 vols. St. Louis: Herder.

———. 1954. *Martin Luther: His Life and Work.* Adapted from the 2nd German ed. by Frank J. Eble. Westminster, MD: Newman.

Hacker, P. 1970. *The Ego of Faith: Martin Luther and the Origin of Anthropocentric Religion.* Chicago: Franciscan Herald Press.

———. 1970a. "Martin Luther's Notion of Faith." In *Catholic Scholars Dialogue with Luther.* Ed. Jared Wicks. Chicago: Loyola University Press.

Hall, Christopher A. 2005. "John Chrysostom." In *Reading Romans Through the Centuries: From the Early Church to Karl Barth.* Ed. J. Greenman and T. Larsen. Grand Rapids: Brazos Press.

Hammond, C. P. 1965. "Notes on the Manuscripts and Editions of Origen's Commentary on the Epistle to the Romans in the Latin Translation by Rufinus." *JTS* 16. Pp. 338–57.

———. 1977. "The Last Ten Years of Rufinus' Life and the Date of His Move South from Aquileia." *JTS* n.s. 28. Pp. 372–429.

———. 1978. "A Product of a Fifth-Century Scriptorium Preserving Conventions Used by Rufinus of Aquileia." *JTS* n.s. 29. Pp. 366–91.

———. 1979. "Products of Fifth-Century Scriptoria Preserving Conventions Used by Rufinus of Aquileia." *JTS* n.s. 30. Pp. 430–62.

Hammond Bammel, C. P. 1981. "Philocalia IX, Jerome, Epistle 121, and Origen's Exposition of Romans VII." *JTS* n.s. 32. Pp. 50–81.

———. 1985. *Der Römerbrieftext des Rufin und seine Origenes-Übersetzung.* Freiburg im Breisgau: Herder.

———. 1992. "Rufinus' Translation of Origen's Commentary on Romans and the Pelagian Controversy." In *Storia ed esegesi in rufino di concordia.* Udine: Arte grafiche friulane. Pp. 131–42.

Hanson, R. P. C. 1959. *Allegory and Event.* Richmond, VA: John Knox Press.

Harl, M. 1958. *Origène et la fonction révélatrice du Verbe incarné.* Paris: Éditions du Seuil.

Harnack, A. 1924. *Marcion: Das Evangelium vom fremden God. Eine Monographie zur Geschichte der Grundlegung der katholischen Kirche.* Texte und Untersuchungen 45. 2nd ed. Leipzig: J. C. Hinrichs; repr. Darmstadt: Wissenschaftliche Buchgesellschaft, 1960.

———. 1958. *Geschichte der altchristlichen Literatur bis Eusebius.* 2 vols. Leipzig: J. C. Hinrichs.

Heither, T. 1990. *Translatio Religionis: Die Paulusdeutung des Origenes in seinem Kommentar zum Römerbrief.* Bonner Beiträge zur Kirchengeschichte 16. Cologne: Böhlau.

Henze, B. 1995. *Aus Liebe zur Kirche Reform: Die Bemühungen Georg Witzels (1501–1573) um die Kircheneinheit.* Münster: Aschendorff.

Iserloh, E., J. Glazik, and H. Jedin. 1980. *Reformation and Counter Reformation.* Trans. A. Biggs and P. W. Becker. History of the Church 5. Ed. H. Jedin and J. Dolan. New York: Seabury.

Jackson, B. 1966. "Sources of Origen's Doctrine of Freedom." *CH* 35.

Jansenius, Cornelius. 1964. *Augustinus.* Frankfurt: Minerva; repr. Louvain: Iacobus Zegerus, 1640.

———. *Augustinus.* Rothomagi 1643.

Keen, R., ed. 1995–96. *Johannes Cochlaeus: Philippicae I–VII.* 2 vols. Nieuwkoop: De Graaf Publishers.

———. 1996. "Political Authority and Ecclesiology in Melanchthon's De Ecclesia Autoritate." *CH* 65. Pp. 1–14.

Kelly, J. N. D., trans. 1955. *Rufinus: A Commentary on the Apostles' Creed.* Ancient Christian Writers 20. London: Newman Press.

———. 1978. *Early Christian Doctrines.* Rev. ed. New York: Harper & Row.

Knoppers, L. L., ed. 2003. *Puritanism and Its Discontents.* Newark: University of Delaware Press.

Kovacs, J. 2002. "Servant of Christ and Steward of the Mysteries of God: The Purpose of a Pauline Letter According to Origen's Homilies on 1 Corinthians." In Blowers (2002). Pp. 147–71.

Küng, H. 1964. *Justification: The Doctrine of Karl Barth and a Catholic Reflection.* New York: Thomas Nelson and Sons.

Lambert, S. 1989. "Richard Montagu, Arminianism and Censorship." *Past and Present* 124. Pp. 36–68.

Lienhard, J. 2000. "Origen and the Crisis of the Old Testament in the Early Church." *Pro Ecclesia* 9:3. Pp. 355–66.

Lies, L. 1985. *Origenes' Eucharistielehre im Streit der Konfessionen.* Vienna: Tyrolia.

Lubac, Henri de. 1996. *Theology in History.* Part 1, *The Light of Christ.* Part 2, *Disputed Questions and Resistance to Nazism.* Trans. A. E. Nash. San Francisco: Ignatius.

———. 1998. *Medieval Exegesis.* Vol. 1, *The Four Senses of Scripture.* Trans. M. Sebanc. Originally published as *Exégèse médiévale, 1 Les quatre sens de l'écriture,* 1959. Grand Rapids: Eerdmans.

———. 2000. *Medieval Exegesis.* Vol. 2, *The Four Senses of Scripture.* Trans. E. M. Macierowski. Originally published as *Exégèse médiévale, 2 Les quatre sens de l'écriture,* 1959. Grand Rapids: Eerdmans.

Marius, R. 1998. "Martin Luther's Erasmus, and How He Got That Way." *Erasmus of Rotterdam Society Yearbook* 18. Pp. 70–88.

Matter, E. A. 1997. "The Church Fathers and the Glossa Ordinaria." In Backus (1997). Pp. 83–111.

McConica, J. 1969. "Erasmus and the Grammar of Consent." In *Scrinium Erasmianum.* 2 vols. Ed. J. Cappens. Leiden: Brill. 2:77–99.

———. 1991. *Erasmus.* Oxford: Oxford University Press.

McCue, J. F. 2001. "Augustine and the Strange Career of Romans 9:10–29." In *For a Later Generation: The Transformation of Tradition in Israel, Early Judaism, and Early Christianity*. Ed. Randal A. Argall, Beverly A. Bow, and Rodney A. Werline. Harrisburg: Trinity Press International. Pp. 169–82.

McGrath, A. 1982. "Forerunners of the Reformation? A Critical Examination of the Evidence for Precursors of the Reformation Doctrines of Justification." *Harvard Theological Review* 75:2. Pp. 219–42.

———. 1986. *Iustitia Dei: A History of the Christian Doctrine of Justification*. 2 vols. Cambridge: Cambridge University Press.

McSorley, H. J. 1969. *Luther: Right or Wrong?* New York: Newman.

Meijering, E. P. 1983. *Melanchthon and Patristic Thought*. Leiden: Brill.

Molland, E. 1938. *The Conception of the Gospel in the Alexandrian Theology*. Oslo: I kommisjon hos J. Dybwad.

Monti. D. V. 1975. "The Way Within: Grace in the Mystical Theology of William of Saint Thierry." *Cîteaux* 26. Pp. 31–47.

Moser, Maureen Beyer. 2005. *Teacher of Holiness: The Holy Spirit in Origen's Commentary on the Epistle to the Romans*. Piscataway, NJ: Gorgias Press.

Murphy, F. X. 1945. *Rufinus of Aquileia (345–411): His Life and Works*. Washington, DC: Catholic University of America Press.

Newman, J. H. 1966. *Lectures on the Doctrine of Justification*. Westminster, MD: Christian Classics.

———. 1969. *Certain Difficulties Felt by Anglicans in Catholic Teaching*. 2 vols. Westminster, MD: Christian Classics.

Nodes, D. 1999. "Origen of Alexandria Among the Renaissance Humanists and Their Twentieth Century Historians." In *Nova Doctrina Vetusque: Essays on Early Christianity in Honor of Fredric W. Schlatter, S.J.* Ed. D. Kries and C. Brown Tkacz. New York: Peter Lang. Pp. 51–64.

Norelli, Enrico. 1997. "The Authority Attributed to the Early Church in the Centuries of Magdeburg and the Ecclesiastical Annals of Caesar Baronius." In Backus (1997). Pp. 745–74.

O'Connor, E. 1980. "The Catholic Response to the Augsburg Confession." *Communio* 7. Pp. 178–86.

Olin, John C. 1979. *Six Essays on Erasmus*. New York: Fordham University Press.

Osborn, E. 1976. "Origen and Justification: The Good Is One, There Is None Good but God (Matt. 19.17 et par.)." *Australian Biblical Review*. Pp. 18–29.

Parmentier, M. 2003. "Pelagius as the Bogeyman of Catholics and Protestants in the Seventeenth Century." *Augustiniana* 53. Pp. 147–58.

Patte, D., and E. TeSelle, eds. 2002. *Engaging Augustine on Romans: Self, Context, and Theology in Interpretation*. Harrisburg: Trinity Press International.

Patterson, L. 1992. "Methodius on Origen in De Creatis." In *Origeniana Quinta*. Ed. R. Daly. Leuven: Leuven University Press. Pp. 497–508.

Payne, J. 1978. "The Significance of Lutheranizing Changes in Erasmus' Interpretation of Paul's Letter to the Romans and the Galatians in His *Annotations*

(1527) and *Paraphrases* (1532)." In *D'histoire de l'exegese biblique au XVIe siècle*. Ed. O. Fatio and P. Fraenkel. Geneva: Droz, 1978.

Payne, J. B. 1990. "Erasmus on Romans 9:2–24." In *The Bible in the Sixteenth Century*. Ed. David C. Steinmetz. Durham: Duke University Press. Pp. 119–35.

Plinval, George de. 1934. "Recherches sur l'oeuvre littéraire de Pélage." *Revue de philologie, de littérature et d'histoire anciennes* 60. Pp. 1–42.

————. 1943. *Pélage: Ses écrits, sa vie et sa réforme. Étude d'histoire littéraire et religieuse*. Lausanne: Payot.

Pusino, Ivan. 1927. "Der Einfluß Picos auf Erasmus." *Zeitschrift für Kirchengeschichte* 46. Pp. 75–96.

Quantin, Jean-Louis. 1997. "The Fathers in 17th Century Anglican Theology." In Backus (1997). Pp. 987–1008.

Quasten, John. 1975. *Patrology*. 4 vols. Allen, TX: Christian Classics.

Quinn, Jerome D. 1985. "The Scriptures on Merit." In *Justification by Faith*. Ed. H. George Anderson. Pp. 82–93.

Rabil, A. 1978. "Erasmus's Paraphrases of the New Testament." In *Essays on the Works of Erasmus*. Ed. R. L. DeMolen. New Haven: Yale. Pp. 145–61.

Reasoner, Mark. 2005. *Romans in Full Circle: A History of Interpretation*. Louisville: Westminster John Knox Press.

Rees, B. R. 1988. *Pelagius: A Reluctant Heretic*. Woodbridge: Boydell.

Renna, Thomas. 1989. "The Jewish Law According to William of Saint Thierry." *Studia Monastica* 31:1. Pp. 49–67.

Rivière, J. 1909. *The Doctrine of the Atonement: A Historical Essay*. Trans. Luigi Cappadelta. 2 vols. St. Louis: Herder.

————. 1925. "Justification." In *DTC* 8: cols. 2085–86.

————. 1946. "Hétérodoxie des pélagiens en fait de rédemption?" *Revue d'histoire ecclésiastique* 41. Pp. 5–43.

Roukema, R. 1988. *The Diversity of Laws in Origen's Commentary on Romans*. Amsterdam: Free University Press.

————. 1989. "Origenes' Visie op de Rechtvaardiging volgens zijn Commentaar op Romeinen. *Gereformeerd Theologisch Tiedschrift* 89:2. Pp. 94–105.

Roussel, B. 1995. "Bèze et Origène." In *Origeniana Sexta*. Ed. G. Dorival and A. Le Boulluec. Pp. 759–72.

Rydstrom-Poulsen, A. 2002. *The Gracious God: Gratia in Augustine and the Twelfth Century*. Copenhagen: Akademisk.

Rylaarsdam, David M. 2006. "Interpretations of Paul in the Early Church." In Aune (2006). Pp. 146–68.

Schär, M. 1979. *Das Nachleben des Origenes im Zeitalter des Humanismus*. Basel and Stuttgart: Helbing & Lichtenhahn.

Schatkin, M. 1970. "The Influence of Origen upon St. Jerome's Commentary on Galatians." *VC* 24. Pp. 49–58.

Schelkle, K. 1954. "Kirche und Synagoga in der frühen Auslegung des Römerbriefs." *Theologische Quartalschrift* 134. Pp. 290–318.

————. 1956. *Paulus, Lehrer der Väter: Die altkirchliche Auslegung von Römer 1–11*. Düsseldorf: Patmos.

Schulze, M. 1997. "Martin Luther and the Church Fathers." In Backus (1997). Pp. 573–626.

Seeberg, R. 1977. *Text-Book of the History of Doctrines*. Trans. C. E. Hay. 2 vols. Grand Rapids: Baker.

Sider, R. 1991. "The Just and the Holy in Erasmus' New Testament Scholarship." *Erasmus of Rotterdam Society Yearbook* 11. Pp. 1–26.

————. 2002. "Early Commentators in Erasmus's Annotations on Romans." In Blowers (2002). Pp. 118–43.

Smith, A. J. 1919. "The Commentary of Pelagius on 'Romans' Compared with That of Rufinus." *JTS* 20. Pp. 127–77.

Souter, A. 1917. "The Sources of Sedulius Scottus' Collectaneum on the Epistles of St. Paul." *JTS* 18. Pp. 184–228.

Stiegman, E. 2001. "William of St. Thierry." In *The Medieval Theologians: An Introduction to Theology in the Medieval Period*. Ed. G. R. Evans. Oxford: Blackwell. Pp. 140–42.

Stupperich, R. 1961. "Die Rechtfertigungslehre bei Luther und Melanchthon, 1530–1536." In *Luther und Melanchthon: Referate und Berichte des Zweiten Internationalen Kongresses für Lutherforschung*. Münster, 8–13 August 1960. Ed. Vilmos Vajta. Göttingen: Vandenhoeck & Ruprecht. Pp. 73–88.

Sungenis, R. A. 1997. *"Not by Faith Alone": The Biblical Evidence for the Catholic Doctrine of Justification*. Santa Barbara: Queenship Publishing.

Tauer, Johann. 1994. "Neue Orientierungen zur Paulusexegese des Pelagius." *Augustinianum* 34. Pp. 313–58.

Teske, Roland J. 1992. "Origen and St. Augustine's First Commentaries on Genesis." In *Origeniana Quinta*. Ed. Robert J. Daly. Leuven: Leuven University Press. Pp. 179–85.

Toner, N. 1957–58. "The Doctrine of Original Sin According to Augustine of Rome (Favaroni) (d. 1443)." *Augustiniana* 7–8. Pp. 100–117, 349–66.

Trueman, Carl. 2006. "*Simul peccator et Justus*: Martin Luther and Justification." In *Justification in Perspective: Historical Developments and Contemporary Challenges*. Ed. B. L. McCormack. Grand Rapids: Baker. Pp. 73–97.

Turner, C. H. 1902–3. "Pelagius' Commentary on the Pauline Epistles and Its History." *JTS* 4. Pp. 132–41.

Tyacke, N. 1987. *Anti-Calvinists: The Rise of English Arminianism c. 1590–1640*. Oxford: Clarendon Press.

————. 2001. *Aspects of English Protestantism, c. 1530–1700*. Manchester: Manchester University Press.

Van den Brink, J. N. 1969. "Melanchthon: De ecclesia et de autoritate Verbi Dei (1539) und dessen Gegner." In *Reformation und Humanismus, Robert Stupperich zum 65. Geburtstag*. Ed. M. Greschat and J. F. G. Goeters. Witten: Luther-Verlag. Pp. 91–106.

Vandiver, E., ed. 2002. *Luther's Lives: Two Contemporary Accounts of Martin Luther.* Trans. and annotated by Elizabeth Vandiver, Ralph Keen, and Thomas D. Frazel. Manchester: Manchester University Press.

Verfaillie, C. 1926. "La doctrine de la justification dans Origène d'après son commentaire de l'Épître aux Romains." Thèse de la Faculté de théologie catholique de l'Université de Strasbourg. Strasbourg.

Völker, W. 1930. "Paulus bei Origenes." *Theologische Studien und Kritiken: Eine Zeitschrift für das gesamte Gebiet der Theologie* 102. Pp. 258–79.

———. 1931. *Das Vollkommenheitsideal des Origenes.* Tübingen: J. C. B. Mohr.

Wagner, M. M. 1945. *Rufinus the Translator: A Study of His Theory and His Practice as Illustrated in His Version of the Apologetica of St. Gregory Nazianzen.* Washington, DC: Catholic University of America Press.

Walsh, P. G., trans. and ed. 1990. *Cassiodorus: Explanation of the Psalms.* Vol. 1, *Psalms 1–51 (50).* New York: Paulist Press.

Wengert, T. 1997. *Law and Gospel: Philipp Melanchthon's Debate with John Agricola of Eisleben over Poenitentia.* Grand Rapids: Baker.

———, and M. Patrick Graham, eds. 1997a. *Philipp Melanchthon (1497–1560) and the Commentary.* Sheffield: Sheffield Academic Press.

———. 1998. *Human Freedom, Christian Righteousness: Philipp Melanchthon's Exegetical Dispute with Erasmus of Rotterdam.* Oxford: Oxford University Press.

———. 1999. "'Qui vigilantissimis oculis veterum omnium commentarios excusserit': Philipp Melanchthon's Patristic Exegesis." In *Die Patristik in der Bibelexegese des 16. Jahrhunderts.* Ed. D. C. Steinmetz. Wiesbaden: Harrassowitz. Pp. 115–34.

Westcott, B. F. "Origenes." In *DCB* 4:96–142.

White, R. A. 1995. "Justification in Ecumenical Dialogue: An Assessment of the Catholic Contribution." Ph.D. diss., Marquette University.

Wiles, M. F. 1967. *The Divine Apostle: The Interpretation of St. Paul's Epistles in the Early Church.* London: Cambridge University Press.

Wilken, Robert L. 1969. "Justification by Works: Fate and the Gospel in the Roman Empire." *Concordia Theological Monthly* 40. Pp. 379–92.

Williams, N. P. 1927. *The Ideas of the Fall and of Original Sin.* London: Longmans, Green.

Wind, E. 1954. "The Revival of Origen." In *Studies in Art and Literature for Belle Da Costa Greene.* Ed. D. Miner. Princeton: Princeton University Press. Pp. 412–24.

Windisch, H. 1908. *Taufe und Sünde im ältesten Christentum bis auf Origenes.* Tübingen: J. C. B. Mohr.

Wörter, F. 1856. *Die christliche Lehre über das Verhältnis von Gnade und Freiheit von den apostolischen Zeiten bis auf Augustinus.* Freiburg im Breisgau: Herder.

Zachman, Randall C. 2006. "Medieval and Reformation Readings of Paul." In Aune (2006). Pp. 167–87.

Index of Passages Cited from Origen's Commentary on the Epistle to the Romans

CRm entries are by book and chapter with Migne (*PG* 14, 833–1292) column numbers given in parentheses. The chapter enumeration of the Hammond Bammel critical edition differs from Migne in books 1, 2, 3, 7, and 8. Scheck's translation of Hammond Bammel's edition preserves the chapter enumeration of Migne.

Origen's *CRm*	Page/Endnote	Origen's *CRm*	Page/Endnote
Pref 1	141 (258n.65)	2.4 (878)	18 (229n.28), 27
Pref 3	57 (238n.217)		(231nn.74, 75), 81
Pref 6	57 (238n.217)		(244n.91)
		2.5(5–7) (885)	111 (251n.41)
1.1 (833)	20 (229n.34)	2.5(5–7) (887)	40 (234n.133), 58
1.3 (845–46)	57 (238n.217)		(238n.221)
1.5 (845)	70 (241n.40)	2.5(5–7) (887–89)	40 (234n.134), 58
1.5(4) (849)	136 (257n.42)		(239n.224)
1.7(5) (849)	109 (250n.32)	2.5(5–7) (888)	58 (238nn.219,
1.9(7) (852)	109 (250n.34)		220)
1.9(11) (855)	26 (231n.66)	2.5(5–7) (889)	41 (235n.145)
1.13(11) (857)	109 (250n.36)	2.6(8) (889)	41 (235n.144)
1.15(13) (859)	41 (235n.142)	2.6(8) (890)	28 (232n.77), 49
1.17(14) (861)	110 (250n.37)		(237n.182)
1.18 (15) (861)	32 (233n.94)	2.7(9) (892)	36 (233n.111)
1.21(18) (865)	25 (230n.59), 25	2.10 (894)	20 (229n.36), 24
	(231n.63), 26		(230n.57)
	(231n.68), 116–17	2.11 (895)	141 (258n.65)
	(252nn.57, 58, 60),	2.12.4 (900)	18 (229n.27)
	143 (258n.74)	2.9(12–13) (900)	45 (235n.161)
1.21(18) (866)	21 (230n.44), 70	2.9(12–13) (901)	110 (250n.38)
	(241n.35)	2.9(13) (901)	36 (233n.112)
1.21(28) (867–68)	33 (233n.101), 52	2.9(12–13) (907)	144 (258n.80)
	(238n.199)	2.9(12–13) (908)	45 (235nn.160,
1.22(19) (870)	70 (241n.36)		161), 58 (239n.224)

Index

Thomas P. Scheck

is assistant professor in pastoral theology at Ave Maria University. He is the first English translator of Rufinus's Latin edition of Origen's *Commentary on the Epistle to the Romans.*